A Dictionary of Communication and Media Studies

Second edition

James Watson
Senior Lecturer in Communication and Education, West Kent
College of Further Education

and

Anne Hill
Lecturer in Communication and Education, West Kent
College of Further Education

Edward Arnold
A division of Hodder & Stoughton
LONDON NEW YORK MELBOURNE AUCKLAND

© 1984, 1989 James Watson and Anne Hill

First published in Great Britain 1984
Second edition published 1989

Distributed in the USA by Routledge, Chapman and Hall, Inc.
29 West 35th Street, New York, NY 10001

British Library Cataloguing in Publication Data

Watson, James, *1936*–
  A dictionary of communication and media studies – 2nd ed.
  1. Communication
  I. Title   II. Hill, Anne, *1952*–
  001.51

  ISBN 0–7131–6585–5
  ISBN 0–7131–6586–3 pbk

Typeset in 8/9 pt Times Roman by
Colset Private Limited, Singapore.
Printed and bound in Great Britain for Edward Arnold, the
educational, academic and medical publishing division of Hodder
and Stoughton Limited, 41 Bedford Square, London WC1B 3DQ by
Richard Clay, Bungay, Suffolk

Preface to the second edition

In preparing a new edition of *A Dictionary of Communication & Media Studies*, we were besieged by some 200 prospective entries pressing for admission – the result of our own greater reading around the subject, developments in media research and more recent contributions from writers in this ever-expanding field of study.

We have had to be stricter than in our first edition with criteria for inclusion. Entries on architecture, art, theatre and music have been deleted: a pity, but other specialist dictionaries readily provide information on these subjects. We have concentrated attention upon material which we consider will more directly relate to the interests of communication and media studies students and the requirements of their course programmes.

Inevitably there were gaps and omissions in the first edition; there were definitions which needed adjusting or improving. We have also had to cut as well as update many first-edition entries. In come several communication models not covered in the first edition. We have expanded the number of entries on interpersonal communication, public address, information technology, communication theory; and we have attempted to flesh out coverage of sociological perspectives. In come BIAS, MAINSTREAMING, NARRATION, FRANKFURT SCHOOL OF THEORISTS, HALO EFFECT, IMPARTIALITY, GLASNOST, PERCEPTION and the SPYCATCHER CASE. AUDIENCE, POWER, LEADERSHIP, STATUS, IMAGE, CONVENTIONS, PREJUDICE, which all represented INFORMATION GAPS in the first edition but have now been included. Our list of abbreviations has been extended. No doubt our net could still be cast more widely and more finely and once more we ask readers to drop us a line, via the publisher, where they consider we have neglected a deserving entry or failed to define our terms with sufficient clarity.

James Watson   Anne Hill

A checklist for use

* Words in SMALL CAPITALS mean that there is a separate entry.
* Source references are usually included in the text of each entry rather than presented in an end-of-dictionary bibliography.
* Use is made of an asterisk (*) at the end of some entries: here books of special interest or value for further reading on the topic are recommended.
* Traditional practice of referring to the city or town where a book was first published has been modified in this dictionary, reference being made to the country of origin (US or UK).
* In order to help the reader pursue research beyond individual entries, and to establish links between entries, the following 14 *collective entries* are included:

BBC	Press
Broadcasting	Radio
Commissions/Committees on the media	Television
	Technology of the media
Communication models	Television
Film	Theories and concepts of communication
Interpersonal communication	Violence and the media
Language	

* Where c. is used it is an abbreviation for *century*. (But see entry under CIRCA.)
* Communication models are listed using the name of the persons who conceived them (e.g. SHANNON and WEAVER MODEL OF COMMUNICATION, 1949), and Commissions/committees on the media are referred to by the name of the chairpersons (e.g. ROSS COMMISSION REPORT ON THE PRESS, 1949).

Acknowledgements

The publishers would like to thank the following for permission to include copyright figures.

Basic Books, Inc. for Robert K. Merton, Leonard Broom, Leonard S. Cottrell, Jr., (eds.): *Sociology Today: Problems and Prospects*, © 1959 by Basic Books, Inc. and reprinted by permission of the publisher; Hans-Bredow-Institut: *The Pyschology of Mass Communication* by G. Maletzke; CBS College Publishing for Elizabeth G. Andersch, Lorin C. Staats and Robert N. Bostrom: *Communication in Everyday Use* 3rd edition, © 1950, 1960 by Holt, Rinehart & Winston, Inc. and reprinted by permission of Holt, Rinehart & Winston, CBS College Publishing; F.E.X. Dance for *Human Communication Theory: Original Essays*, Holt, Rinehart & Winston (NY) 1967, 288–300 © F.E.X. Dance; Journalism Quarterly for B.H. Wesley and M.S. MacLean 'A conceptual model for communications research', *Journalism Quarterly* 34, 1957 and for 'Bass's double action model of internal news flow', *Journalism Quarterly* 46, 1969 and for 'McNelly's model of news flow', *Journalism Quarterly* 36, 1959 and for 'White's gatekeeper model', *Journalism Quarterly* 27, 1950; Longman for three diagrams from *Communication Models for the Study of Mass Communication* by D. McQuail and S. Windahl; McGraw Hill Publishing Company for a figure from *The Dynamics of Human Communication* by Myers and Myers; Mouton Publishers (a division of Walter de Gruyter & Co.) for Johnnye Akin, Alvin Goldberg, Gail Myers and Joseph Stewart: *Language Behaviour: A Book of Readings* in K.K. Sereno and C. D. Mortensen (eds): *Foundations of Communication Theory*; Sage Publications Inc. 'A Dependency model of mass media effects', *Communication Research* 3 (1976); The University of Illinois Press for Schramm: 'How Communication Works', *Process and Effects of Mass Communication* and Shannon and Weaver: *Mathematical Theory of Communication* and the University of Minnesota and Professor Samuel L. Becker for 'What rhetoric (communication theory) is relevant for contemporary speech communication?' in *The University of Minnesota Spring Symposium in Speech Communication*, 1968.

Useful abbreviations: a selection

AA	Advertising Association
ABC	American Broadcasting Company
ABE	Association of British Editors
ABS	Association of Broadcasting & Allied Staffs
ABSA	Association for Business Sponsorship of the Arts
ACADE	Association for Computers in Art Education
ACARD	Advisory Council for Applied Research & Development
ACS	Associations for Cultural Studies
ACTT	Association of Cinematography, Television & Allied Technicians
ADP	Association of Directors & Producers
ADP	Automatic Data Processing
AEB	Associated Examining Board
AFC	Assistant Film Cameraman
AFFIRM	Alliance for Fair Images & Representation in the Media
AFR	Assistant Film Recordist
AI	Amnesty International
ALCS	Authors' Lending & Copyright Society
ALGOL	Algorithmic Language
AIDS	Architectural Informations Distribution Service
AMSO	Association of Market Survey Organizations
AP	Associated Press
APA	Association of Production Artists
AR	Audience Research
ATV	Associated Television (Associated Broadcasting Company)
BABT	British Approvals Board for Telecommunications
BAFTA	British Academy of Film & TV Arts
BAPLA	British Association of Picture Libraries & Agencies
BARB	Broadcasters Audience Research Board
BASIC	Beginners All-Purpose Symbolic Instruction Code
BBC	British Broadcasting Corporation
BBFC	British Board of Film Classification
BCC	Broadcasting Complaints Commission
BFFS	British Federation of Film Societies
BFI	British Film Institute
BFMP	British Federation of Master Printers
bit	binary digit
BLEND	Birmingham & Loughborough Electronic Network Development
BMWA	Black Media Workers Association
BPC	Broadcasting Press Guild
bps	bits per second
Brad	British rate & data
BREEMA	British Radio & Electronic Equipment Manufacturers Association
BSB	British Satellite Broadcasting
BSC	British Society of Cinematography; Broadcasting Standards Council
BSI	British Standards Institute
BT	British Telecom
BTA	British Theatre Association
BTUA	British Telephone Users Association
BUFV	British Universities Film and Video Council
BVA	British Videogram Association
CADA	Confederation of Art & Design Associations
CADCAM	Computer Aided Design–Computer Aided Manufacture
CAM	Communications Advertising & Marketing Educational Foundation
CAP	Code of Advertising Practice
CAOW	Computer Assisted Office Work
CARM	Campaign Against Racism in the Media

CBA	Commonwealth Broadcasting Association
CCCS	Centre for Contemporary Culture Studies (University of Birmingham)
CCD	Charge-Coupled Device
CCDP	Community Communications Development Project
CCIR	International Consultative Committee for Radio
CCITT	International Consultative Committee for Telephone & Telegraphy
CD	Compact Disc
CDV	Compact Disc Video
CMCS	Computer Mediated Communication Systems
COBOL	Common Business Oriented Language
COI	Central Office of Information
COMCOM	Community Communications Group
CPBF	Campaign for Press & Broadcasting Freedom
CPU	Commonwealth Press Union
CRTC	Canadian Radio-TV Commission
CRW	Children's Rights Workshop
DAMM	Defence Against Media Manipulation
DBS	Direct Broadcasting Satellite
DICE	Digital Intercontinental Conversion Equipment
DP	Data Processing
DSK	Dvorak Simplified Keyboard
DTP	Desk Top Publishing
EAVA	European Audio Visual Aids Association
EBU	European Broadcasting Union
EDP	Electronic Data Processing
ELF	Extra Low Frequency
EMA	Editorial Media Analysis
ENG	Electronic News Gathering
FAB	Federation of Alternative Booksellers
FACT	Federation Against Copyright Theft
fax	Facsimile
FM	Frequency Modulation
FRB	Federation of Radical Booksellers
FWW	Federation of Worker Writers
GBNE	Guild of British Newspaper Editors
GCHQ	Government Communications Headquarters
GIGO	Garbage In, Garbage Out (computer operator's acronym.)
GSR	Galvanic Skin Response
HDTV	High-Definition Television
HDVS	High-Definition Video System
HF	High Frequency
HMSO	Her Majesty's Stationery Office
IBA	Independent Broadcasting Authority
IBI	Intergovernmental Bureau of Informatics
IBM	International Business Machines
IFFI	International Foundation for Freedom of Information
IFJ	International Federation of Journalists
IFRB	Inter-Frequency Regulation Board
IFVA	Independent Film & Video Makers Association
ILR	Independent Local Radio
In-mar-sat	International Maritime Satellite Organization
In-tel-sat	International Telecommunications Satellite (Consortium)
IPA	Institute of Practitioners in Advertising
IPC	International Publishing Corporation
IPDC	International Programme for the Development of Communication
IPI	International Press Institute

IPR	Institute of Public Relations
Iras	Infra-red astronomy satellite
ISBN	International Standard Book Number
ISN	International Services Digital Network
IT	Information Technology
ita	initial teaching alphabet
ITA	Independent Television Authority (now IBA; until 1990)
ITAP	Information Technology Advisory Panel
ITCA	Independent TV Companies Association
ITU	International Telecommunications Union
ITV	Independent Television
IV	Interactive Video
JICNAR	Joint Industrial Council for Newspaper Audience Research
JICPAR	Joint Industrial Council for Poster Audience Research
JICTAR	Joint Independent Committee for TV Advertising Research
JICRAR	Joint Industrial Committee for Radio Audience Research
LA	Library Association
LAN	Local Area Network
Laser	Light amplification by stimulated emission radiation
LBR	Laser Beam Recording
LED	Light Emitting Diode
LFF	London Film Festival
LGMG	Lesbian & Gay Media Group
MAC	Multiplexed Analogue Components
MBS	Mutual Broadcasing System
MIS	Management Information System
MISP	Microelectronic Independent Support Programme
MO	Mass Observation
MOMI	Museum of the Moving Image
modem	modulator-demodulator
MR	Motivation Research
NAHBO	National Association of Hospital Broadcasting Organizations
NASB	National Associaton of Student Broadcasting
NATSOPA	National Society of Operative Printers, Graphical & Media Personnel
NBC	National Broadcasting Company (US)
NBL	National Book League
NCCL	National Council for Civil Liberties
NCU	National Communications Union
NECCTA	National Educational Closed-Circuit Television Association
NFA	National Film Archive
NFFC	National Film Finance Corporation
NFT	National Film Theatre
NGA	National Graphical Association
NHMF	National Heritage Memorial Fund
NIVC	National Interactive Video Centre
NPA	Newspaper Proprietors Association (UK)
NT	National Theatre
NUJ	National Union of Journalists
NVLA	National Viewers & Listeners Association
NWICO	New World Information & Communication Order
OB	Outside Broadcast
OCR	Optical Character Recognition
OFTEL	Office of Telecommunications
OU	Open University
PA	Press Association
PABX	Private Automatic Branch Exchange

PCM	Pulse Code Modulation
PCW	Personal Computer Word Processor
PDC	Publications Distribution Cooperative
PEN	Poets/Playrights/Editors/Essayists/Novelists: PEN International
PITCOM	Parliamentary Information Technology Committee
PLR	Public Lending Rights
PLQ	Perfect Letter Quality
POLIS	Parliamentary Online Information System
PSI	Para-Social Interaction
PSN	Public Switched Network
RDS	Radio Data System
RDU	Remote Detection Unit
RI	Reaction Index
RP	Received Pronunciation
rpm	revolutions per minute
RSC	Royal Shakespeare Company
RTS	Royal Television Society
RTSA	Royal Television Society Awards
Satstream	British Telecom business satellite service
SEFT	Society for Education in Film & Television
SEM	Scanning Electronic Microscope
SIGINT	Signals Intelligence
SLADE	Society of Lithographic Artists, Designers & Engravers
SLR	Single Lens Reflex
SOGAT	Society of Graphical & Allied Trades
SPREd	Society of Picture Research & Editors
SSPS	Satellite Power Station
STC	Standard Telephone & Cables
STD	Subscriber Trunk Dialling
SYNCOM	Synchronous Communication Satellite
TAM	Television Audience Measurement
TASS	Telegraph Agency of the Soviet Union
T & SG	Television & Screen Writers Guild
TNAUK	Newspaper Association of the United Kingdom
TTL	Through the Lens
UHF	Ultra High Frequency
UKUSA	United Kingdom/United States Signals Intelligence treaty (1947), also signed by Allied states
Unesco	United Nations Educational Scientific and Cultural Organization
UNO	United Nations Organization
VDU	Visual Display Unit
VHF	Very High Frequency
VHD	Video High Density
VHS	Video Home System
VTA	Video Trade Association
WAMM	Women Against Media Myths
WARC	World Administrative Radio Conference
WP	Word Processing
wpm	words per minute
WSET	Writers & Scholars Educational Trust
WPFC	World Press Freedom Committee

AA-certificate, A-certificate See CERTIFICATION OF FILMS.

ABC Trial, 1978 British journalists Crispin Aubrey, John Berry and Duncan Campbell (A,B,C) co-wrote an article in *Time Out* entitled 'The Eavesdroppers' in May 1976 which referred to the Government communications HQ at Cheltenham and its activities in electronic surveillance. The authors were charged on nine counts under the OFFICIAL SECRETS ACT. The court judge eventually dismissed the case in September 1978. Not to be outdone, British security brought a case against *Peace News* which had revealed the name of a secret witness at the trial – Colonel 'B'. For breaching Official Secrets (Colonel 'B' was a member of British security, so it was forbidden to publish his real name), *Peace News* was fined £500. See CENSORSHIP; SECRECY.

Aberrant decoding See DECODE.

ABX model of communication See NEWCOMB'S ABX MODEL.

Acceleration factor What results from the speed-up of forms of transportation, thus having far-reaching impact upon communities, nations and cultures. Marshall MCLUHAN preached that the combination of accelerated modes of transport communication and the rapid development of electric communication – TELEPHONE, TV – was having the effect of reducing the world to a 'global village'. 'All meaning,' says McLuhan in *Understanding the Media* (UK: Routledge & Kegan Paul, 1964), 'alters with acceleration, because all patterns of personal and political interdependence change with any acceleration of information.' Ultimately, McLuhan believed, the acceleration of electric/electronic media would not only outpace transport communication but make it substantially redundant.

Action research Some social science research is motivated by the desire to alter and improve a social situation. Action research aims not only to collect and analyse information but also to bring about practical social change. See GLASGOW UNIVERSITY MEDIA GROUP.

Active participation Occurs in situations where media interest in a news story becomes involvement, and the story takes on a media-induced direction. An appetite for stories of scandal and sensation, and the cut-throat competition for circulation, can lead newspapers into playing the role of agent provocateur, as handy with the chequebook as the reporter's notebook.

Actuality Material from real life – the presentation in a broadcast programme of real events and people to illustrate some current theme or practice. RADIO, in parallel with film DOCUMENTARY, pioneered actuality in the 1930s. Producers such as Olive Shapley and Harry Harding were early innovators in this field. The radio programme *Time to Spare*, made in 1934, documented unemployment, broadcasting the voices of the unemployed and their families and creating an impact that was both moving and disturbing.

Actualization See MASLOW'S HIERARCHY OF NEEDS.

Adaptors See NON-VERBAL BEHAVIOUR REPERTOIRE

Admass Term credited to J.B. Priestley to describe high-pressure ADVERTISING and publicity across the media to stimulate sales; representing a harmful influence upon the CULTURE of society.

Advertising The extent of the *reliance* of all forms of mass media upon advertising can be gauged by glancing at any monthly edition of Brad, which comprises some 400 to 500 pages of information on where advertisements can be placed and how much they will cost. Everything is there – the national and local PRESS, TV and RADIO, cinema, POSTERS, bus shelters, parking metres, litter bins and transport advertising.

If advertising merely sold products, it would cause less critical concern than it does. But it also sells images, dreams, ideal ways of life; it sells, then reinforces time and again, VALUES – those of consumerism; and it trades in stereotypes. In *The Shocking History of Advertising* (UK: Penguin, revised edition, 1965), E.S. Turner states that 'Advertising is the whip which hustles humanity up the road to the Better Mousetrap.'

On the credit side, advertising has speeded the introduction of useful inventions to a wide as distinct from a select circle of consumers; it has spread markets, reduced the price of goods, accelerated turnover and kept people in employment. But the 'relentless propaganda on behalf of goods in general', as J.K. Galbraith puts it in *The Affluent Society* (UK: Hamish Hamilton, 1958), is considered by many a dangerous mode of BRAINWASHING in that advertising's central function appears to be to create desires that previously did not exist, or rather *anxieties* which response to the ad (by going out and buying the advertised product or service) helps to assuage - but only temporarily. V.L. Leymore in *The Hidden Myth* (UK: Heinemann, 1975) argues that, like MYTH, advertising reinforces accepted modes of behaviour and acts as an anxiety-reducing mechanism resolving contradictions in a complex and confusing society: 'To the constant nagging dilemmas of the human condition, advertising gives a simple solution . . . [It] simultaneously provokes anxiety and resolves it'. (See ANOMIE).

The many modes of advertising may be categorized as follows: (1) Commercial consumer advertising, with its target the mass audience and its CHANNEL the mass media. (2) Trade and technical advertising, such as ads in specialist magazines. (3) Prestige advertising, particularly that of big business and large institutions, generally selling image and good name rather than specific products (See PR: PUBLIC RELATIONS). (4) Small ads, directly informational, which are the bedrock support of local periodicals and are the basis of the many giveaway papers which have been published in recent years. (5) Government advertising – health warnings, for example. (6) Charity advertising, seeking donations for worthwhile causes at home and abroad. (7) Advertising through sponsorship, mainly of sports, leisure and the arts. This indirect form of advertising has been a major development; its danger has been to make recipients of sponsorship come to rely more and more heavily on commercial support. Sponsors want quick publicity and prestige for their money and their loyalties to recipients are very often short-term.

The effect upon newspaper and BROAD-CASTING editorial and programme content is rarely overt; rather it is a process of media people 'internalizing' advertisers' demands. Ad-related newspaper features have grown enormously in the post-2nd World War period, especially in the 'quality Press', such as *The Times, Guardian* and *Daily Telegraph*, which derive over half their revenue from advertising. In press advertising, numbers count for less than the estimated purchasing power of the target readership. This explains why two major newspapers with big circulations – the *Daily Herald* (See MIRACLE OF FLEET STREET) and the *News Chronicle* – were closed down in the 1960s. They simply did not appeal to the advertisers. Competition for advertisements in today's FLEET STREET has never been more desperate. In TV advertising, however, quantity (of audience) tends to count for more than quality.

Advertising has suffused our CULTURE and our LANGUAGE; its influence has been felt in modern art movements such as *pop art*; its snappy techniques as developed for TV have been widely adopted in the cinema. It has drawn into its service actors, celebrities, artists, photographers, writers, designers and FILM makers. It is often said that on TV the adverts are better than the programmes; there is a grain of truth here as there is in the claim that it is *because* of the adverts, and the goals of those who commission and make them, that the programmes are not better, more original or more challenging. See AIDA MODEL; CONSUMPTION BEHAVIOUR; GRAPHIC REVOLUTION; HARMONIOUS INTERACTION; SUBLIMINAL.

* G. Dyer, *Advertising as Communication* (UK: Methuen, 1982).

Advertising: mainstreamers, aspirers, succeeders and reformers Target audiences for ADVERTISING have traditionally been defined along lines of social CLASS. Research into consumer habits and tastes produced, in the 1980s, a classification entitled, in the UK, the *Four Cs* (*C*ross-*c*ultural *c*onsumer *c*haracterization), indicating the belief that these days we are all consumers now and that class differences count less than personal aspiration. A BBC QED programme, *It's Tough Being a Dolphin* (May 1988) gave currency to this new approach to discovering and satisfying consumer needs. Adman John Banks described four categories of consumer. (1) *Mainstreamers* make up some 40% of consumers; security is what characterizes them in terms of their central needs, thus they buy well-known, tried brand names. (2) *Aspirers* are those for whom personal status is of prime importance; they go for what is smart and fashionable and is perceived to contribute towards the aspirer's image. (3) *Succeeders* have already arrived rather than being still on their way up; what characterizes them is their need for control – in their lives, their work, in their consumption. Advertisements which stress power and control are targeted at them. (4) *Reformers* are those who tend to put the quality of life before mere monetary acquisition. They are people, John Banks explained, who wish to change life for the better. They tend to be readers of the *Guardian*, teachers, doctors, workers in caring services generally. They are the health food and the 'Real Ale' people and constitute potentially powerful lobbies as consumer 'watchdogs'. See HIDDEN NEEDS; MASLOW'S HIERARCHY OF NEEDS.

Aesthetic Code See CODES

Affect displays See NON-VERBAL BEHAVIOUR: REPERTOIRE

Affective See COGNITIVE (AND AFFECTIVE).

Affiliates So-called subsidiaries of the three major US BROADCASTING networks: ABC, CBS and NBC. Between them, these organizations control 6/7 of the country's 750 commercial TV stations.

Agenda setting Term used to describe the way the media set the order of importance of current ISSUES, especially in the reportage of news. Closely linked with the process of GATE KEEP-ING, agenda setting defines the context of transmission, establishes the terms of reference and the limits of debate. In BROADCASTING the agenda is more assertive than in newspapers where the reader can ignore the order of priorities set by the paper's editorial team and turn straight to the small ads. or the sports page. Broadcasting is linear – one item following after another – and its agenda unavoidable (except by switching off). Interviewers in broadcasting are in *control* of pre-set agenda. They initiate, formulate the questions to be asked and have the chairperson's power of excluding areas of discussion. Very rarely does an interviewee break free from this form of control and succeed in widening the context of debate beyond what is 'on the agenda'. See McCOMBS and SHAW AGENDA SETTING MODEL OF MEDIA EFFECTS, 1976.

Agit-prop The Department of Agitation and Propaganda was created in 1920 as part of the Central Committee Secretariat of the Communist Party of the Soviet Union. Its responsibility was to use all available media – especially FILM – to disseminate information and ideas to the population of the world's first Communist state. The term agit-prop has come to be used to describe any unashamedly political propagandizing.

AIDA model Guide to the principal stages of ADVERTISING a product or service: A – create Awareness; I – create Interest; D – promote Desire; A – stimulate Action or response.

Alexandra Palace Birthplace of TELEVISION in the United Kingdom. The first TV broadcasting took place from London's 'Ally Pally' on 2 November 1936. Initially the service reached only a few hundred privileged viewers in and around the capital. Some 400 TV sets, costing around £100 – the price of a small car – were in use. With the coming of the 2nd World War, TV broadcasts came to an abrupt end on 1 September 1939, by which time there were an estimated 20,000 TV sets in operation. The Alexandra Palace studios opened for business again on 7 June 1946 but had to briefly shut down transmission again in early 1947 because of the acute fuel crisis. The Alexandra Palace studios remained in service until 1955. See BROADCASTING; TELEVISION.

Alienation As a concept, derives largely from the work of Karl Marx (1818–83), who argued that the organization of industrial production robbed people of opportunities for meaningful and creative work, performed in cooperation with others and over which they had some control. Researchers have posed the question whether the mass character of the modern communications industry produces a sense of alienation in its own workers. Lewis Coser in *Men of Ideas* (US: Free Press, 1965) believes that the industrial mode of production within media organizations hamstrings the individual producer by denying his or her creativity in the quest for a mass CULTURE and that this results in alienation.

The term has a wider application. Alienation is seen as a socio-psychological condition which affects certain individuals. William Kornhauser in *The Politics of Mass Society* (US: Free Press, 1959) argues that the breakdown and decline of community GROUPS and the extended family in modern society produces feelings of isolation and increases the possibility that people will be influenced by the appeals of extremist political groups. Alienation might therefore be a significant variable in determining an individual's receptivity to certain types of communication. See ANOMIE; INTERVENING VARIABLES; MASS SOCIETY.

Allegory A narrative which seeks to convey MEANING by representing abstract ethical concepts or historical/political events indirectly in the guise of certain characters, settings or plots. Historical allegory treats contemporary themes which may not be discussed openly, by presenting an historical work which implicitly involves the same themes. It is therefore a popular means of registering political protest in a repressive regime. Jean-Paul Sartre (1905–80), for example, re-wrote the classical legend of Orestes and Electra, which is concerned with the theme of freedom, in *Les Mouches* (The Flies), performed in 1943 whilst France was still under German occupation.

Alternative press See UNDERGROUND PRESS.

Amplitude See NEWS VALUES.

Amsats Amateur satellites; costing a fraction of their 'professional' counterparts. Since the Russian SPUTNIK led the way into space in 1957, over 20 satellites, built by amateurs, have been launched. First was Oscar 1, battery-operated and weighing 4.5kg, given a free piggy-back into orbit during 1962 with a US Air Force spy satellite. A thriving international Amsat organization has flourished since its repeated MORSE CODE 'Hi' transmissions were picked up around the world by RADIO HAMS. The Spacecraft Engineering Research Unit at the University of Surrey built two 50kg 'Vosat' satellites for under £500,000, both launched by the Americans. The cost compares dramatically with that of establishing a commercial communications satellite NETWORK, which is estimated to require £100m funding and five years from planning to launch. Both VoSats pass over Europe several times a day transmitting scientific data on the earth's magnetic field and the radiation pouring in from the sun. With a home computer and the appropriate software package, anyone can tune in for data. More than 900 UK schools and 3000 GROUPS worldwide regularly obtain data from this extremely cost-effective satellite engineering. See SATELLITE TRANSMISSION.

Anabasis From the Greek, 'going up'; in the theatre, the rising of action, the crescendo to a climax or dénouement.

Anagnorisis From the Greek, 'recognition'. A term used by Aristotle in his *Poetics* to describe the moment of recognition – of truth – when ignorance gives way to understanding, as for example when Othello – too late – discovers how Iago has betrayed him and how profoundly mistaken his jealousy of Desdemona has been.

Analogy A comparison of similarities between two things which are basically unalike, in order to clarify or support a point made. Analogies can be drawn between the branches of a tree and of a family, between the brain and a computer, between a stage performance and the 'performance' that constitutes a well-run restaurant. An analogy can be a useful means of clarification but there is a certain amount of risk involved in using analogies to support arguments because somewhere along the line in an argument the comparison breaks down and an opponent might point this out. All metaphors and similes are based upon analogy. Often, the analogy gathers power by being *emotive*. Thus, 'the hooligans behaved like animals' colours the expression but weakens the argument because careful scrutiny of animal behaviour might locate very little evidence to indicate that animals behave like hooligans. A case might be made for calling a truce in analogy-making on references to pigs, cows, cats, ageing goats, rams and toads.

Analysis – modes of media analysis See DISCOURSE ANALYSIS; FUNCTIONALIST; MARXIST; SOCIAL ACTION (MODES OF MEDIA ANALYSIS).

Anamorphic lens Movie camera lens which 'squeezes' a wide picture on to standard FILM. In a projector it 'unsqueezes' the image to fill a wide screen.

Anarchist cinema Epitomized in the work of French FILM maker Jean Vigo (1905–34) who was 12 when his anarchist father, known as Miguel Almereyda, was found strangled in a French police cell in 1917. In *A propos de Nice* (1930), Vigo expressed the anarchist's views on inequality, contrasting the luxurious, suntanned life of wealthy holidaymakers with the underfed, deformed bodies of slum children. In his comic masterpiece *Zéro de Conduite* (Nought for Conduct) produced in 1932, Vigo used anarchist friends as actors. His theme was the rebellion of schoolchildren against the rigidity of the school authorities. It was immediately banned by the French authorities. Vigo was a direct inspiration for the 'anarchistic' film of a modern, public school rebellion in Lindsay Anderson's *If*, made in 1968. (Anarchy: complete absence of law or government.)

Anchorage The part that captions play in helping to frame, or anchor, the meaning of photographic images, as reproduced in newspapers and magazines. French philosopher Roland Barthes used this term to describe the way captions help 'fix' or narrow down the *choice* of meanings of the published image. He defines the caption as a 'parasitic message designed to connote the image'.

Andersch, Staats and Bostrom model of communication, 1969 Environmental or contextual factors are at the centre of the communication model devised by Elizabeth G. Andersch, Lorin C. Staats and Robert N. Bostrom and presented in *Communication in Everyday Use* (US: Holt, Rinehart & Winston).

Like BARNLUND'S TRANSACTIONAL MODEL this one stresses the *transactional* nature of the communication process, in which messages and their meanings are structured and evaluated by the Sender and subjected to reconstruction and evaluation on the the the part of the Receiver, all the while interacting with factors (or stimuli) in the environment. See COMMUNICATION MODELS.

Anecdote A short narrative, usually of a personal nature, used to illustrate a general issue. Anecdotes are often used in media coverage to heighten the emotional aspect of an issue. Colin Seymour-Ure in *The Political Impact of the Mass Media* (UK: Constable, 1974) recounts the use made of one such anecdote by the politician Enoch Powell in his efforts to bring the immigration issue to public attention during 1967 and 1968. Powell claimed to have received a letter from a correspondent in Northumberland expressing concern about an elderly widow in Wolverhampton who feared harassment by newly arrived immigrants in the area. This anecdote was widely reported by the PRESS, yet, despite strenuous efforts, no trace of the elderly widow could be found. The story did, however, do much to fuel the emotive manner in which the immigration issue was discussed in the popular press.

Animal communication See COMMUNICATION, ANIMAL.

Animatic Sequence of drawings representing the story of a TELEVISION advertisement, prior to filming. Another term for STORYBOARD.

Animation The process of filming still drawings, puppets, etc. in sequence to give the illusion of movement; also the actual direct drawing and painting on to positive or negative stock or on to clear celluloid itself. Long before CINEMATOGRAPHY was invented devices were in use which gave drawings the illusion of movement. By 1882 Emile Reynauld had combined his *Praxinoscope* with a projector and a decade later opened the Théâtre Optique in the Musée Grevin in Paris.

Live-action cinema became all-important once the Lumière brothers had shown its possibilities in 1895, but animation soon captured interest, from 1908 onwards, with the work of J. Stuart Blackton in the US and Emile Cohl in France. *New York Herald* cartoonist Winsor McCay made *Gertie the Dinosaur* in 1909, and in 1919 the first animated feature, *The Sinking of the Lusitania*. In November 1928 Walt Disney (1901–66) presented Mortimer, later Mickey Mouse to the world – using SYNCHRONOUS SOUND, in *Steamboat Willie*, along with his

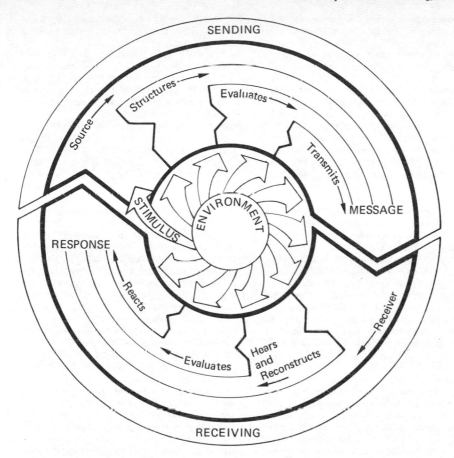

SENDING

Source

Structures

Evaluates

Transmits

STIMULUS

ENVIRONMENT

MESSAGE

RESPONSE

Reacts

Evaluates

Hears and Reconstructs

Receiver

RECEIVING

Andersch, Staats and Bostrom model of communication, 1969

Skeleton Dance (1929) one of the true classics of animation film.

The laboriousness of producing thousands of drawings for filming has been dramatically altered in the 1980s by the introduction to animated FILM making of COMPUTER GRAPHICS.

* R. Stephenson, *Animation in the Cinema* (UK: Zwemmer, 1967); D. Crafton, *Before Mickey. The Animated Film, 1898–1928* (US: MIT Press, 1982).

Annan Commission Report on Broadcasting, 1977 Historian Lord Annan chaired the Royal Commission on the Future of Broadcasting whose main task was to decide what should happen to the BROADCASTING industry once the right to broadcast of the RADIO and TV companies lapsed at the end of July 1979. Also, the Annan Commission was asked to make recommendations on a fourth television channel.

Annan favoured the continuance of much of the existing broadcasting system, though the

Report suggested that both the BBC and IBA should lose their local radio stations to a new Local Broadcasting Authority.

Annan also proposed a BROADCASTING COMPLAINTS COMMISSION, empowered to award costs if a complaint were upheld, and a Public Enquiry Board for Broadcasting. The task of the Board would be to hold seven-yearly public audits of the way each authority had met its responsibilities and to conduct hearings on specific ISSUES, particularly the award of FRANCHISES. A further recommendation was for an Open Broadcasting Authority to operate the fourth channel 'more as a publisher of material provided by others'.

What Annan wanted above all was a shift from DUOPOLY to a more diverse system of broadcasting in Britain: 'We want the broadcasting industry to grow. But we do not want more of the same. . . . What is needed now are programmes for the different minorities which add up to make the majority.'

Annan also declared that there was 'a widely shared feeling that British broadcasting is run like a highly restricted club – managed exclusively by broadcasters according to their own criteria of what counts as good television and radio'.

The then Labour Government published a white paper, *Broadcasting* (July 1978), in response to Annan, declaring itself against the Local Broadcasting Authority and the Public Enquiry Board but in favour of the Complaints Commission and the Open Broadcasting Authority. Before there was time for legislation, the Conservatives came to power in May 1979. The Queen's Speech promised the fourth channel to COMMERCIAL TELEVISION and the proposal for an Open Broadcasting Authority was rejected. See CHANNEL FOUR; COMMISSIONS/COMMITTEES ON THE MEDIA.

Anomie It was Emile Durkheim (1858–1917), a French sociologist, who first used this term to describe a state of 'normlessness' in which the individual feels that there are no effective social rules governing behaviour or that those rules and VALUES to which he/she is exposed are conflicting and therefore confusing. The anomic state is most likely to occur when contact with others is limited. Durkheim linked anomie with the disturbance caused by social change and upheaval and saw it as a temporary social phenomenon. Several contemporary observers consider it a more permanent feature of modern industrial society.

MASS SOCIETY theorists have tended to view those suffering from anomie as being particularly vulnerable to over-influence by MASS COMMUNICATION. Observers have also found that some behaviour that was considered anomic was in fact SUB-CULTURAL. Another feature of anomie is that the individual may react to it by becoming ceaselessly ambitious and this in some cases can lead to severe agitation and discontent. Dissatisfied ambition is a target for much ADVERTISING and is often seen as a desirable trait in modern capitalist societies – a perspective reinforced by some of the outpourings from the mass media. A question of concern is, then, the contribution of the mass media and in particular advertising to the condition of anomie. Anomie can lead to extensive personal as well as social breakdown, to suicide and mental illness as well as to crime, delinquency, drug addiction and alcoholism.

Anti-language A term used to refer to those languages which express opposition and resistance to the dominant order, the DOMINANT CULTURE and its linguistic order. These languages stem from oppositional sub-cultures, such as deviant sub-cultures. They also serve to express, maintain and reinforce the solidarity of members of the sub-culture and to exclude outsiders. An example of such an anti-language would be the LANGUAGE of the Rastafarian sub-culture. See DOMINANT DISCOURSE; SUB-CULTURE.

Antonym A word that means the opposite of another. *Synonym* is a word that means approximately the same as another. In media terms, the antonym of broadcast would be narrowcast (See CODES). Synonyms for *sender* would be *encoder* or *addresser*.

Apache silence The complex meanings of silence, as observed by the North American Apache tribes, have been tabulated by K.H. Basso in 'To give up words: silence in western Apache culture' in P. Giglioli, ed., *Language and Social Context* (UK: Penguin, 1972). Basso describes Apache silence as 'a response to uncertainty and unpredictability in social relations'. Often baffling to the outsider, Apache silence was an important element in the courtship process; when meeting strangers; even when greeting children back from a long journey; and in the presence of other people's grief. See COMMUNICATION, NON-VERBAL.

Applaudable messages See VERBAL DEVICES IN SPEECH-MAKING.

Apocryphal stories Those of doubtful origin, false or spurious. See FOLK DEMONS; LOONY LEFTISM; MYTH; RUMOUR.

Arbitrariness One of the characteristic features of human LANGUAGE is that between an object described and the word that describes it, there is a connection which is purely *arbitrary*, that is, the speech sound does not reflect features of the object denoted. For example, the word *chair* describes the object, chair, because the English have arbitrarily decided to name it thus as a matter of convention. In contrast, ONOMATOPOEIC expressions are *representative* rather than arbitrary in that they reflect properties of the non-linguistic world (for example, *clatter, buzz, flap* – and *snap, crackle* and *pop*).

'Areopagitica' Title of a tract or pamphlet by the English poet John Milton (1608–74) in defence of the freedom of the PRESS, published in 1644. Milton spoke out, with eloquence and courage, following the revival of CENSORSHIP by parliamentary ordinance in 1643 (traditional press censorship had broken down with the Long Parliament's abolition of the Star Chamber in 1641). The title was taken from the Greek, *Areopagus* – the hill of Ares or Mars in Athens, where the highest judicial court held its sittings; a 'behind closed doors' court.

Milton celebrated the power and influence of the printed word: books 'do preserve, as in a vial, the purest efficacy and extraction of that living intellect that bred them. I know they are as lively, and as vigorously productive, as those fabulous dragon's teeth; and being sown up and down, may chance to spring up armed men. And yet, on the other hand, unless wariness be used, as good almost kill a man as kill a good book: who kills a man kills a reasonable creature, God's image; but he who destroys a good book, kills reason itself, kills the image of God, as it were, in the eye.'

Argot See SLANG.

Ariane European communications space satellite, rival for space business to the US space shuttle and three-stage launchers, the Thor-Delta and the Atlas Centaur. Developed at a cost of about £940 million by the 10 Western European countries making up the European Space Agency (ESA), the Ariane project received a major setback in September 1982 when the satellite launcher crashed into the Atlantic 13 minutes into its first operational flight. It was successfully re-launched in 1987. The most prominent investors in the Ariane programme have been France (60%) and West Germany (20%). The other countries subscribing to the venture are the UK, Belgium, Denmark, Italy, the Netherlands, Spain and Sweden.

Artefacts Things made by human workmanship; in a communication sense, the adornments which are worn which 'say something' about the wearer: dress, hairstyles, jewellery, make-up; or objects which we possess – such as motor cars – are indicators of our SELF-CONCEPT. See OBJECTICS.

Article 10 of the European Convention Declares 'Everyone has the right to freedom of expression. This right shall include the freedom to hold and to receive and impart information and ideas without interference by public authority and regardless of frontiers.' The European Court of Human Rights exists to sit in judgement on cases brought by litigants from nations who are signatories to the Convention in the light of certain qualifications to that freedom (such as national security, territorial integrity, or public safety). The UK government adheres to the Convention but its formulations have not been incorporated into English law.

Article 19 A global pressure group, centred in London, using electronic media to monitor state CENSORSHIP around the world. The group derives its name from the United Nations Declaration of Human Rights, Article 19 of which asserts that 'Everyone has the right to freedom of opinion and expression. . .'. Computer data bases have been established by Article 19 on the current state of freedom of information, PRESS laws, official secrets legislation, CODES, cases and practices in all countries.
* *Article 19 World Report: Information, Freedom and Censorship* (UK: Longman, 1988).

Artillery of the press Term used by James Reston in his *The Artillery of the Press* (US: Harper, 1966), to refer to the potential power

the PRESS has by virtue of the range of information in its possession, which it may or may not publish. Influence can be exercised by withholding information from the public – an example of negative power. See CENSORSHIP.

Aspect ratio Ratio of the width to the height of the FILM or television image.

Aspirers See ADVERTISING: MAINSTREAMERS, ASPIRERS, SUCCEEDERS, AND REFORMERS

Assertiveness training To be assertive is to be able to communicate one's thoughts, feelings, beliefs, ATTITUDES, positions and so on in a clear, confident, honest and direct manner; it is in short to be able to stand up for oneself whilst also taking into consideration the needs and rights of other people. Being assertive differs from being aggressive in that aggressiveness involves a standing up for one's own rights and needs at the expense of others. In recent years there has been much interest in assertiveness training – that is, in enabling people to develop techniques and strategies, verbal and non-verbal, for INTERPERSONAL COMMUNICATION which will encourage them to assert themselves in social situations. The ability to be assertive is linked to self-esteem and self-confidence and thus to a positive SELF-CONCEPT. Such training provides the opportunity for considerable exploration of the relationship between the self-concept and interpersonal behaviour.

Assign Part of a family or category of SIGNS to which MEANING is 'assigned'. An example of an *assign* is the ancient Egyptian Dodo. We say 'As dead as the Dodo', fully aware of the meaning of the phrase but probably unfamiliar with either the appearance of the Dodo bird, or why it came to signify what it does.

Attention See PERCEPTION

Attitudes We all hold a range of attitudes on a variety of topics and ISSUES. An attitude, according to Milton Rokeach in 'The Nature of Attitudes', *Encyclopædia of the Social Sciences* (UK: Collier-Macmillan, 1965), is '. . . a relatively enduring organization of beliefs around an object or situation predisposing one to respond in some preferential manner'. Attitudes are learned from direct experience or through SOCIALIZATION and are capable of being changed. Attitudes may vary in their direction (that is, they may be positive, negative or neutral), their intensity and in the degree of importance attached to them. It is possible to discern three component elements of an attitude: the *cognitive* component, that is the knowledge one has, true or false, about a particular subject which may have been gathered from a wide range of sources; the *affective* component, that is, one's emotional response or feelings towards a particular subject which will be linked to one's beliefs and VALUES; and the *behaviour* component, that is, how one reacts with respect to a certain subject. Attitudes cannot be seen. Their existence can only be inferred from what people say or do. It is for this reason that accurate attitude measurement is considered to be highly problematic: people may not be that willing to communicate what they really think or feel. It is basically through communicating with others that one develops attitudes. Attitudes, once developed, influence the way in which we perceive other people and thus how we behave towards them. The mass media may shape, reinforce or challenge attitudes. For example, in conveying STEREO-TYPES, mass media messages may shape peoples' attitudes towards GROUPS with which they have had little, if any, contact. CAMPAIGNS, such as ADVERTISING campaigns, may be designed to change people's attitudes towards a certain product. See DIFFERENTIAL PERCEPTION; DISSONANCE; NOISE; REINFORCEMENT; SELECTIVE EXPOSURE.

Attribution theory Concerned with the psychological processes by which individuals attribute causes to behaviour. Such attribution can be *dispositional* – behaviour attributed to such factors as personality and attitude – or *situational* – behaviour attributed to factors in the situation. We may, for example, blame a person's failure to gain employment on his/her laziness (dispositional attribution) or on the state of the economy (situational attribution). Ernest R. Hilgard, Richard C. Hilgard and Rita L. Hilgard in *Introduction to Psychology* (US: Harcourt Brace Jovanovich, 1975) argue that we tend to overestimate the influence of dispositional factors in the behaviour of other people and underestimate the influence of situational factors. They further argue that dispositional attribution can be difficult to change and that we are unwilling to discard dispositional attributions even when they are discredited. This may help explain the persistence of STEREOTYPES and PREJUDICE.

Audience The student of Communication Studies recognizes the term *audience* as overarching all the reception processes of MESSAGE sending. Thus there is the audience for theatre, TELEVISION and cinema; there is the RADIO listener. There is the audience for a pop concert or at a public meeting. Communicators shape their messages to fit the perceived needs of their audience: they calculate the level of receptiveness, the degree of readiness to accept the message and the mode of delivery. Audience is readership too and the success in meeting audience/readership needs relies extensively on FEEDBACK. When students of the Associated Examining Board A Level in Communication Studies design their second year Project, they have to make sure there is an audience for their chosen theme and mode of presentation: they have to *pre-test* their idea on

a potential audience and when the Project is complete, *post-test* it and write a report on the feedback obtained.

Sometimes there is an extra factor in the communicator–audience situation. This might be the *client*. An advertising agency, for example, is employed by a client (a company wishing to have its products advertised) to create a commercial whose audience is the television-watching public:

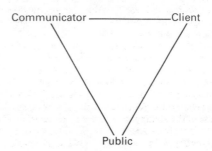

Communicator —————— Client

Public

Of course audience needs are not the only criterion for the communicator or the client but they are central to a process which is essentially interactive and subject to a wide range of social, cultural, economic, political and environmental influences. It might be argued that the advertiser's job is to *create* a need which his or her client's product or service will fulfil. See AUDIENCE RESEARCH; BROADCASTING RESEARCH; CATALYST EFFECT: CONTAGION EFFECT; CONTENT ANALYSIS; DECODE; DEPENDENCY THEORY; DOMINANT, SUBORDINATE, RADICAL; EXPECTATIONS; IDENTIFICATION; INHERITANCE FACTOR; MALETZKE'S MODEL OF THE MASS COMMUNICATION PROCESS, 1963; OPINION POLL; MOTIVATION RESEARCH (MR); PACKAGING; PARA-SOCIAL INTERACTION; PASSIVITY; PREFERRED READING; PR: PUBLIC RELATIONS; RATINGS; SOCIAL ACTION (MODE OF MEDIA ANALYSIS); USES AND GRATIFICATIONS THEORY; WESLEY AND MACLEAN'S MODEL OF COMMUNICATION, 1957.

Audience differentiation Like the 'mass', audiences – for RADIO, TELEVISION, the cinema or readers of the PRESS – are often simplistically regarded as a homogeneous lump. It is easier to make generalizations that way; but misleading. Audience differentiation works from the premise that analysis of audience response to media messages can only be purposeful if it recognizes that the mass is a complex of individuals, differentiated by gender, age, social class, profession, education and CULTURE. See ANALYSIS – MODES OF MEDIA ANALYSIS; AUDIENCE RESEARCH.

Audience Measurement Service See BROADCASTING RESEARCH.

Audience needs See USES AND GRATIFICATIONS THEORY.

Audience Reaction Service See BROADCAST-ING RESEARCH.

Audience research (AR) Investigation of the impact of the mass media, initially concerned with the size and structure of the audience for each particular MEDIUM of communication. The Department of Mass Communications of Unesco has an active programme for collecting basic statistical data on the development of MASS COMMUNICATION and the size of audiences throughout the world. Interest in audience research is particularly strong in the US where the mass media are heavily supported by commercial ADVERTISING revenues. The standard approach is to use sample surveys to measure audience size, composition and response.

The evolution of AR has been one of the refining its instruments of research and analysis. To the simple measurement categories of age, gender, social class, occupation etc. have been added the scrutiny of social and psychological characteristics and the *context*, social, political and cultural, in which the interaction between media and audience takes place.

The three major research methods are: experimental studies, both laboratory and quasi-laboratory; surveys based upon interviews or questionnaires and intensive case studies employing PARTICIPANT OBSERVATION, informal and group interviews, personal documents and other sources of documentation. BARB, the Broadcasting Audience Research Board, monitors 3000 homes in the UK, comprising approximately 7500 people. Each TV set or VCR is continuously metered and data are transmitted automatically each night by telephone line into a central computer. This quantitative measurement is backed up by measurement of audiences' appreciation of programmes based upon the responses of a panel of 3000 individuals, aged 12 and over. There is a separate children's panel of 1000. Each panellist completes a booklet covering seven days' viewing on all channels, scoring each programme seen on an interest/enjoyment scale. See ANALYSIS – MODES OF MEDIA ANALYSIS; BROADCASTING RESEARCH; CONTENT ANALYSIS.

Audience research into broadcasting See BROADCASTING RESEARCH.

Aura That which gives art its distinctive individuality, its uniqueness, and indeed its social separateness. The age of reproduction has gone a considerable way to dismissing this aura and rendering art much more of a collective experience.

* Walter Benjamin, 'The work of art in the age of mechanical reproduction' in J. Curran, Gurevitch and J. Woollacott, eds., *Mass Communication and Society* (UK: Edward Arnold, 1977).

Autobiography The poet Robert Southey is generally considered to be the first to use this term in 1809, to describe an account of a man or woman's own life.

Autocue Or teleprompt. A device which uses angled mirrors to project the words of a script on to a screen just below the lens of the TV camera. This enables a presenter to 'read' a script without looking down.

Autonomy the capacity to be self-governing, self-controlling and to be able to act in an independent manner. The term can be applied to individuals, GROUPS or institutions. Debate normally centres on the degree of autonomy a particular individual, group or institution has; an example here would be debate about the degree to which the BBC can act independently of the government of the day. See IMPARTIALITY.

Avant-garde The innovative, advance guard in any art form; usually assaulting tradition and boundaries of acceptability. The phrase was used as early as 1845 by Gabriel-Désiré Laverdant, and the anarchist Michael Bakunin named a periodical *L' Avant-garde* in 1878.

Back projection Process by which actors in a studio can be made to appear as though performing against a real moving background through the use of a rear projection process. In the US, it is termed 'rear projection'.

Back region, front region See IMPRESSION MANAGEMENT.

Bad news See GLASGOW UNIVERSITY MEDIA GROUP.

Baker-Nunn camera Large telescopic CAMERA for photographing orbiting satellites.

Balance See BALANCED PROGRAMMING; CONGRUENCE THEORY.

Balanced programming The PILKINGTON REPORT, 1962, put forward three criteria for the creation of balance in TV programmes. Balance would be achieved, Pilkington stated, if channels provided the widest possible range of subject matter; if the fullest treatment was given to each subject within the range and if SCHEDULING did not create imbalances by concentrating certain types of popular programmes at peak viewing times while relegating others, deemed less accessible, to inconvenient times. Paragraph 95 of Pilkington says, 'If service meant providing a wide enough choice of programmes of different kinds, then (it was submitted to us) there was a specially marked failure to do so in peak viewing hours.'

Balance has a more controversial, political CONNOTATION, when it is seen as a device to counter and control *bias*. More than any other MEDIUM public BROADCASTING aspires to equilibrium. Being fair to all sides can have paradoxical results: if one programme, for example, condemns Apartheid in South Africa, must the balance be sustained by allowing a programme which defends Apartheid? It is questionable whether fairness is actually achieved by giving air-time to ideas which flout the very principle of fairness.

Balance might ultimately mean always sitting on the fence; it may indicate a position which considers all standpoints to be tenable. Yet the balanced position – the fulcrum, as it were – from which other viewpoints are presented, has to be decided by *someone* whose impartiality in turn might be questioned by others. See IMPARTIALITY

Ball–Rokeach and Defleur's dependency model of mass communication effects, 1976 See also, DEPENDENCY THEORY. Ball-Rokeach and Defleur's model poses the question, to what extent is contemporary society dependent, for information and for viewpoints, on the all-pervasive mass communication industry and, arising from this question, how far are we dependent on the media for our orientation towards the world beyond our immediate experience? In 'A Dependency model of mass media effects' in *Communication Research*, 3 (1976), the authors argue that the nature and degree of dependency relate closely first to the extent to which society is subject to change, conflict or instability and second to the functions of information provision and attitude shaping of the mass media within those social structures:

The model emphasizes the essentially interactive nature of the processes of media effect. The societal and media systems interact and influence audience responses which in turn

influence media and society. The *cognitive* effect is that which relates to matters of the intellect and the *affective* to matters of emotion. In the cognitive area, the following areas of effect or influence are identified: creation and resolution of ambiguity; attitude formation; AGENDA SETTING; expansion of people's belief systems; value clarification. Under the affective heading, the media may be perceived as creating fear or anxiety; increasing or decreasing morale and establishing a sense of alienation. In terms of the third category, behaviour, the effects may be to activate or de-activate; formulate ISSUES and influence their resolution. They may stimulate a range of behaviours from political demonstrations to altruistic acts such as donating money to charity (see GLOBAL JUKEBOX; SOCIAL ACTION BROADCASTING). The authors cite the model as avoiding 'a seemingly untenable all-or-nothing position of saying either that the media have no significant impact on people or society, or that the media have an unbounded capacity to manipulate people and society'.

Where the model is open to most serious criticism is in its assumption that the societal structure and the media structure are independent of one another and that these are in some sort of equilibrium with audience. In many cases the media are so interlinked with power structures that a free interaction is more likely in theory than in practice. See CULTURAL APPARATUS; HEGEMONY; MEDIATION; POWER ELITE.

* D. McQuail and S. Windall, *Communication Models for the Study of mass communications (UK: Longman, 1981)*.

Band-wagon effect See NOELLE-NEVMANN'S SPIRAL OF SILENCE MODEL OF PUBLIC OPINION, 1974.

Bandwidth Range of frequencies available for carrying data and expressed in hertz (cycles per second). The amount of traffic a communication CHANNEL can carry is roughly proportional to its bandwidth. A TELEPHONE system, for example, requires a bandwidth of 4 Kilohertz while a 625-line TV channel requires around 8 Megahertz.

Bardic television A concept developed by John Fiske and John Hartley in *Reading Television* (UK: Methuen, 1978) in which they suggest TV performs functions in a modern society similar to those that the bard – poet, minstrel – performed in earlier times. The authors list seven functions of TV, which include the role of articulating the main lines of the established cultural CONSENSUS about the nature of reality; of involving audiences in the dominant value-system of the CULTURE and transmitting a sense of cultural membership through a sense of security and involvement.

BARB Broadcasters' Audience Research Board; limited company jointly owned by the BBC and

Ball-Rokeach and Defleur's dependency model of mass communication effects, 1976

ITCA. See BROADCASTING RESEARCH.

Barnlund's transactional model of communication, 1970 In 'A transactional model of communication' in K.K. Sereno and C.D. Mortensen, eds., *Foundations of Communication Theory* (US: Harper & Row, 1970), Dean C. Barnlund attempts to address the 'complexities of human communication' which present 'an unbelievably difficult challenge to the student of human affairs'. His model pays due respect to this complexity. For Barnlund communication both describes the evolution of MEANING and aims at the reduction of uncertainty. He stresses that meaning is something 'invented', 'assigned', 'given' rather than something 'received': 'Meanings may be generated while a man stands alone on a mountain trail or sits in the privacy of his study speculating about internal doubt.'

Within and around the communicant are *cues* of unlimited number, though some carrying more weight – or valence – than others at any given time. Barnlund's model indicates three sets of cues, each interacting upon one another. These are *public cues, private cues* and *behavioural cues*. DECODING and ENCODING are visualized as part of the same spiralling process – continuous, unrepeatable and irreversible. The use of +, 0 and – against the various cues denotes their weighting, as stimulating a positive, neutral or negative response or reading.

Public cues Barnlund divides into *natural* – those supplied by the physical world without the intervention of people, such as atmospheric conditions, natural occurrences – and *artificial*, those resulting from people's modification and manipulation of their environment. For example, Barnlund places his communicant, Mr A, in a doctor's waiting room which contains many public artificial cues – a pile of magazines, a smell of antiseptic, a picture by Joan Miró on the wall. Private cues emanate from sources not automatically available to any other person who enters a communicative field: 'Public and private cues may be verbal or non-verbal in form, but the critical quality is that they were brought into existence and remain beyond the control of the communicants.' The third set of cues – Behavioural – are those initiated or controlled by the communicant him/herself and in response to public and private cues, coloured by the communicant's 'sensory-motor successes and failures in the past, combined with his current appetites and needs' which will establish 'his set towards the environment'.

In the second diagram INTRA-PERSONAL COMMUNICATION becomes INTERPERSONAL COMMUNICATION, with the multiplication of cues and the introduction of the MESSAGE (M).

Barnlund emphasizes the *transferability* of cues. Public cues can be transformed into private ones, private cues may be converted into public ones, while environmental and behavioural cues may merge. In short, the whole

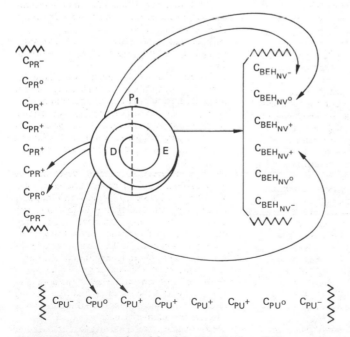

Barnlund's transactional models of Communication, 1970

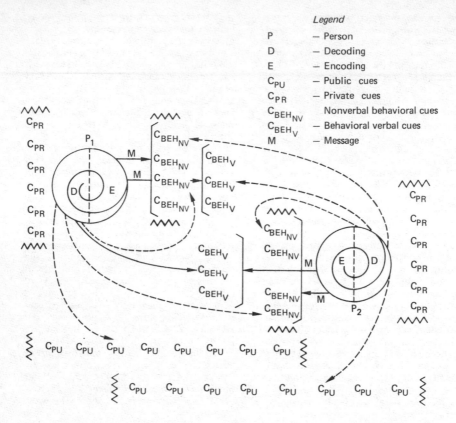

Legend

P	— Person
D	— Decoding
E	— Encoding
C_{PU}	— Public cues
C_{PR}	— Private cues
$C_{BEH_{NV}}$	Nonverbal behavioral cues
C_{BEH_V}	— Behavioral verbal cues
M	— Message

process is one of *transaction*, and few models have explored so impressively the inner dynamics of this process as Barnlund's, which also has useful application to the dynamics of MASS COMMUNICATION. See COMMUNICATION MODELS.

Barrier signals Used as personal defence mechanisms in communication situations, GESTURES such as the placing of hands and arms across the body, or folding the arms. In the business world, the classic defensive barrier is the desk. On its role in the relationship between the executive and this modern version of the old moated castle and drawbridge, much has been written – about the size and dominance of the desk, its angle to the office door, the distance between the desk and the chair placed for those who approach the boss's territory. In *Manwatching: A Field Guide to Human Behaviour* (UK: Jonathan Cape, 1977), Desmond Morris would have us believe of the executive desk that 'many a businessman would feel naked without one and hides behind it gratefully every day, wearing it like a vast wooden chastity belt.'

Basic cable Term used in the US to describe the original type of cable system servicing areas where 'off-air' RADIO and TV reception was poor. Basic cable eventually provided in

America a package of useful additional services – local as well as long-distance transmissions and special services such as Cable News Network (CNN), all for a flat-rate subscription by the viewer. The system makes possible a range of interactive services, allowing the viewer to communicate with banks and other agencies for personal business including hotel, holiday and theatre booking. See CABLE TELEVISION; COAXIAL CABLE; HF MULTIPAIR CABLE; OPTICAL FIBRE CABLE.

Basic needs See MASLOW'S HIERARCHY OF NEEDS.

Bass's 'double action' model of internal news flow, 1969 A development of two earlier classic models addressing the processes of media news production – WHITE'S GATEKEEPER MODEL, 1950 and McNELLY'S MODEL OF NEWS FLOW, 1959. In his article, 'Refining the gatekeeper concept' in *Journalism Quarterly*, 46(1969), A.Z. Bass argues that the most important 'gates' in the exercise of GATEKEEPING are located within the news organization. Bass divides the operation into a news *gathering* stage and a news *processing* stage:

Writers, reporters and local editors are closer to the 'raw' news, the event, than those

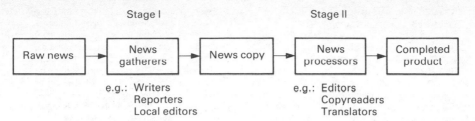

Bass's 'double action' model of internal news flow, 1969

involved in Stage II of the gatekeeping process, while those involved at Stage II are closer to the power centre of the organization and therefore more subject to the organization's NORMS and VALUES and to pressures from competing stories.
See MALETZKE'S MODEL OF THE MASS COMMUNICATION PROCESS, 1963.

Baton signals Chiefly manual GESTURES with which we beat time to the rhythm of spoken expression and which give emphasis and urgency. They are the stock-in-trade of declamatory communication, especially that of politicians. Not only the hands are employed in baton signals, but the head, shoulders and feet.
See NON-VERBAL BEHAVIOUR: REPERTOIRE.

BBC See BBC ORIGINS; RADIO BROADCASTING; RADIO: BROADCASTING IN THE 90s; REITHIAN. *See also* BROADCASTING COMPLAINTS COMMISSION; 'BROADCASTING IN THE SEVENTIES'; CONGLOMERATES; IMPARTIALITY; MONOPOLY, FOUR SCANDALS OF; PILKINGTON COMMITTEE REPORT ON BROADCASTING, 1962; PUBLIC SERVICE BROADCASTING; RADIO BALLADS; RECEIVED PRONUNCIATION; SATELLITE TRANSMISSION; SCHEDULING; SELSDON COMMITTEE REPORT ON TELEVISION, 1935; 'TASTE AND STANDARDS IN BBC PROGRAMMES'; THIRD PROGRAMME; ULLSWATER COMMITTEE REPORT ON BROADCASTING, 1936; WORLD REPORTER.

BBC, origins The BBC began life as the British Broadcasting Company, incorporated on 15 December 1922 and receiving its licence to broadcast on 18 January 1923. It was a private company made up chiefly of manufacturers of BROADCASTING equipment. The Company was incorporated with 100,000 shares of stock worth £1 each. Any British wireless manufacturer could join by purchasing one or more shares, making a £50 deposit and agreeing to the terms that had been drawn up by the negotiating manufacturers and the Postmaster General.

The six largest manufacturers, in return for guaranteeing the continuing operation and financial solvency of the company, were given control. Although other manufacturers could buy stock and be admitted to membership, the principals could choose six of the Company's nine directors and these in turn had the power to select its chairman.

Each wireless set owner had to pay a 10 shilling (50 p.) licence fee to the Post office annually and the government agreed to issue licences only to people using receivers made by members of the company. Thus the manufacturers were guaranteed protection against competition.

The company was to establish eight broadcasting stations in different parts of the British Isles. Only news originating from four established NEWS AGENCIES (such as the Press Association and Reuters) could be used in broadcasting and there was to be no ADVERTISING.

By April 1923 the Postmaster General had appointed a seven-man investigating committee to review the status of the British Broadcasting Company, headed by Sir Frederick Sykes, with a mandate to consider 'broadcasting in all its aspects'. The Sykes Committee faced questions on widespread evasions of the equipment monopoly and condemnation by Beaverbrook newspapers of the control of the Six. After 34 meetings, the Committee recommended – and the government accepted – a single receiver licence of 10 shillings to cover all types of radios, and the ban was raised on foreign receivers.

Most important, Sykes forecast the eventual replacement of private by public operation: '. . . we consider that the control of such a potential power [of broadcasting] over public opinion and the life of the nation ought to remain with the State, and that the operation of so important a national service ought not to be allowed to become an unrestricted commercial monopoly.'

A new committee under the chairmanship of the Earl of Crawford and Balcarres, set up in 1925, led to the Charter and Licence which created the British Broadcasting Corporation and authorized it to broadcast for 10 years from 1 January 1927. It was established on three principles which were to apply to British broadcasting until the coming of COMMERCIAL TELEVISION: broadcasting became a monopoly, financed by licence fees and administered by an independent public corporation.

* A. Briggs, *The History of Broadcasting in the United Kingdom* (UK: Oxford, vol. 1 1961; vol. 2, 1965, vol. 3 1979, vol. 4 1979).

'BBC Radio in the Nineties' A discussion paper published in November 1982 setting out the way BBC RADIO might develop. The paper elaborates proposals for a five-service plan for the BBC, four UK networks and a full pattern of English Local and National Regional Radio – 'in effect' Radio Five – being a system of some 40 English stations primarily BROADCASTING locally-orientated programmes, news and information but also carrying elements of popular drama, light music, continuing education and programmes of minority or ethnic interest. See 'BROADCASTING IN THE SEVENTIES'.

Beamwidth The angular width of a RADIO or RADAR beam.

Becker's mosaic model of communication, 1968 Messages are rarely single, coming along one line, so the concept of a *mosaic* as a model of the communication process is a useful variant on the linear theme. S.L. Becker in 'What rhetoric (communication theory) is relevant for contemporary speech communication?' a paper presented at the University of Minnesota Spring Symposium in Speech Communication, 1968, posed the theory of a 'communication mosaic' indicating that most communicative acts link MESSAGE elements from more than the immediate social situation – from early impressions, previous conversa-tions, from the media, from half-forgotten comments: a mosaic of source influences.

The layers of Becker's mosaic cube correspond to layers of information. Some elements of the mosaic assert themselves, others are blocked out. The model illustrates the complexity of the many layers of the communication process and the interaction between its 'cubes' or 'tesserae' of information, showing the internal as well as the external world of communication; that which is isolated or unique, that which is recurring in a dense and ever-changing pattern. See COMMUNICATION MODELS.

Behavioural cues See BARNLUND'S TRANSACTIONAL MODEL OF COMMUNICATION.

Behaviourism A school of psychological thought which maintains that a scientific understanding of human behaviour can only be attained from objective, observable *action*. Consciousness, feeling and other subjective aspects of human behaviour are not regarded as suitable bases for investigations.

Berlo's SMCR model of communication, 1960 David K. Berlo, who studied with Wilbur Schramm (See SCHRAMM'S MODELS OF COMMUNICATION) at the University of Illinois, produced the following model in his *The Process of Communication: An Introduction to Theory and Practice* (US: Holt, Rinehart & Winston, 1960). It is a development in a sociological direction of the SHANNON AND WEAVER MODEL OF COMMUNICATION:

Features of the process have been made

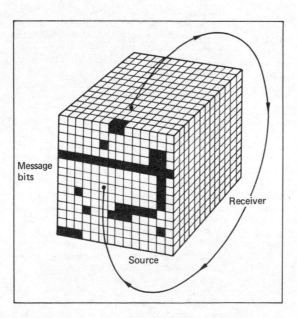

Becker's mosaic model of communication, 1968

explicit, due acknowledgment being made of the significance to both Source and Receiver of CULTURE and the social system in which the act of communication takes place. Berlo's model does not record the *flow* of communication, though the assumption must be that it is conceived as linear – in a line from Source to Receiver. Both FEEDBACK and the *interaction* of elements are implied rather than made explicit. In a successful act of communication, Berlo's model suggests, the skills of Source and Receiver must, to a considerable extent, *match* each other. The same may be said for attitudes or VALUES; and Knowledge must be *acknowledged*. The model rewards analysis and testing out, especially its elegant portrait of the MESSAGE. See COMMUNICATION MODELS.

Beveridge Committee Report on Broadcasting, 1950 Both from a theoretical and a practical point of view the Committee chaired by Lord Beveridge conducted the most thorough examination of BROADCASTING in Britain since its inception. Beveridge went to considerable lengths to identify and discuss the dangers of broadcasting monopoly, as then held by the BBC. Nevertheless proposals for *competitive* broadcasting were rejected on the grounds that programmes would deteriorate in quality if there were rival corporations.

Beveridge was equally firm in believing that broadcasting should be independent of government control, and declared against suggestions that the power of the BBC should be curbed through closer parliamentary supervision.

To prevent broadcasting becoming an uncontrolled bureacracy, Beveridge recommended more active surveillance of output by the BBC's Board of Governors and a 'Public Representation Service' to bridge the gap between the BBC and the general public. Additionally, the Committee proposed regional and functional devolution of some of the corpora-

tion's activities, more comprehensive reports by the BBC on its work, and five-year reviews by small independent committees.

A major recommendation which made no headway was that the monopoly of broadcasting be extended to local authorities and universities, allowing them to operate FM RADIO stations.

Commercial broadcasting in the US style was not approved of: 'Sponsoring . . . puts the control of broadcasting ultimately in the hands of people whose interest is not broadcasting but the selling of some other goods or services or the propagation of particular ideas.' Interestingly, four of the 11 committee members (including Lord Beveridge) dissented from the majority verdict against any form of commercial ADVERTISING. See COMMISSIONS/COMMITTEES ON THE MEDIA.

Bias From the French, *biais*, slant; a one-sided inclination of the mind. The student of communication approaches this word with extreme caution, for bias generally belongs to the realm of PERCEPTION, and other people's perceptions at that: like beauty, bias lies in the eye of the beholder whose vision is coloured by VALUES and previous experience. The accusation of bias tends to be predicated on the assumption that there is an opposite – OBJECTIVITY; that there is an attainable ideal called IMPARTIALITY; that freedom from bias is not only possible but desirable. To speak, publish or broadcast without bias would imply the use of LANGUAGE which is *value-free*. Yet however careful we might be in what we say we disclose something of ourselves, what shaped and formed us; what counts with us, what we value. When other people appear to call that value into question, we may be tempted to classify them as biased.

Bibliotherapy Or 'book therapy'; help with human problems by means of books. Used chiefly with young people, bibliotherapy has

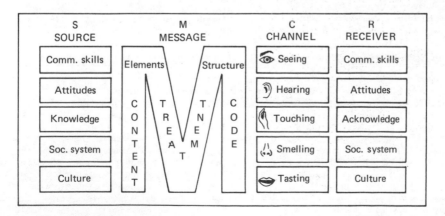

S SOURCE	M MESSAGE		C CHANNEL	R RECEIVER
Comm. skills	Elements	Structure	👁 Seeing	Comm. skills
Attitudes			👂 Hearing	Attitudes
Knowledge	C O N T E N T	T R E A T / N E M T / C O D E	👆 Touching	Acknowledge
Soc. system			👃 Smelling	Soc. system
Culture			👄 Tasting	Culture

Berlo's SMCR model of communication, 1960

also successfully been introduced to the elderly in long-stay hospital wards or other institutions.

As children grow up and develop they encounter a multitude of problems stemming from cultural conflicts, religious differences, family mobility, hospital confinement, parental separation, etc. Some of their concerns arise mainly within themselves while others evolve from outside events. To help children attain some degree of understanding of their personal problems, there are books that offer solace, help, clarification. Bibliotherapy, aims to create a dynamic interaction between literature and the personality of the reader.

Therapeutic bibliotherapy attempts to tackle existing difficulties and problems while **Preventative bibliotherapy** sets out to anticipate problems in the future. IDENTIFICATION is an almost universal experience of young readers and therapy can begin through affiliation with a real or fictional character in literature (See PARA-SOCIAL INTERACTION). Once identification has taken place, the reader – or listener – is then prepared to gain a purging effect from learning more about a set of circumstances outside the book. The hoped-for result is *insight*, arising from the fusion of intellectual perception and emotional drive.

Among the elderly, bibliotherapy, according to Daniel Sweeney ('Bibliotherapy and the elderly' in R.J. Rubin, ed., *Bibliotherapy Source Book*, UK: Oryx Press Monsell Publishers, 1978), taps the 'capacity to experience joy in life'; it restores morale, encourages activity and rekindles feelings of competence by reminding old people of past skills, goals and ambitions achieved. Not the least, it provides a valuable CHANNEL for reminiscence – joy and laughter are remembered, and unresolved hurts or regrets aired.

* James Marr, 'The capacity for joy' in the *Nursing Times* (21–7 September, 1983).

Bifurcation of belief See IMPARTIALITY

Billy Blue Collar Trade parlance in the US to describe the typical member of the 'massest' of mass audiences.

Binary opposition See SEMANTIC DIFFERENTIAL

Bit See COMPUTER LANGUAGE.

Black comedy In art, literature and cinema, a mode which extracts humour from serious matters such as death, murder, madness and sexual perversion. Leslie Halliwell in his *Filmgoer's Companion* (UK: Paladin, first published 1972) believes Black comedy to be 'enjoyed chiefly by those with sophisticated tastes'. A classic FILM Black comedy – enjoyed by sophisticated and unsophisticated alike – is the Ealing Studios' production *Kind Hearts and Coronets* (1949), directed by Robert Hamer and starring Denis Price as the poor relation of a rich, aristocratic family who murders his way to the dukedom, and Alec Guinness playing all eight of Price's victims, male and female. Master of the Black comedy in the cinema is Spanish director Luis Buñuel (1900–83) who, in films such as *The Criminal Life of Archibaldo de la Cruz* (1959), subjects religion and the social pretensions of the bourgeoisie to merciless scrutiny. Black comedy is a familiar theme in the theatre. In recent times, in the UK, Joe Orton (1933–67) excelled in the idiom. In plays such as *Entertaining Mr Sloane* (1964) and *Loot* (1966) he treated crime, sexual perversion and violence as hilariously comic. In *Loot*, a young criminal secretes loot from a burglary in his mother's coffin, and from this act a macabre and complicated farce develops.

Black documentary Not to be confused with FILM NOIR. The term refers to a GENRE of DOCUMENTARY produced in Iron Curtain countries, particularly Poland, in the middle and late 1950s during a period in which the reins of government CENSORSHIP were loosened. The black documentaries represented a rawer, more searching, more implicitly critical subject matter than the rose-tinted morale-booster films that had predominated since the 2nd World War (1939–45). Typical of the style was Jerzy Bossak's *Warsaw 56* (1956), a FILM that captures the terror faced by the 'cliff-dwellers', Warsaw people continuing, long after the war, to live in city ruins, while not far away is the extravagant 'Stalin-style' Palace of Culture.

BLEND The Birmingham and Loughborough Electronic Network Development; advanced experiment in the networking of research data electronically. See MEDIA TECHNOLOGY.

Blimp A sound-proof cover fixed over a camera during shooting, to absorb running noise.

Body language See COMMUNICATION, NON-VERBAL; GESTURE; INTERPERSONAL COMMUNICATION; NON-VERBAL BEHAVIOUR: REPERTOIRE; PROXEMICS; TOUCH.

Boom A movable trolly with a telescopic arm to which a microphone is attached during BROADCASTING or FILM-making, to allow positioning of the microphone.

Boomerang response Effect of a mass media MESSAGE which, in terms of audience reaction, proves to be the opposite of that which was intended.

Bowdlerize To extract from text what is deemed offensive; to expurgate. The word comes from the surname of Dr Thomas Bowdler who, in 1818, published *The Family Shakespeare* which censored 'those words and expressions which cannot with propriety be read aloud in a family'. Not only 'bad language' is bowdlerized: harmful or subversive *sentiments* can be removed or toned down, very often when a wider audience for a work is being considered. In *Subculture: The Meaning of Style* (UK/US: Methuen, 1979), D. Hebdige observes that the original messages conveyed by early jazz music – those of anger at the negro's position in US society, and sexual eroticism – were bowdlerized (or laundered) as Jazz was fed into the mainstream popular CULTURE of the country in the 1920s and 1930s.

B-Picture In the 1940s and 1950s it was cinema practice to put on two films, the main feature – the A-Picture – and a cheaply and quickly made supporting FILM – the B-Picture. The equivalent of the 'flip-side' of a popular record, the B-Picture, or B-movie was invariably *B*udget and almost invariably *B*ad. Time, however, lends enchantment and film enthusiasts often have a soft spot for a 'GENRE' the like of which just is not made any more. Examples are Joseph H. Lewis's *Gun Crazy* (1949), Nathan Juran's *Attack of the 50 Foot Woman* (1958) and Roger Corman's *Little Shop of Horrors* (1960), which the director claimed to have made in two days.

Braille Himself blind, Louis Braille (1809–52) conceived and developed the *Braille system* of printing for the blind. It consists of embossed characters printed on special paper, recognizable by TOUCH and formed by using varying combinations of six dots. In 1982 the Auto-Braille Printing Press, designed and made in the UK, was introduced. Not only has it doubled the speed of braille printing, but the machine cuts, embosses, collates and folds.

Brainwashing Concerted effort to change attitudes using a wide range of techniques; specifically refers to the 'washing out' of political beliefs and the attempt to replace these by the political beliefs of the group, party, movement or nation responsible for the brainwashing. A similar word is *indoctrination*. It is held that brainwashing works most effectively when the subject is *isolated* and when the treatment is *intense*; collaboration is induced through systems of rewards and punishments.

Edgar H. Schein of the Massachusetts Institute of Technology in 'The Chinese indoctrination program for prisoners of war: a study of attempted "brainwashing" ', in R.A. King, ed., *Readings for an Introduction to Psychology* (US: McGraw-Hill, 1961), lists the following general principles which underlay the various phases of the Chinese indoctrination programme: (1) Repetition. (2) Pacing of demands – starting with easy demands, then making them harder: 'This was particularly effective in eliciting confessions, self-criticism, and information during interrogation'. (3) Insistence on constant participation on the part of the prisoner. (4) Emphasis upon inserting new ideas into 'old and meaningful contexts'. (5) Systematic reward for cooperation, punishment or threats of punishment for non-cooperation. (6) Use of prestige suggestion – eliciting collaboration through pleas for acceptable philosophies: anti-war sentiments strongly appealed to war-weary soldiers. (7) Use of manipulative tricks, for example, to 'require signatures, photographs, or personal information for a purpose which sounded legitimate, then using them for another purpose'.

Brakelight function In American communications parlance, a signal to audience that a speaker is about to conclude his or her speech. The brakelight could be a word, phrase, sentence, gesture or movement.

Breakfast-time television In the UK, the BBC was ahead of its rival, COMMERCIAL TELEVISION, when it launched its early weekday morning programme *Breakfast Time* in 1983. TV-AM, the company given the early morning FRANCHISE by the IBA followed with *Good Morning Britain*.

Bribery 'Subsidies' by government to British newspapers in the late 18th and early 19th c. were extensive. Sir Robert Walpole, the first 'true prime minister', who held power from 1721 to 1742, made bribery a form of government. In the last decade of his administration £50,000 was paid out in bribes to newspapers and pamphleteers in return for giving his government a quiet and supportive PRESS. Walpole's example set the tone for the future. In 1797, *The Times* with a circulation of 2000 received a government subsidy of £8,112. At the same time, direct payments were made to journalists, and the government also spread its patronage by placing adverts in newspapers of which it approved. Today, bribery is a thing of the past – except for the offering of knighthoods to the editors of some newspapers, and not others. See NEWSPAPERS, ORIGINS.

British Board of Film Censors Set up in 1912 to approve films for public showing. The right of local authorities to ban films had been granted in the Cinematography Act of 1909. This had resulted in a chaos of contradictory judgements. The Cinematograph Exhibitors Association and the main production companies set up their own vetting office – the BBFC. The Board consists of a president and a secretary, both appointed by the FILM industry. Like most CENSORSHIP bodies, the Board lagged behind public tastes for decades and was susceptible to influence by government. Under the more liberal regime of John Trevelyan (1958–71) the Board acquired a new image, casting off its earlier reputation for over-cautiousness. Since then the general trend of the Board's activity has been towards greater toleration while at the same time maintaining a protective attitude towards children. See CERTIFICATION OF FILMS; WILLIAMS COMMITTEE REPORT.

British Broadcasting Company See BBC, ORIGINS.

British Broadcasting Corporation See BBC; BBC, ORIGINS.

British Code of Advertising Practice Rule book of the Advertising Standards Authority, whose CAP Committee devises parameters of ethics and taste beyond which advertisers are expected not to stray. The code is spelt out in detail and responsive to evolving and changing public attitudes. For example in the sixth edition, rules governing the ADVERTISING of alcoholic drink forbid the association of drink with driving or dangerous machinery, and 'Advertisements should not encourage or appear to condone over-indulgence. Repeated buying of large rounds should not be implied'.

British Film Institute An outcome of the Report of the Commission on Educational and Cultural Films, financed chiefly by the Carnegie trustees (1929–32), the BFI was set up in 1933 to foster the use of FILM for educational purposes to preserve the cultural heritage of commercial film in the vaults of the National Film Library. Today the BFI's services to film in the UK are enormous. They include: the NATIONAL FILM ARCHIVE; the National Film Theatre on London's South Bank; the financing of films by British directors; a network of regional film theatres; widening commitments to film education and the publication of works on cinema.

British Film Production Fund UK Treasury official Wilfred Eady devised this means of raising funds for FILM production in 1950. The so-called Eady Levy or Eady Plan imposed a levy on cinema admissions to support film making. Initially a voluntary system, it became statutory under the Cinematograph Act, 1957. In 1985 the Conservative Government replaced the National Film Finance Corporation, responsible for the distribution of monies to production, with a private-sector body. State funding of £1.5m a year for five years was proposed; the private-sector body to match that for a period of three years.

Broadcast and narrowcast codes See CODES.

Broadcasting See BBC, ORIGINS; BBC RADIO IN THE NINETIES; CABLE TELEVISION; COMMERCIAL RADIO; COMMUNITY RADIO; PIRATE RADIO; RADIO BROADCASTING; RADIO: BROADCASTING IN THE 90s; SATELLITE TRANSMISSION; TELEVISION BROADCASTING; WIRELESS TELEGRAPHY. *See also:* ANNAN COMMISSION REPORT ON BROADCASTING, 1977; BREAKFAST-TIME TELEVISION; BROADCASTING ACT, 1980; BROADCASTING COMPLAINTS COMMISSION; 'BROADCASTING IN THE SEVENTIES'; 'BROADCASTING IN THE '90s': GOVERNMENT WHITE PAPER, 1988; BROADCASTING RESEARCH; BROADCASTING STANDARDS COUNCIL; CAMPAIGN FOR PRESS & BROADCASTING FREEDOM; CB – CITIZEN'S BAND RADIO; CELLULAR RADIO; CONGLOMERATES; DEVOLUTION; FORMULA BROADCASTING; FOURTEEN-DAY RULE; FRANCHISES FOR INDEPENDENT TELEVISION; FREE COMMUNICATIONS GROUP; FREQUENCY; GATE KEEPING; GENERAL ADVISORY COUNCILS: HUNT COMMITTEE REPORT ON CABLE TELEVISION, 1982; HYDE PARK OF THE AIR; ILR; IMPARTIALITY; LONGFORD COMMITTEE REPORT ON PORNOGRAPHY, 1972; MARINE BROADCASTING (OFFENCES) ACT, 1965; MINORITY REPORT OF MR SELWYN LLOYD; NETWORK; PILKINGTON COMMITTEE REPORT ON BROADCASTING, 1962; POLITICS OF ACCOMMODATION (IN THE MEDIA); PUBLIC SERVICE BROADCASTING; RADIO NORTH-SEA; REFLECTIVE-PROJECTIVE THEORY OF BROADCASTING & MASS COMMUNICATION; REITHIAN; SANIEL PEDWAR CYMRU; SCHEDULING; SELSDON COMMITTEE REPORT ON TELEVISION, 1935; SINCERITY TEST (BY THE MEDIA); SINS OF OMISSION; SOCIAL ACTION BROADCASTING; SOUND BROADCASTING ACT, 1972; STATUS QUO; STEREOTYPE; STUDENT RADIO; TELETEXT; 'TELEVISION PROGRAMME GUIDELINES'; 'THIRD AGE OF BROADCASTING'; THIRD PROGRAMME; TIME-SHIFT VIEWING; TRIVIALITY; ULLSWATER COMMITTEE REPORT ON BROADCASTING, 1936; VIDEO; 'WAR OF THE WORLDS'; WESTMINSTER VIEW; WIRELESS TELEGRAPHY ACT, 1904.

Broadcasting Act, 1980 Receiving its Royal Assent on 13 November 1980, the Act extended the life of the IBA until the end of 1996; defined the Authority's responsibility for the new CHANNEL FOUR; set out special measures for the Fourth Channel in Wales, Saniel Pedwar Cymru (S4C) and contained a number of other important provisions relating to the future of BROADCASTING, including the establishment of a BROADCASTING COMPLAINTS COMMISSION.

Broadcasting Complaints Commission In October 1971 an independent Programmes Complaints Commission was set up by the BBC, but disbanded in 1981 when the government-formed Broadcasting Complaints Commission began work under Part IV of the Broadcasting Act of 1980. Five commissioners appointed by the Secretary of State were empowered to consider and adjudicate on unjust or unfair treatment in sound or TV programmes and unwarranted infringements of privacy; consequently to oblige the offending BROADCASTING body to publicly acknowledge a proved complaint within a specified period. The Commission reports annually on its findings. Complaints can be made by any person or persons in writing.

'Broadcasting in the Seventies' Published by the BBC in 1969, with a foreword by Lord Hill of Luton, its Chairman, the report describes a long-term programme for BROADCASTING in which the BBC proposed to undertake some of the newly defined needs of RADIO. The purpose of the plans were, in Lord Hill's words, 'to adapt our service to a changing world to meet changing tastes and needs'. The publication acknowledged the altered habits of the listening audience: 'for most people radio is now mainly for the day time. They see it less as a medium for family entertainment, more as a continuous supplier of music and information'.

Radio had also opened up from the centre into the regions, indicating in the audience 'a growing resistance to the apparently inexorable magnetism of London'. A restructuring of the BBC's English regions was proposed, from six to eight smaller 'and more socially logical regions', based on Birmingham, Bristol, Leeds, Manchester, Newcastle, Norwich, Plymouth and Southampton. At the same time, the BBC proposed to develop local radio 'as a major element in the BBC's services', setting a target of approximately 40 stations servicing nearly 90% of the population of England.

See 'BBC RADIO FOR THE NINETIES'; RADIO: BROADCASTING IN THE 90s.

'Broadcasting in the '90s': Government White Paper, 1988 What *The Observer* called 'the biggest bomb put under British TV in half-a-century' (13 November 1988), the Tory government's White Paper on the future of broadcasting in the UK, *Broadcasting in the '90s: Competition, Choice and Quality* promises a vast increase in broadcasting channels; and the keynote of this new regimen would be competition. Published in November 1988, and announced in Parliament by Home Secretary Douglas Hurd, the White Paper proposes a fifth TV channel, an expansion of Direct Satellite Broadcasing (DBS), more local TV stations, three new national RADIO networks and a growth in localized radio.

The Independent Broadcasting Authority (IBA) will be replaced by an Independent Broadcasting Commission 'with a lighter touch than the IBA'. All independent TV services – cable, satellite and terrestrial – will come under the orbit of this single agency. Most controversial of the White Paper's proposals is the decision to auction off the independent TV franchises to the highest bidder. There will be a 'quality threshhold'.

Channel 5 would be expected to provide a diverse programme service appealing to a variety of tastes and interests and to ensure that a minimum of 25% of original programming came from independent producers. As for the BBC, the White Paper states that the licence fee will eventually be replaced by a system of subscription, though not before the renewal of the Corporation's Royal Charter and Licence in 1996.

Questions arising from the proposals are: will the future of broadcasting lie exclusively in the hands of multinational media corporations? Will broadcasting come increasingly to resemble the tabloid press in content and presentation?

Most importantly, will the principles of *public service* in broadcasting be sustainable once market forces dominate the airwaves? See DEREGULATION; MAINSTREAMING.

Broadcasting legislation The first act of its kind in the world was the Wireless Telegraphy Act of 1904, in which the British government commanded substantial powers over the regulation of wireless TELEGRAPHY. The Act gave the Postmaster General the duty to licence all wireless telegraphy apparatus. The British Broadcasting Company received its licence from the Post Office in 1923. The TELEVISION ACT, 1954 created COMMERCIAL TELEVISION in the UK with the formation of the Independent Television Authority (later the Independent Broadcasting Authority). ADVERTISING was to be kept separate from programming. Requirements were laid down to govern programming content. The Copyright Act, 1956 initiated copyright protection of broadcast material. In 1972 the Sound Broadcasting Act inaugurated COMMERCIAL RADIO and the ITA became the IBA. The Independent Broadcasting Authority Act, 1979 empowered the IBA to create CHANNEL FOUR, while the Broadcasting Act (1980), among other regulations, created the BROADCASTING COMPLAINTS COMMISSION. In 1984 came the VIDEO RECORDING ACT requiring the certification of all new VIDEO releases. The CABLE and BROADCASTING ACT of the same year set up the Cable Authority whose task was to select operators for particular areas and to oversee organizational and programming stipulations. See BROADCASTING STANDARDS COUNCIL; CINEMA LEGISLATION.

Broadcasting research Daily measurements of RADIO audiences have been conducted by the BBC since December 1931, and of TV audiences since 1952. In 1981 the BBC and ITV companies launched a system of TV audience measurement, BARB, a limited company jointly owned by the BBC and ITCA, with two major branches – the *Audience Measurement Service* and the *Audience Reaction Service*. The first provides continuous monitoring of the size of TV audiences, the amount of viewing and demographic profiles of viewers etc.; the other monitors the reaction of audiences to each programme and, for selected programmes, provides detailed analysis of this critical reaction. The BBC's *Broadcasting Research Department* is data supplier to BARB for the Reaction Service. This yields an approximate 2500 sample size per viewing day of the population aged 12 and over. Opinions are obtained through a self-completion booklet *What You Think Of What You Watch* placed with the Department's Daily Survey correspondents and returned by post.

For radio, audience sizes are measured through the Department's Daily Survey, a sample survey in which some 1000 people aged four

and over are interviewed daily in their homes. Audience reactions to radio programmes are obtained through a panel of about 3000 listeners, each week receiving a questionnaire on a selection of the following week's broadcasts. As in the case of the TV audience, the panel members are requested not to vary their normal pattern of radio listening. See AUDIENCE RESEARCH.
* *Annual Review of Broadcasting Research Findings* (BBC Publications).

Broadcasting Standards Council Created in 1988 by the Conservative government in the UK to monitor sex and violence on British TELEVISION screens. Former editor of *The Times* and former vice-chairman of the BBC, Sir William Rees-Mogg was appointed the Council's first chairman. According to Douglas Hurd, the Home Secretary, the initially non-statutory Council's remit would be 'taste and decency' not political CENSORSHIP. Speaking in the House of Commons for the Labour opposition, Roy Hattersley feared the BSC was 'the thin end of a highly authoritarian wedge'. See BROADCASTING.

Brute A high-intensity spot lamp.

Bubble memory A means for storing the digitized visual information of an all-electronic camera; bubble memories are low-cost ultra high-density devices within which upwards of one hundred million bubbles can be implanted in one square in a garnet crystal, the bubbles being charged or not charged according to the information received from the charge-coupled device (CCD) array.

Butterfly In films, a net stretched over an outdoor scene to soften the sunlight.

Button apathy When a TV viewer cannot be bothered to switch off a programme, or to switch from one CHANNEL to another, he/she is probably suffering from 'button apathy'. This is a challenge to programmers to trap audience interest rapidly and early. Very often, apathy – or lethargy – does the rest, and the viewer stays loyal. See SCHEDULING.

By-line Use of the journalist's/author's name on a report or article. These are very common now in the PRESS but at one time the granting of by-lines was a rare honour, to distinguish top writers or as a reward for outstanding reportage.

Cable and Broadcasting Act, 1984 Drawn up by the UK Conservative government with the intention of facilitating the 'cabled society', the Act followed most of the recommendations of the HUNT COMMITTEE REPORT ON CABLE EXPANSION AND BROADCASTING POLICY, 1982, which proposed a cable NETWORK for Britain with the minimum of rules and regulations.

The Act set up a Cable Authority to select cable operators for particular areas and to maintain an overview on general matters of organization and programming. See BROADCASTING LEGISLATION.

Cable television Underground cable networks were established in the 1930s in the UK to relay RADIO broadcasts. These were later adapted to transmit TV to areas which received poor 'off-air' signals; reception problems were also the reason for the US 'cabling up' in the 1950s.

Until the election of the Conservative government in 1979, the commercial potential of cable in developing information technology had stimulated only modest interest. In March 1982 the Tory Cabinet's Information Technology Advisory Panel (ITAP), appointed in July 1981 by the prime minister Margaret Thatcher, recommended a rapid and substantial expansion of cable networks, to be established and operated by private companies, with a minimum capacity of 30 channels each. The operator of each NETWORK should, ITAP advised, be given monopoly control over the programmes transmitted. The Panel considered that it would cost some £2.5bn to wire up the homes of Britain's chief cities, the finance coming from private companies. Such recommendations came essentially from a body of men with vested interests in MEDIA TECHNOLOGY, such as Charles Read, director of Inter-Bank Research Organization, involved in the planning of electronic home banking and I.H. Cohen, managing director of the Mullard company owned by Philips which, through its Visionhire subsidiary, is the UK's second largest cable operator. The Panel confessed that it had 'not done any detailed market research' and information was not elicited from trades unions, political parties or consumer organizations. In short, there was no concrete evidence that there was a public *demand* for a vast increase of cable networks and the subsequent flood of new programmes these would make possible.

ITAP reported swiftly; the HUNT REPORT was made public in September 1982, also urging the 'wiring up' of the nation, with a minimum of rules and regulations. In 1983 the Home Secretary in Mrs Thatcher's newly elected government, Leon Brittan, issued special government licences prior to a full-scale spread of cable networks.

Mindful of the dominance of quantity over quality in programmes, as typified by TV in the US, the ANNAN REPORT, 1977 perceived cable to be a 'ravenous parasite'. The fear was that more did not necessarily mean better. However, 'more' is obviously to be the keynote of BROADCASTING in the 1980s onwards.

SATELLITE TRANSMISSION is internationalizing broadcasting; cable and VIDEO are diversifying it but also calling into question the concepts and practice of PUBLICE SERVICE BROADCASTING. In the UK the traditional DUOPOLY of the control of broadcasting, between the BBC and the IBA is at its curtain-call. DEREGULATION will change the face of broadcasting.

Vast profits from cable subscriptions are far from a certainty. Cabling is massively expensive and in turn cable services will not come cheaply to consumers. For this reason, cable (unlike Public Service Broadcasting) may prove discriminatory – between region and region, between rural and urban areas, between society's 'haves' and 'have-nots'. The ISSUES concern production, distribution, exchange and regulation. A prime worry expressed by commentators is that far from giving communities of interest a say in their own networks – which cable ideally could provide – what will happen will mirror developments in the US where every sector of the cable TV industry is in the grip of multi-national corporations. See BASIC CABLE; COAXIAL CABLE; HF MULTIPAIR CABLE; OPTICAL FIBRE CABLE.

Caddy Special sleeve to protect the LASERVISION VIDEO-disc.

Cahiers du Cinéma French FILM magazine founded by André Bazin in 1951; associated with, and very often written by, the *Nouvelle Vague*, or New Wave directors such as Claude Chabrol and François Truffaut. The young critics of *Cahiers* reacted against the current ideological conservatism in the film world, against its reluctance to face up to or to express the facts of contemporary life.

Calotype Process of photographic print-making invented by William Henry Fox Talbot (1800–77). The Calotype method produced negatives on coated paper from which any number of paper prints could be made. Talbot celebrated his invention in his book *The Pencil of Light* (1844). See PHOTOGRAPHY, ORIGINS.

Camcorder A VIDEO camera and miniature sound recorder combined in a single unit.

Camera The first photographic camera on sale to the public was produced by London optician Francis West, for 'Photogenic Drawing' (1839). In the same year Baron Séguier introduced a lightweight bellows camera with three 'firsts' in equipment – a darkroom tent, a photographic tripod and a ball-and-socket head. Binocular-type cameras were introduced as early as 1853, by John Benjamin Dancer of Manchester. In 1858 Thomas Skaife introduced his 'Pistolgraph': a spring shutter worked by rubber bands was released by a trigger. He once aimed his Pistolgraph at Queen Victoria and was nearly arrested for an attempt on her life. 1880 saw the first twin-reflex camera, a quarter plate with a roller-blind shutter attached to the taking lens, made by R. & J. Beck of London.

George Eastman produced the first camera incorporating roll-film, calling it the Kodak (1888). The simplicity of this camera ('Pull the string – turn the key – press the button') made mass photography possible, especially as Eastman recommended the return of the camera to the factory for development and printing.

Miniature cameras, as scientific precision instruments, were produced from 1924 (the Ermanox made by the Ernemann Works of Dresden). In 1912 George P. Smith of Missouri produced a 35-mm camera taking one by one-and-a-half inch pictures on cine-FILM which was being mass produced at the time. The prototype of the Leica was constructed by Oskar Barnack in 1914; Rolleiflex was put on the market by Franke and Heidecke Braunschweig in 1947 and Voigtländer's ZOOM LENS was introduced in 1959.

In the 1960s and 1970s the application of electronics revolutionized camera and lens design. The silicon chip allowed amazing feats of miniaturization. In 1963 Eastman Kodak introduced the 126 'instant loading' cartridge, a modernization of an old idea going back to the Expo Watch camera of 1905. In 1972 they produced the pocket 110, an ultraminiature cartridge-load camera. Polaroid, in the same year, launched the SX-70 instant photo system which abandoned the method whereby a protective covering had to be peeled off the print. With SX-70, the photo image develops automatically in the light, protected by a plastic coating.

1976 saw Canon introduce its famous AE-1, a fully automatic SLR camera incorporating very advanced digital electronic technology, produced by automated methods. In the early 1980s Kodak launched its disc-camera. Three-dimensional (3-D) cameras also came on to the market at this time. See PHOTOGRAPHY, ORIGINS; POLAROID; HIGH-SPEED PHOTOGRAPHY.

Camera cue Red light on a TV camera which is illuminated when that camera is transmitting. Known also as a 'tally light'.

Camera obscura Latin for 'dark chamber'; an early means of projecting an image – a box or room with a lens at one end and at the other a reflector which throws an external image upon a screen or table. Antonio Canaletto (1697–1768) used the *camera obscura* to considerable effect in his paintings of Venice, though the device was referred to as early as Aristotle. It was French army officer Joseph Nicéphore Niépce (1765–1833) in 1826 who first exposed a metal plate coated with a layer of bitumen to the image in a camera obscura. The light hardened the bitumen which was washed away to reveal the fixed image. Photography, or as Niépce termed it, the 'Heliograph' – sun drawing – was born.

Where the camera obscura possessed a reflector, the **camera lucida** had a prism. When placed in front of an artist's eye the prism projects image onto paper, thus allowing accurate copying. See CAMERA; PHOTOGRAPHY, ORIGINS.

Caméra-stylo Alexandre Astruc in 'Le Caméra-stylo' in *Écran français* (March 1948) likened the FILM camera to a pen in the hand of the film maker – an extension of his/her heart and mind.

Camera, television A TV studio camera is electronic and produces instant pictures. It works with a system of mirrors and lenses which distinguish three primary colours, red, blue and green, in colour cameras (or shades of black, white and grey in the case of monochrome) and reflects them on three separate camera tubes. These lenses are coated with a light-sensitive material which produces an electrical charge according to the amount of light falling on it. This is then scanned by an electron beam converting the electrical charge into an electrical signal, one for each tube. The three-tube outputs combine to make a colour picture which is transmitted 'live' or recorded on videotape.

Campaign This term is most often used in the media studies context to refer to a conscious, structured and coordinated attempt at persuading those members of the general public who utilize the mass media. The goals of such persuasion are varied. ADVERTISING campaigns for example aim to change people's choice of product or to persuade them to buy new products. Election campaigns aim to reinforce or change people's voting behaviour. Pressure GROUPS use campaigns to alert the public to a particular issue, to influence the public's opinion on that issue, to mobilize support and pressurize those in power to take some desired action. Access to the mass media is often crucial for a pressure group's successful campaign. Media personnel may also initiate campaigns to raise their audience's awareness of certain ISSUES – child abuse, for example. Indeed such campaigns can be seen as part of the mass media's AGENDA SETTING role. One focus for media research has been the measurement of how effective campaigns are.

Campaign for Press and Broadcasting Freedom UK organization formed in 1979 as a broad-based non-political party pressure group dedicated to making Britain's media more open, diverse and accountable. Specifically the Campaign has worked for the RIGHT OF REPLY, a Freedom of Information law and more community-based and 'alternative' newspapers. The Campaign publishes a bi-monthly bulletin, *Free Press*. See PRESS.

Candid Camera Playfully sadistic TV series originated in the US by Allen Funt, using concealed cameras and microphones, with the intention of taking people off guard; became popular in the UK in the 1960s and elsewhere.

An example of the cinema as *catalyst*. See CATALYST EFFECT; CINÉMA VÉRITÉ.

Cans Headphones worn by the crew of a TV camera unit, for example, so that they can hear instructions from the control room.

Cards See CIGARETTE CARDS; PICTURE POST-CARDS.

Caricature A distorted representation of a person, type or action. Though we generally associate caricature with humorous CARTOONS, the process of distortion has played an important role in art. Known to the Egyptians and Greeks, CARICATURE was revived by Italian artists of the Renaissance and developed throughout Europe in the 18th c. In England artists such as James Gillray (1757–1815) and Thomas Rowlandson (1756–1827) combined high quality draughtsmanship with trenchant social and political satire. Though the most famous, *Punch* was only one among many magazines carrying cartoons in the 19th c. In England, *Vanity Fair* (founded 1868) proved a rival. In the US *Puck* (1876), in France, *Le Rire* (1894), in Germany, *Simplicissimus* (1896), made the cartoon the most impactful form of printed illustration prior to the regular use of photography. Best known of all US magazines carrying cartoons, the *New Yorker*, was founded in 1925.

E.H. Gombrich, in *The Story of Art* (UK: Phaidon, 1958), writes, 'Caricature had always been "expressionist", for the caricaturist plays with the likeness of his victim, and distorts it to express just what he feels about his fellow men.' Gombrich emphasizes the *serious* nature of caricature and its particular significance in EXPRESSIONISM, which set people protesting rather than laughing: 'As long as these distortions of nature sailed under the flag of humour nobody seemed to find them difficult to understand. Humorous art was a field in which everything was permitted, because people did not approach it with the prejudices they reserved for Art with a capital A.'

Among the artists who used caricature to express and evoke feelings of pain rather than pleasure, was the Norwegian Edvard Munch (1863–1944). His lithograph, *Shouting* (1895) communicates, through distortion, a sense of acute anguish – a key emotion in much Expressionist art.

Car telephone See CELLULAR RADIO.

Cartoons In fine art, a cartoon is the final preparatory drawing for a large-scale painting, tapestry or mosaic. The Leonardo cartoon in the National Gallery, London, is a notable example – ready for final working, but never completed by the artist. In modern terms, the cartoon is a humourous illustration or strip of illustrations. In 1841 a series of fine art cartoons was designed for paintings in the new

Houses of Parliament in London. The satirical magazine *Punch*, founded in that year, poked fun at the drawings, with sketches entitled '*Punch's* Cartoons'.

According to Alan Coren in his Foreward to W. Hewison's *The Cartoon Connection* (UK: Elm Tree Books, 1977), cartoons were born 'in the far Aurignacian days of 20,000 BC', when 'a squat, hirsute, browless man one morning dipped his stick in a dark rooty liquid, bent straight again, and, on the cave-wall of Lascaux, drew a joke about men running after buffalo'.

Hewison calls the cartoon 'drawn humour' and poses the following cartoon categories: (1) Recognition humour (where the viewer recognizes the workings of human nature); (2) Social comment (very often Recognition humour with a MESSAGE); (3) Visual puns; (4) Zany (or screw-ball); (5) Black humour (or sick, or bad taste); (6) Geometric (where, for example, lines are made to fall in love with dots); (7) Faux Naif (pretended naivety) – 'When an ideas man *can* draw but cannot develop a satisfactory comic style of *cartoon* drawing, he quite often throws in the towel and adopts a deliberately childlike style' – and (8) the Strip cartoon the originator of which was Wilhelm Busch (1832–1904).

In *The Cartoon: A short history of graphic comedy and satire* (UK: David & Charles, 1972), J. Geipel writes that 'Cartoons may be called the slang of graphic art. Like verbal slang, they tend to rely for their impact on spontaneity, playfulness, popular imagery and often deliberate vulgarity . . .' providing 'a most suitable outlet for man's healthy and irresistible urge to poke fun at his fellows, his institutions and himself'. Of the scores of outstanding cartoonists in the English-speaking world during the modern era there is space here to mention only a few: for comic fantasy, William Health Robinson and Rowland Emett; for the world of horses and the horsey, Norman Thelwell; for political satire, Sir David Low, who invented the embodiment of the diehard reactionary, 'Colonel Blimp' and the *Guardian*'s current chief cartoonist, Les Gibbard; for the creation of one of the great cartoon family sagas, Carl Giles; for services to the comical aspects of music, Gerard Hoffnung; for cartoons which scream with anguish rather than laughter, Gerald Scarfe and Ralph Steadman.

On the screen, Walt Disney has dominated the field of the ANIMATED cartoon but there have been many others: Paul Terry's 'terrytoons', Pat Sulliven's Felix the Cat, Bob Cannon's Gerald McBoing-Boing, Ernest Pintoff's Human Rectangle, Flebus, Tex Avery's Chilly Willy, the endlessly warring Tom and Jerry created by William Hanna, Joe Barbera and Fred Quimby, along with countless others such as Top Cat, Scooby Doo and the Flintstones; Walter Lantz's Woody Woodpecker and Terry Gilliam's Monty Python's Flying Circus. Among those artists who have attempted to push the cartoon on FILM in an innovative direction are the Hungarian John Halas and his wife Joy Batchelor, Richard Williams and Bob Godfrey.

Case study Generally a process in problem-solving in which students, trainee supervisors, managers, etc. examine a specific case with a view to arriving at a solution, either by action or decision. An industrial case study may require students to analyse a particular dispute at work – a walk-out, a conflict between personnel, a breakdown in communication – and, individually or in GROUPS, offer explanations for the dispute and ways of solving it.

In the Associate Examining Board's A-Level in Communication Studies, Paper 2 is made up of case studies. These provide a range of materials or a set of situations requiring the student to apply communication skills in sifting, perceiving, organizing, and eventually *processing* the material for some target audience or recipient.

* N. McKeown, *Case Studies and Projects in Communication* (UK: Methuen, 1982).

Catalyst effect Where a book, newspaper, FILM, TV or RADIO programme has the effect of modifying a situation, or taking a *mediating* role. The actual presence of TV cameras may, it is believed, influence the course of events. The debate continues as to whether such effects are substantial or marginal, for reliable proof is hard to come by. See MEDIATION.

Catharsis From the Greek, 'purging'. *Catharsis* is the effect upon an audience of tragedy in drama or the novel. The Greek philosopher Aristotle perceived the function of great tragedy to be the release of pent-up emotions in the audience. As a consequence, the mind is cleansed and purified. See BIBLIOTHERAPY; CATHARSIS HYPOTHESIS; COMMUNICATION, FUNCTIONS.

Catharsis hypothesis Belief that violence and aggression on films and TV has a therapeutic effect. Exponents of this idea argue that the involvement in fantasy aggression may serve as a *displacement*, providing a harmless 'release' from hostile impulses which might otherwise be acted out. See EFFECTS OF THE MEDIA.

CB – Citizens' Band Radio Originally conceived in the US, then authorized in a number of countries, CB was legalized in the UK in 1981. It is a two-way RADIO communication system available to technically unqualified members of the public once a £10 licence has been purchased from the Post Office. Two-way transceivers (rigs) are available from around £50 upwards. Most equipment works on 27MHz, though the 934MHz band, providing more private and better quality contact, is available at a higher cost. The transmission for hand-held CB radio is about a mile, from vehicle to vehicle five miles and from home-based stations ten miles.

B. Cowlan in 'A revolution in personal communications: the explosive growth of Citizens Band radio' in G. Gumpert and R. Cathcart, eds., *Inter/media: Interpersonal Communication in a Media World* (US/UK: Oxford University Press, 1979), writes 'People . . . have found, in CB, a medium for *themselves*; they are tuning to it in ever increasing numbers; they are devising their own protocols for its use; they are developing a formidable political lobby to ensure its development. The CB radio system is a medium which puts the citizen in control of the communication process.' See CELLULAR RADIO; COMMUNITY RADIO; PIRATE RADIO; 10-CODES.

CD – Compact disc The GRAMOPHONE equivalent of LASERVISION, the compact disc is a quarter the size of the traditional long-playing record. CDs can store an hour's music on one side, and they will never wear out and do not require painstaking cleaning. To produce such a disc, every second in a musical passage is sampled over 44,000 times, each sampling given a simple digital code which is then printed on a disc as a series of reflective pits. A small laser is beamed at the revolving disc. The code is consequently reflected back into the CD player and then converted into sound via a semiconductor chip.

Ceefax Trade name of the TELETEXT service offered by the BBC since September 1974, giving viewers access to information on a wide range of services. At the push of a button appropriate information is displayed on the TV screen. Each page of information resembles a tele-printed MESSAGE and carries such items as the latest weather forecast, stock market prices and train schedules. The IBA equivalent is ORACLE. See MEDIA TECHNOLOGY.

Celebrity The modern version of the old hero; though while the hero was distinguished by *achievement*, the celebrity is distinguished by his/her *image*. As Daniel J. Boorstin writes in *The Image* (UK: Penguin, 1963), 'The hero was a big man; the celebrity is a big name . . . the creature of gossip, of public opinion, of magazines, and the ephemeral images of movie and television screen.' The passage of time 'creates and establishes the hero' but it 'destroys the celebrity. One is made, the other unmade, by repetition.'

Cell Name of each of the many thousands of individual drawings which make up an ANIMATION film.

Cellular radio Comprises RADIO frequencies divided up into 'cells' of air waves facilitating, in particular, personal communications systems. For example, anyone operating a car TELEPHONE will be switched automatically from one radio frequency to another as the operator passes through the air wave cells. The system is already in wide use in the US and operates on a restricted basis in the UK. It is believed that cellular radio could be worth £300 m. in equipment sales by 1990. Its potential is enormous – personal communications systems for pedestrians, telephones in trains, systems where drivers are provided with display units in cars giving business instructions or map guidance or the latest financial data. See MEDIA TECHNOLOGY.

Celluloid A decisive technological breakthrough for still and movie photography came in 1865 with the creation by British metallurgist Alexander Parkes of a plastic substance from nitro-cellulose, camphor and alcohol, which he named Parkesite. The material, which provides an ideal medium for carrying images, was later modified by his associate Daniel Spill and called Xylonite. An improved version – celluloid – is credited to John W. Hyatt, a printer of Albany, New York State (1869).

Censorship Pre-emptive censorship is censorship *before* the event; punitive, *after* the event. They often work in tandem: one punishment serves as a warning to others. Censorship involves the curtailment, usually by or on behalf of those in authority, of the major freedoms – of belief, expression, movement, assembly and access to information.

The most common form of censorship is that applied by the *self*. A thing is not expressed because of the risk of external censorship – from the law, from organizations and institutions, from pressure GROUPS. Thus we have censorship by omission or evasion.

Few if any communities tolerate completely free expression. In the UK, for example, laws of DEFAMATION exist to protect persons against acts of communication which may offend or injure them, or their reputation in the community. Equally protective are restrictions upon material transmitted to children (See CERTIFICATION OF FILMS).

Such forms of censorship meet with general agreement, but they represent only the tip of a large legal ice-berg. The UK's OFFICIAL SECRETS ACT is one of the most far-reaching weapons of legal censorship ever devised. The act (or Acts, 1911–39) makes it an offence for anyone to obtain and communicate documents and information which could be harmful to the safety and interest of the state. Such is the extent of the Official Secrets Act that, while protecting the state against the passing of crucial military secrets to the enemy, it could also prohibit the publication of the Prime Minister's lunchtime menu at Number 10 Downing Street. Employees in state services often have to sign a declaration agreeing not to disclose any information to which they have access (See LEAKS).

In addition, the state protects a commonality of interests with a wide range of laws. The Public Order Act of 1936 restricted the way we behave, or what we say, in public. If an individual uses threatening or insulting words, likely to cause a breach of the peace, this is a punishable offence. The common law offence of Sedition, of long standing, protects the sovereign, the government and its institutions from individual or groups causing intentional discontent and hatred, while the Incitement to Disaffection Act of 1934 made it an offence to try to persuade a member of the armed forces to an act of disloyalty. Equally, the Police Act of 1964 made it an offence to promote unfaithfulness by a police officer towards his duties.

It remains an offence to issue a Blasphemy – that is, to speak or communicate in writing, etc. matter which may cause hatred, contempt, insult or ridicule against the Church. It is a rarely used law but a law's potency lies in its existence, in the knowledge that it can always be used when free speech appears to be getting out of hand.

Obscenity too has occupied the minds of lawmakers. Since the 17th c. certain types of indecent expression or behaviour have been subject to punishment by the law. Material considered likely to 'deprave and corrupt' has often been subject to punitive legal censorship (See OZ TRIAL). Defining what is obscene and what is liable to deprave and corrupt has proved immensely difficult. The WILLIAMS COMMITTEE REPORT ON OBSCENITY AND FILM CENSORSHIP, 1979 is probably the most level-headed attempt to resolve this problem, and to suggest what to do about censorship generally in the UK.

The targets of censorship tend to be those actions or expressions which appear to endanger by subversion, ridicule, defiance or just plain disrespect, the VALUES and value systems of the dominant HIERARCHY of society – its ESTABLISHMENT. In the UK the 'sacred cows' are the Monarchy, the Church, Nationality, the Family, Defence, each a SYMBOL in some way or other of law and order; of *control*. Censorship is a weapon to counter the ever-present threat – real or imagined – of social, and therefore political, destabilization.

To concentrate attention solely on the activities of the law in the process of censorship is to risk overlooking the immense pervasiveness of indirect censorship: 'back-door' censorship rather than crude, head-on tactics. Indeed a regularly identifiable characteristic of censorship is the difficulty of getting to the bottom of things, that is, *who* is responsible, and *why* the censorship has taken place and what the motives behind the act of censorship are. See ABC TRIAL; 'AREOPAGITICA' ARTICLE 19; BRAINWASHING; BROADCASTING STANDARDS COUNCIL; DATA PROTECTION; D-NOTICES; ECONOMIC LEAGUE; FOURTEEN-DAY RULE; HAYS OFFICE; INDEX; LONGFORD COMMITTEE REPORT; LORD CHAMBERLAIN; 'OH CALCUTTA!'; SECTION 28; SPYCATCHER CASE; TAXES ON KNOWLEDGE; THALIDOMIDE CASE; WORLD PRESS FREEDOM REVIEW; ZIRCON AFFAIR.
* *Censorship: Six Assignments for Individuals and Small Groups* (UK: Amnesty International British Section Education Project, Unit 7, 1983); *Index on Censorship* (UK: Writers & Scholars International, six issues a year); M. Scammell, 'Censorship and its History', in *Article 19 World Report: Information, Freedom and Censorship* (UK: Longman, 1988).

Centrality Within the communication *structure* of any social group some members will derive certain advantages or disadvantages resulting from their position in that structure; in particular, from the FREQUENCY with which they communicate with other members of the group. By using a SOCIOGRAM such as that illustrated below, the *centrality* of a person within the communication structure can be measured:

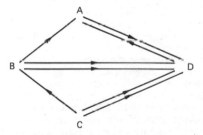

The sociogram indicates that D's *centrality index* is highest; it is arrived at by taking the total number of communication links between group members and then dividing that by the total number of such links between one member and the other members of the group. In the diagram, D's centrality may arise because of his/her status, role, articulacy, personality etc.

The concept of a centrality index enables observers to estimate quantitively the degree of influence members of the group may have by virtue of their position in the group. The more central a member is in a communication NETWORK, the sooner he/she will be in possession of all the information at the disposal of the group. *Influence* is closely related to possession of information because the possessor has the power to choose what information to pass on, and to whom. Communication networks differ in the degree of centrality and the number of levels of centrality possible within them.

Centres for research into the media See RESEARCH CENTRES (INTO THE MEDIA).

Certification of films For several years until December 1982, the BRITISH BOARD OF FILM CENSORS had the following system of certification: *X*, denoting films with high sex and violence content or other disturbing subject-matter to which those under 18 were not permitted; *AA* films from which children under 14 were barred; *A* films to which children were admitted if accompanied by an adult, and *U*-certificate films admitting all. The new 1982 categories are *18* (permitting admission for those 18 and over); *15* (replacing *AA*, and raising the admission age from 14 to 15); *PG* (Parental Guidance, a symbol used in the US, and intended to show that a FILM contains some scenes which individual parents may feel unsuitable for children), and *U* as before. See H-CERTIFICATE.

Chamberlain, Lord See LORD CHAMBERLAIN.

Change-over cue Small dot or other mark in the top right hand corner of the FILM frame to signal to the cinema projectionist that the film reel is coming to an end and it is almost time to switch from one projector to another.

Channel Each MESSAGE carrying signal requires its route along which it is transmitted from the sender to the receiver and along which FEED-BACK may be obtained. Channels may be physical (our voices or bodies) technical (the TELEPHONE) or social (our schools, media etc.) In business organizations or institutions they may be vertical, hierarchical, formal and predominantly one-way – from the boss downwards; or horizontal, democratic, informal and two-way as between workmates and GROUPS with common tasks, interests and sympathies. Like country paths, channels need to be kept open and frequented – and sometimes repaired – if they are to continue to be recognized as viable. See JAKOBSON'S MODEL OF COMMUNICATION; COSMOPOLITE AND LOCALITE CHANNELS; PHATIC COMMUNICATION; SHANNON AND WEAVER'S MODEL OF COMMUNICATION.

Channel capacity C.E. Shannon and W.E. Weaver use this term to describe the upper limit of information that any communication system can handle at a given time. To discover this limit, it is first essential to know how much uncertainty – or *entropy* – a given signal will eliminate. See REDUNDANCY.

Channel Four Under the direction of Jeremy Isaacs, C4 became the UK's fourth TV channel in 1982. It is a commercial system controlled by the IBA. C4 began auspiciously, providing a rich variety of programmes to challenge the mind and the senses, catering for minorities and acting as patron for DOCUMENTARY and FILM makers.

Inevitably, within weeks, there were protests about 'bad language' in programmes: this was another way of saying that C4's open-door policy towards alternative and sometimes radical social and political ideas was being seen as potentially 'subversive'.

Perhaps C4's earliest achievement was to break through the conventions of *who* should be broadcasting; ethnic minorities suddenly discovered access; youth was given the opportunity to express itself in other than mere consumer terms or as potential deviants; the 'statutory' representation of women in serious debate was replaced by real and equable representation; even the voice of organized labour got direct access as opposed to *mediated* access.

C4 became the first channel to provide a full hour of news daily. In 1988 Michael Grade – from the BBC – succeeded Isaacs as controller. The Welsh Fourth Channel is called Saniel Pedwar Cymru (S4C). See ANNAN COMMISSION REPORT.

Characteristics of mass communications See MASS COMMUNICATIONS, SEVEN CHARACTERISTICS.

Charter 77 State repression in Czechoslovakia gave rise to a movement in the country comprising artists, writers, musicians and academics dedicated to the struggle for human rights, in particular freedom of expression. The Charter 77 Declaration, dated 1 January 1977, was signed by 243 citizens and the Charter's first spokesmen were philosopher Jan Patočka, playwright Václav Havel and former foreign minister Jiří Hajek. Hundreds of human rights documents have been produced over the years on social, cultural and economic themes; on rights to education; freedom of speech and worship; and hundreds have been victimized through arrest, interrogation and imprisonment as a result of their commitment.

Chequebook journalism A EUPHEMISM for bribery – newspapers paying someone for exclusive rights on his or her story. The police pay their 'snouts' or 'grasses' for the common good; the PRESS pay their informants for tomorrow's headline, to serve the public's 'right to know' and to boost sales in the war of circulation.

Children's Film Foundation Set up in 1944 by J. Arthur Rank as the Children's Entertainment Films Division of the Rank Organization. The British FILM industry took over the project in 1951, naming it the CFF. In the Cinematograph Films Act of 1957, the CFF was guaranteed an annual grant from the BRITISH FILM PRODUCTION FUND. Films specially for children have been produced ever since – low-budget features, shorts and serials, shown at children's matinees and for the families of servicemen and women, never at ordinary public showings or on TV.

Cigarette cards A US company, Allen Ginter, produced the forerunner of the first British cigarette card when they packed with their Richmond Gem brand a pair of oval cards held together by a stud, one section of which was a calendar for 1884, with UK parcel postage rates on the back. By the 1890s the larger British tobacco companies were issuing cards, beginning with advertisements then progressing to series on particular themes such as soldiers, ships, royalty, sport and famous beauties.

The first company to issue photographic cigarette cards on a large scale was Ogdens who, in 1894, began their Guinea Gold and Tabs cards covering, in the next 13 years, practically every facet of life of that period. In the early 1900s there were around 50 companies issuing cards in the UK and Ireland. Reflecting the dominance of the British Empire, the cards represented many military issues, along with major inventions of the time – the motor car and the aeroplane. Exploration and discovery, and the Edwardian craze for collecting things – bird's eggs, butterflies, porcelain – were prominently reflected in the choice of subject matter as were the music hall and the scouting movement.

Early in the 1st World War (1914–18) the Wills company actually issued cards as miniature recruiting POSTERS while Gallahers put out several series of *Victoria Cross Heroes*, in 1915 and 1916. Carreras issued *Women on War Work* and *Raemaker's War Cartoons* portraying the Germans as barbarians.

Later examples of these cultural ephemera were Gallahers' *Boy Scouts*, *Fables and Their Morals*; Wills' *Cinema Stars* and *Radio Celebrities*. Ogdens produced a series on *Broadcasting*. With the approach of the 2nd World War (1939–45) Carreras produced *Britain's Defences* (1938), Players issued *Aircraft of the RAF* in the same year and in 1939 *Modern Naval Craft*. The most ambitious cigarette card enterprise of the period was the Imperial Tobacco Company's *Air Raid Precautions*, made available in a variety of cigarette brands.

Cigarette card production remained popular in the post-war era, though the 1960s saw a marked decline. In the 1970s came the much sought-after series from Player, *The Golden Age of Motoring*, packed in Doncella cigars. The Golden Age continued with *Steam* (1976), *Flying* (1977) and *Sail* (1978). See PICTURE POSTCARDS.

Cine-clubs Played an important role in the development of cinema in many countries. Where, in the commercial FILM theatres, popular entertainment monopolized programmes, the cine-clubs showed new experimental and often non-fictional work. John Grierson (1898–1972) organized the first British showing of Sergei Eisenstein's *Battleship Potemkin* at the London Film Society (formed in 1925) in 1929, along with his own seminal DOCUMENTARY *Drifters*. Minister of Propaganda in Nazi Germany, Goebbels, outlawed all cine-clubs because of their 'subversive' nature and a similar fate befell the cine-club movement in pre-2nd World War Japan.

The Depression and the failure of the media to meet head on the causes of depression, helped give belated birth to the US cine-club movement. The Workers' Film and Photo League, soon renamed the National Film and Photo League, was formed in New York in 1930. Members of the League made films as well as watched them, concentrating on filming the hunger marches and other mass protests of the time. Among their creations was a Workers' Newsreel which the League persuaded some commercial cinemas to screen.

Cinema See CINEMATOGRAPHY, ORIGINS; FILM.

Cinema legislation The first legislation in the UK relating to cinema use was the Cinematograph Act of 1909. It concerned the licensing of exhibition premises and the safety of audiences. In 1922, the Celluloid and Cinematograph Film Act drew up safety rules for premises where raw CELLULOID or cinematograph FILM was stored and used. The Cinematograph Film Production (Special Loans) Act, 1949 established the National Film Finance Corporation and in the same year came the British Film Institute Act.

The Cinematograph Films Act, 1957 provided a statutory levy on exhibitors and exhibitions to be collected by Customs and Excise and paid to the British Film Fund Agency which would use the monies to support film production in the UK and support the Children's Film Foundation. This made the formerly voluntary levy (See BRITISH FILM PRODUCTION FUND) compulsory. The Cinematograph (Amendment) Acts of 1982 extended provision of the 1909 Act to include 'all exhibitions of moving pictures for private gain', bringing under regulation pornographic cinema and video 'clubs'. The Acts exclude from regulation *bona fide* film societies. The Films Act, 1985 abolished the Cinematograph Films Council, the Eady Levy and dissolved the National Film Finance Corporation, replacing it with the British Screen Finance Consortium. The government provided a 'starter' of £1.5m for five years to the loan fund of the BSFC whose function would be to raise funds independently of state support. See BROADCASTING LEGISLATION.

Cinemacy Word coined by Thorold Dickinson to equate with literacy. His view was that education sadly neglects the cinema as a serious area of study. In the 1980s this neglect is being redressed, with the introduction into schools and colleges of communication, FILM and media studies, and into universities and polytechnics of degree courses in the media field.

CinemaScope Wide-screen process copyrighted by 20th Century Fox in 1953 but invented much earlier by Henri Chretien. See ANAMORPHIC LENS.

Cinématographie Word first used by G. Bouly in 1892 in a French patent specification for a movie camera.

Cinematography, origins Among the earliest moving-picture inventions was the *Thaumatropical Amusement* of Englishman Henry Fitton (1826). Exploiting the phenomenon of PERSISTENCE OF VISION the Thaumatrope consisted of a round box inside of which was a number of discs each with a design on it. When the discs were twirled round, the images merged and gave the impression of a single movement.

Joseph Plateau's *Phenakistoscope* (1833), a circular design opposite a mirror, worked the same little miracle. The ZOETROPE or 'wheel of life', invented by Englishman W.G. Horner (1834) offered a revolving drum with strip sequences inside, enabling figures to jump, gallop or even do cartwheels. Emile Renauld's *Praxinoscope* of 1877 improved on the Zoetrope by removing the slots of the drum and using mirrors to reflect the images, thus avoiding the dizziness to viewers caused by the Zoetrope; and the wonder of this device was extended with the *Projecting Praxinoscope* using a revolving disc-blade shutter to project animated images on to a screen.

The main impetus in the development of cinematography came, however, from another direction. Working in the US, English photographer Eadward Muybridge (1830–1904) in the 1870s took multiple photographs of animals, birds and humans in movement. His most famous experiment was the one in which a line of cameras, using exposures of less than one thousandth of a second, 'filmed' a galloping horse. The horse triggered each camera as it passed – and proved, incidentally, that there *are* moments in a horse's movement when all its hooves are clear of the ground.

The next step was the projection of these in-sequence pictures. William Friese-Green (1855–1921) in 1890, revealed the potential of moving film when he set up a small slide projector in which the usual slide carrier had been replaced by a glass disc bearing a ring of pictures. Friese-Green's revolving disc was later demonstrated, to eager crowds, in the window of his studio in Piccadilly.

In France meanwhile Etienne Jules Marey (1830–1904) had invented a photographic 'gun' (1882) to take pictures of birds in flight and soon followed this with a camera capable of snapping 60 pictures a second on a paper-based film. In the US Thomas Alva Edison (1847–1931) produced his *Kinetograph* to take moving pictures and his KINETOSCOPE to show them. The viewer looked through a peephole in the foot-high box. The 50 feet of FILM ran for about 13 seconds. 'Kinetoscope parlours' were set up in which people could view films by putting a coin in the slot.

The most important year in the development of cinematography was 1895, with the invention of projectors in the US by Thomas Armat and Woodville Latham, in France by the Lumière brothers – Auguste (1862–1954) and Louis (1864–1948) – and in the UK by Robert Paul. With the arrival of the Lumières on the scene, the cinema was truly born. Their vision and entrepreneurialism turned experiment into performance, private screenings into public, commercial profit. 'What did I do?' Louis Lumière is reported to have said. 'It was in the air.'

Auguste Lumière was less modest than Louis: 'My brother,' he said, 'invented the cinema in one night.' On 28 December 1895, the Lumières, already highly successful in the photographic business, opened in the Salon Indien, in the Grand Café on the Boulevard des Capuchines. Seats were priced at one franc. Within weeks they were a worldwide success. Immediately the Lumières trained a brigade of cameramen-cum-projectionists and sent them abroad to several foreign countries; in quick time, some 1200 single-shot films were produced, including the Diamond Jubilee procession in London.

Cinéma vérité Or *Catalyst* cinema. DOCUMENTARY film maker Jean Rouch made the notable *Chronique d'un Été* (Chronicle of a Summer) in 1961 which pushed DIRECT CINEMA techniques into a new, CANDID CAMERA approach. Instead of simply being observed in their daily routines, Parisians were faced with camera and tape recorder and asked, 'Tell us, are you happy?' Rouch and co-producer Edgar Morin were suddenly on-camera participants; and so were their subjects – invited to see FILM rushes of their interviews. Their discussion of these was filmed and recorded and used as part of the end-product.

The style was named cinéma vérité in homage to the Russian movie pioneer Dziga Vertov (See SPINNING TOP), and translated from the term used by Vertov and his associates, *kino pravda*, film truth. E. Barnouw in *Documentary* (UK: Oxford University Press, 1974), writes, 'The direct cinema documentarist took his camera to a situation of tension and waited hopefully for a crisis; the Rouch version of cinéma vérité tried to precipitate one. The direct cinema artist aspired to invisibility; the

Rouch cinéma vérité artist was often an avowed participant'.

Cinemiracle A wide-screen system similar to CINERAMA but without the drawback of joining-lines between the projected images: 'seamless cinerama'.

Ciné-poème Dutch FILM maker Bert Haanstra used this expression to describe his DOCUMENTARY, *Glass* (1958), one of the most celebrated of all short films: lyrical, evocative – indeed a piece of poetry on CELLULOID. The ciné-poème was fashionable among documentary film makers in the years following the 2nd World War (1939–45).

Cinerama Extra-wide screen system invented by Fred Waller and first demonstrated in *This is Cinerama* (1952). Three projectors, electronically synchronized, created a three-section picture on the screen, giving a disturbing visual wobble at the joins. The first FILM story using the process was *How the West Was Won* (1962). Shortly afterwards the three-camera system was abandoned in favour of 'single-lens Cinerama', practically identical to CINEMASCOPE, though with higher definition.

Circa Latin for 'about' or 'around'; most often used in reference to dates, such as births and deaths, when these are not known exactly. The word is almost invariably abbreviated to a single letter: thus, Vivaldi (*c.* 1676–1741). In this dictionary, however, c. is generally employed as an abbreviation for *century*.

Citizens' Band radio See CB – CITIZENS' BAND RADIO.

City symphonies Early FILM DOCUMENTARIES, usually Surrealist in approach, concentrating on the rhythms and patterns of city life. Walter Ruttman's *Berlin: Symphony of a City* (1927) set a fashion, taken up by many directors in the early 1930s, among whom was Jean Vigo (1905–34), who made *Apropos de Nice* (On the subject of Nice) in 1929, released 1930, with Boris Kaufman, youngest brother of AVANT-GARDE documentarist Dziga Vertov. In the US Ralph Steiner and Willard Van Dyke directed *The City* (1939), a notable exposition, not of the symphony of city life, but of urban crisis.

Civil inattention Phenomenon of INTERPERSONAL COMMUNICATION observed by Erving Goffman in *Behavior in Public Places* (US: Free Press, 1963), where, after initial EYE CONTACT a person quickly withdraws visual attention from another to avoid any further recognition or need for further contact. As Goffman says, 'In performing this courtesy the eyes of the looker may pass over the eyes of the other, but no "recognition" is typically allowed.' The ritual of civil inattention Goffman says is one that 'constantly regulates the social intercourse of persons in our society'. See INDICATORS; REGULATORS.

Clapper board See SHOT.

Claptrap See VERBAL DEVICES IN SPEECHMAKING.

Class A factor of vital importance in the analysis of interpersonal and mass communication is the concept of *class*; and the most significant impact on the development of that concept was made by the German philosopher Karl Marx (1818–83). For him, class denoted a relationship to the *means of production* in any given society. Marx identified two main classes: the owners of the means of production (land, factories) whom he called the *bourgeoisie*, and those who were obliged to sell their labour to the owners to make a living the *proletariat*. Although aware of other classes, he considered them of minor importance.

Marx argued that as a result of their position in the economic order, members of each class shared common experiences, lifestyles and certain political and economic interests. He believed that there was and would remain, in a capitalist society, an inevitable *conflict* between the interests of the bourgeoisie and the proletariat. He further argued that GROUP identity, class-consciousness and collective political and economic action would develop in the course of economic and political conflict. Proletarian class-consciousness was particularly likely to emerge as its members were thrown into serious difficulties and close daily associations at work.

The dominant class – the bourgeoisie – would, according to Marx, seek to impose its CULTURE upon the rest of society. Its culture would become the *dominant* culture, its IDEOLOGY the dominant ideology. Consequently the communication systems of society would reflect the dominant culture of the bourgeoisie and also the conflict between the two classes. From a Marxist viewpoint, control of many facets of the mass media by the ownership of capital gives that class the opportunity to disseminate its own culture and ideology. Such control, in Marxist terms, plays a vital role in the maintenance of HEGEMONY.

The term is also commonly used when what is meant is *social class*. Social class membership is based, primarily, upon occupation rather than ownership or non-ownership of the means of production.

For the ADVERTISING industry and media management, social class is a significant factor in the profile of their audience. The *Daily Mail*, for example, on its inception was aimed, according to Lord Northcliffe at the '£1000 a year man' or as Northcliffe admitted '. . . well . . . they like to imagine themselves £1000 a year people'. Market researchers are primarily interested in income and spending power. For those media organizations which are dependent on advertising revenue the social class composition of its audience is of obvious importance.

The inter-relationships between the social class structure and the communication processes of society are complex and research in this area is wide-ranged. Of particular concern is whether the narrowness of social class backgrounds of those who control and work in the media is reflected in its output. See ADVERTISING: MAIN-STREAMERS, ASPIRERS, SUCCEEDERS AND RE-FORMERS; CODES; CONGLOMERATES; ELITES; ESTABLISHMENT; MARXIST (MODE OF MEDIA ANALYSIS).

Clause 28 See SECTION 28.

'Clean up TV' movement Brought together in Birmingham in 1963 by Mary Whitehouse and others; later called itself the National Viewers' and Listeners' Association (NVLA). Over the years the movement has succeeded in gaining access to practically every forum in which the ISSUES of BROADCASTING are discussed; additionally, the NVLA has been active as a 'morality watchdog' in other arts, especially the theatre and publishing.

The basis of NVLA thinking is that of traditional Christian ethics; the belief that the VALUES of chastity and the family underpin all that's best in western society, and that such values are constantly under threat and have to be protected.

Of equal concern to the NVLA is the increase in the display, in FILM, on TV and in the theatre, of scenes of violence. See BROADCASTING STANDARDS COUNCIL; CENSORSHIP; LONGFORD REPORT; MORAL ENTREPRENEURS.

Climax order In the process of persuading others, the *order* in which arguments and evidence are placed is of considerable importance. Research has been conducted into the *climax order* and *anti-climax order*, that is when the best point of an argument is reserved till last (climax) or used at the outset (anti-climax). The two orders have varying advantages depending on the particular conditions under which the communication is presented, including the audience's predisposition and the type of matter being transmitted. Similar concepts are the Law of PRIMACY and the Law of Recency.

Clique A close-knit group of people within a SOCIAL SYSTEM whose communication is largely with each other. *Clique analysis* is used to determine communication groupings within a social system and its main tool is SOCIO-METRICS.

Closed text See OPEN, CLOSED TEXTS.

Closure Occurs in a communication situation when one participant, usually the receiver of information, closes down attention, and thus deflects or rejects the MESSAGE or the messenger. The reasons for closure may relate to the unacceptability of the message: it may conflict with the attitudes, beliefs or VALUES of the receiver; it may be an 'uncomfortable truth' which causes

the receiver a feeling of DISSONANCE. Also, it may have something to do with the messenger rather than the message – personal dislike of the sender on the part of the receiver or a simple unwillingness to receive *this* kind of message from *this* messenger. The means of closure will involve NVC (Non-verbal communication) as well as verbal strategies. See COMMUNICATION, NON-VERBAL; PREFERRED READING.

Clothing signals Indicators of our attitudes to ourselves and to others – our CLASS, beliefs, roles, status, priorities, etc. – through what we wear. See COMMUNICATION, NON-VERBAL; INTER-PERSONAL COMMUNICATION.

Coaxial cable Has a wider BANDWIDTH than HF MULTIPAIR CABLE. The inner conducting core is surrounded by a second conducting mesh – both usually being made of copper. Coaxial cable is commonly used in the US and Canada. Its original 12-channel capacity was increased in the 1970s to a potential 100 channels. Coaxial has a narrower bandwidth than OPTI-CAL FIBRE CABLE. See CABLE TELEVISION.

Cocktail party problem In *On Human Communication* (US: MIT Press, 1966), Colin Cherry writes 'One of our most important faculties is the ability to listen to, and follow, one speaker in the presence of others. This is such a common experience that we may take it for granted; we may call it "the cocktail party problem". That is, how do we filter out a barrage of communication messages, selecting one to concentrate upon?' Cherry experimented with two different taped readings being played at once, with the instruction to the subject to concentrate on one and ignore the other. Though the tapes produced a 'complete babel', and though very wide-ranging texts were used, considerable success in deciphering the MES-SAGE was demonstrated, illustrating the importance of 'our ingrained speech habits at the acoustic, syllabic, or syntactic levels'. Cherry and his colleagues also experimented to see what happened when a subject was asked to read a text out loud while simultaneously listening to another one. This process, of testing the subject's ability to select from competing message channels, they called 'shadowing'.

Code of Advertising Practice See BRITISH CODE OF ADVERTISING PRACTICE.

Codes A code is generally defined as a system into which signs are organized, governed by consent. The study of codes – other than those *arbitrary* or fixed codes such as mathematics, chemical symbols, MORSE CODE, etc. – emphasizes the social dimension of communication. We have codes of conduct, ethical, aesthetic and LANGUAGE codes (See ELABO-RATED AND RESTRICTED CODES).

Non-verbal communication is carried on through what have been classified as **presentational codes:** GESTURE, movement of the eyes, expressions of the face, tone of voice. A **representation code** can be speech, writing, music, art, architecture, etc. Speech itself has non-verbal characteristics: **prosodic codes** affect the MEANING of the words used, through expression or pitch of voice.

The media are often referred to as employing **broadcast** and **narrowcast codes** in gearing content, level and style to expected audiences. In *Introducing Communication Studies* (UK: Methuen, 1982), John Fiske writes, 'Narrowcast codes have acquired the function in our mass society of stressing the difference between "us" (the users of the code) and "them" (the laymen, the lowbrows). Broadcast codes stress the similarities among "us" (the majority)'. In the case of TV, *Coronation Street* would represent the broadcast code and a production of Shakeskeare's *King Lear* a piece of narrowcasting, though economically speaking, in terms of ADVERTISING, narrowcast may simply indicate the target audience of the advertiser.

Aesthetic codes are crucially affected by their cultural context, some of it highly conventional, some AVANT-GARDE, subject to textual rather than commonly recognized cues to meaning. Much modern ART, for example, has been ENCODED in visual languages accessible only to a small number of people. However, over time, innovative aesthetic encoding becomes *conventionalized*. The obscure code has become familiar. A case in point is SURREALISM, whose intention was to shock cultural convention, yet whose dream symbols and often disturbing juxtapositions of objects have become a commonplace of mass advertising. What began as a code specific to itself has been transformed to one given its meaning by cultural convention. See DECODE; DOMINANT, SUBORDINATE, RADICAL; ELITE; HIGHBROW; OPERATIONAL CODE; SEMIOLOGY/SEMIOTICS.

Cognitive (and Affective) That area or domain of human behaviour which can be described as intellectual – knowing, understanding and reasoning – is often referred to as the *cognitive*. A substantial amount of media communication is aimed at producing cognitive responses in the receiver. That area which is involved with attitudes, emotions, VALUES and feelings is termed the *affective*. Obviously the two overlap and intertwine. Whether the content of a MESSAGE is cognitive or affective in its orientation will greatly influence the mode chosen for its communication. If the content of a message is judged to be of cognitive intent, then LANGUAGE will generally be couched in neutral terms; presentation will strive after objectivity and *balance*. An affective message will be more likely to be framed in EMOTIVE LANGUAGE, its imagery directed towards emotional responses.

However, much recent media research has been directed towards a more critical analysis of the allegedly objective modes of cognitive messages. There is concern as to whether the dissemination of apparently neutral information – especially if that dissemination is of some FREQUENCY and CONSISTENCY of treatment – influences an audience's perception of national and world events. From the mass of available information, the media select and and reject. They give emphasis – and legitimacy – to some ISSUES rather than others, and they set the order of priorities (See AGENDA SETTING) as well as seeking to establish links between occurrences and their causes in the minds of the audience. If, for example, trade unions only appear in media coverage as sources of social and political conflict, both the cognitive and affective responses of audiences are likely to become unfavourable to the concept or even the existence of trade unionism. See EFFECTS OF THE MASS MEDIA; GLASGOW UNIVERSITY MEDIA GROUP.

Cognitive capture See IMPARTIALITY.

Cognitive dissonance See CONGRUENCE THEORY; DISSONANCE.

Cold media, hot media See HOT MEDIA, COLD MEDIA.

Cold-type technology Money-saving alternative to labour-intensive hot metal PRINTING. Copy is keyboarded into a computer terminal whose output is 'cold type' photographic paper, ready for page assembly. Once layout is complete, pages are photographed and the negative made into a flexible polymer printing plate. See TECHNOLOGY OF THE MEDIA.

Collocation The tendency of words to occur in regular association; words set together through customary usage such as 'fair' and 'play', 'auspicious' and 'occasion'.

Collodion or wet-plate process See PHOTOGRAPHY, ORIGINS.

Colloquialism An expression used in common, informal speech, but not as far removed from acceptable modes as SLANG. If your comments 'cut no ice' with somebody, that is a colloquialism; if you are told to 'keep yer 'air on', that is slang. It is a modest distinction, for as R. Ridout and C. Witting say in *The Facts of English* (UK: Pan Reference Books, 1973), 'the slang of yesterday becomes the colloquialism of today'. See DIALECT; JARGON; REGISTER.

Colour TV The first regular TV service in colour began in the US in 1954; 1960 saw the first colour service in Japan, seven years ahead of Britain. In 1969 there were 100,000 colour sets in use in the UK; by the same month in 1972 there were 1.6m and twice that 12 months later. Ferguson produced the first full-size colour receiver using transistors throughout, in 1967. Transistors consumed a quarter the power of traditional valve receivers. They ran cooler and were more reliable. Later came integrated circuits doing away with many discrete components. The surface acoustic wave (SAW) filter further refined the accuracy of colour reception as did improved SHADOW-MASK TUBES. Here stripes of colour rather than dots achieved registration of the picture's red, green and blue components without the need for any of the many correction-circuits previously required.

Comics The first newspaper comic-strip is generally considered to be that which appeared on 16 February 1896 in the *New York Sunday World*. It was a three-quarter page feature in colour called 'The Great Dog Show in M'Googan's Avenue'. Kids in the city's slum backyards were organizing their own dog show; the hero, dressed in a bright yellow nightgown, soon became the 'Yellow Kid' and 'Hogan's Alley' achieved immediate popularity as a long-running comic strip.

The idea was not new. English cartoonist Thomas Rowlandson (1757–1827) created a comic character, Dr Syntax, who was popular with the public, and considerably earlier William Hogarth (1697–1764) included speech 'balloons' in his engravings satirizing London life.

George Orwell took comics seriously enough to write about them. In 'Boys' Weeklies' (1939), published in *Selected Essays* (UK: Penguin, 1957), Orwell analyses the social and political connotations of early publications in the GENRE.

What seems to characterize comics, in Orwell's day or our own, is their social change-lessness, deep down if not in the surface detail. Orwell did find differences between the older and the new generation of weeklies, however: in the new, 'better technique, more scientific interest, more bloodshed, more leader-worship'; in 'social outlook there is hardly any advance'.

As life appears to have become more complex, and society more complicated, the STEREOTYPE of the hero has had a sustaining appeal. Picture-strip heroes such as Clark Kent, alias Superman, who first made his appearance in *Action Comics* (1938) in the US, have not only led popular (and charmed) lives on the printed page but have translated into immensely popular FILM heroes.

See CARTOONS.

Comint See SIGINT.

Commercial laissez-faire model of (media) communication In their Introduction to *The Manufacture of News* (UK: Constable, 1973) joint editors S. Cohen and J. Young cite two general, and polarized, models which attempt to explain the intentions and impact of media on their audiences – the *Mass manipulative model* and the *Commercial laissez-faire model*. In the first, 'the public is seen as an

atomized mass, passive receptacles of messages originating from a monolithic and powerful source.' From the perspective of the political Left it is big business – the hierarchy of capitalism – which is the seemingly all-powerful manipulator. From the perspective of the political Right, the media in this model are seen as manipulating 'standards' by lowering them.

Drawn from the laissez-faire (leave well alone) model of the economy, the Commercial laissez-faire model mirrors the freedom of the market place where producers compete with one another to sell their products to consumers. Thus media corporations are seen as having to compete for the attention and loyalty of their consumers – the audience.

Researchers using this model tend to argue that the consumer is sovereign and that media corporations have to tailor their products to suit consumer wishes, tastes and needs. The focus of their research is, therefore, often upon the mechanisms by which such tailoring is achieved.

The Commercial laisses-faire model emerged as a critique of the Mass manipulative model. It is generally the PREFERRED READING of journalists and media people themselves. Because there is competition, the argument goes, there is consequently 'variety and diversity in information and opinions presented in the mass media and that such variation minimizes the chances of manipulation'. This summary having been made in Cohen and Young's Introduction, the rest of the book's fascinating collection of reports and analyses is a remorseless exposé of fallacies perceived in the Commercial laissez-faire model. See COMMUNICATION MODELS; EFFECTS OF THE MASS MEDIA.

Commercial radio Though PIRATE RADIO attempted to buck the BROADCASTING monopoly of the BBC during the 1960s, legitimate commercial broadcasting in the UK was not in operation till the 1970s, following the Conservative government's Sound Broadcasting Act of 1972. IBA had, by 1983, 37 commercial RADIO stations operating under licence throughout the UK and plans for over 60 commercial stations.

In the US the first commercial radio was KDKA of Pittsburg which went on the air on 2 November 1920 with a broadcast of the returns of the Harding–Cox presidential elections. In 1921 there were eight commercial radio stations, by 1922, 564. Development of radio in the US was spectacular and chaotic. In 1927 (the year that the BBC, by Royal Charter, was given a monopoly of radio broadcasting in the UK) Congress passed a Radio Act setting up the Federal Communications Commission to allocate wavelengths to broadcasters. Four radio networks were created as a hedge against monopoly – National Broadcasting Commission (NBC), Columbia Broadcasting Service

(CBS), Mutual Broadcasting System (MBS) and the American Broadcasting Company (ABC), while the FCC worked towards the growth of projects of educational interest.

Despite the BBC's monopoly in the UK, commercial broadcasts in English were transmitted from abroad as early as 1925. Radio Paris, broadcasting from the Eiffel Tower, presented a fashion talk in English, sponsored by Selfridges. Only three listeners wrote to the station to say they had heard the broadcast but the commercial lobby was undaunted. In the 1930s Captain L.F. Flugge, who had arranged the fashion talk, formed and ran the International Broadcasting Company. The IBC's Radio Normandy transmitted 15-minute shows for several hours a day from 1931 and by the following year 21 British firms were paying sponsorship money for commercial broadcasting, and the UK was being beamed at commercially from Holland, Spain and Luxembourg.

The IBC actually set up offices in Portland Place, London, and had its own outside broadcasting vehicles, each painted black with 'Radio Normandy 274 metres' on the side. An important part of the company's operations was the International Broadcasting Club, formed in 1932, with free membership. By 1939, the IBC had 320,000 members.

Radio Luxembourg began broadcasting on 1191 metres long wave in 1933, its first two sponsors being Zam Buk and Bile Beans. Though the Post Office conducted a sustained campaign to close down these commercial stations, it was Adolf Hitler and the 2nd World War which did the trick: many transmitters were either destroyed by the Nazis or taken over. Radio Luxembourg became Hitler's major PROPAGANDA weapon against the British. The notorious Lord Haw-Haw (William Joyce), an Irishman committed to the German cause, broadcast daily recommendations to the British to lay down their arms, from the most powerful transmitter in Europe.

Of the commercial stations, Luxembourg was the only one to start up again after the war. The first accredited commercial radio station on British soil was Manx Radio which began broadcasting in 1964.

With the election of the Conservatives in 1970, the Minister of Posts and Telecommunications produced a White Paper, *An Alternative Service of Broadcasting* proposing a network of about 60 commercial stations under the Independent Television Authority (to be renamed the Independent Broadcasting Authority). Opposition Spokesman Ivor Richards called it 'nothing more than the establishment of 60 pop stations'.

From the beginning, in 1972, local independent radio was to broadcast on stereo VHF as well as medium wave. The first FRANCHISES were awarded in 1973, to bring into existence the all-news London Broadcasting Company (LBC) and Capital Radio for London, with regional stations following soon afterwards.

Additional franchises were granted by the IBA in 1981. By 1988 there were 40 independent local radio stations (compared to 27 BBC local stations). See COMMUNITY RADIO; RADIO: BROADCASTING IN THE 90s.

Commercial television Although TV in the US was commercial – relying on ADVERTISING for its revenues – from the beginning, TV in the UK was a PUBLIC SERVICE BROADCASTING monopoly until the TELEVISION ACT, 1954, which gave birth to Independent Television. The ITA's first term ran from 1954 to 1964. It became the IBA from 1972, when the second term lasted until 1981. The third term, from 1982, was marked by the inauguration of CHANNEL FOUR and BREAKFAST TIME TELEVISION. ITV programme companies were appointed by the IBA for an eight-year contract period, serving modified areas and with two fresh dual regions.

The UK regions – until the 1990s (see BROADCASTING IN THE 90S: GOVERNMENT WHITE PAPER 1988) – are served as follows: East of England (Anglia TV), Scottish borders (Border TV), East and West Midlands (Central), Channel Islands (Channel), North Scotland (Grampian), North West England (Granada), Wales and West of England (Harlech – HTV), London, weekends (London Weekend TV), Central Scotland (Scottish TV), London, weekdays (Thames), South West England (TSW – Television South West), South and South East of England (TVS – Television South), North East England (Tyne Tees), Northern Ireland (Ulster TV) and Yorkshire (Yorkshire).

Programmes are made by or commissioned by the individual companies who obtain their revenue from the sale of advertising time in their own transmission areas and pay the IBA a rental to cover its costs in administering the system and operating the national network of transmitters as well as the financing of Independent TV News. The companies also pay a levy on profits to the government and subscribe to the running of Channel Four.

The five largest ITV companies – Central, Granada, LWT, Thames and Yorkshire – provide a core of ITV schedules throughout the country as well as programmes specifically for their own regions. All outputs are carefully monitored by the IBA's Programme Policy Committee, presided over by the chairperson of the Authority.

Informative programmes must comprise a third of the entire TV output and over 80% of programmes must originate in the UK or EEC, with a ceiling of 14% on productions from the US and elsewhere outside the Common Market. Narrative programmes – drama, films, series etc. – also approximate to a third of output; the rest is loosely classifiable as entertainment and music (20%), plus sport (8%). See COMMERCIAL RADIO; FRANCHISES FOR INDEPENDENT TELEVISION; TELEVISION PROGRAMME GUIDELINES.

Commissions/committees on the media See ANNAN COMMISSION REPORT ON BROADCASTING, 1977; BEVERIDGE COMMITTEE REPORT ON BROADCASTING, 1950; BROADCASTING COMPLAINTS COMMITTEE; BROADCASTING STANDARDS COUNCIL; HANKEY COMMITTEE REPORT ON TELEVISION, 1943; HUNT COMMITTEE REPORT ON CABLE EXPANSION AND BROADCASTING POLICY, 1982; LLOYD COMMITTEE REPORT, 1967; MACBRIDE COMMISSION; MCGREGOR COMMISSION REPORT ON THE PRESS, 1977; PILKINGTON COMMITTEE REPORT ON BROADCASTING, 1962; ROSS COMMISSION REPORT ON THE PRESS, 1949; SELSDON COMMITTEE REPORT ON TELEVISION, 1935; SHAWCROSS COMMISSION REPORT ON THE PRESS, 1962; SYKES COMMITTEE REPORT ON BROADCASTING (SEE BBC, ORIGINS); ULLSWATER COMMITTEE REPORT ON BROADCASTING, 1936; WILLIAMS COMMITTEE REPORT ON OBSCENITY AND FILM CENSORSHIP, 1979.

Commoditization of information The notion that information is something upon which the possessor can put a price; thus information is bought and sold because it is a commodity rather than a public service. The process constitutes an important ISSUE, and might also be termed the *privatization* of information. Herbert I. Schiller in 'Critical Research in the Information Age', in *Journal of Communication* (Summer 1983), writes, 'The privatization of information is observable in all sectors of society . . . A new international division of labour, no less inequitable than its predecessor, is being created practically before our eyes'. Schiller refers to a 'gale of technological and industrial change whipping across the United States and other industrialized countries' which is having far-reaching effects on the way we regard, and use, information: 'In sum, long-term, deep structural forces are making communication the central process in global, national and local social organization. At the same time, the most powerful national and transnational decision-making groups are initiating and deploying new information technologies to consolidate and extend their positions'. See ELITE; HEGEMONY; INFORMATION GAPS; MEDIA IMPERIALISM; POWER; POWER ELITE; TECHNOLOGICAL DETERMINISM.

Commonality In terms of LANGUAGE, beliefs, CULTURE, general outlook, that which is *shared* within a community; that which most elements of the community have in common.

Communication While the definitions of communication vary according to the theoretical frames of reference employed and the stress placed upon certain aspects of the total process, they all include five fundamental factors: an initiator; a recipient; a mode or vehicle; a MESSAGE and an effect. Simply expressed, the communication process begins when a *message* is conceived by a *sender*. It is then ENCODED – translated into a signal or sequence of signals – and *transmitted* via a particular MEDIUM or CHANNEL to a *receiver* who then DECODES it and interprets the message, returning a signal in some way that the message has or has not been understood.

What has been termed NOISE, or interference, may impede the message. This may be internal (resistance to the message or to the sender, for example, on the part of the receiver) or external (actual noise, distraction, LANGUAGE level, etc.). During the communication process, sender, message and receiver are subject to a multitude of *cues* which influence the message, such as a person's appearance, his/her known status or the expression on his/her own face as the message is communicated or responded to (See BARNLUND'S TRANSACTIONAL MODEL).

While INTERPERSONAL COMMUNICATION is that which occurs between two or more people, INTRAPERSONAL COMMUNICATION is what you say within and to yourself. Inner thoughts, impressions, memories interact with external stimuli – the decor of a room, a painting on the wall, a beautiful landscape, a row of slum houses, a jostling crowd, a teacher at the front of the class, your friend's good or bad mood – to create a silent DISCOURSE, continuously changing and renewing itself and influencing your perceptions of self and the world.

It is important to hold in mind, as Raymond Williams points out in *Keywords* (UK: Fontana, 1976), the 'unresolved range of the original noun of action, represented at its extremes by "transmit", a one-way process, and "share" . . . a common or mutual process'. This polarity of meaning – of the one-way process as against aspects of *communion* – is fundamental to the analysis of communication, hence the attempt to generalize the distinction in such phrases as *manipulative communication* and *participative communication*.

Frank Dance in 'Toward a theory of human communication' in the book he edited, *Human Communication Theory: Original Essays* (US: Holt, Rinehart & Winston, 1967), observes that communication is something that changes even while one is in the act of examining it; it is therefore an interaction and a *transaction*. F. Dance and C. Larson in *The Functions of Human Communication: A Theoretical*

Approach (US: Holt, Rinehart & Winston, 1976), detail their examination of 126 definitions of communication. They specify notable differences but common agreement that communication is a *process*. The authors conclude with a definition of their own: 'The production of symbolic content by an individual, according to a CODE, with anticipated consumption by other(s) according to the same code'. Or as Colin Cherry succinctly puts it in *On Human Communication* (US: MIT Press, 1957), communication is 'essentially a social affair'.

Of course a painter or a poet may quarrel with this definition. He/she might claim that the process of communication is between artist–materials–subject-matter–artist's self or poet–words–feelings in an act of self-address, and that the eventual viewer of the painting or reader of the poem is of little account at the moment of encoding. It is open to debate whether, if the painting is stored in an attic or the poem burnt, any meaningful communication has taken place. Also, the painter or poet's work, once presented for consumption by others may be decoded – interpreted – in as many ways as there are people, each one re-processing the work of art according to his/her own needs, NORMS, VALUES, CULTURE, EXPECTATIONS and SOCIALIZATION.

T.R. Nilson in 'On defining communication' in *Speech Trainer*, 1957, and reprinted in K.K. Sereno and C.D. Mortensen, eds., *Foundations of Communication Theory* (US: Harper & Row, 1970), distinguishes between communication which is *instrumental*, that is intended to stimulate a response, and *situational* in which there need not be any intention of evoking a response in the transmission of stimuli.

As early as 1933, Edward Sapir differentiated between, *explicit* and *implicit* modes of communication, a perspective supported by Baker Brownell in *The Community: Its Philosophy and Practice for a Time of Crisis* (US: Harper & Bros., 1950) who speaks of *direct* and *indirect* communication. The latter Brownell defines as being a '. . . process wherein something converted into symbols is carried over from one person to another', while the former is a function of the '. . . identification of people with one another'.

A precept that few commentators would challenge is that it is *impossible not to communicate*. By saying nothing, by remaining blank-faced, by keeping our hands stiffly to our sides, we are still communicating, however negatively. We are still part of the interaction whether we like it or not. For Jurgen Ruesch, communication is 'all those processes by which people influence one another' (in 'Values, communication and culture', J. Ruesch and G. Bateson, eds., *The Social Matrix of Psy-*chiatry, US: W.W. Norton, 1951). At first we may resist the claim that whatever we do we are exerting an influence. Yet by trying *not* to influence we are arguably still affecting the patterns of communicative action, interaction and transaction. In our absence from the scene – from our family or work group, for example – as well as in our presence, we may still exert influence, however little, however unintended. See COMMUNICATION, ANIMAL; COMMUNICATION, FUNCTIONS; COMMUNICATION MODELS; MASS COMMUNICATION; THEORIES AND CONCEPTS OF COMMUNICATION.

Communication, animal The study of the way animals communicate, involving as it does a wide variety of disciplines ranging from bio-acoustics and biochemistry through anatomy to sensory physiology, neurophysiology, zoology, anthropology and LINGUISTICS, is gathered under the title of *Zoosemiotics*, a word coined by Thomas A. Sebeok writing in *Language* (39, 1963).

The science of Zoosemiotics lies at the intersection of general SEMIOLOGY/SEMIOTICS and ethology, the biological study of behaviour. In addition to the more well-known vocal mode (e.g. barking), animals communicate via the following systems: chemical (via pheremones), optical and tactile (TOUCH). Bio-acoustic systems relate to modes of communication by means of mechanical vibrations, as with insects and birds. Mammals which communicate in this way are bats, shrews, rodents, deer, seals, carnivores, monkeys and anthropoid apes. Such systems may also operate under water among crustacea, aquatic insects, fishes, whales and other cetacea.

It is generally agreed that research has only scratched the surface as far as understanding animal communication is concerned, and interpretation of it has tended to be anthropomorphic, that is viewed from a human point of view – thus a bird singing is considered 'happy'. Four main message-by-sound categories have been defined: food-getting, avoiding enemies, reproduction and group movements. Visual messages as expressed by movement, stance, facial set, colouration and, as in the case of the firefly, the production of light, represent a vast and complicated LANGUAGE, and much of our interpretation of it is guesswork.

One classic subject for study is the honey bee. Austrian biologist Karl von Frisch, for example, in *The Dancing Bees* (US: Harcourt, Brace & World, 1965) describes how worker bees used a series of dance movements to help them communicate the direction and distance of food sources to other members of the hive. Another well known subject is the chimpanzee. Numerous attempts have been made during this century to investigate the capacity of the chimp – claimed to be so close in the scale of evolution to humankind – for acquiring human language.

One recent experiment has been with a chimp called Washoe. The directors of Project Washoe, Allen and Beatrice Gardner of the University of Nevada, attempted to teach Washoe American Sign Language. The experiment began when she was about a year old and continued until she was about five, by which time Washoe could understand and use several hundred signs and could combine a number of them in sequences which were similar to the sentences of a two-year-old child. In the 1980s a pigmy chimp called Kanki amazed scientists at the Language Research Centre near Atlanta, USA. He combined skills in understanding spoken language with an ability to communicate with, and show comprehension of, geometric symbols, using a keyboard – feats extensively documented in the *New York Times*.

Communication, functions Many and varied listings have been made by communications analyists. The following eight functions are usually quoted as being central: instrumental (to achieve or obtain something); control (to get someone to behave in a particular way); information (to find out or explain something); expression (to express one's feelings or put oneself over in a particular way); social contact (participating in company); alleviation of anxiety (to sort out a problem, ease a worry about something); stimulation (response to something of interest), and role-related (because the situation requires it). See JAKOBSON'S MODEL OF COMMUNICATION.

Communication integration See INTEGRATION.

Communication, interpersonal See INTERPERSONAL COMMUNICATION.

Communication, intrapersonal See INTRAPERSONAL COMMUNICATION.

Communication models See ANDERSCH, STAATS AND BOSTROM MODEL OF COMMUNICATION, 1969; BALL-ROKEACH AND DE FLEUR'S DEPENDENCY MODEL OF MASS COMMUNICATION EFFECTS, 1976; BARNLUND'S TRANSACTIONAL MODEL OF COMMUNICATION, 1970; BASS'S DOUBLE ACTION MODEL OF INTERNATIONAL NEWS FLOW, 1969; BECKER'S MOSAIC MODEL OF COMMUNICATION, 1968; COMMERCIAL LAISSEZ-FAIRE MODEL OF COMMUNICATION; DANCE'S HELICAL MODEL OF COMMUNICATION, 1967; DONOHEW AND TIPTON'S INFORMATION-SEEKING MODEL, 1973; GALTUNG AND RUGE'S MODEL OF SELECTIVE GATEKEEPING, 1965; GERBNER'S MODEL OF COMMUNICATION, 1956; HYPODERMIC NEEDLE MODEL OF COMMUNICATION; JAKOBSON'S MODEL OF COMMUNICATION, 1958; LASSWELL'S MODEL OF COMMUNICATION, 1948; MALETZKE'S MODEL OF THE MASS COMMUNICATION PROCESS, 1963; McCOMBS AND SHAW

AGENDA SETTING MODEL OF MEDIA EFFECTS, 1976; McNELLY'S MODEL OF NEWS FLOW, 1959; NEWCOMB'S ABX MODEL OF COMMUNICATION, 1953; NOELLE-NEUMANN'S SPIRAL OF SILENCE MODEL OF PUBLIC OPINION, 1974; ONE-STEP, TWO-STEP, MULTI-STEP FLOW MODELS OF COMMUNICATION; RILEY AND RILEY MODEL OF MASS COMMUNICATION, 1959; SCHRAMM'S MODELS OF COMMUNICATION, 1954; SHANNON AND WEAVER MODEL OF COMMUNICATION, 1949; S-IV-R MODEL OF COMMUNICATION; WESLEY AND MACLEAN'S MODEL OF COMMUNICATION, 1957; WHITE'S GATEKEEPER MODEL, 1950.

* These and other models not included in the Dictionary – such as Comstock's Psychological model of Television Effects on Individual Behaviour, 1978, De Fleur's Model of the American Mass Media System, 1970, and Gieber and Johnson's Model of Source–Reporter Relations, 1961 – may be read about in detail in *Communication Models for the study of mass communications* (UK: Longmanm 1981, impression, 1986) by Denis McQuail and Sven Windahl.

Communication, Non-verbal (NVC) A *presentational* code of communication, also called 'Body language'. Michael Argyle in 'Non-verbal communication in human and social interaction' in R. Hinde, ed., *Non-Verbal Communication* (UK: Cambridge, 1972) lists 10 such CODES of NVC: bodily contact; proximity (or PROXEMICS); orientation (how we angle ourselves to others); appearance; head nods; facial expression; GESTURES (or KINESICS); posture and eye movement/eye contact and PARA-LINGUISTICS. Varyingly NVC conveys much of what we wish to say, and much of what we would wish to withhold.

Affiliation, sexual attraction, rejection, aggression, dominance, submission, appeasement, fear, grief, joy are often best expressed – and in some cases can only be expressed – through NVC. The amount of NVC in the repertoire of different peoples and nations varies considerably in range, emphasis and frequency.

See NON-VERBAL BEHAVIOUR: REPERTOIRE.

* M. Argyle, *The Psychology of Interpersonal Behaviour* (UK: Penguin, 1972) and *Bodily Communication* (UK: Methuen, 1975); E. Hall *The Silent Language* (US: Anchor Books, 1973).

Communication postulates See POSTULATES OF COMMUNICATION.

Communication theory See THEORIES AND CONCEPTS OF COMMUNICATION.

Communications capability The linking, electronically, of equipment to gain access to additional resources (e.g. main frame computers) and the facility to transmit data to another room, building, city or country.

Communications conglomerates See CON-
GLOMERATES.

Communications gap Failure of understanding usually as a result of a lack of
information, especially between different age
GROUPS, economic CLASSES, political factions
or cultural groups.

Communicative negligence See LAW OF THE
TOTAL SITUATION.

Communicology The study of the nature, process and meanings systems of all forms of
communication in what Dean C. BARNLUND has
described as 'the totality of time, space, personality and circumstance' (in 'A transactional
model of communication', K.K. Sereno and
C.D. Mortensen, eds., *Foundations of Communication Theory*, US: Harper & Row, 1970).

Community radio Because RADIO BROAD-
CASTING is the cheapest form of MASS COM-
MUNICATION it lends itself to 'grass roots' use
by communities of interest – geographical,
cultural, political. Its potential is to be run by
and for local communities, special interests and
followings. The development of local RADIO in
the UK has made some progress towards the
community ideal, but full independence, in
terms of appointments, policy, financing, programming, etc. remains at levels other than the
local one.

Though the term *community radio* was probably first used by Rachel Powell in a pamphlet
Possibilities for Local Radio (UK: Centre for
Contemporary Cultural Studies, University of
Birmingham, December 1965), the idea goes as
far back as the BEVERIDGE REPORT 1950 which
proposed the use of VHF frequencies to 'establish local radio stations with independent programmes of their own. How large a scope there
would be in Britain for local stations broadcasting programmes controlled by Universities
or Local Authorities or public service organizations is not known, but the experiment of setting up some local stations should be tried
without delay.'

In 1962 the PILKINGTON REPORT recommended that the BBC provide 'local sound
broadcasting' on the basis of 'one service in
some 250 localities', stations having a typical
range of five miles. The 1971 government
White Paper launched COMMERCIAL RADIO, but
radio BROADCASTING through the next decade
was to remain under the DUOPOLY of the BBC
and IBA.

Pressure to produce a 'third' force in broadcasting in the UK, to consist of highly individual and genuinely local stations, has grown
in the 1980s. Throughout the country groups
dedicated to the furtherance of community
radio have multiplied, providing information,
exerting pressure at national and local levels – and very often with transmitters at the
ready (or actually broadcasting illegally).

A flourishing example of community radio
has been set by France since the election of
President Mitterand. For 18 months there was
a free-for-all on the airwaves, a 'solution' to
which was announced in July 1982 after a year
of enquiry by a special commission. Frequencies on VHF were allocated to a host of special-
interest broadcasters – Gaullists, newspaper
interests, Jews, English-speakers, a Christian
station shared between Catholics and Protes-
tants and two immigrant stations.

A last-minute slot was allocated to *Fre-
quence Gaie* (Gay Radio) after a protest march
in Paris following its initial exclusion. Gay
Radio had featured in the top four in the listening charts.

The French government ban on ADVERTISING
on these community channels poses the problem of finance, which is having to be found
through grants and cultural events.

See RADIO: BROADCASTING IN THE 90s.

Commutation test A useful device for the
analysis of the MEANING and impact of communication presentations such as photographs,
paintings and advertisements. We may look at
a newspaper picture of inner city riots. By
commuting elements – images or words – in
the picture, removing them and replacing them
by others, how is the meaning of the picture
transformed?

Compact disc See CD – COMPACT DISC.

Competence In LINGUISTICS, a term used to
describe a person's knowledge of his/her own
LANGUAGE, its system of rules; his/her competence in understanding an unlimited number
of sentences, in spotting grammatical errors,
etc.

Completion point See VERBAL DEVICES IN
SPEECH-MAKING.

**Compliance, identification and internali-
zation** See INTERNALIZATION.

Computer graphics Truly one of the wonders
of the modern world: art by numbers – computer numbers – capable of feats of design of
astonishing virtuosity and potential. Computer
capability in the field of graphics is vast,
ranging from representation of three-dimensional technical design, complete with depth
cueing, to simulations of space exploration and
of nuclear conflict. Computer graphics supply
the visual wizardry of Space Invader-type computer games and are also capable of producing
ANIMATION in the manner of Walt Disney. In
1982, the Disney studios produced the first feature film using this technique, *Tron*. A quarter
of the film is conventional live-action; the rest
is computer graphics or a mixture of computer-
generated images with live action. Director of
Tron, Steven Lisburger has said of animation
by computer, 'It gives you a whole world, an
entire geography, an entire physics, all from
the mind of the computer.'

The implications of this technology do not apply merely to animation film: the computer can 'draw' backgrounds and figures so real, it can simulate everyday objects so accurately, and three-dimensionally that the movie set of the future might exist only in an electronic console. In science and medicine computer graphics are applied microscopically, simulating, for example, molecular constructs and interaction, thus opening up possibilities in the development of new drugs. Macroscopically, computer graphics have reconstructed in detail, in wire frame (line drawing), the entire city of Chicago and are serving an increasing role in space design testing. They are also opening up fresh areas of expression for artists as well as scientists.

Computers in communication Of the hundred or so forms of computer LANGUAGE approximately a dozen are in common use. Most familiar is BASIC (Beginners All-purpose Symbolic Instruction Code) developed at Dartmouth College for time-sharing of campus computer resources by students. At a higher level, the most popular computer language for commercial work is COBOL (Common Business Oriented Language), while FORTRAN (Formula Translation) was developed for scientific and technical problem solving in which mathematics is used. APT (Automatically Programmed Tools) is used for control of machine tools, GPSS (General Purpose Simulation System) for design and manufacturing problems and RPG (Report Program Generation) for structuring the production of business reports. Such languages are considered either procedure-oriented or problem-oriented, the one with a wide range of applications, the other for particular applications.

Bit is an elementary unit of computer information, taking the value 0 or 1. *Byte* is eight bits, the usual length of computer encoded character and unit of measurement for computer storage. *Compiler*, in the form of both hardware or software (computer programs) translates from a programming language such as BASIC or COBOL to the bit-code understood by the computer. Each language requires its own compiler for each type of computer.

The *Daisy wheel* is a printer mechanism to produce high quality results from a computer; its petal-like characters are held at the ends of a print wheel. The *Disk* is a high-capacity storage MEDIUM enabling direct and speedy recall of information. Hard disks have high capacity and are costly while so-called *floppy disks* are cheaper and of lower capacity. The *Dot Matrix* is printed computer read-out made up of tiny dots. *K* is the abbreviation for 1000 (Kilo): 1K bytes of memory represent 1000 (or in some computer texts, 1024) characters.

Large, high cost, wide capacity computers are *Mainframe*. The *Microcomputer* is similar in size to personal computers but designed particularly for business or industrial use. Central to the operation of personal or microcomputers is the *Microprocessor*, the silicon chip which does the computer calculations as distinct from memory chips which hold information. The *Minicomputer* comes between mainframe and microcomputer in cost and size, again for business use, while the *Personal computer* is now familiar in home and school, with ever-expanding potential.

The *Program* is the detailed sequence of instructions which controls the computer – the *Software* as opposed to the *Hardware*. *Applications software* refers to programs that are written by users to accomplish specific jobs such as working out a firm's wages. *Systems software* serve to make the overall computer system work, while *Control software* is made up of programs to control the orderly flow of both applications and systems programs.

RAM is Random Access Memory – silicon chips used to memorize computerized information – which can be easily changed. *ROM* is Read Only Memory in which silicon chips are used to memorize information that does not change. *Multiprocessing* refers to the use of more than one computer doing the same job; *Multiprograming* is the programing of two or more jobs by a single computer and *Time sharing* is the use of large processing facilities by many simultaneous users at different locations, each interacting directly with the computer. See WORD PROCESSING.

* J. Cayford, *Computer Media: Living & Working with Computers* (UK: Comedia, 1987).

Computer sketchpad Means by which a scientist or engineer can communicate directly with a computer via a special cathode ray tube and a 'light' pencil, stating a problem, query or proposition in much the same way as he/she might 'sketch' his/her thinking with paper and pencil. 'In this way,' writes Professor Arthur Porter in *Cybernetics Simplified* (UK: English Universities Press, 1969), 'a sort of man–machine dialogue is established and this means that the capabilities of man on the one hand and machine on the other are being used to the full capacity – the human as an intuitive and inductive thinker, the machine as an ultra high-speed data processor and computer'. See CYBERNETICS.

Conative function of communication See also JAKOBSON'S MODEL OF COMMUNICATION, 1958.

Concurrence-seeking tendency In GROUPS, the cohesiveness of members may produce a tendency to agree at all costs, even when the decisions brought about by that unanimity may turn out to be disastrous. In *Groupthink*.

Psychological Studies of Policy Decisions and Fiascos (US: Houghton Mifflin, 1972) Irving L. Janis identifies the concurrence-seeking tendency as being one which, developing unchecked in a group's decision-making processes, causes a 'deterioration of mental efficiency, reality testing, and moral judgement'.

Concurrent printing A facility in WORD PROCESSING which allows the typist to enter fresh text while simultaneously printing out something else, thus avoiding frustrating waits between jobs.

Confederates See SLIDER.

Confrontation dressing Vivien Westwood, fashion designer, used this term to describe the phenomenon, especially evident in the PUNK youth SUB-CULTURE, of assembling everyday objects into fashion outfits in such a way as to subvert their original use and thus their social MEANING. One example of this has been the use, by some followers of the Punk youth culture, of razor blades, tampons and clothes pegs as 'jewellery'. The overall effect is to display a mode of dress which symbolically challenges, confronts, the accepted modes of dress and, at a deeper level, the existing VALUES and ideologies of society. See IDEOLOGY; STYLE.

Conglomerates The increasing cost of entering the media market has, in part, fostered a concentration of ownership in the various sectors of the communications industry. Graham Murdock in 'Large corporations and the control of the communications industries' in M. Gurevitch, T. Bennett, J. Curran, and J. Woollacott, eds., *Culture, Society and the Media*, (UK: Methuen, 1982) notes that 'At the present time . . . the communications industries are increasingly dominated by conglomerates with significant stakes in a range of major media markets giving them an unprecedented degree of potential control over the range and direction of cultural production. Moreover, the effective reach of these corporations is likely to extend still further during the 1980s, due to their strategic command over the new information and video technologies . . .'

A *communications conglomerate* is an amalgam of corporations which operate mainly or wholly with communications or leisure interests – like the Granada group which operates the Granada TV network, a large TV rental chain and a paperback publishing company and has interests in the cinema, music publishing and numerous other entertainment outlets. Significant sectors of the communications industry are, however, part of general conglomerates whose main business concerns are outside the communications field.

The mass media can be seen as related to the industrial system in two ways: firstly they are part of it as large-scale buyers and sellers and makers of profit; secondly they are preachers of its (industry's) messages. Much of the communications industry is in the control of *multinational* corporations, that is companies which have large-scale investment in many different countries. Thus the multinationals keep a substantial 'finger in the pie' of these countries' information systems (See MEDIA IMPERIALISM).

The concentration of ownership, the increased potential for power which it facilitates, and the interrelationship between the communications industry and other industrial and commercial interests constitute important areas of current media research. See ELITE; ESTABLISHMENT; NEWS AGENCIES; SOCIOMETRICS.

Congruence theory The basic premise of congruence or *balance* theory is that in the case of two people who like or dislike each other, some patterns of the relationship will be balanced – in congruence – and some will be unbalanced, as when a person dislikes the object which is liked by a liked person. You have congruence if a person you like approves of a cause or affirms a position with which you are in sympathy.

The principle of congruity as advanced by Charles Osgood and Percy Tannenbaum in 'The Principle of Congruity in the Prediction of Attitude Change', *Psychological Review* 62(1955) holds that when change in evaluation or attitude occurs it always occurs in the direction of *increased* congruity with the prevailing frame of reference.

The opposite of cognitive balance is *cognitive dissonance*, a notion analysed by L.A. Festinger in *A Theory of Cognitive Dissonance* (US: Row Peterson, 1957). The theory predicts that people will seek out information which confirms existing attitudes and views of the world or reinforces other aspects of behaviour. Similarly it predicts that people will avoid information which is likely to increase DISSONANCE. If you dislike a person, and you dislike his/her views, what he/she says is unlikely to cause cognitive dissonance, for there is a congruence here. Dissonance is acute when a liked person says something seemingly 'out of character' or fails to accord with expectations or the image held of him/her. See COGNITIVE AND AFFECTIVE; DEFENSIVE COMMUNICATION; EFFECTS OF THE MASS MEDIA; NEWCOMB'S ABX MODEL OF COMMUNICATION, 1953; RESONANCE; SYMMETRY, STRAIN TOWARDS.

Connotation Roland Barthes's second order of SIGNIFICATION in the transmission of messages. The second order comprises connotation and MYTH. **Denotation**, the first order of signification, is simply a process of identification. The word 'green' represents a colour; but green, at a higher level, can **connote** the countryside, permission to go ahead, the Irish, etc. Connotation is the act of adding information, insight, angle, colouration, value – MEANING, in fact, to denotation.

* R. Barthes, *Mythologies* (UK: Paladin, 1973).

Consensual validation H.S. Sullivan in *Concepts of Modern Psychiatry* (US: White Psychiatric Foundation, 1940) uses this phrase to describe the ready-made interpretations or meanings of things passed down through a CULTURE; matters about which there is CONSENSUS. Agreed definitions of MEANING within a society are, of course, easier to claim validity for than to prove, especially if we take into consideration such factors as HEGEMONY and notions of DOMINANT DISCOURSE.

Consensus That which is generally agreed; an area or basis of shared agreement among the majority. Three elements crucial to the function of consensus are: common acceptance of laws, rules and NORMS; attachment to the institutions which promulgate these laws, rules and norms; and a widespread sense of identity or unity, of similar or identical outlook. The opposite term is *dissensus*. The elements obviously vary independently, yet the strength of any one helps to strengthen the others.

Consensus, states the *International Encyclopaedia of Social Sciences* (ed. D.L. Sills; US: Macmillan and Free Press, 1968) 'operates to restrict the extension of dissensus and to limit conflict . . .' Beliefs about consensus 'usually concern the rightness and the qualifications of those in authority to exercise it' and thus relate to the legitimacy of institutions, accepted standards and practices, and dominant principles. They tend to affirm existing patterns of the distribution of authority.

Consensus, therefore, is largely defined by those who have the power and the means to disseminate their definition; and the definition is employed as a means of acknowledging and reinforcing the legitimacy of the powerful. Equally important in this context is the close affinity of outlook of the central cultural system with the central institutional system. Stuart Hood in *Hood on Television* (UK: Pluto, 1980) says 'It is the essence of the idea of consensus that it attempts, at a conscious and unconscious level, to impose the view that there is only one "right" reading. This assumption derives from the view that we – that is the audience and the broadcaster – are united in one nation in spite of class or political definition'. See CULTURAL APPARATUS; IMPARTIALITY.

Consent, manufacture of The American philosopher and linguist Noam Chomsky has defined the *manufacture of consent* as a complex process whereby powerful interests inside democracies such as the US and the UK create in the public mind patterns of acceptance. In an article written for *Index on Censorship*, 1(1987), entitled 'No anti-Israeli vendetta', Chomsky refers to 'devices of thought control' in democratic societies 'which are more pertinent for us than the crude methods of totalitarian states'. The devices arise from such aspects of the media process as control over resources and the locus of decision-making in the state and private economy. Where state policy on an issue such as the Arab–Israeli conflict, or with regard to Central American politics, is rigorously committed to one side or the other, alternative options which the public might be interested in considering, are declared out of bounds – through what Chomsky describes as 'suppression, falsification, and Orwellian manipulation'.

Consistency There is general agreement among research analysts that the greater the degree of consistency in media coverage, the greater is the likelihood that audiences will absorb the projected version – adopt the PREFERRED READING – of reported situations. See EFFECTS OF THE MASS MEDIA; FREQUENCY; INTENSITY.

Consonance, hypothesis of See NEWS VALUES.

Conspiracy of silence The tacit agreement among those with significant information to keep 'mum' about it – say nothing. An early use of the phrase, perhaps even the first as far as BROADCASTING was concerned, is ascribed to the head of BBC News in 1938 at the time of the Munich crisis, when the BBC failed to broadcast any close examination of Neville Chamberlain's policy of appeasement towards Nazi Germany. See CENSORSHIP.

Conspiracy theory Not so much a theory, more a hunch or suspicion. As far as the media are concerned, the 'conspiracy' relates – in the view of those who claim it exists – to the practice of manipulating MESSAGES in order to support those who own the means of communication, their social CLASS (i.e. middle and upper) and their interests. The conspiracy theorists argue that in a capitalist society where the media are owned or strongly influenced by the capitalist ESTABLISHMENT, information is shaped to underpin existing social, economic and political conditions.

In his Introduction to the GLASGOW UNIVERSITY MEDIA GROUP publication *Bad News* (UK: Routledge & Kegan Paul, 1976), Richard Hoggart ventures to locate two levels or forms of conspiracy theory, High and Low, the one aligning with the Marxist view of media operation, the other with the generality of people who at some time or another suspect that the media project the interests and the value systems of those who own, control or run them. See HEGEMONY.

Constituency Term generally applied to an electoral area which returns a parliamentary candidate, but it is also used by researchers to refer to the readership of a newspaper and carries with it the implication that the reader's political views may be influenced by the paper's coverage of events. The notion of audience as constituency was particularly prevalent in the age of PRESS BARONS such as Lords Northcliffe, Rothermere and Beaverbrook, who claimed access to political decision-making on the strength of the constituency of their papers' readership.

Consumer sovereignty A phrase used in the PEACOCK REPORT, 1985, summarizing the attitude towards BROADCASTING of the Committee on Financing the BBC. The Committee took the market-place view that the customer knows best and that consumer tastes should be the guiding principle of RADIO and TELEVISION programming. See PUBLIC SERVICE BROADCASTING.

Consumption behaviour Term used by researchers for how audiences respond to product marketing: attitudes towards ADVERTISING, knowledge of commercials and people's buying behaviour. At the nub of market research into consumption behaviour is *motivation*. Why do people watch a TV commercial, what makes them pay attention and heed the MESSAGE? Regularly cited are three major reasons for a positive audience response: (1) *Social utility* – watching commercials in order to gain information about the 'social significance' of products or brands, and the association of advertising objects with social ROLES and lifestyles; (2) *Communication utility* – watching in order to provide a basis for later INTERPERSONAL COMMUNICATION; (3) *Vicarious consumption* – participating at second-hand in desired lifestyles as a means of indirect association with those people possessing glamour or prestige. See ADVERTISING: MAINSTREAMERS, ASPIRERS, SUCCEEDERS & REFORMERS.

Contagion effect Power of the media to create a craze or even an epidemic. Examples of this are the so-called Swastika Epidemic of 1959–60 where an outbreak of swastika daubing in the US was accelerated by media coverage, and the UK Mods v. Rockers seaside battles in the 1960s. Debate continues on whether media coverage 'worsened' or provoked the street riots in several British cities in 1981, often named Copycat Riots.

Stanley Cohen in 'Sensitization: the case of the Mods and Rockers' in S. Cohen and J. Young, eds., *The Manufacture of News* (UK: Constable, 1973), writes, 'Constant repetition of the warring gangs' image . . . had the effect of giving these loose collections a structure they never possessed and a mythology with which to justify the structure' and the court scenes at which those arrested by the police were tried were 'arenas for acting out society's morality plays'. See MEDIA IMAGES; MORAL PANIC.

Contempt of Court Act, 1981 Part of the armoury of CENSORSHIP in the UK, this act restricts the reporting of court cases before they come to trial. It was first used in 1983 when several newspapers published articles on Michael Fagan, who had climbed into the Queen's bedroom at Buckingham Palace. The publishers of the *Sunday Times* and the *Daily Star* were found guilty of printing stories which ran a substantial risk of prejudicing the trial of Fagan.

Lord Chief Justice Lord Lane, Lord Justice Achner and Lord Justice Oliver held that the *Star's* fault was a mistake which had slipped through its system of checks – and the newspaper was not fined. However, the *Sunday Times* had published several errors of fact but had not seriously disrupted the outcome of the trial. It was fined £1000. The *Sun, Sunday People* and *Mail on Sunday* were cleared of Contempt and the Attorney-General was ordered to pay the legal costs of these papers. The *Sunday Times* and the *Star* were ordered to pay costs.

Content analysis Research into mass media content identifies, categorizes, describes and quantifies short-term and long-term trends. An early and most valuable descriptive trend study was that of Ernst Kris and Nathan Leites in 1947. In 'Trends in 20th century propaganda' in B. Berelson and M. Janowitz, eds., *Reader in Public Opinion and Communication* (US: Free Press, 1947), the authors traced the trend in PROPAGANDA from the 1st World War (1914–18) to the 2nd (1939–45), identifying a changing style towards a less emotional, less moralistic and more truthful orientation.

Content analysis serves an important function by comparing the same material as presented in different media within a nation, or between different nations; or by comparing media content with some explicit set of standards or abstract categories. On the basis of the existing body of quantitative and qualitative research, several broad generalizations may be hazarded about the content of MASS COMMUNICATION: what is communicated by the mass media is a highly selected sample of all that is available for communication; what is received and consumed by the potential audience is a highly selected sample of all that is communicated; more of what is communicated is classifiable as entertaining rather than informative or educative, and, because the mass media are aimed at the largest possible audience, most material is simple in form and uncomplicated in content. See AUDIENCE RESEARCH; GLASGOW UNIVERSITY MEDIA GROUP.

Control group In comparative research methods, the neutral body against which a test group is measured. Thus, in the case of AUDIENCE RESEARCH, the test group is exposed to a TV programme, for example, and their responses analysed against identical monitoring of the control group who have not seen the programme.

Control of the media See MEDIA CONTROL.

Control room Nerve centre of a studio broadcast or recording in which all the technology of production is operated.

Conventions Established practices within a particular CULTURE or SUB-CULTURE. Conventions are identifiable in every form of communication and behaviour, some strict, like rules of grammar, others open to wider application, such as dress. Conventions are largely culture-specific and context-specific. It is an accepted convention that a candidate dress smartly for a job interview yet it would be deemed unconventional if he or she appeared on the beach clad in the same manner. Media practices have established many conventions which have become so familiar they appear 'the natural way to do things'. TELEVISION news holds to the convention of having on-screen news-readers; documentaries generally hold to the convention of having a voice-over narration. Innovators – for example in the arts – break with convention. The shock of the new often stirs among the conventional a sense of affronted VALUES. The chances of the new becoming conventionalized will depend on various factors, such as OPINION LEADERS, prevalent tastes and fashions, even NEWSWORTHINESS. See REDUNDANCY.

Co-orientation approach See McCOMBS and SHAW AGENDA SETTING MODEL OF MEDIA EFFECTS, 1976.

Copycat effect See CONTAGION EFFECT.

Cosmopoliteness In most social structures there are individuals who have considerable awareness of other social situations and frequent contact with those outside their own social structure; that is, there are some individuals who are **cosmopolite**. In general the more cosmopolite an individual is the more receptive he/she is to messages containing new ideas.

Cosmopolite and localite channels The situation in which the sender and receiver of a MESSAGE belong to different SOCIAL SYSTEMS or sub-systems is referred to as **cosmopolite**. **Localite** CHANNELS are those in which both sender and receiver belong to the same social system or sub-system.

Counter-culture A type of SUB-CULTURE firmly antagonistic to the dominant or prevailing CULTURE of a community. The term is generally used to describe the collection of mainly middle-class youth cultures which developed in the 1960s and whose central feature was the call for the adoption of alternative social structures and lifestyles. In 'Sub Cultures, cultures and class', J. Clarke and others in S. Hall and T. Jefferson, eds., *Resistance Through Rituals* (UK: Hutchinson, 1976) explore some of the distinguishing features of such a counter-culture as compared with other types of youth sub-cultures. Its opposition to the dominant cultures takes very open political and ideological forms and goes beyond the registering of complaint and resistance to the elaborate construction of alternative institutions.

Further resistance continues beyond the teenage years and its ideologies permeate all areas of life – work, home, family, school and leisure – and thus blurs their boundaries, whereas in many working class youth sub-cultures such boundaries are rigorously maintained. The HIPPY movement, for example, embraced political protest – most notably in the form of demonstrations for peace – and developed coherent alternative philosophies; it established some alternative institutions such as an UNDERGROUND PRESS. It also proposed radical, democratic structures for the organization of work, school and the family. Although the resistance of the counter-culture is usually more open and confident than that of the sub-culture, it still contains important symbolic elements such as dress and hair STYLE.

Corporate commitment See IMPARTIALITY.

Crab and track See SHOT.

Crisis (definition) How do we know when a crisis is a crisis? One answer is – when the media tell us it is a crisis. Their capacity for AGENDA SETTING, of selecting the front-page headlines or the lead stories, can not only crystallize the notion of crisis in the public mind but in some cases help precipitate one, at least in the sense that people in authority – such as governments – can be forced into a crisis response to a crisis stimulus.

A classic example of a media-fostered crisis is the handling of the speech made by Enoch Powell MP on 20 April 1968 about the imminent 'crisis' in society caused by immigration. Delivered in Birmingham to an audience of under 100, Powell's so-called 'Rivers of Blood' speech was transmitted via the media to 95% of the adult population of the UK (according to a Gallup poll). The crisis – in race relations in Britain – received its legitimacy; its definition. See EFFECTS OF THE MASS MEDIA.

* C. Seymour-Ure, chapter 4: Enoch Powell's 'earthquake', *The Political Impact of Mass Media* (UK: Constable, 1974).

Cryptography Secret LANGUAGE; the transfer of messages into secret CODES. A cryptograph is anything written in *cypher*. See DATA PROTECTION.

Cued speech A method of using hand shapes in communication with the hearing-impaired to indicate pronunciation. It sorts out the word and speech sounds that look identical as they are pronounced or are completely hidden in lip-reading. R. Orin Cornelt developed cued speech in the US in the mid-1960s.

Cues See BARNLUND'S TRANSACTIONAL MODEL OF COMMUNICATION.

Cultivation As used by US communication analyst George Gerbner, the term describes the way that the mass media system relates to the CULTURE from which it grows and which it addresses. The media 'cultivate' attitudes and VALUES in a culture. For example, audiences are cultivated into rejecting certain acts of violence while at the same time being cultivated into accepting or tolerating others. See MAINSTREAMING.

* G. Gerbner, 'Cultural indicators: the case of violence in television drama', in *Annals of the American Association of Political and Social Science*, 338 (1970).

Cultivation differential The difference between the perceptions of heavy and light viewers on a particular aspect of social reality. Several researchers have focused upon the influence of TV upon an individual's perception of social reality. George Gerbner and others in 'The demonstration of power: violence profile No. 10' in *Journal of Communication*, 29 (1979), report on findings regarding the effect of TV portrayal of violence on certain viewers' perceptions of the incidence of real violence. They found that heavy viewers of TV were more likely to be influenced by, more likely to accept, the image of reality presented by TV programmes than light viewers. See EFFECTS OF THE MASS MEDIA.

Cultural apparatus 'Taken as a whole,' writes C. Wright Mills in *Power, Politics and People* (US: Oxford University Press, 1963), 'the cultural apparatus is the lens of mankind through which men see; the medium by which they interpret and report what they see.' It is composed of 'all the organizations and *milieux* in which artistic, intellectual and scientific work goes on, and of the means by which such work is made available to circles, publics and masses'.

The cultural apparatus features large in the process of guiding experience, defining social truths, establishing standards of credibility, image-making and opinion forming, and is 'used by dominant institutional orders'. It confers prestige and the 'prestige of culture is among the major means by which powers of decision are made to seem part of an unchallengeable authority'. Wright Mills goes on to argue that, no matter how internally free the 'cultural workman' as he names the artist or intellectual, he/she is instrinsically part of the cultural apparatus which tends in every nation to become a 'close adjunct of national authority and a leading agency of nationalist propaganda'. CULTURE and authority overlap and this overlap 'may involve the ideological use of cultural products and of cultural workmen for the legitimation of power, and the justification of decisions and policies'. See CONSENSUS.

Cultural Indicators research project See MAINSTREAMING.

Cultural industry See FRANKFURT SCHOOL OF THEORISTS.

Culturalist studies of the media See CULTURE.

Cultural modes The *literate* mode is rooted in the written word; the *oral* mode is spoken or visual. Traditionally they have been aligned to CLASS differences; that is, the upper, better educated classes have lived by a literate mode of cultural interaction – the *dominant* CULTURE, while the more 'untutored' classes have relied upon oral modes. With the advent of electronic media the oral mode has become increasingly dominant. It is essentially the mode of FILM and TELEVISION, though both media still tend to be run by a class educated in the literate mode and whose perceptions are conditioned by such a mode. In *Culture and Society* (UK: Penguin, 1958), Raymond Williams describes the oral, working class mode as 'the basic collective idea' while the bourgeois, literate culture represents the 'basic individualist idea'. See BARDIC TELEVISION.

Culture The sum of those characteristics which *identify* and *differentiate* human societies – a complex interweave of many factors. The culture of a nation is made up of its LANGUAGE, history, traditions, climate, geography, arts, social, economic and political NORMS, and its system of VALUES; and such a nation's size, its neighbours and its current prosperity condition the nature of its culture.

There are cultures within cultures. Thus reference is made to *working class culture* or *middle class culture*. Organizations and institutions can have their own cultures (See ORGANIZATION CULTURES). We refer to **cultural epochs** which are the result of developments – social, political, industrial, technological – which create cultural change.

Mass production and the mass media have contributed immensely to cultural change, giving rise to what critics have termed *mass culture* and disapprovingly portrayed as manufactured, manipulated, force-fed, marketed like soap powder and, because of its unique access to vast audiences, open to abuse of the mass by the powerful. Alan Swingewood in *The Myth of Mass Culture* (UK: Macmillan, 1977) argues, however, that there 'is no mass culture, or mass society; but there is an ideology of mass culture and mass society'. The IDEOLOGY is real enough, but the thing itself he describes as MYTH: 'If culture is the means whereby man affirms his humanity and his purposes and his aspirations to freedom and dignity then the concept and theory of mass culture are their denial and negation.'

Culture is transmitted through SOCIALIZATION to new members of a social group or society. The media play an important role in this process. A central concern of culturalist studies of the media is the degree to which the media's output may both reflect and communicate the culture of the more powerful social GROUPS in that society at the expense of the less powerful. By asserting one culture against others, the media help to nurture a *dominant culture* and relegate rival cultures into the realms of DEVIANCE. See CONSENSUS; COUNTER-CULTURE; CULTURAL APPARATUS; HEGEMONY; STREET CULTURE; SUB-CULTURE; YOUTH CULTURE.

* R Williams, *The Long Revolution* (UK: Chatto & Windus, 1961, and Penguin, 1965) and *Culture* (UK: Fontana, 1981); R. Hoggart, *The Uses of Literacy* (UK: Penguin, 1958); M. Gurevitch, T. Bennett, J. Curran and J. Woollacott, eds., *Culture, Society and the Media* (UK: Methuen, 1982); R. Collins, J. Curran, N. Garnham, P. Scannell, P. Schlesinger and C. Sparns, eds, *Media, Culture and Society* (UK: Sage, 1986).

Cultures of organizations See ORGANIZATION CULTURES.

Cultures, The two The novelist C.P. Snow in 1959 delivered the Rede Lecture in Cambridge, and deplored the widening gap between the Two Cultures, that of the humanities and that of the sciences and technology.

Cut-off In INTERPERSONAL COMMUNICATION, actions which block – cut off – incoming visual signals when people are under stress: hands over eyes, deflected glance, glazed look, eyes shut, etc. See GESTURE.

Cybernetics The study of communication FEEDBACK systems in human, animal and machine. Taken from the Greek for 'Steersman', the term was the invention of American Norbert Wiener, author of *Cybernetics; or Control and Communication in the Animal and the Machine* (US: Wiley, 1949). Essentially an interdisciplinary study, Cybernetics ranges in its interest from control systems of the body to the monitoring and control of space missions. Cybernetics concerns itself with the analysis of 'whole' systems, their complexity of goals and hierarchies within contexts of perpetual change. The Greek steersman used the feedback of visual, aural and tactile indicators to chart his passage through rough seas. Today we have computers: the potential for accuracy and rapidity of feedback and control is vastly greater, and so is the potential for disaster should the feedback systems go wrong.

Cylinder or rotary press The most important technical development in PRINTING history following the invention of moveable type was the steam-driven cylinder press invented by Friederich Koenig. Born in Saxony, Koenig moved to London in order to set up a works to manufacture the new machines (1812). He demonstrated that a cylinder press machine could take off impressions at the rate of over 1000 an hour. On 28 November 1814 one of the presses was used to print *The Times*. Its editor, John Walter, described the press as 'the greatest improvement connected with printing since the discovery of the art itself'. As a result of its advantage in using Koenig's press, *The Times* became the dominant and most influential newspaper of the 19th c. in the UK. See MEDIA TECHNOLOGY.

Daguerrotype Early photograph produced in the manner of Louis Jacques Mandé Daguerre (1789–1851) a French theatrical designer who teamed up with Joseph Nicéphore Niépce (1765–1833), a founding father of photography, in 1830. Niépce died three years later but Daguerre continued their work, fixing images on metal plates coated with silver iodide, which he treated with mercury vapour in a darkroom. Daguerre was eventually able to reduce the exposure time of a photograph from eight hours to between 20 and 30 minutes. His Daguerrotype was taken up by the French government in July 1839 and revealed to the world at a meeting of the Académies des Sciences in August. No prints could be made from a Daguerrotype; thus Daguerre's method was a cul-de-sac in photography, though a vastly successful one at the time. See PHOTOGRAPHY, ORIGINS.

Daisy wheel A print-head rather like a daisy in shape, on each 'petal' of which is a character. Easily interchangeable, with tolerance for high-speed impact printing, the daisy wheel has come to rival the famous IBM 'golfball' on modern quality typewriters. It is used in computer print-out machinery when speed and 'top' copy standards are required.

Dance's helical model of communication, 1967 The earliest communication models were *linear*; their successors were *circular*, emphasizing the crucial factor of FEEDBACK in the communication process. Frank E. X. Dance in 'A helical model of communication', in the book he edited, *Human Communication Theory* (US: Holt, Rinehart & Winston, 1967), commends the circular model as an advance upon the linear one but faults it on the grounds that it suggests that communication comes

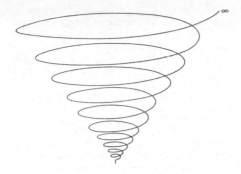

back full-circle, to exactly the same point from which it started, an assumption which is 'manifestly erroneous'.

The helix or spiral, for Dance, 'combines the desirable features of the straight line and of the circle while avoiding the weaknesses of either'. He goes on, 'At any and all times, the helix gives geometric testimony to the concept that Communication while moving forward is at the same moment coming back upon itself and being affected by its past behaviour, for the coming curve of the helix is fundamentally affected by the curve from which it emerges.'

Dance's helical model parallels theories of education put forward by Jerome Bruner, and generally referred to as the *spiral curriculum*. See COMMUNICATION MODELS.

Data processing Generally referred to as DP, it is the handling of data – letters, words, numbers, statements, etc. – in a sequence of operations designed to obtain a specific result. Computer programs provide the sequence of operations controlling the processor. The hardware comprises *input* and *output* devices, a *processor* – computer, minicomputer or microcomputer – and storage facility. Other parts of the system are printers and video display units (VDUs). See COMPUTERS IN COMMUNICATION.

Data protection The increasing use of computers and sophisticated INFORMATION TECHNOLOGY has greatly magnified the harm to individual privacy that can occur from any collection, storage or dissemination of personal information, and many countries have legislated against data abuse. Sweden, Denmark, Norway, Luxembourg, West Germany and France have all legislated to protect both the public and private sectors of society. In the US and Canada data protection legislation only applies to the public sector and compliance with it is voluntary.

In the UK, the report of the Lindop Committee (*Report of the Committee on Data Protection*, 1978) urged the need for individuals to have a right of veto on what information was passed on about them, and how this would operate in the context of 'the interests of the rest of society, which include the efficient conduct of industry, commerce and administration'. In 1984, the DATA PROTECTION ACT entered the Statute Book, and began operation in 1987 (See next entry).

Cryptography, or what in modern parlance is termed *privacy transformation*, can be employed to 'scramble' data prior to storage in order to guard against accidental or deliberate disclosures of information. The problem here is how the key or code to the scrambling process is to be protected. In the US, the Hellman-Diffie method allowed for different keys for the scrambling and unscrambling processes. An alternative to this is the so-called *electronic signature* which works by reversing the roles of scrambling and unscrambling keys. Another mode is PIN – personal identity number, where everybody would be issued with a personal key. PIN is already in use for the authorization of electronic funds transfers.

Data Protection Act, 1984 The purpose of the Act is 'to regulate the use of automatically processed information relating to individuals and the provision of services in respect of such information'. From 11 November 1987 the public has been able to check if any organization holds information on them; to see a copy of that information, known as personal data; to complain to the Data Protection Registrar about the way the data were collected or are being used; to have inaccurate computer records corrected or deleted in certain circumstances and to claim compensation through the courts if the 'Data subject' has suffered damage by the loss or destruction of personal data, or through an unauthorized disclosure or because of inaccuracy.

Designed to bring Britain into line with the Council of Europe Convention for the Protection of Individuals with regard to Automatic Processing of Personal Data, the Act provides for the establishment of a data watchdog, the Data Protection Registrar, and outlines eight DATA PROTECTION PRINCIPLES.

The test of any act protecting the citizen is the size and scope of the exceptions. There are three unconditional exemptions from registration: personal data required to be exempt for the purpose of safeguarding national security; data which its user is required by law to make public and personal data held by an individual and 'concerned with the management of his personal, family or household affairs or held by him only for recreational purposes'.

Subject access is barred on matters of prevention or detection of crime, the apprehension or prosecution of offenders or the assessment or collection of any tax or duty.

* *The Data Protection Act, 1984*, Office of the

Data Protection Registrar, Springfield House, Water Lane, Wilmslow, Cheshire SK9 5AX.

Data Protection Principles Listed in the DATA PROTECTION ACT, 1984 are the following eight principles governing data protection for computer users handling personal data: computer users must (1) obtain and process the information fairly and lawfully; (2) register the purposes for which they hold the data; (3) not use or disclose the information in a way contrary to those purposes; (4) hold only information which is adequate, relevant and not excessive for the purposes; (5) hold only accurate information and, where necessary, keep it up to date; (6) not keep any information longer than is necessary; (7) give individuals access to information about themselves and, where appropriate, correct or erase the information; (8) take appropriate security measures. Persons feeling that any computer user has broken one or more of the above principles may complain to the Data Protection Registrar. See PRIVACY; SECRECY.

Decipher See ENCODE; DECODE.

Decisive moment French photographer Henri Cartier-Bresson (b. 1908) used this term to describe the instant when pressing the shutter release button produced the desired image. Indeed Cartier-Bresson's timing, his ability to be at the ready when destiny appeared to be bringing highly photogenic elements together, is legendary and uncanny. Some critics claim that this instinct for the decisive moment makes Cartier-Bresson the finest of all photographers.

Declaration on the Mass Media (Unesco General Council, 1978) See MEDIA IMPERIALISM.

Decode The process of interpreting, analysing and understanding the nature of messages – written, spoken, broadcast, etc. This requires not just an understanding of the words, signs or images used but also a sharing of the VALUES and assumptions which underpin their ENCODING into a MESSAGE by the transmitter. A focus for research in communication studies is the extent to which the receiver decodes the message in the way the encoder or sender would prefer. This is an important element in the debate on the power and influence of the media.

 Aberrant decoding is a term used by Umberto Eco in 'Towards a semiotic inquiry into the television message' (translation) in *Working Papers in Cultural Studies* No. 3 (UK: Birmingham University Centre for Contemporary Culture Studies, 1972) and also in *Communication Studies*, J. Corner and J. Hawthorn, eds., (UK: Edward Arnold, 1980). In this case the artist or broadcaster – the encoder – encodes a message designed to elicit

an expected audience response. If the message is received by an audience which does not share the same CODES or values as the sender, it will be interpreted in an 'aberrant' way, that is, a different meaning will be assumed than that which was intended. In short, it is a difference of 'reading' the message derived from a difference of experience, perception or evaluation.

 A simple illustration of this might be the response of an employer when a candidate arrives for a job interview in sweatshirt and jeans. The interviewee is perhaps intending to assert his individuality, his character, his attitude; whereas the employer may aberrantly decode the message as one of implied insult to the conventions of interview.

Deep focus FILM making technique in which objects close to the camera and those far away are both in focus at the same time.

Deep structure Though the term was first used by Charles Hockett (b. 1916), the concept was given widest currency by fellow US linguist Noam Chomsky (b. 1928) in 'Current issues in linguistic theory' in J. Foder and J. Katz, eds., *The Structure of language: Readings in the Philosophy of Language* (US: Prentice-Hall, 1964). In its original form, *deep structure* is an underlying abstract level of sentence organization, which specifies the way a sentence should be interpreted. It is an abstract representation of SYNTAX. Surface grammar is the final stage in the syntactical representation of a sentence – the nearest one gets to the actual spoken or written form of a sentence (arrived at via the phonological – sound component – or graphological – written component – of the grammar).

 The deep structure is made manifest through a process of 'transformation'. For Chomsky the deep and surface structures, and the relationship between them, provide the essential bases of LANGUAGE which, far from being merely a sequence of words strung together, is rather a series of *organized structures* (see STRUCTURALISM). This deep structure, or level, supplies information that enables the reader or listener to distinguish between alternative interpretations of sentences which have the same surface form, or sentences which have different surface forms but have the same underlying MEANING.

 When, for example, a publisher replies to a budding author, 'I will waste no time in reading your manuscript', he presents a surface structure with alternative possible meanings. Yet by altering the surface structure of the sentence 'The dog chased the cat' to 'The cat was chased by the dog', the underlying idea is not altered. The transformations that might occur between deep and surface structure can be *passive* ('My father was warned by the doctor to give up smoking'), *negative* ('My father was not warned to give up smoking'), in *question* form ('Was my father warned to give up smoking?') or as an *imperative* ('Father was told – "Stop smoking!" '). There are many more possibilities.

* N. Chomsky, *Language and mind* (UK: Harcourt Brace Jovanovitch, 1968).

Deep throat Journalists' parlance for 'anonymous sources'. Perhaps the most famous in recent times was the unknown telephone informant calling himself 'Deep throat' who set *Washington Post* reporters Bernstein and Woodward on the trail in the WATERGATE scandal which eventually led to the resignation of President Richard Nixon. See PRESS.

Defamation Any statement made by one person which is untrue and may be considered injurious to another's reputation, causing shame, resentment, ridicule or financial loss is regarded as defamation under the Defamation Act of 1952. In permanent form, such as expressed in print, records, films, tapes, photographs, images or effigies, defamation is classed as *libel*. In temporary form such as in spoken words or gestures, defamation is classified as *slander*.

Defamation is a tort – or private wrong – which enables the victim to sue for compensation if the untrue statement is 'published', that is, made to a third person, for example by a newspaper to its readers. If a libel is likely to cause a breach of the peace then the defamation ceases to be a private wrong; it becomes a public wrong, and thus a crime. Slander must normally be proved to result in the victim suffering some loss, for example a publican accused by the slanderer of watering down his beer, and thus losing custom as a result. Libel on the other hand does not require loss or injury to be proved; it is 'actionable *per se*', that is, without proof of loss.

However, there are instances when slander is actionable without proof, such as when a false assertion is made that the plaintiff has been guilty of a criminal offence punishable by imprisonment or when an imputation is made that any woman or girl is unchaste. There are several defences for those accused of defamation. These include: (1) Where what was said was substantially true; this defence is referred to as *justification*. (2) Where what was said was honestly believed; termed *fair comment*. (3) *Privilege* exists in certain cases and certain places where the law cannot be exercised against those felt to be guilty of defamation. Absolute privilege exists for statements made during parliamentary proceedings, during court proceedings and communications between a solicitor and his/her client. Qualified privilege exists for reports of parliamentary and judicial proceedings and in cases where an employer gives a reference about the character and capabilities of an ex-employee. In such cases, only if *malice* is proved can qualified privilege be breached.

No legal aid is granted to plantiffs or defendants in defamation cases, thus persons even with the most genuine case for grievance at reports about them in the PRESS etc. must think twice before deciding to incur vast legal expenses in defending their reputation. See CENSORSHIP.

Defensible space Term used in architecture – domestic, community and town-planning design – to describe the practice of physically defining personal and public space (See PROXEMICS). Such definers may be walls, fences, hedges, paths; such areas of defensible space, gardens and courtyards where visual or physical access to individual and family privacy, or to the sense of residential group community, is restricted.

A contemporary architectural trend has been to create building developments like the old western wagons formed in tight squares or circles to fend off marauding Red Indians. Such enclosed spaces do not necessarily provide either a sense of community or of security; the more space is closed in, the more corners and angles are built against the outside world, the greater – very often – is the potential for isolation.

Defensive communication Occurs when people hear what they do not wish to hear. DISSONANCE arises when messages cut across, or contradict, VALUES and assumptions and the reaction varies from not concentrating on the MESSAGE to deliberately misrepresenting or misunderstanding the sender's motive as well as his/her message.

Climates of threat create defensive tactics just as supportive climates help reduce them. If we know that we are being tested or evaluated, for example, our communication response will be guarded. Equally we might resort to defensive tactics if we feel the communicator of the message is intent on winning control, exerting superiority. We are less defensive in situations in which spontaneity, empathy, equality and a sense of open-mindedness about the nature of the message are predominant.

Defensiveness The tendency to protect our ideas, ATTITUDES, views, and so on against a real or imagined attack from others. Such a reaction often occurs in communication situations in which we do not feel safe and is usually accompanied by a feeling that aspects of our SELF-CONCEPT are under threat. Defensiveness may occur when we receive negative FEEDBACK about our self-image; it may lead us to be wary about self-disclosure.

* G.E. Myers and M.T. Myers, *The Dynamics of Human Communication*, (US: McGraw-Hill, 1985 edition).

Demographic analysis The collection and interpretation of data about the characteristics of people other than their beliefs, VALUES and attitudes. Specifically, *demography* is the study of population, while *demology* is the theory of the origin and nature of communities. See DOMESDAY PROJECT.

Denotation See CONNOTATION.

Dependency theory The degree to which audiences are dependent upon the mass media constitutes one of the chief debates about the functions and effects of modern communication systems. In 'A dependency model of mass media effects' in G. Gumpert and R. Cathcart, eds., *Inter/Media: Interpersonal Communication in the Media* (US/UK: Oxford University Press, 1979), S.J. Ball-Rokeach and M. DeFleur believe 'The potential for mass media MESSAGES to achieve a broad range of cognitive, affective, and behavioural effects will be increased when media systems serve many unique and central information systems.' The fewer the sources of information in a media world, the more likely the media will affect our minds and thoughts, our attitudes and how we behave. Further, that influence will have increased potential 'when there is a high degree of structural instability in the society due to conflict and change'.

However, just as the audience may be changed by information/messages it receives, in turn the media systems themselves are changed according to audience response. It is not one-way traffic. In the COGNITIVE or intellectual sphere, the authors cite the following possible media ROLES: (1) The resolution of ambiguity, and relatedly limiting the range of interpretations of situations which audiences are able to make. (2) Attitude formation. (3) AGENDA SETTING. (4) Expansion of people's systems of beliefs (for example, the tremendous growth in awareness of ecological matters). (5) Clarification of VALUES, through the expression of *value conflicts* (See DEVIANCE; DEVIANCE AMPLIFICATION).

The authors emphasize that 'it is difficult to imagine the cognitive effect of attitude formation without accompanying affective effects', that is, emotional effects. 'In periods of intense social conflict the police may form a number of attitudes from media characterization about groups with which they have to deal,' suggest Ball-Rokeach and DeFleur. 'If the media-derived attitudes contain affective elements, such as anger, hostility and frustration, it may retard the ability of the police to keep their cool when the encounter actually comes.'

The media play a significant role in the establishment and maintenance of 'we feeling', that is, communal solidarity and oneness; equally they may work towards the ALIENATION of sections of the population who are traditionally discriminated against – women, blacks, etc.

In terms of the way the media may affect audience behaviour, the authors pose the following possibilities: *activation* stimulated by media-communicated messages; or *deactivation* as a result of such messages.

Certainly at critical decision making times, such as elections, people have become increasingly dependent on the media, especially TV, for election information and guidance. Ball-Rokeach and DeFleur argue that the greater the uncertainty in society, the less clear are people's frames of reference; consequently there is greater audience dependence on media communication. See BALL-ROKEACH and DE FLEUR'S DEPENDENCY MODEL OF MASS COMMUNICATION EFFECTS, 1976; EFFECTS OF THE MASS MEDIA; THEORIES AND CONCEPTS OF COMMUNICATION.

Deregulation Describes the process whereby channels of communication, specifically RADIO and TV, are opened up beyond the existing FRANCHISE-holders (e.g. BBC and IBA). Another term in current use, 'privatization', emphasizes the practical nature of the shift, from public to commercial control, accelerated by the development of VIDEO and CABLE TELEVISION. A typical example of deregulation was the British government's decision, in 1982, to permit the private sector to compete with British Telecom in SATELLITE TRANSMISSION, in the shape of the privately-financed Mercury company.

Deregulation has profound implications for national and international communication systems. Critics fear that it will favour the powerful – companies or nations – and lead the less powerful into positions of dependence upon the powerful. See BROADCASTING; 'BROADCASTING IN THE 90s': GOVERNMENT WHITE PAPER, 1988.

Desensitization Process by which audiences are considered to be made immune, or less sensitive, to human suffering as a result of relentless exposure to such suffering in the media. A constant media diet of violence – real or fictional – is widely believed to 'harden up' people's tolerance of violence. Like the DISPLACEMENT EFFECT, the notion of desensitization remains a conjecture rather than a theory substantiated by proof.

What has been of particular concern to analysts is the habit practised by the media of 'legitimizing' certain acts of violence, and indeed celebrating them. A case in point is the assault on the Iranian Embassy in London by the Special Air Services (SAS) after the embassy had been occupied by Iranian dissidents in 1980. The whole affair was treated like a John Wayne movie.

In 1982, with the Falklands war, repeated pictures in the PRESS and on TV of preparations

for war, of soldiers, ships, guns, etc. helped
'sensitize' the nation to the approaching conflict. It would be difficult to argue, however,
that such coverage 'desensitized' the nation to
the awesome dangers of such a war, nor made
the deaths (on both sides) less intolerable. See
CULTIVATION.

Design features Term used by US linguist
Charles Hockett (b. 1916) to describe the
essential properties and characteristics of
human speech. He cites 13 of these in 'The origin of speech', *Scientific American*, 203 (1960)
and in later publications adds three more.
These range from the feature of the *Vocal-
auditory channel* to what he calls *Prevarication*
(the use of LANGUAGE to deceive or deliberately
talk nonsense), *Reflexiveness* (the capacity of
language to communicate about language
itself) and *Learnability* (the feature that, to
know one language is to be capable of learning
another).

Detachment, ideology of See IMPARTIALITY.

Determinism The argument that most social
and cultural phenomena are profoundly
shaped and directed by – that is, determined
by – other powerful underlying forces within
society. Theorists of this school of thought
differ over which factors should be regarded as
possessing determinist power but those put
forward include widespread technological
change (as argued by Thorstein Veblen) or the
economic base and the structure of economic
relations within society (as argued by Karl
Marx). The determinist perspective is criticized
for being simplistic in its explanation of the
relationships between social structures, processes and change.

Developmental news That which developing
nations consider will help rather than harm
their prospects. 'Western news' is seen by
developing nations as essentially the pursuit of
'bad' news; and bad news hurts. In November
1976 Tanzania announced the foundation of its
new national news agency, TNA, responsible
for 'counter-measures against imperialist news
dissemination' and to 'uphold, support and
justify confidence' in the government of
Tanzania. The example is typical of a general
3rd World response to the way Western nations
have reported their affairs in the past.

The term implies government monopoly of
information flow in the interests of giving a
developing country a 'good name' and runs
counter to Western notions of free comment.
The aspirations to a reporting tradition of
social responsibility rather than sensation-
seeking are honourable; and the dangers – of
PRESS subservience to government – obvious.
See INFORMATION SOCIETY; MEDIA IMPERIALISM;
NEW WORLD INFORMATION ORDER.

Deviance Social behaviour which is considered
unacceptable within a social community is

deviant; and the defining of what constitutes
deviance depends upon what NORMS of conduct
prevail at any given time in a society. Of primary interest in the analysis of deviance is the
question – who defines deviance and why?
There are two main views on this: the first
maintains that the definition of what is deviant
behaviour stems from a general CONSENSUS
within society; the second argues that it is the
most powerful GROUPS within a society who
define as deviant behaviour that which may
constitute a threat to themselves or their dominant position in society. Particular interest
has been focused on the role of the media in
shaping definitions of deviance and then
responding to those definitions (See DEVIANCE
AMPLIFICATION). While from a moral standpoint the media may disapprove of deviant
behaviour, there is at the same time a reliance
upon it: normative behaviour rarely makes a
good headline; but seaside battles between
'deviant' mods and rockers or punch-ups
between 'deviant' soccer hooligans are food
and drink to the PRESS and TV. It might be
argued that if deviance did not exist, it would
be necessary for the media to invent it. See
SENSITIZATION; SIGNIFICATION SPIRAL; STEREO-
TYPE.

* R.V. Ericson, P.M. Baraueh and J.B.L.
Chan, *Visualizing Deviance: A Study of News
Organizations* (UK: Open University, 1987).

Deviance amplification Several studies of
DEVIANCE have been concerned with the role of
the mass media in both the definition and
amplification of deviance. Leslie Watkins first
outlined the concept of deviance amplification
in 'Some sociological factors in drug addiction
control', D. Wilner and G. Kassebaum, eds.,
Narcotics, (US: McGraw Hill, 1965). He
argues that the way in which a society defines
and reacts to deviance may in fact encourage
those defined as deviant to act in a more
deviant manner – this would be particularly
true for deviants excluded from or restricted in
participation in normal social activities. If societal reaction to deviance is strong it can lead to
greater deviance which in turn may lead to
stronger societal reaction and so on, establishing a **deviancy amplification spiral** in which
each increase in social control is met by an
increase in the level of deviancy.

Jock Young in 'The amplification of drug
use', in S. Cohen and J. Young, eds., *The
Manufacture of News: Deviance Social Problems and the Mass Media* (UK: Constable,
1973) examines the role of the media in both
precipitating and shaping such a deviancy
amplification spiral. Young argues, from the
evidence of this study of marijuana smoking in
London's Notting Hill (1967–69), that the
media can in fact play an important role in the
creation of such a spiral. It is through the

media that the public are alerted to the existence of certain types of deviance and if the coverage is sensational, as it was in this case, a MORAL PANIC may flare up. This results in the police and the courts being put under greater pressure to solve the problem and their attempts to do so can be, as in this case, the beginning of the spiral escalation.

Young found that the media acted as an important source of information for each group, about the other group. Also, the media's portrayal of the situation in terms of stereotypical behaviour and its sensational treatment of the problem helped to create circumstances which pushed the deviants to behave more in accordance with the STEREOTYPES provided by the media itself. See DEPENDENCY THEORY.

Deviant See SLIDER.

Devolution A recurring theme with regard to the monolithic edifices of the BBC and IBA: should these vast corporations be **devolved** into smaller elements, each with its own independence? So far, BROADCASTING devolution in the UK has made as little progress as devolution for Scotland or Wales. However, government plans outlined in 'BROADCASTING IN THE 90S' will change all that. See COMMERCIAL RADIO; HUNT REPORT.

Diachronic linguistics The study of LANGUAGE through the course of its history. In contrast, **synchronic** LINGUISTICS takes a fixed instant as its point of observation (chiefly a contemporary one). The distinction was first posed by Swiss linguist Ferdinand de Saussure (1857–1913).

Dialect A dialect is usually regionally based and is a variation within a LANGUAGE which differs from the accepted *standard* in vocabulary, pronunciation and idiom. In post-war years (from 1945) regional dialects have become increasingly accepted for their own inherent value. The study of dialect further illuminates connections between CLASS background and language usage in that until recently the use of standard English was associated with an individual of high social status. Dialects, whilst adding richness and variety to a language can also, of course, form a barrier to communication. See COLLOQUIALISM; JARGON; REGISTER; SLANG.

Diary stories See SPOT NEWS.

Differential perception The perceptions of each individual or social group are influenced by a number of factors: knowledge, experience, social environment, and personality, for example. The precise nature of the influence these factors have varies with each individual or social group. Thus individuals and social GROUPS are likely to perceive the same information, the same MESSAGE, quite differently. See SELECTIVE EXPOSURE.

Diffusion The process by which innovations spread to the members of a social system. Diffusion studies are concerned with messages that convey new ideas, the processes by which those ideas are conveyed and received, and the extent to which those ideas are adopted or rejected. Appropriateness of CHANNEL to MESSAGE is particularly important. For example, mass media channels are often more useful at creating awareness – knowledge – of new ideas, but interpersonal channels are considered to be more important in changing attitudes towards innovations.

The rate and success of diffusion is very much affected by the NORMS, VALUES and social structures in which the transmission of new ideas takes place. See EFFECTS OF THE MASS MEDIA.

Digital communications Process whereby the transmission of information – letters and numbers, voice, FACSIMILE or VIDEO – is coded into discrete on/off electronic signals, in contrast to analog transmission in which a signal is a measure of time of a continuous flow of electricity.

Digital retouching Or electronic retouching; process whereby laser and computer technology are combined to retouch or recreate photographs. A laser beam scans and measures images and pigmentations, then reduces them into a series of 'pixels', or minute segments. These are then recorded in digital form and stored in the computer's memory for eventual reproduction, which permits the rearrangement of the picture, a re-creation – or just plain faking.

Diorama The word is derived from the Greek, to 'look through'; a diorama is a three-dimensional exhibition usually viewed through an aperture. A flat or curved backcloth bears a painted or photographed scene: objects are then placed in front of the screen and a coloured or transparent gauze or screen is used to heighten the three-dimensional effect. The diorama was invented by one of the pioneers of photography, Louis Daguerre (1789–1851). It was exhibited in Paris in 1822 and in Regent's Park, London, the following year. See CINEMATOGRAPHY, ORIGINS.

Direct cinema Term used to describe the work of post-2nd World War DOCUMENTARY film makers in the US, such as Albert Maysles (*Salesman*, 1969 and *Gimme Shelter*, 1970), who coined the phrase, Stephen Leacock (*Don't Look Back*, 1968) and Frederick Wiseman (*High School*, 1968). New, lightweight equipment and improved SYNCHRONOUS SOUND recording facilities made the work of these observer-documentarists an inspiration for FILM makers in many other countries. Direct cinema went out into the world and recorded life as it happened, in the 'raw'. An earlier, and British, link with this mode of film making was *Free cinema*, a short-lived 'collective' of directors in London, organized by Karel Reisz (*Momma Don't Allow*, 1956) and Lindsay Anderson (*O Dreamland*, 1953). Direct cinema film-makers had the technical edge on Free cinema because of the availability of superior sound recording. See CINÉMA VÉRITÉ.

Dirty medium Term used of TV by Richard Dyer and quoted by Stuart Hall in 'Television and culture', *Sight and Sound*, Autumn 1976, to describe the way TV lives off other media and other forms of entertainment, snatching, jackdaw-fashion, styles and approaches from cinema, THEATRE, concert hall, circus, stage shows, music hall, cabaret, public lectures, after-dinner conversations, etc.

Discourse A form, mode or GENRE of LANGUAGE-use. Each person has in his/her repertoire a whole range of possible discourses – the language of love, of authority, of sport, of the domestic scene. In a media sense, an example of a discourse would be the News, reflecting in its choice of language and STYLE of presentation the social, economic, political and cultural context from which the discourse emanates. See DOMINANT DISCOURSE.

Discourse analysis Form of MASS COMMUNICATION analysis which concentrates upon the *ways* in which the media convey information, focusing on the LANGUAGE of presentation – linguistic patterns, word and phrase selection (lexical choices), grammatical constructions and story coherence. In particular, discourse analysis sets out to account for the textual form in which the mass media present IDEOLOGY to readership or audience. See CONTENT ANALYSIS; MODES OF MEDIA ANALYSIS; NEWS AS IDEOLOGY.

* M. Coulthard and M. Montgomery, eds., *Studies in Discourse Analysis* (UK: Routledge & Kegan Paul, 1981).

Discursive communication Susanne Langer in *Philosophy in a New Key* (US: Harvard University Press, 1942) differentiated between what she named discursive communication – prose and logic – and non-discursive communication, such as poetry, music and ritual.

Disembodiment Phenomenon recognized by Scottish psychiatrist and writer, R.D. Laing (b. 1927), who suggests that we live in an age where people rarely TOUCH each other. See COMMUNICATION, NON-VERBAL; PROXEMICS.

Disenfranchisement (of readership) Researchers have commented on the extent to which some newspapers reflect an assumption – possibly that of the owners and editors – that their readership is totally uninvolved and uninterested in the political processes and events of the country. It is as if the readers were politically **disenfranchised**, not able to participate in the political process, and thus news of political affairs was of no concern to them. Such papers aim to entertain, to concentrate on stories of human interest and drama rather than to inform. See PRESS.

Disinformation Derives from the Russian, 'Dezinformatsiya', a term especially associated with the Soviet Union's secret service, the KGB. It applied to the use of forgery and other techniques to discredit targeted governments, persons or policies. The process of disinformation is, of course, as old as mankind, and sowing the seeds of disinformation is matched by accusing the *opposition* of spreading disinformation.

A classic example in the UK of the operation of disinformation is the case of the ZINOVIEV LETTER, 1924.

It was published on the Saturday before polling day, when the *Mail* bugled forth with the headline 'Civil War Plot By Socialists' Masters'. This sensational piece of disinformation (it was probably concocted by Russian émigrés in Berlin) was swallowed and regurgitated by the entire British Press, with the exception of the *Daily Herald*. While the victor of the election, Stanley Baldwin, is reported to have thought the letter 'materially assisted' but did not 'vitally affect' the Conservative triumph, it needs to be pointed out that the letter was the culmination of a Red Scare campaign, not the beginning of one – and though Labour lost 50 seats the party gained one million votes. See EFFECTS OF THE MASS MEDIA.

Displacement Applied in a linguistic sense, one of 16 DESIGN FEATURES of human LANGUAGE suggested by Charles Hockett (b. 1916), American linguist. It describes the characteristic of language whereby we can talk about things which are displaced in time and space. We can speak of people who are not present, of events from the past or of things to come – a feature almost exclusive to human communication. One of the rare known examples of displacement in non-human communication is that of bees when they convey information about the location of nectar.

Displacement effect Refers to the reorganization of activities which takes place with the introduction of some new interest or attention-drawer, such as TV. Activities such as reading may be cut down, or stopped altogether, to make time for viewing. New media 'displace' or adjust the placement of other media. Cinema-going habits have been substantially affected by the introduction of TV, even more so with access to films on VIDEO.

The notion of *functional similarity* has often been applied as a yardstick to measure the extent and nature of displacement: if the new is functionally similar to the old, then the old is likely to be displaced. Functionally dissimilar activities are likely to hold their own. The difficulty is in establishing what functions a MEDIUM actually serves, which means that displacement is all the more difficult to assess. As a result of TV, do people talk less, read less, go out with friends less, socialize less? Does TV mop up marginal activities, displace real with second-hand experience; does it displace 'day-dreaming'? Evidence concerning people's reactions to programmes is so open to influence from INTERVENING VARIABLES that it is difficult to use it as a basis for reliable theory. That people stay in and watch TV more instead of dining out at a restaurant may have nothing to do with TV and everything to do with financial necessity. See EFFECTS OF THE MASS MEDIA; USES AND GRATIFICATIONS THEORY.

Disqualifying communication A form of self-protection, or DEFENSIVE COMMUNICATION when, in a situation causing embarrassment, anxiety or uneasiness, people talk aimlessly about, say, the weather, or go into a variety of non-verbal responses in order to avoid direct communication. The politician's version of this is 'No comment'. See INTERPERSONAL COMMUNICATION.

Dissolve A process in camera-work by which one picture fades out and the following scene fades in on top of it. Also called a 'mix'. See SHOT.

Dissonance Occurs when two COGNITIVE inputs to our mental processes are out of line. The result is a certain amount of psychological discomfort. Action is usually taken to resolve the dissonance and restore balance. Several strategies are commonly employed in order to achieve this: downgrading the source of dissonance; compliance with rather than acceptance of new expectations and ideas; changing one's previous ideas and attitudes; and avoidance of the source of dissonance.

All MESSAGES, particularly those conveyed to a mass audience, are potentially a source of dissonance to someone. If they disturb the intended receiver(s), then they may well be ignored or rejected. The need for messages intended for a mass audience to be successful, however, ensures that such messages are often well 'laundered' in order to reduce their potential offensiveness. See CONGRUENCE THEORY; SELECTIVE EXPOSURE.

Diversification In media terms, the spread of ownership and control into a wide range of associated, and often unassociated, products and services. Thus newspapers have moved into TV share-holding; TV companies into set rentals, bingo and social clubs and motorway catering services. In parallel, great corporations have moved into media ownership – oil companies buying up newspaper chains and investing in BROADCASTING interests, book publishing and record production. The result of diversification is often, paradoxically, concentration of control, and a real danger to a

newspaper, FILM company or publishing house of being just another 'product' on the shelf of the multi-national conglomerate whose objective is profit maximization above all other considerations. See CONGLOMERATES.

Division of labour A feature of many societies: instead of one person doing a wide range of work activities, it is considered more efficient for people to concentrate on specialized tasks. The division of labour is particularly noticeable in industrial societies where attempts to streamline production have often resulted in the manufacturing process being broken down into very specific jobs; the communications industry is no exception.

Such specialization is reflected in other areas of society. Within the family unit, for example, there is often a division of labour, with women, men and children being responsible for the performance of certain jobs. The degree of such specialization varies widely between different occupational sectors of society, and between social CLASSES.

D-Notices Defence notices; British government memoranda requesting newspapers not to publish specific items of information considered by authority to pose a security risk if widely disseminated. Notices are issued by the Services, Press and Broadcasting Committee. They have no binding force at law, even in wartime, but a newspaper or BROADCASTING station defies the D-Notice at its peril.

A form of pre-emptive CENSORSHIP, the D-Notice system was most famously challenged in recent years by the *Daily Express* on 21 February 1967, with its headline story 'Cable Vetting Sensation' based upon evidence that copies of private cables were carried off for routine inspection by the security services. Colonel L.G. Logan of the D-Notice Committee had declared that publication of the information contravened the D-Notice memoranda of 1956 and 1961 against revealing 'secret intelligence or counter-intelligence methods and activities in or outside the United Kingdom'.

The then Labour government set up a Committee of privy counsellors under Lord Radcliffe to investigate. Radcliffe reported that the *Express* story was 'not inaccurate in any sense' and that no secret information had been revealed. The government took no further action except to produce a face-saving White Paper, *The D-Notice System* in June 1967. It is difficult to ascertain whether D-Notices have worked more effectively or less effectively since that time because, by the very nature of the system, we only hear about it when it breaks down. See OFFICIAL SECRETS ACT.

Documentary Any mode of communication which, in addressing an audience, **documents** events or situations – books, RADIO, theatre, photography, FILM or TV. Usually based upon recorded or observable fact, the documentary may aim for objectivity or PROPAGANDA; it may, however, in terms of *human* documentation, be highly subjective. 'Even when temperate,' writes William Stott in *Documentary Expression and Thirties America* (US/UK: Oxford University Press, 1973), 'a human document carries and communicates feeling, the raw material of drama.'

British film director, producer and theorist John Grierson (1898–1972) is thought to have been first to use the word Documentary, in a New York *Sun* review (1926) of Robert Flaherty's film *Moana*, a study of the way of life of the South Seas islanders. In fact, 'documentary' is as old as the cinema itself. Louis Lumière's early short films of 1895, one showing the demolition of a wall, another of a train coming into a station, can be described as documentaries.

The founding father of documentary film making in the UK and later in Canada, Grierson never claimed scientific objectivity for such films. For him the documentary was far more than a straightforward reconstruction on film of reality. He spoke of the 'creative use of actuality' in which the director re-formed fact in order to reach towards an inner truth.

Indeed when documentarists have felt it necessary to get at the truth of a subject as they perceive it, they have not held back from fictionalization, often using actors, often turning the real-life person into an actor recreating a scene.

In the 1930s film documentary ran parallel with radio documentary – the BBC showed considerable innovative enterprise in this field, especially its Manchester studio – and, in the US, many impressive publications combined documentary evidence with outstanding photography. The themes were very often those of the Depression: concern at the plight of the poor, the unemployed, the alienated; and the mode was largely to have the people speak for themselves rather than distance the impact of their experience by using the MEDIATION of a commentator.

The documentary approach has been a recurring feature in modern theatre, especially from the 1960s. Historical or contemporary events on stage are far from new: Aeschylus dramatized the victory of Marathon (490 BC) and Shakespeare reconstructed history, often to fit the perceptions of the Tudor monarchy, in a third of his output. German dramatist Rolf Hochhuth (b. 1932) won worldwide attention with his documentary drama *The Representative* in 1963, on the subject of the Papacy and the Jews during the 2nd World War (1939–45). He followed this up with *Sol-*

diers (1967) based upon the alleged involvement of British Prime Minister Winston Churchill in the wartime death of the Polish General Sikorski. In the UK, Peter Brook's highly successful *US* (1966) was an indictment of American involvement in the Vietnam war.

On-stage documentaries – in the US often termed the *Theatre of Fact* – have frequently been presented with the aid of official and PRESS reports, original diaries, projected photographs, tape recordings and NEWSREEL films. In the case of the Royal Court production, *Falkland Sound* (1983), a moving – and damning – recollection of the Falklands War (1982) was presented through the letters home of a young naval officer killed in action.

Faction or *Dramadoc* are terms mainly associated with TV documentaries in which actors recreate historical lives, such as the BBC's *The Voyage of Charles Darwin* (1978) or play the part of famous people of the immediate past, such as Thames Television's *Edward and Mrs Simpson* (1978), Southern TV's *Winston Churchill – The Wilderness Years* (1981), and ITV's *Kennedy* (1983). To TV producers faction has come to represent an ideal synthesis of education, information and entertainment, albeit highly selective and deeply coloured by contemporary perspectives. See BLACK DOCUMENTARY; CINEMATOGRAPHY, ORIGINS; CINÉMA VÉRITÉ; DIRECT CINEMA; FLY ON THE WALL; NEW JOURNALISM; RADIO BALLADS.

* J. Corner, ed., *Documentary and the Mass Media* (UK: Edward Arnold, 1986).

Dogma This term refers to a doctrine, tenet, principle, or article of faith, particularly one laid down by those in authority. The term dogmatism generally refers to a narrow-minded, rigid adherence to a particular dogma or opinion. The inflexibility inherent in a dogmatic attitude may serve to enhance an individual's sense of security in his or her view of the world or aspects of it but it is likely to lead to many problems when communicating with others – a refusal to listen to other people's arguments being just one example. Also, messages from the mass media are likely to be ignored or rejected out of hand if they contradict a dogmatically held opinion or belief.

Dolby Noise Reduction System Introduced in 1970, substantially reduces the amount of hiss and crackle in magnetic tape playback. See GRAMOPHONE.

Dolly A trolley on which a camera unit can be soundlessly moved about during shooting; can usually be mounted on rails. A 'crab dolly' will move in any direction.

Domesday Project The 20th c. electronic equivalent of the Domesday Book, the project was the creation of the BBC, a compilation of information on the United Kingdom contributed to by more than a million people. In 1985 a research and report exercise was begun which was to result in a vast bank of data – texts, maps, charts, photographs, for use on the BBC's advanced INTERACTIVE VIDEO system, a combination of TELEVISION monitor, microcomputer and VIDEO disc player. The information on the two discs – the Community Disc and the National Disc (containing more official reference data) – was gathered by schoolchildren from 14,000 schools, along with many other volunteer organizations, such as scouts, guide troops and women's institutes.

Dominant culture See CULTURE.

Dominant discourse In a general sense, discourse is talk; converse; holding forth in speech and writing on a subject. We are referring both to the content of communicative exchanges and to the level at which those exchanges take place, and in what mode or STYLE as well as to whom the discourse is addressed. A dominant discourse is that which takes precedence over others, reducing alternative content, alternative approaches to 'holding forth' to *subordinate* discourses. All public discourse is socially and culturally based, thus it follows that the dominant discourse is usually that which emanates from those dominant in the social and cultural order:

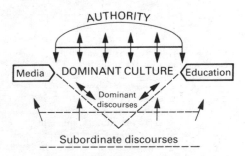

See ELITE; HEGEMONY; POWER ELITE.

Dominant, subordinate, radical Three categories of response in terms of the *reading* of media MESSAGES on the part of audience, posed by Frank Parkin in *Class, Inequality and Political Order* (UK: Paladin, 1972). Do we accept what is told us, only half accept or substantially reject it? Parkin argues that it is our place in the social structure which conditions our response. Stuart Hall in 'The determination of news photographs' in S. Cohen and J. Young, eds., *The Manufacture of News* (UK: Constable, 1973) supports Parkin's view, with the same categories but different terminology.

The **dominant** system of response (Hall calls it a *dominant* CODE) signifies that the dominant VALUES and existing society are wholly accepted by the respondent; the **subordinate** response (Hall's *negotiated code*) indicates

general acceptance of dominant values and existing social structures, but the respondent is prepared to argue that a particular group – blacks, unemployed, women – within that structure may be unfairly dealt with and that something should be done about it. The **radical** response (Hall's *oppositional code*) rejects the PREFERRED READING of the dominant code and the social VALUES that produced it.

David Morley's researches into audience response, published in *The Nationwide Audience* (UK: British Film Institute, 1980), give substance to Parkin and Hall's division of response, but also emphasize other response-conditioning factors such as education, occupation, political affiliation, geographical region, religion and family. See EFFECTS OF THE MASS MEDIA.

Donohew and Tipton's Information-Seeking Model, 1973 In L. Donohew and L. Tipton, 'A conceptual model of information seeking, avoiding and processing' in P. Clarke, ed., *New Models for Communication Research* (US: Sage Publications, 1973) a model is proposed which tentatively explores the way individuals deal with information. It is useful to consider some of the definitions used, before discussing how the model works.

The 'Image' or 'image of reality' here comprises an individual's life experiences and the goals, beliefs and knowledge he or she has acquired; the individual's self-image; the individual's information-using 'set' which governs the way in which the individual seeks and processes information. The individual may choose from among several information-seeking strategies when looking for information. The model distinguishes between a broad focus and a narrow focus strategy. When employing the broad focus strategy the individual firstly draws up a list of possible, available sources of information and then makes a choice as to which one to use. If the narrow focus strategy is employed, one single source of information is used as a starting point and this source is then used as a base for further exploration. 'Closure' is the point at which the individual stops looking for more information. The diagram opposite shows a representation of Donohew and Tipton's model taken from Denis McQuail and Sven Windahl's *Communication Models for the study of mass communications* (UK: Longman, 1986 edition).

The authors do not intend this model to be tightly prescriptive and the steps may not always be taken in the order outlined but it does give some useful insights into the factors and relationships involved in information-seeking.

As McQuail and Windahl point out, the model does tend to concentrate attention on the intrapersonal aspect of information-seeking and the wider influences from the indi-

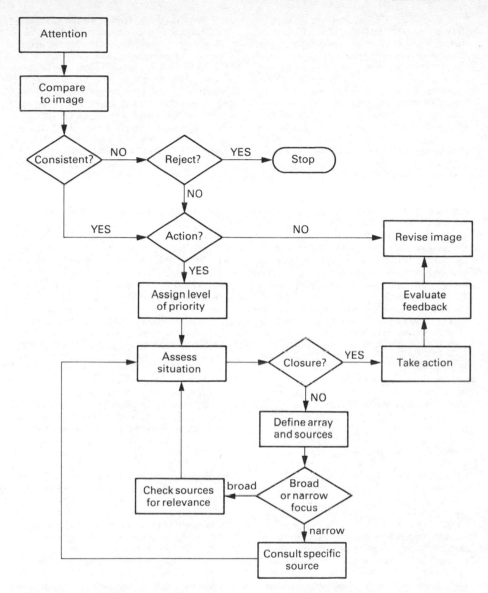

Donohew and Tipton's information-seeking model, 1973

vidual's environment need to be considered too, when using this model.

Double exposure Two pictures superimposed upon one another on the same piece of FILM. Like reverse motion, double exposure in filming began by being a simple visual curiosity before it became a fully fledged means of artistic expression. It was first used in still photography, where double or multiple exposure images produced what was described as 'spirit photography'. Georges Meliès (1861–

1938) used it in his films from 1908. It has been used dramatically to achieve many effects, chiefly that of suggesting the supernatural and of conveying the process of thought and of spirituality.

Dramadoc See DOCUMENTARY.

Dry-run TV programme rehearsal in which action, lines, cues, etc. are tried out prior to the final rehearsal.

Dual-audio TV US innovation, developed by Terry Barton, provides a secondary auditory

CHANNEL to the TV set, enabling children to obtain greater understanding from the enormous amount of potentially useful information contained in TV programmes. In 'Dual-audio television', *Harvard Educational Review*, 41 (1974) Barton argues that children normally fail to understand much of what they hear partly because the LANGUAGE level used is beyond their own and partly because the programmes fail to provide children with opportunities to discover how information that is received could be used. Most programmes also do not give the child any form of FEEDBACK against which to check his/her understanding.

The channel reaches the child either via a transistor RADIO equipped with an ear inset or via a radio receiver already in the room. The announcer makes comments during pauses in the original dialogue. This facility can be utilized in a variety of ways: (1) Words can be repeated, defined and explained; thus promoting vocabulary acquisition. (2) Titles, actors' names and various signs that appear on the screen can also be read out. (3) Explanations can be given of those events which the child might normally have difficulty in understanding. (4) Children can be encouraged to participate in the programme by being asked direct questions.

Dualism See RELATIVISM.

Dub In FILM making, to blend speech, music, incidental sound and sound effects on to film or videotape. At a later stage, the LANGUAGE of the 'home' AUDIENCE may be dubbed on to the sound track in preference to subtitles.

Dubbing See POST-SYNCHRONIZATION.

Dumping World-wide practice, led by the US, of saturating foreign markets with BROAD-CASTING material, extremely cheap to hire in comparison with the cost of home companies making their own original programmes. See MEDIA IMPERIALISM.

Dunning process An early method in the cinema of filming actors in the studio against a moving background which has been photographed elsewhere. With the advent of colour FILM, the process was superseded by BACK PROJECTION.

Duopoly A monopoly held by two organizations rather than one. In BROAD-CASTING, the term is used to refer to the duopoly of the BBC and IBA. See MEDIA CONTROL.

Dyad A communication dyad consists of two persons interacting and is the elemental unit of INTERPERSONAL COMMUNICATION.

Dynamic mediation See IMPARTIALITY.

Eady Plan, or Eady Levy See BRITISH FILM PRODUCTION FUND.

Early Bird satellite Owned by the US Communications Satellite Corporation, Early Bird was the first of its kind to be used in the operation of long-distance intercontinental TELEPHONE services. It went into service on 28 June 1965.

Eastmancolor Colour filmstock now used universally in FILM making.

Effects of the mass media Can be broadly defined as any change induced directly or indirectly by the recording, filming or reporting of events. Analysts of effects, or impact, are concerned with the modification of attitudes and of behaviour of individuals and GROUPS – and the process of measuring these effects is immensely complicated, as the ground upon which the measurements are taken is constantly shifting.

The **actual effect** of the media on audiences, so far as it can be ascertained, is arguably less significant than the **perceived effect**. In the 19th c. those in authority were of the view that access by the mass of the population to the printed word might turn docility into uprising. The new mass MEDIUM of the cinema was similarly accused of a wide range of 'effects', while TV, in the eyes of some, is responsible for many of the ills of our time, as though such media could be somehow divorced from the social, political and cultural environment which produce them.

A few generalized hypotheses about effects can be tentatively posited: the media are probably more likely to modify and reinforce attitudes than change them; media impact will be greater among the uncommitted ('floating voters') than the committed; impact will be more influential if all the media are saying more or less the same thing at the same time (CONSISTENCY); equally, if the media are concentrating on a small rather than diverse number of stories (INTENSITY) and if they are repeating messages, images, viewpoints over and over again (FREQUENCY).

'The timing of communication processes,' writes C. Seymour-Ure in *The political impact of mass media* (UK: Constable, 1974) 'is probably one of the most important determinants of mass media effects.' If the timing is right, the media can often be the arbiters of crisis, by being in the most prominent position to define it. Because of their AGENDA SETTING capacity, the media have influence upon the criteria which, in the public domain, decide what is important and what is not, what is normal and what is DEVIANT, what is CONSENSUS and what is *dissensus*, what is significant, or newsworthy and what is marginal.

Thus *negative* influence can be as effective as *positive* influence. During the debate on Britain's entry into the Common Market, leading up to the national referendum (1972), only one newspaper, the *Daily Express*, argued for the country to withdraw from the EEC, so full, frank and detailed debate went, as far as the media were concerned, by default.

No summary of effects, however brief, should neglect the role played – some would say most powerfully – by the media in supporting, reinforcing and cementing patterns of social control, not the least by maintaining and sometimes fashioning the symbols of legitimate government. See ALIENATION EFFECT; AUDIENCE RESEARCH; CATALYST EFFECT; CATHARSIS HYPOTHESIS; COGNITIVE (AND AFFECTIVE); CENSORSHIP; DEVIANCE AMPLIFICATION; DISPLACEMENT EFFECT, FRANKFURT SCHOOL OF THEORISTS; HYPHENIZED ABRIDGMENT; INTERCULTURAL INVASION (AND THE MASS MEDIA); INTERVENING VARIABLES (IV); LOONY LEFTISM; MAINSTREAMING; McCOMBS AND SHAW AGENDA SETTING MODEL OF MEDIA EFFECTS, 1976; MEAN WORLD SYNDROME; MEDIATION; MULTIPLIER EFFECT; NARCOTICIZING DYSFUNCTION; PSEUDO-CONTEXT; RESONANCE; REINFORCEMENT; SLOW-DRIP; SOCIALIZATION; SOCIOMETRICS (AND MEDIA ANALYSIS); USES AND GRATIFICATIONS THEORY.
* O. Boyd-Barrett and P. Braham, eds., *Media Knowledge and Power* (UK: Open University, 1987; P. Golding, G. Murdock and P. Schlesinger, eds., *Communicating Politics: Mass communication and the political process* (UK: Leicester University Press, 1986); D. McQuail, *Mass Communication Theory: An Introduction* (UK: Sage, 2nd edition, 1987).

Egocentrism The tendency to perceive ourselves as the centre of any exchange or activity; an over concern with the presentation of ourselves to others.

Elaborated and Restricted Codes In *Class, Codes and Control* Vol. 1 (UK: Paladin, 1971), Basil Bernstein posed a now-famous classification of LANGUAGE codes, the *Elaborated* and *Restricted* codes based upon researches into the language-use of children. Bernstein maintains that there are substantial differences in speech between middle CLASS and working class children, the former using the Elaborated Code, the latter the Restricted Code.

The determinant of the code in each case is the nature of the social relationships and influences to which the child is exposed. A close-knit, traditional working class community, Bernstein argues, tends to use the **Restricted Code** because a high degree of shared MEANING is assumed. In the more typically loose-knit middle class communities there are fewer grounds for making assumptions about shared meaning and therefore a more *explicit*, **Elaborated**, Code is used. This is not to say that the middle class do not possess their own Restricted CODES in particular social or professional situations. The important point is that the middle classes can move with ease from a Restricted to an Elaborated code.

The Restricted Code tends to be less complex than the Elaborated, with a small vocabulary and simpler sentence structure. It tends to be spoken rather than written. It is easy to predict (high in REDUNDANCY) whereas the Elaborated Code is less easy to predict (high in ENTROPY). The Restricted Code is orientated towards social relations, towards COMMONALITY, while the Elaborated Code represents a great emphasis on individuality and individual differences.

The one is the language of the street, the home, the playground, the pub; the other – very largely – the language of school; the language of formal education. Thus, Bernstein indicates, within the educational context, the user of the Restricted Code is placed at a disadvantage.

Bernstein does not argue that the Elaborated Code is superior to the Restricted Code, only that it is different and more useful for upward social mobility.
* B. Bernstein, 'Social class, language and socialization', an extract from his major work, in J. Corner and J. Hawthorn, eds., *Communication Studies* (UK: Edward Arnold, 1980); S. Rogers, 'The language of children and adolescents and the language of schooling' S. Rogers, ed., *They Don't Speak Our Language* (UK: Edward Arnold, 1976).

Electronic democracy See INTERACTIVE TELEVISION.

Electronic mail The dream of a paper-less office became a reality in the 1980s when many companies or departments within companies began to exchange mail electronically, using computer terminals. By operating a screen and keyboard, a business person in the UK, using the TELEPHONE system may dial British Telecom's electronic mail computer, Telecom Gold. Within seconds correspondence is transmitted to the receiver's terminal; a special bleeper may warn of incoming messages.

Every microcomputer is a potential electronic mail terminal and in 1983 a new Micro-mail service gave access to TELECOM GOLD to personal computer users. See INFORMATION TECHNOLOGY; VIEWDATA; WIRED WORLD.

Electronic man Term coined by Marshall MCLUHAN to contrast with *typographical man*, or Gutenberg man, whom electronic man has substantially superseded. For centuries CULTURE has been dominated by the printed word, and the print MEDIUM has shaped the ways of thought and behaviour of that culture. Now the electronic media of RADIO, TV, etc. have created a world of the instantaneous where everything is speeded up, causing fundamental changes of personal and communal perception and behaviour.

Electronic newsgathering Referred to as ENG, the gathering of sound and vision news reports electronically, usually transmitted via TELEPHONE links or from transmitter vans. Much lighter and more compact than traditional FILM or TV cameras, electronic equipment records on to cassette, by-passing the film processing stage: pictures from the scene of action can be transmitted directly or stored electronically. Electronic newsgathering saves time and cuts labour – hence its wary acceptance by film technicians and their union representatives. EFP – Electronic Field Production – is an advance on ENG, making location programmes of all kinds possible without having the cameras tied to an outside broadcasting (OB) vehicle.

Electronic newspaper At the push of a TV button – all the nation's newspapers; a fast-approaching possibility. Already VIDEO and CABLE TELEVISION are being seen as electronic bookstalls. It is too early to predict that in future paper will stay in the trees for it will be difficult if not impossible by electronic means to create the flexibility of the newspaper in terms of *where* it can be read. See BLEND; TELETEXT; VIEWDATA.

Electronic publishing The replacement of traditional modes of PRINTING, storage and dissemination of paper by electronic means. See ELECTRONIC MAIL; VIEWDATA; WORD PROCESSING.

Electrophone 'Piped' entertainment through the CHANNEL of a TELEPHONE line, and thence through headphones, was available in the UK as early as 1895, 27 years before regular RADIO, 41 years before regular TV broadcasts, and over 80 before CABLE TELEVISION. The Electrophone Company of Gerrard Street, London, provided for a modest outlay a year's programmes of nightly selections of THEATRE performances, shows from the music halls and concerts, plus dozens of Sunday services.

Formed in 1894 by H.S.J. Booth, the company had 50 subscribers in London by 1896, 100 by 1919 and over 2000 by 1923. The coming of 'wireless' rendered the success of Electrophone short-lived, though transmission continued in Bournemouth till 1937.

Elite A small group within a society who may be socially acknowledged as superior in some sense and who influence or control some or all sectors of the society. Several definitions of the term elite exist and these influence the precise focus of research into the relationship between the media, elites, and society.

Early writers generally see the elite as a ruling elite or oligarchy whose power is general and affects most aspects of society. Writers, such as Vilfredo Pareto (1848–1923) and Gaetano Mosca (1848–1941) regarded elites as being inevitable, whatever the political system.

C.W. Mills in a study of elites in US society entitled *The Power Elite* (US: Oxford University Press, 1956) points to the similarity of backgrounds, attitudes and VALUES, and power skills of the members of the three elites which, he argues, dominate American Society: the military, the economic and the political. He also comments on the degree of personal and family contacts between elite members and the interchangeability of personnel between top posts in the military, economic and political elites from which the 'power elite' is recruited. This concept of **elite cohesion** has been of interest to several media researchers who have sought to investigate links between members of economic and political elites and those who own or control the media, and the effect such links might have on media output.

The notion of a ruling elite or oligarchy contrasts with the Marxist concept of a ruling CLASS. Whilst elite theorists point out the necessity for the elite to recruit from outside itself, to remain accessible to the influence of the non-elite and to maintain a CONSENSUS among the non-elite which legitimates the elite's right to rule, Marxist analysis stresses the continuing and increasing *polarization* or separation of the ruling from the ruled class. Marxist analysis of the media therefore concentrates upon the role of the media in propagating the ideas of the dominant class in order to create a false consciousness, or to create HEGEMONY, which is instrumental in subjugating the rest.

The concern that the mass media are used by an elite to manipulate the masses is not only to be found in Marxist critiques of the media. Much early research into media effects centred on the notion that the media could become a powerful PROPAGANDA tool by which the few could control the socially isolated citizens of a MASS SOCIETY.

Anthony Sampson in *Anatomy of Britain Today* (UK: Hodder & Stoughton, 1965) suggests that an elite is any socially visible group of individuals who possess some valued characteristic and power within a limited area of human behaviour. Sampson argues that power in Britain resides in a loose-knit cluster of specific elites – intellectual, military, administrative and moral rather than in a cohesive 'power elite'. Further, whilst there may be some contact between the members of the various specific elites, these elites may also at times be in competition with one another. Those who own and control the media can thus be seen as constituting one particular elite which may have links with other elites but which may also be in competition with them.

This perspective is akin to that of the liberalist – PLURALIST school of analysis which sees the media as a kind of FOURTH ESTATE pressuring governing elites and reminding them of their dependency on majority opinion. Other commentators have pointed to the role social elites play in media *coverage*. Stuart Hall in 'The determination of news photographs', in S. Cohen and J. Young, eds., *The Manufacture of News: Deviance, Social Problems and the Mass Media*, (UK: Constable, 1973), comments that 'Newspapers are full of the actions, situations and attributes of elite persons.' Other commentators have also argued that the unequal distribution of power in Britain, and thus the eliteness of the power holder, are reflected in the degree of attention paid to such people in the media. Similarly, considerable space is devoted to the activities of elite, powerful nations.

Elite persons often serve as objects of general IDENTIFICATION; the elite can be used to say something about situations or events which affect everybody. In the UK the Royal Family are regularly used for this purpose. See ESTABLISHMENT; NEWS VALUES; POWER ELITE.

Elite-concentration See NEWS VALUES.

Email See ELECTRONIC MAIL.

Emancipatory use of the media Term employed by Hans Magnus Enzensberger in 'Constituents of a theory of the media' in D. McQuail, ed., *Sociology of Mass Communication* (UK: Penguin, 1972) to contrast with what he defines as the **Repressive use of the media**. He characterizes the Emancipatory use of the media as follows: decentralized programme (as opposed to the Repressive mode of a *centrally* controlled programme); each receiver a potential transmitter (as opposed to one transmitter, many receivers); mobilization of the masses (as opposed to immobilization of isolated individuals); interaction of those involved, and FEEDBACK (as opposed to passive consumer behaviour); a political learning process (as opposed to depoliticization); and collective production, social control by self-organization (as opposed to production by specialists, control by property owners or bureaucracy). See DOMINANT, SUBORDINATE, RADICAL.

Embargo Restriction set upon a news item, indicating when that item can be published or broadcast. A PRESS release from government or industry, for example, will be headed 'Not for publication/broadcasting until . . .' and give a specific date.

Emblem See NON-VERBAL BEHAVIOURAL: REPERTOIRE.

Emotional dynamization Russian film director Sergei Eisenstein (1898–1948) used this expression to describe the collision of different images and actions brought about by the editing of FILM to detonate emotional response,

both in relation to the theme of the film and its cinematic or aesthetic intent. See MONTAGE.

Emotive language To describe a crowd as a 'mob' or a 'rabble' is to be emotive, to convey not only information but one's own attitude towards the crowd and one's intention of influencing the receiver's attitude towards it. Emotive LANGUAGE tells as much about the communicator as the MESSAGE. It reveals *what* he/she thinks and very often *how* he/she thinks.

IDEOLOGY is the root and inspiration of the media use of emotive language. Newspapers use it on those they disagree with, who appear somehow to threaten what the newspapers wish to preserve. Thus, while trades unions might consider they are striking 'in defence of hard-won rights', they may be accused in banner headlines of 'holding the nation to ransom'. Here the intention of emotive language is to isolate the strikers, to establish a CONSENSUS against them and thus bring them into line. In times of national emergency such as a war, emotive language is used to whip up support and fervour for the cause and to forge a sense of national unity. During Britain's Falklands war with Argentina (1982), the *Sun* encapsulated the nature of emotive language in one word: 'Gotcha!'

Empathy The ability to put oneself into another person's position, into another person's shoes, and to attempt to understand his/her behaviour and perspectives without filtering them through one's own value system. It is not possible totally to avoid such filtering but to be emphathetic requires that an individual makes an effort to avoid judging others on the basis of his/her own subjective experiences and perspectives, and makes an attempt to see things from the other person's point of view, whilst retaining his/her own perspectives, VALUES and so on. Clearly empathy has an important role to play in effective interpersonal communication.

Empirical Based upon *experience*. Empirical research in the social sciences centres upon fieldwork – the collection of evidence about observable human behaviour. Such enquiry usually lacks or does not make explicit the theory guiding its procedures. Its evidence may be used to establish an isolated proposition, to test certain theoretical analysis against observable behaviour, or to gain insight into certain behaviours. Such evidence may itself generate hypotheses, concepts, models, and theories.

Encipher See ENCODE.

Encode We communicate by means of a variety of visual and aural signals which are assembled according to certain rules or CODES. If Person A wishes to convey to Person B a MESSAGE which Person B is likely to understand, then the message has to be *encoded* with Person B's ability to DECODE the message-carrying signals well in mind. The MEANING of a message is something the receiver assigns in the act of decoding which is itself a part of an interaction with the encoder.

A glance at the ANDERSCH, STAATS AND BOSTROM MODEL OF COMMUNICATION, 1969 helps here. This emphasizes the stages through which the act of encoding passes. There is a stimulus to a message, which is structured – put together – and evaluated for its possible effect on the receiver before it is transmitted. The same process occurs on the part of the receiver: the message is registered; it is reconstructed according to the decoder's perception of the message and of the encoder who has delivered the message; then the response is evaluated prior to transmission.

This is only the beginning of a continuing circle of sending and receiving, encoding and decoding. Contributory to the perceptions of encoder and decoder in the process of communication are such factors as previous experience, the current and future context of the interaction and the feelings, opinions, assumptions and values of the encoder and decoder. The terms *encipher* and *decipher* are sometimes used instead of encode and decode. See DEEP STRUCTURE; ELABORATED AND RESTRICTED CODES.

Encompassing situation Term coined by W.E. Brockriede in 'Demonstrations of the concept of rhetoric', *Quarterly Journal*, 54 (1968) to describe the *context* of each and every act of communication, specifically the elaborate set of conventions and rules imposed upon an individual's behaviour in social situations.

Enigma, code of See HERMENEUTICS.

Entropy See REDUNDANCY.

Enunciation The pronunciation and articulation of words and other communicative sounds; an aspect of vocal delivery.

Ephemera In communications terms, publications such as CIGARETTE CARDS, PICTURE POSTCARDS and POSTERS produced for the moment, conveying information for immediate use. Ironically such ephemera are now collector's items, illuminating records of our past.

Escalation Where a person or group is initially committed to an action in a small way and, gradually, because of that initial commitment, increases – escalates – that action.

Esperanto LANGUAGE invented in 1887 by Louis Zamenhof (1859–1917) of Poland. Meaning 'hopeful', Esperanto was intended to serve as a universal language. It was an improvement upon an earlier artificial language, VOLAPÜK, being more regular and more flexible. An international delegation of scholars in 1907 produced *Ido* as a substantially advanced form of Esperanto, but this was not adopted by the main body of Esperantists.

Establishing shot Opening shot or sequence showing the location of a FILM scene or a juxtaposition of characters in action to follow.

Establishment It has been argued by many political and social commentators that in the UK, among other countries, there exists a ruling ELITE known as the Establishment. This is not readily recognizable as a ruling CLASS but is composed of people who because of wealth, birth or position in government are able to exercise considerable power and influence. Generally the term is applied to those who are not directly, democratically answerable in their positions of power.

Ethnic Term generally used in the social sciences to refer to a community of people possessing its own CULTURE. The characteristics which identify an ethnic group may include a common LANGUAGE, common customs and beliefs, and a cultural tradition. A society may contain several ethnic GROUPS some of whom, but not all, may also be racial groups.

Ethnocentrism The use of one's own CULTURE as a yardstick by which to measure, to judge, the attributes and activities of other cultures. Such judgement bears the implicit or explicit assumption that one's own culture is superior. Robert Levine and Donald Campbell in *Ethnocentrism: Theories of Conflict, Ethnic Attitudes and Group Behaviour* (US: Wiley, 1972) argue that there is a tendency for all social GROUPS and societies to be ethnocentric. If this is the case, then such a tendency could be expected to have considerable impact upon the way in which MESSAGES about other cultures are interpreted and the way in which other cultures are discussed in any one culture. There has been increasing concern about the possible effects of ethnocentrism upon the media's coverage of race relations in the UK and elsewhere. See ETHNIC; MEDIA IMPERIALISM.

Ethos In communication terms, the ethos of a communicator determines the image one has of him or her at any given time – either one person or a GROUP. In their paper 'A summary of experimental research in ethos', *Speech Monographs*, 30, (1963) Kenneth Anderson and Theodore Clevenger Jr refer to research findings which point to two general categories of ethos: *extrinsic* and *intrinsic*. The first is the image, say, of a speaker as it exists prior to a given speech; the second is the image derived from elements during the presentation of a speech, consciously or unconsciously provided by the speaker. The final impression is a mixture of extrinsic and intrinsic factors.

The prestige of a speaker, his/her appearance, likeableness, credibility, social CLASS, voice, etc. contribute to his/her ethos.

Anderson and Clevenger assert that evidence from research proves 'that the ethos of the source is related in some way to the impact of the message' and that this applies 'not only to political, social, religious and economic issues but also to matters of aesthetic judgement and personal taste'.

Etymology The science, or investigation, of the derivation and original SIGNIFICATION of words.

Euphemism In polite circles, 'belly' is not referred to, but 'stomach' is acceptable. That is a *euphemism*, the rendering of blunt, harsh or unpleasant terms in mild, inoffensive or quaint LANGUAGE. Thus 'to die' may be rendered euphemistically as 'to pass away'; a 'bookie' may prefer to seek more status by calling him/herself a 'turf accountant'. In ADVERTISING 'budget items' are preferred to 'cheap goods'. In business, people are not 'sacked' but 'the labour force is slimmed'.

Some euphemism is justifiable in INTER-PERSONAL COMMUNICATION, for example at times of grief and tragedy; some is an insult to language and to human intelligence and dignity, such as the terminology of the arms race where (in so-called *Pentagonspeak*) 'demographic targeting' means the destruction of our cities by nuclear weapons; 'support structure' is civilians and 'collateral damage' is dead civilians. See NEWSPEAK; NUKESPEAK.

Euphony Derived from the Greek, euphony means 'having a pleasant sound'; applies both to the sound as it is heard and in relation to its ease of pronunciation (for example, *appreciable* rather than *appreciateable*).

Euronet A consortium of national computer interests in nine European countries, working towards the creation of a mutually compatible interconnection of European data bases. EURONET is designed for reasons as much political as economical, as a method of ensuring that in the long term the economic control of Europe remains in European hands, and thus, inextricably, the control of information. The consortium is a defence against the computer-information HEGEMONY of the US and specifically of IBM which, by 1980, was responsible for 70% of the world's computer installations.

Excessive generality Term used by Richard Hoggart in *Speaking to Each Other* (UK: Chatto & Windus, 1970) to describe the over-extension or over-use of a STEREOTYPE to the point at which it no longer conveys any MEANING to the audience. **Excessive particularity** on the other hand results from the gearing of communication to too small a section of the audience, thus alienating most of it. Several commentators claim that the need to avoid this leads to a mass media output characterized by generality, artificiality and neutrality in order to appeal to the widest number of people; and programmes and articles which present a nice, harmless and lifeless image of the range of human experience. See MID-ATLANTIC SOLUTION.

Exnomination Roland Barthes uses this term in *Mythologies* (UK: Paladin, 1973) to describe the assumption on the part of the communicator, usually the mass media, that certain VALUES are so basic and so widely shared, indeed so natural, that they are beyond question and need not be referred to or justified. Exnomination is integral to the working of IDEOLOGY, representing the dominant CODE of a society. See MYTH.

Expectations People come to have a collection of ideas about what is expected of them in terms of their behaviour in certain social situations and, in turn, of what they should expect concerning the behaviour of others and of their treatment in society generally. Research into human PERCEPTION has highlighted the important influence expectations have on an individual's perception of new information. Expectations are formed from personal experience and by information received from various other sources. Information received from these other sources may modify previous expectations or play a particularly crucial role in shaping expectations about persons or social situations of which the individual has no direct experience. An item of information will be more readily accepted if it is compatible with existing ideas and expectations; if it is not then DISSONANCE may occur and the information may be rejected or ignored.

The media are an important source of information about many social and political events of which the individual has little or no first-hand experience. Several researchers have therefore sought to investigate the role played by the media in shaping audience's expectations about certain persons, social GROUPS or social situations – those related to social unrest for example – of which the audience has little or no direct experience against which to test the validity of the media's presentation. The matter of concern here is that in such cases individuals are more than usually vulnerable to PROPAGANDA. Also of interest is the role of the media in creating STEREOTYPES by engendering a set of expectations and beliefs about particular individuals, social groups or social situations.

Experimental group A research term for the group within an experiment to whom the experimental treatment is applied (for example, the group may be asked to conform to a particularly rigorous procedure of communication whilst performing a set task). The results from this group are then compared to those from a comparable CONTROL GROUP which was not subjected to the experimental treatment. The control group provides the base-line against which the effectiveness of the treatment can be judged. Changes which take place in the behaviour of the experimental group but not the control group are likely to be seen as resulting from the treatment. See MEDIA ANALYSIS.

Exploitation A trade word covering all phases of FILM or other media-product publicity, public relations and promotion. **Exploitation pictures** are movies with little or no discernible merits apart from the capability of being sensational, very often cashing in on current trends or specific events.

Extra A crowd player in a FILM, with no lines to speak.

Extrapersonal communication That which takes place without human involvement: machine to machine communication, for example; a major growth industry of communications with the coming of computers, increased automation and the development of robotics. See INTERPERSONAL COMMUNICATION; INTRAPERSONAL COMMUNICATION.

Eye contact Perhaps the most subtle and significant feature of non-verbal communication (See COMMUNICATION, NON-VERBAL). 'So complex is mutual eye contact,' writes C. David Mortensen in *Communication: the Study of Human Interaction* (US: McGraw-Hill, 1972), 'that a whole vocabulary is necessary to distinguish among the ways people look at each other.' We stare, glower, peep, pierce, glance, watch, gaze and scan; and we do it directly or indirectly, provocatively or furtively, confidently or nervously.

Centring is when we fix our gaze upon the eyes or face of another centrally, as an initiator of relationship. The impression of being looked at depends not simply on the directness of the eye-line but upon the relation between eye movements and that of head, facial and bodily orientation to others.

Eye contact is rarely constant, nor is it necessarily mutual. It may be maintained longer when relationships are close or where there is a sustaining activity between participants. When innocuous subjects are discussed, eye contact is likely to be more prolonged than when conversation turns upon personal matters. Women, it is held, engage in more mutual glancing than men do.

Factors of psychological dominance and submissiveness are reflected in the extent and nature of eye contact. A single glance may be all that is required for an individual to assert him/herself over others, take initiative or leadership. Eye contact indicates awareness and signals interest in further contact: it can open a relationship, further it, or, by *avoidance*, close that relationship down.

Looking behaviour provides a valuable means of eliciting information from another person. As Mortensen says, 'While virtually any non-verbal cue may serve as an indicator of individual response to message cues, the fact is . . . that the area of the human eye is the *most visible* and richly revealing of all sources of expressive meaning.' See CIVIL INATTENTION; INDICATORS; PROXEMICS; REGULATORS.

Facsimile Exact copy; today, facsimile (or fax) is the transmission of a printed or handwritten page or image by electronic means. As early as 1842 Scotsman Alexander Bain proposed the first facsimile system though it was not until the 1920s that the process was generally employed for the transmission of news, photographs, weather maps and maps for military purposes.

Newspaper editions can be transmitted across continents for simultaneous publication; the pictures of wanted criminals can be relayed instantly to practically every police force in the world while the facsimile machine can combine with the domestic TV receiver to provide a permanent record of news and other items appearing on the screen.

Most facsimile data is carried over ordinary TELEPHONE wires. Acoustic coupling of fax machines to telephone lines is achieved by placing the phone handset into a cradle on the machine. The number of the receiver is dialled and the connection made. For higher transmission rates electronic coupling must be done to protect the fax equipment and the telephone plant from each other. Whether by wire or by RADIO, transmission is free of the danger of error in transit. Facsimile transmission was used, for example, when the Anglo-French Concorde project was undertaken in Bristol and Toulouse. Backed by voice and TELEPRINTER circuit, a two-way facsimile link provided minute-to-minute contact over design matters.

A facsimile transmission system can be equipped with a document feeder which, combined with associated memory, can be programmed to handle data *automatically*, without the presence of a human operator. See MEDIA TECHNOLOGY.

Fact, theatre of See DOCUMENTARY.

Faction See DOCUMENTARY.

Fade in Gradual emergence of a scene from blackness to clear, full definition. The term is used in RADIO as well as FILM and TV.

Family Viewing Policy See 'TELEVISION PROGRAMME GUIDELINES'; VIOLENCE ON TV: CODES OF PRACTICE.

Fax See FACSIMILE.

Federal Communications Commission (FCC) Set up by the US federal government in 1934; a body empowered to regulate interstate and foreign communications – such as RADIO and TV- originating in America.

Federal Radio Commission Formed in the US in 1927 by government to exercise statutory authority and regulation over RADIO BROADCASTING which, until then, had been a free-for-all.

Feedback According to *Chambers Twentieth Century Dictionary* (ed. A.M. Macdonald, UK, 1972), feedback is the 'return of part of the output of a system to the input as a means towards improved quality or self-correction of error'; in *A Dictionary of New English, 1963–1972*, (eds., C.L. Barnhart, S. Steinmetz and R.K. Barnhart, US/UK: Longman, 1973), feedback is 'a reciprocal effect of one person or thing upon another; a reaction or response that modifies, corrects, etc., the behaviour of that which produced the reaction or response'. Without feedback – the signal which is stimulated by an act of communication, biological, mechanical, human or animal – meaningful contact halts and cannot make progress.

Feedback is the regenerative circuit, or loop, of communication. A student who submits his/her essay to the teacher expects feedback in terms of comments and a mark. Unless this feedback occurs, the student lacks guidance for the future; more, he/she is likely to be demotivated and draw back from further communicative interaction.

When the student's essay *is* returned it may contain **positive** or **negative feedback**: harsh comments, without encouragement, and a low mark might well be more demotivating than not receiving any feedback at all. Praise and supportive criticism on the other hand are likely to produce a positive response – of greater effort and motivation.

Central to the purpose of feedback is *control*; that is, feedback enables the communicator to adjust his/her MESSAGE, or response, to that of the sender, and to the context in which the communicative activity takes place. At the interpersonal level feedback is transmitted by voice, expression, GESTURE, sight, hearing, TOUCH, smell, etc. The greater the distance between communicators, the fewer of the 'senses' being employed to 'read' and return feedback, the more difficult it is to arrange and control, and the more difficult it is to assess its nature and meaning. See CYBERNETICS.

Fibre-optic technology One of the wonder-products of the INFORMATION AGE, fibre-optic cable is fine-spun glass, a mixture of silicon and oxygen, through which digital CODES are passed in pulsing light. Its impact on TELEPHONE technology has been immense and its potential for this, CABLE TELEVISION, and many other purposes, turns so rapidly into achievement and new possibilities that even the experts find it difficult to plan for fibre's accelerating capacity.

By 1990 over 50% of cabling in the UK will be fibre-optic, replacing the traditional copper-based coaxial wire.

Fibre-optic cable can carry 10 times further than coaxial without requiring a booster. Over 7500 different channels can operate along a single pair of optical fibres, though the potential number lies in millions. Because fibre-optic transmission is free from electrical interference, cable can be cheaply laid along existing railway lines; it can follow existing electricity pylons, enclosed in the earth wire. Fibre-optic cable has already been laid across the English Channel, and 1989 saw the first submarine cable across the Atlantic. All forms of cable are limited in terms of the span of the NETWORKS by the number of cable terminals. In contrast, SATELLITE TRANSMISSION has a global reception capacity. The future will see a closer linkage between satellite technology and fibre-optics. See TECHNOLOGY OF THE MEDIA.

Film See ANARCHIST CINEMA; ANIMATION; BLACK DOCUMENTARY; BRITISH BOARD OF FILM CENSORS; BRITISH FILM INSTITUTE; BRITISH FILM PRODUCTION FUND; CAMÉRA STYLO; CATALYST EFFECT; CELLULOID; CERTIFICATION OF FILMS; CINEMATOGRAPHY, ORIGINS; CINÉMA VÉRITÉ; DIRECT CINEMA; DOCUMENTARY; DOUBLE EXPOSURE; DUNNING PROCESS; EMOTIONAL DYNAMIZATION; FILM CENSORSHIP; FILM NOIR; FLASHBACK; FLY-ON-THE-WALL; FRONT MONEY; HAYS OFFICE; HIGH-SPEED PHOTOGRAPHY; HOLLYWOOD; KINETOSCOPE; KULESHOV EFFECT; LLOYD COMMITTEE REPORT, 1967; MARCH OF TIME; IMAX; MCGUFFIN; MINIMAL CINEMA; MONTAGE; MULTIPLE IMAGE; MUSICAL – FILM MUSICAL; NATIONAL FILM ARCHIVE; NEO-REALISM; NEWSREEL; NEW WAVE; ODORAMA; OMNIMAX; PARASOCIAL INTERACTION; PERSISTENCE OF VISION; PROJECTION OF PICTURES; SCHÜFFTAN PROCESS; SEMIOLOGY/SEMIOTICS; 16 MM; SLOW MOTION; SOVIET MANIFESTO, 1928; SOVKINO; SPAGHETTI WESTERNS; SPECIAL EFFECTS; SPINNING TOP; SQUANDERBUG; STORY-BOARD; SUBTITLE; THAUMATROPE; TWO-REELER; TYPAGE; VAMP; VIDEO; VISTAVISION; VITAPHONE; WESTERN; WILLIAMS COMMITTEE REPORT ON OBSCENITY AND FILM CENSORSHIP, 1979; WIPE; ZOETROPE; ZOOM LENS; ZOÖPRAXOGRAPHY.

Film censorship See CENSORSHIP; CERTIFICATION OF FILMS; WILLIAMS COMMITTEE REPORT ON OBSCENITY AND FILM CENSORSHIP, 1979.

Film noir Term used by French FILM critics, notably Nino Frank, to describe a particular kind of dark, suspenseful thriller. A classic of the GENRE is French director Marcel Carné's *Le Jour se Lève* (1939) – 'Day Arises', starring Jean Gabin. We see the last doomed hours of a man wanted by the police for murder. He has barred himself in his attic bedroom in an apartment block. He is totally surrounded. He has no chance; but then, Carné makes clear, the man never did have a chance. At dawn he shoots himself and, as he lies dying, his alarm clock goes off, reminding him of his otherwise intolerable life as a worker.

Described as 'symbolism with a three o'clock in the morning mood', *film noir* also gained currency in the US with films such as John Huston's *Maltese Falcon* (1941).

Filmless camera Launched by the Japanese in 1987, the all-electronic camera is instant, avoids the need for chemical processing, can project its pictures from a standard TELEVISION monitor and even permits its images to be transmitted down a TELEPHONE line or fed into a computer for further processing. Paper pictures can be swiftly produced from VIDEO printers. However, picture quality on FILM promises to remain superior to anything produced by solid-state cameras for the foreseeable future.

First impressions There is evidence that we tend to give too much attention to the initial information we may receive about an individual, and relatively less to later information that may be contradictory; that is, we are biased towards primacy effects. (See PRIMACY, THE LAW OF). There is some evidence that negative first impressions in particular can be resistant to change.

First impressions can clearly count in situations where most of the information is received about a person in a fairly short, discrete period of time, as in an interview. In this instance there might be little opportunity for first impressions to be modified.

In some circumstances – as when a considerable time gap intervenes between sets of information received about an individual or when there is regular, close contact with that individual – first impressions can be modified. Here the later information received may have greater impact. This is known as the *recency* effect, because it is the more recent information which is the more influential.

Fish-eye lens Camera lens of extremely short focal length and wide subject area. Some fish-eye lenses produce only a circular image; others give a full rectangular image.

Flashback A break in the chronology of a narrative in which events from the past are disclosed to the reader, listener or viewer, and which have a bearing on the present situation. Flashback was a device used very early in the history of the cinema. D.W. Griffith's epic *Intolerance* (1916) is made up of four flashbacks. Used with a narrator, the form achieved its greatest popularity in the cinema in the 1930s and 1940s. Orson Welles's *Citizen Kane* (1941) is made up entirely of a dazzling series of flashbacks. Equally inventive is the flashback narrative of the Ealing comedy, Robert

Hamer's *Kind Hearts and Coronets* (1949). See FILM.

Fleet Street Until the 1980s, the home of most of Britain's major national newspapers; indeed the name had become the generic term for the nation's PRESS; a figure of speech (see METONYMY). The advent of new technology linked with the cost-cutting ambitions of newspaper owners, both of which led to bitter conflict with the PRINT UNIONS, caused an exodus from 'The Street' of all the major titles. See PRESS BARONS.

* L. Melvern, *The End of the Street* (UK: Methuen, 1986).

Fly on the Wall Popular title given to a GENRE of DOCUMENTARY film making, for the cinema or TV, in which the camera remains concealed, or is handled so discreetly that the subjects forget they are being filmed. Richard Denton, producer of the BBC documentary series *Kingswood: A Comprehensive School* (1982) describes the approach in 'Fly on the wall – designed to invade privacy', *Listener* (13 January, 1983) as attempting 'to remove the process of filming so far from the consciousness of the contributors that they will, in theory, forget its existence and so behave in a markedly more natural, truthful and realistic manner'. Denton speaks of two distinct problems: 'The first concerns the question of accuracy and context. . . . The second, and probably more important, problem concerns privacy.' An outstanding example of the fly on the wall approach was the BBC's *Police* series (1982), the work of Roger Graef and Charles Stewart. See CINÉMA VÉRITÉ; DIRECT CINEMA.

Folk culture Term generally applied to the CULTURE of pre-industrial societies. Such societies have certain distinguishing features which are thought to affect the elements of their culture: work and leisure are undifferentiated; there is relatively little DIVISION OF LABOUR; the communities are small and social action is normally collectivist as opposed to individualist. Thus folk songs, for example, are usually firmly rooted in the everyday experience and beliefs of both the audience and the performer.

Folk devils Stanley Cohen in *Folk Devils and Moral Panics* (UK: MacGibbon & Kee, 1972), argues that societies are subject to periods of MORAL PANIC in which certain GROUPS are picked out as being a special threat to the VALUES and interests of society. The media and in particular the PRESS play an important role in transmitting this sense of outrage to the general public. These groups or individuals are usually those transgressing the values of the dominant HIERARCHY, as for example did the mods and rockers and the PUNKS. It is further argued by Cohen and others that the castigation of such groups – such folk devils – by the media is a mechanism by which adherence to dominant social NORMS is strengthened along with support for the forces of law and order and an extension of their powers. See LOONY LEFTISM.

* S. Cohen and J. Young, eds., *The Manufacture of News: Deviance, Social Problems and the Mass Media* (UK: Constable, 1973).

Footage Length of FILM expressed in feet.

'Footprint' Term used to describe the area in which a signal from a communications satellite can be received. See SATELLITE TRANSMISSION.

Formula broadcasting In the search for success measured in terms of the universality of appeal of their programmes, many TV companies, according to some critics, have been reduced to finding standard recipes – formulas – for most programmes in order to attract and hold very large audiences. Formula broadcasting displays a minimum range of styles, maximum inoffensiveness of content and little variation in characters, plot or situation. Such standardization can be found in drama and documentaries as well as serials and variety programmes. See EXCESSIVE GENERALITY; PATTERN OF BROADCASTING.

Formula-written Usually refers to novels written to popular formulas with the intention of selling in vast numbers and internationally; aggressively marketed and linked with FILM or TV versions, and promotional programmes.

Four Cs See ADVERTISING: MAINSTREAMERS, ASPIRERS, SUCCEEDERS and REFORMERS.

Fourteen-Day Rule In the period after the 2nd World War (1939–45) the BBC entered into an agreement with government whereby it would not try to usurp the functions of the House of Commons as the supreme forum of the nation by BROADCASTING on ISSUES due to be debated in Parliament. An embargo was placed upon all such issues until 14 days after Parliament had debated them. It was a crippling intrusion upon the editorial rights of the corporation, and the BEVERIDGE REPORT called for the abandonment of the Rule. Nevertheless, successive governments held tenaciously to it.

In 1956 the House of Commons set up a Select Committee to investigate the workings and effects of the Rule: it recommended a reduction to seven days. Pressure from broadcasters and the PRESS continued unabated and within a year the Rule was abandoned altogether (1957). See CENSORSHIP.

Four Theories of the Press See PRESS, FOUR THEORIES OF.

Fourth Estate Title often ascribed to – and claimed by – the PRESS; that is, the press is said to play a vital social or community role in the context of the First Estate (government), the Second Estate (the judiciary), and the Third Estate (the church). Its claim to be an independent watchdog on behalf of the citizen, incorruptible guardian of the rights of all CLASSES, needs to be weighed against arguments which suggest that the press in the main speaks for rather more vested interests – those of ownership, of the ELITE classes. Few would argue, for example, that the press sets out to be the guardian of trade union rights. See MEDIA CONTROL; WATCHDOGS.

Franchise Contractual agreement; most commonly associated with the licensing to broadcast, for fixed periods, of COMMERCIAL TELEVISION and COMMERCIAL RADIO companies. See FRANCHISES FOR INDEPENDENT TELEVISION (UK).

Franchises for Independent Television (UK) Royal Assent to the TELEVISION ACT, 1954 was received on 30 July and on 4 August the Independent Television Authority (later to become the Independent Broadcasting Authority) was set up by the Postmaster General under the chairmanship of Sir Kenneth Clark, and the first COMMERCIAL TELEVISION franchises were issued in 1955, with the Associated Broadcasting Company (ATV) beginning its first London transmissions on 24 September 1955, and its first midlands transmission on 17 February 1956.

The other original franchise holders were: Associated Rediffusion (broadcasting weekdays in London; starting date, 22 September 1955), Granada Television Network (weekdays, North of England; 3 May 1956), Associated British Picture Corporation (Midlands 18 February 1956 and North of England, 5 May 1956), Scottish Television (Central Scotland, 31 August 1957), TWW, Television Wales and West (South Wales and West of England; 14 January 1958), Southern Television (South of England; 30 August 1958), Tyne Tees Television (North-East England; 15 January 1959), Anglia Television (East of England; 27 October 1959), Ulster Television (Northern Ireland; 31 October 1959), Westward Television (South-West England; 29 April 1961), Border Television (Borders, 1 September 1961 and Isle of Man, 23 March 1965), Channel Television (Channel Islands; 1 September 1962), Grampian Television (South-East Scotland; 30 September 1961) and Wales (West and North) broadcasting in Wales and North Wales from 14 September 1962. A subsidiary of ABC (Associated British Corporation), Associated British Cinemas (Television) became that franchise holder's programme contractor and in January 1964 Wales (West and North) became a subsidiary of TWW.

On 30 July 1964 all the contracts were renewed to run till 1967. Then, on 27 January 1966, it was announced that the contracts would be extended to 31 July 1968. From July

1968 some franchise areas were altered. Wales and West England – the Harlech Consortium (HTV) – took in TWW. Harlech began transmissions on 4 March 1968 using TWW's schedules and eventually introduced its own programmes on 20 May 1968. New areas in 1968 were the Midlands (Associated Television Network – ATV), Lancashire (Granada Television), Yorkshire (Yorkshire Television, originally Telefusion Yorkshire and Yorkshire Independent Television; first transmission date 29 July 1968) and two London franchises: London weekends (London Weekend Television; 2 August 1968) and London weekdays (Thames Television, including ABC Television and Rediffusion; 30 July 1968). All of these contracts were extended to run to 31 December 1981.

The IBA publicly announced its decision on new franchises on Sunday 28 December 1980, the contracts to run from 1 January 1982, for eight years. The authority, under the chairmanship of Lady Plowden, announced that Southern Television and Westward Television would lose their franchises and be replaced respectively by South and South Eastern Communications Ltd (TVS – Television South) and Television South West Ltd – TSW. Major share changes or other restructuring was insisted upon for Yorkshire Television and ATV Midlands (subsequently called Central Independent Television).

The franchise holders from 1982 were: Border Television, Scottish Television, Channel Islands Communications (Television), Central (East and West Midlands), Anglia, London Weekend, Thames, Grampian, Tyne Tees, Granada, TVS, Television South West, Harlech, Yorkshire and Ulster. Following the UK government's White Paper, 'BROADCASTING IN THE 90S', a radical shake-up in the system of franchise allocation – by auction – will occur, under the supervision of a new 'light touch' regulatory body, the Indepedent Broadcasting Commission (IBC).

Frankfurt school of theorists Founded in 1923, the Institute for Social Research in Frankfurt became the meeting point of several young Marxist intellectuals among whom were Theodor Adorno, Herbert Marcuse and Max Horkheimer. The members of the 'school' placed at the forefront of their thinking and analysis the CENTRALITY of the role of IDEOLOGY in mass communication. When Hitler came to power in 1933, the Institute moved to New York and until 1942 it was affiliated to the Sociology Department of the University of Columbia. In 1949, Horkheimer led the Institute back to Frankfurt, though Marcuse remained in America.

The Frankfurt school posed the questions: why had the prospect of radical change in society so little popular or natural support? Why was there so little consciousness of the need for politically radical change – indeed how had that sense of need been apparently eliminated from popular consciousness? Marcuse, in *One Dimensional Man* (UK: Sphere Books, 1968), contends that in advanced societies capitalism appears to have proved its worth; by 'producing the goods' it is deemed a successful system and therefore one which has rendered itself immune to criticism: 'The products indoctrinate,' writes Marcuse, 'and manipulate; they promote a false consciousness which is immune against its falsehood. . . . Thus emerges a pattern of *one-dimensional thought and behaviour* in which ideas, aspirations, and objectives that, by their content, transcend the established universe of discourses and action are either repelled or reduced to the terms of this universe.'

The Frankfurt school believed that CULTURE – traditionally transcendent of capitalist ethic and thus in many ways potentially subversive of it, had been harnessed by the mass media (See HEGEMONY). Classical art had been popularized, yes; but in the process of media-adoption, it had been deprived of its *oppositional* value (See DOMINANT, SUBORDINATE, RADICAL). The Frankfurt school has had considerable influence upon thinking about the media and its influence upon culture, but has been criticized for condemning existing reality without proposing how it might be changed for the better. See CULTIVATION; CULTURAL APPARATUS; DOMINANT DISCOURSE; HYPHENIZED ABRIDGEMENT; MASS SOCIETY; PSEUDO-CONTEXT.

Frequency In a non-technical sense, and as used in relation to the media, *frequency* is the degree of repetition of topics of news or information in the PRESS, on RADIO or TV. The more frequently a topic inhabits news headlines and news stories, the more likely it is to continue to do so; to be defined and accepted as 'important', and to have media impact.

If there were no daily reference to the doings of Parliament in news columns or broadcasts, or to the activities of the Royal Family, or the latest industrial conflict, the media would be accused (by the politicians if not by the Royal Family) of neglecting their duty – that is, to reinforce through frequency the acceptance of established institutions, not the least the WESTMINSTER VIEW of British politics.

Negative frequency operates when stories are overlooked, or edged to the margins of attention. Consequently they rarely have the chance either to improve their status as news or impart the full weight of their argument. The term may also be used to refer to the way in which news items fit the frequency – the time scale – of the mode of communication; thus the daily newspaper is more interested in time-limited events such as murders and disasters than, for example, monthlies whose reporting of such events would be dated, or overtaken by other events. See CONSISTENCY; EFFECTS OF THE MASS MEDIA; IMMEDIACY: INTENSITY: PERIODICITY.

Front money That percentage – usually 70% – of the monies required for the production of a FILM to go ahead. This comes largely from the banks and other major investors. The remainder of the investment is called *end money* and comes from, for example, the British Film Institute, the Arts Council or artistic trusts of one kind or another.

Front region, back region See IMPRESSION MANAGEMENT.

Functionalist (mode of media analysis) Interprets social behaviour in terms of its contribution to the assumed overall goals of society, recognizing a CONSENSUS within society of common NORMS and VALUES. The main focus of functionalist analysis is upon the ways in which social systems maintain *equilibrium*. A functionalist would consider any social or cultural element in relation to its contribution to the survival, integration or stability of society. The communication process features as a major component in the 'servicing' of equilibrium.

Structural functionalism, a mode of analysis developed by US sociologist Talcott Parsons, identifies common features of a complex industrial society which are central to its survival. These include the delineation and maintenance of boundaries (social, cultural, etc.); the definition of major structural units of society and the connections between them; and an overriding concern with system maintenance. This school of analysis has been particularly strong in the US.

Within the functionalist perspective, activities which contribute to the survival of a system are known as **eufunctions**; those which contribute to disturbance are known as **dysfunctions**. A distinction is also made between manifest and **latent functions**, the one intended and recognized by the participants, the other neither intended nor recognized.

The functionalist approach makes challengeable assumptions about consensus over the goals of society, leaving untouched important questions about the *source* of these goals and the degree to which an identified source may influence the nature of the social structure and social action. Its tendency is to legitimize the STATUS QUO and to emphasize the predominance of the whole over the parts, overlooking alternative means of achieving the same or similar functions. See MARXIST; SOCIAL ACTION (MODES OF MEDIA ANALYSIS).

Functions of communication See COMMUNICATION, FUNCTIONS.

Galtung and Ruge's Model of Selective Gatekeeping, 1965 Whenever 'newsworthiness' is discussed and analysed the names of Johan Galtung and Mari Ruge are likely to be mentioned before all others. Their article, 'The structure of foreign news: The presentation of the Congo, Cuba and Cyprus crises in four foreign newspapers' in the *Journal of International Peace Research*, 1 (1965) and reprinted in *The Manufacture of News* (UK: Constable, 1973), edited by Stanley Cohen and Jock Young, has proved a focal point for those who ask the questions, what qualifies as news? and what makes one item of news predominate over another?

The model represents the way in which events pass through the GATEKEEPING processes of the media – initially the perceptions of media people as to whether the event qualifies as news, then the selection according to a set of news criteria (I to IX) alone or in combination. For details of the criteria identified by Galtung and Ruge, see NEWS VALUES.

Gate keeping To reach its intended target, every MESSAGE has to pass through many 'gates'; some will be wide open, some ajar,

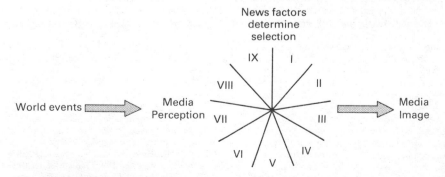

News factors determine selection

World events ⟹ Media Perception

IX I
VIII II
VII III
VI IV
V

Media Image

Galtung and Ruge's model of selective gatekeeping, 1965

some tightly closed. At work, the boss's secretary is the archetypal gate keeper. She may be under instruction to welcome callers or delay them, by letter, by TELEPHONE or physically by 'guarding' the boss's door. Writing about **gate keepers** in the media, Stuart Hood in 'The politics of television' in D. McQuail, ed., *Sociology of Mass Communications* UK: Penguin, 1972) says 'A news bulletin is the result of a number of choices by a variety of "gatekeepers". They include the editor who decides on the day's coverage, or the organizer who briefs the camera crews and reporters and allocates assignments, the film editor who selects the film to be included in the bulletin, the copytaster who chooses the stories from the tape to accompany the film, the sub-editor who writes the story and the duty editor who supervises the compilation of the bulletin, fixes the running order of the stories and gives it its final shape.'

The selection or rejection of material is made according to a set of criteria determined by a number of factors – the gate keeper's CLASS background, upbringing and education and his/her attitudes to the world – VALUES; plus the values, NORMS and traditional wisdom of the organization for which the gate keeper works.

Hood believes that a substantial majority of media gate keepers practice 'middle-class consensus politics' and it is this which colours their perceptions of news and influences the selection process. He goes on to point out that the narrow range of social background from which TV staff come, coupled with organizational pressures such as the need to safeguard jobs and the importance of team spirit, are 'sufficient to ensure that the ground rules of consensus politics are not broken'. See CONSENSUS; GALTUNG AND RUGE'S MODEL OF SELECTIVE GATE-KEEPING, 1965; MR GATE; NEWS VALUES; WHITE'S GATEKEEPING MODEL, 1950.

Gay News: The Love That Dares to Speak Its Name Denis Lemon, editor of *Gay News,* received an 18-month suspended jail sentence in 1977, and was heavily fined, for publishing James Kirkup's poem *The Love* etc. which a court jury found to be guilty of blasphemous libel. Judge Alan King-Hamilton presided. It was the first case of its kind to be tried in the courts since 1922. Nicholas de Jongh of the *Guardian* summarized the offending poem as 'the fantasy of a homosexual Roman centurion about homosexual acts between himself and Jesus. At the close of the poem the centurion for the first time accepts the divinity of Jesus, and the fact that he loved all variety of men.' Five of the lines, said the judge, were the ultimate profanity. See CENSORSHIP; SECTION 28.

Gender The cultural construction of differences expected in typically 'male' or 'female' behaviour. Gender differences are thus those between male and female human behaviour, or expectations of male and female behaviour, which arise from CULTURE rather than nature. Messages about such assumed differences abound in human communication. One particular recent focus for research has been the degree to which mass media products shape, reflect and reinforce cultural definitions of gender differences. See MALE-AS-NORM; NORMS.

Gender signals Male and female signals in interpersonal conduct and appearance that label or place emphasis upon the sex of the signaller. See GESTURE; PROXEMICS.

General Advisory Councils Both the BBC and the IBA have General Advisory Councils for the purposes of monitoring public opinion. The members of these councils are appointed by the institutions themselves.

The BBC's council was established in 1934, 'to secure the constructive criticism and advice of representative men and women over the whole field of its activity and to use their influence in helping towards a further understanding of the BBC's problems and policy on the part of the general public'. The council periodically issues papers for the public, for example on tastes and standards in BBC programmes.

The IBA's council was established in 1964, 'to keep under review the programmes of independent television and to make comments to the Authority thereon; to advise the Authority on the general pattern and content of programmes and to consider such other matters affecting the independent television service as may from time to time be referred to it by the Authority.'

In addition to these general councils both institutions have a number of regional and specialist Advisory Committees and the BBC has National Broadcasting Councils for Scotland and Wales.

The IBA has a dozen or so committees to provide advice in specialist areas such as education. The BBC has 55 advisory bodies to deal with general programmes and specialist subjects, an Engineering Advisory Committee and a Committee on the Social Effects of Television. See BROADCASTING RESEARCH; BROADCASTING STANDARDS COUNCIL.

General Council of the Press See PRESS COUNCIL.

Genre Particular styles of artistic expression – genres – exist within all art forms. The WESTERN, for example, is a genre of FILM.
* 'Genre and cinema', in T. Bennett *et al,* eds., *Popular Television and Film* (UK: British Film Institute/Open University, 1981).

Gerbner's model of communication, 1956 This is described by Denis McQuail in *Communication* (UK: Longman, 1975) as perhaps 'the most comprehensive attempt yet to specify all the component stages and activities of communication'. Below is a modified version of George Gerbner's model as presented in 'Towards a general model of communication', in *Audio Visual Communication Review*, 4.

M is responder to E (event) and may be human or machine (such as a microphone or camera). Gerbner's emphasis is upon the considerable *variability* in the perception of an event by a communicating agent and also in the way the MESSAGE is perceived by a receiver. He speaks of the essential 'creative, interactional nature of the perceptual process'. Equally important is the stress placed upon the importance of *context* to the 'reading' of messages, and of the *open* nature of human communication.

For Gerbner the relationship between form and content in the communication process (S = Signal) is dynamic and interactive. It is also concerned with *access* and *control,* dimensions which inevitably affect the nature and content of communication messages – their selection, shaping and distortion. At the level of the mass media this is obvious, but access and control also operate at the level of INTERPERSONAL COMMUNICATION – teachers in classrooms, for example, speakers at public meetings, parents in the home situation.

Back on the horizontal axis, Gerbner stresses the importance of *availability*. A literate electorate may have the capacity to read all the facts about a political situation, all the pros and cons of an industrial dispute but that

capacity can only operate, and the pros and cons be properly weighed, if the necessary facts are made available.

What Gerbner's model does not do is address itself fully satisfactorily to the problems of how MEANING is generated. The form or CODE of the message (S) is taken for granted, whereas the advocate of SEMIOLOGY/SEMIOTICS would argue that meaning is of the essence. See COMMUNICATION MODELS.

Gestuno Sign LANGUAGE created by the World Federation of the Deaf, for use at international conferences and meetings of deaf people. Like ESPERANTO, it is not intended to replace other languages, but to serve as a second language for international communication.

Gesture In *Manwatching: A Field Guide to Human Behaviour* (UK: Jonathan Cape, 1977), Desmond Morris defines a gesture as 'any action that sends a visual signal to an onlooker'. *Incidental* gestures may be unintentional, accidental, but they still communicate messages – such as mood information. *Primary* gestures are those which are intended – a wave, a nod, a wink. Morris offers six categories of gestures: (1) *Expressive;* shared by other animals as well as humans, and including facial expression and manual gesticulations. (2) *Mimic* gestures; exclusively human, 'The essential quality of a Mimic Gesture is that it attempts to copy the thing it is trying to portray'.

This category Morris subdivides into *Social* mimicry (or 'putting on a good face'); *Theatrical mimicry; Partial* mimicry (pretending

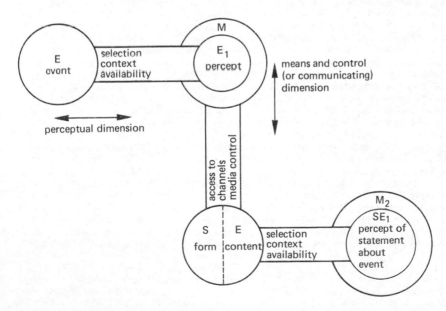

Gerbner's model of communication, 1956

your hand is a gun, for example), and what he terms *Vacuum* mimicry – gestures to indicate hunger or thirst. (3) *Schematic* gestures are those in which imitations become abbreviated or abridged; a gestural shorthand. (4) *Symbolic* gestures represent moods and ideas – such as the sign to indicate that you consider someone is 'round the twist'. (5) *Technical* gestures constitute specialized signal systems recognized only by those in the trade or profession, such as those employed by a TV studio manager or a fireman to his colleagues. (6) *Coded* gestures are based upon formal systems, such as Deaf-and-Dumb Sign Language, Semaphore and the Tic-tac signalling of the race course.

Many gestures carry universal MEANING but in general the gesture is critically dependent upon the cultural context in which it is made and specific contexts of timing and situation as well as the combination of gestures, for rarely do they exist alone, or without vocal accompaniment. See BARRIER SIGNALS; BATON SIGNALS; CLOTHING SIGNALS; COMMUNICATION, NON-VERBAL; CUT-OFF; GENDER SIGNALS; GUIDE SIGNS; INSULT SIGNALS; METASIGNALS; NON-VERBAL BEHAVIOUR: REPERTOIRE; POSTURAL ECHO; PROXEMICS; RELIC SIGNALS; SALUTATION DISPLAY; SHORTFALL SIGNALS; TIE-SIGNS.

Ghost-writer One who does literary work for someone else who takes the credit. The practice of publishing autobiographies and memoirs by the famous, written by ghost-writers, is widespread (not the least, it is believed, among sports persons).

Glasgow University Media Group Set up with a grant from the UK Social Science Research Council, the Group has published research findings which have won considerable attention and, not unexpectedly, drawn fire from the media under investigation. By 1982, the Group had published three major works tabulating its exhaustive research into the way TV handles the news. First came *Bad News* (UK: Routledge & Kegan Paul, 1972), which exploded the generally held image of broadcasters being substantially more objective and reliable in news reporting than the press. 'Our study,' wrote the eight authors of the original study, 'does not support a received view that television news is "the news as it happens".' The Group had monitored all TV news broadcasts over a six-month period, from January to June 1975. Notable among the Group's findings was a bias in TV against the activities of organized labour and a relentless emphasis upon effects rather than causes.

Later publications by the Glasgow University Media Group have been *More Bad News* (UK: Routledge & Kegan Paul, 1980), *Really Bad News* (UK: Writers and Readers' Publishing Co-operative, 1982) and *War and Peace*

News (UK: Open University Press, 1985) about media coverage of the Falklands War, the Miners' Strike and Northern Ireland. The theoretical base from which the Group works may be summarized by a quotation from *More Bad News:* 'news is not a neutral and not a natural phenomenon: it is rather the manufactured production of ideology'. See BROADCASTING RESEARCH; RESEARCH CENTRES (INTO THE MEDIA).

Glasnost Openness; Russian term for greater freedom of expression and less state SECRECY. The word became universal currency with the election to leadership in the Soviet Union of Mikhail Gorbachev, who welcomed rather than shunned world publicity and demonstrated an openness within the Russian nation and in communication with other countries not experienced since the early days of the Russian Revolution. Linked with *glasnost* has been *perestroika*, meaning reconstruction, reform in relation to government practices and expectations.

Global village See ACCELERATION FACTOR; MCLUHANISMS.

Gold See TELECOM GOLD.

Graffiti The poor man or woman's tilt at literary immortality; writings in public but forbidden places attempting crudely or pithily or both to summarize some of life's basic truths, such as 'Suicide is the most sincere form of self-criticism', or pertinent advice, such as 'let's keep incest in the family' or even historical analysis, such as 'Emmanuel Kant but Ghengis Khan'. Ultimately, of course, 'Graffiti should be obscene and not heard', and specially-provided blank walls for graffiti writers such as Sweden has provided rob the 'art' of the thrill of doing something illegal.

Gramophone Originally the Phonograph, invented by Thomas Alva Edison (1847–1931), his first sketch of which was published in the *Scientific American,* 22 December 1877. His 'talking tinfoil' led to the creation in 1878 of the Edison Speaking Phonograph Company, and soon a single exhibition phonograph could earn as much as US$1800 a week. Concurrently, Edison designed different models, including a disc machine with a volute spiral which anticipated later developments.

Commercial recordings began in 1890, though sound reproduction remained exceedingly poor and the wax cylinders could only play for two minutes maximum and there was no way of mass producing the cylinders. Machines were driven by cumbersome, heavy-duty batteries and were very expensive to purchase – that is until Thomas Hood Macdonald, a manager of Graphophone, rival company to Edison's, put on sale the first mechanical phonograph (1894), retailing at $75.

The Columbia company were the first to manufacture double-sided discs (1908), though the next major innovation was electrical recording, initiated by Lionel Guest and H.O. Merrimen in 1920 when they recorded, by electrical process, the Unknown Warrior burial service in Westminister Abbey. Bell Laboratories in the US proved substantial pioneers in this area, which they termed *orthophonic* recording.

The miraculous rise of the gramophone was eventually hit by the more popular mass appeal of RADIO and the 1930s were lean years, though the record industry in Europe did not plumb the depths to the extent it did in the US where, by January 1933, the record business was practically extinct. However, in September 1934, the RCA Victor sales department offered the Duo Junior, consisting of an electrically powered turntable and a magnetic pickup, primitive but popular, and by 1935 the notion of 'high-fidelity' was born. Station W2XR (later WQXR) in New York began 'high fidelity broadcasting' in 1934, in truth, as much high publicity as hi-fi.

The 2nd World War (1939–45) cut non-military use of shellac – the material for the discs – principally imported from India, and record production was severely curtailed. 1944 saw the first examples of Decca's 'ffrr' sound reaching British ears. This was 'full frequency range reproduction' achieving standards of reproduction never previously heard.

In 1941, 127 million discs were sold; in 1947, 400 million – a year before Columbia Records in the US launched the unbreakable microgrove disc, with a playing time of 23 minutes per side. The LP (Long Playing) Record had arrived. It bore between 224 and 300 grooves per inch compared to 85 grooves on the ordinary disc; and it moved on the turntable at $33\frac{1}{3}$ rpm instead of the traditional 78. Not to be outdone, RCA Victor hit back with the 45 rpm record, thus beginning the so-called Battle of the Speeds, diminishing trade in what turned out to be a period of consumer uncertainty. It was the period too when recording by magnetic tape was rapidly expanding.

Neither ousted the other: in fact they proved complementary and expanded together in the dynamic growth period of Rock and Roll and the radio disc jockey.

Stereophonic sound, or 'two-eared listening', had been possible since the Bell Laboratories had put on binaural demonstrations at the Chicago World's Fair of 1933, and Walt Disney's film *Fantasia* (1940) showed the possibilities of multi-source music reproduction in a cinema. The stereo effect was caught first on high-quality magnetic tape. Then in 1957 the Westrex Company devised a successful method of putting two stereo channels into a single groove. By September of the following year every major record company in the US was offering stereo discs for sale.

The tape cassette emerged from Philips who demonstrated its potential at the 1963 Berlin Radio Show. They improved it substantially and in 1970 along came the DOLBY NOISE REDUCTION SYSTEM just at the time when tape machines were becoming popular as in-car entertainment.

An innovation in gramophone technology which has never quite caught on is Quadrophony, using four speakers rather than two, the additional channels intended to convey 'ambient' sound – fractionally delayed impulses reflected from the rear of the recording hall. Digital recording is now with us. The trusty stylus is being eased into history by the laser, and discs as we have known them banished by new developments in miniaturization. 'A partisan historian', 'writes Roland Gelatt of the gramophone, 'could perhaps be forgiven for claiming it as the chief marvel and solace of the century'. See CD – COMPACT DISC.

Graphic revolution Daniel Boorstin in *The Image* (UK: Penguin, 1963) uses this term to describe the accelerated importance of the visual image in the post 2nd World War period. Presented in photography and moving pictures, with all the backing of modern technological wizardry, the image has more impact in the 'graphic revolution' than the word; further, the image has become more interesting, more vivid and dramatic than the original: 'the shadow becomes the substance' and suddenly reality cannot match up to its image. See ADVERTISING.

Graphophone See GRAMOPHONE.

Gregg shorthand See SHORTHAND.

Grip Person in a FILM crew responsible for laying *tracks*, portable 'railway lines' for the smooth movement of the camera mounted on a DOLLY.

Groups A good deal of communication takes place within groups of one type or another. Charles H. Cooley, one of the initiators of research into group behaviour and communication, in his work, *Social Organization* (US: Scribner, 1909), classifies groups into two main types. **Primary groups** such as the family are defined as groups in which there is face-to-face communication; in which NORMS and MORES are produced; in which ROLES are allocated and in which a feeling of solidarity is enjoyed. **Secondary groups,** such as social CLASS groups, are much larger aggregates. Several researchers have sought to determine the communication processes which take place within groups and in particular the inter-relationship between a group's CULTURE, roles, structure, size, and type and its communication processes.

R.F. Bales in 'Channels of communication in small groups', *American Sociological Review,*

16 (1951), argues that the inequality of participation among the members of a small group increases as the group size increases.

In terms of the effect of a group's communication structure upon its task performance, several studies have shown that a restriction of communication leads to more efficient performance of straightforward tasks. Less restricted communication does, though, seem to result in a higher morale among group members according to H. Leavitt in 'Some effects of certain communication patterns on group performance', *Journal of Abnormal and Social Psychology,* vol. 46 (1951). Further, Marvin Shaw argues in 'Some effects of problem complexity upon problem solution efficiency in different communication nets', *Journal of Experimental Psychology,* 48 (1954), that when a task involves the solution of a complex problem, creativity and a discussion of alternative solutions, the less restricted communication NETWORK is more effective.

A small **primary group** particularly has the potential to influence the perceptions of its individual members and thus the way in which they interpret and respond to communication from sources both within and outside the group. For example, Shils and Janowitz in 'Cohesion and disintegration in the Wehrmacht in World War II', *Public Opinion Quarterly,* vol. 12 (1948), found that the German forces were relatively immune to Allied PROPAGANDA because of the effectiveness of primary group cohesion. Only when the primary group structure was disrupted were German military personnel accessible to persuasion and the weakening of resolve. The role an individual is allocated within a group, particularly a primary group, can also affect both the quality and quantity of his/her contribution to the group's communication processes.

Secondary groups are not without influence either, in the communication process. Basil Bernstein argues, in 'Social class, language and socialization', P. P. Giglioli, ed., *Language and Social Context,* (UK: Penguin, 1972) that a relationship exists between membership of a social class group and the LANGUAGE code adopted. See CONCURRENCE-SEEKING TENDENCY; GROUPTHINK.

Groupthink Term used by Irving L. Janis in *Groupthink. Psychological Studies of Policy Decisions and Fiascos* (US: Houghton Mifflin, 1972) to describe the operation of group decision-making which is dominated by a CONCURRENCE-SEEKING TENDENCY, 'a mode of thinking that people engage in when they are deeply involved in a cohesive in-group, when the members' strivings for unanimity override their motivation to realistically appraise alternative courses of action'.

Group decisions, Janis concedes, are often better thought through than those arrived at by individuals alone, 'yet the advantages of having decisions made by groups are often lost because of psychological pressures that arise when members work closely together, share the same values, and above all face a crisis situation in which everyone is subject to stresses that generate a strong need for affiliation. In these circumstances, as conformity pressures begin to dominate, groupthink and the attendant deterioration of decision-making set in.' See GROUPS; VALUES.

Grub Street Description of any form of literary or journalistic drudgery. According to Dr Johnson (1709–84) Grub Street was 'originally the name of a street near Moorfields in London, much inhabited by writers of small histories, dictionaries and temporary poems, whence any mean production is called grub-street'.

GSR Galvanic skin response: a measure of stress and emotion caused to individuals by others, especially when spatial territories have been invaded – that is, someone coming too close for psychological comfort. See PROXEMICS; SPATIAL ZONES.

Guide signs Actions indicating direction, sometimes called Deictic Signals: finger pointing, head pointing, eye pointing. Thumbs down and thumbs up come into this category, and all the GESTURES of beckoning as well as repelling. See NON-VERBAL BEHAVIOUR: REPERTOIRE.

Gum print 19th c. mode of photograph printing which made the pictures resemble oil painting.

Hacker Just as the tomb robbers of ancient Egypt broke into seemingly impregnable pyramids and underground tombs, so the 'hacker' breaks into computer CODES and computer systems. All the hacker needs is a personal micro, know-how and persistence and some of the world's most closely guarded information banks can be penetrated.
* H. Cornwall, *Datatheft Computer Fraud, Industrial Espionage and Information Crime* (UK: Heinemann, 1987).

Halo effect In initial encounters we tend to pick out one or two characteristics of a person and let these influence our general impression of him or her. For example, at an interview, it may be assumed that someone who is well qualified, neatly dressed and pleasant in manner will necessarily perform well in the job and work hard. Such generalizations from one or two characteristics are based on our implicit personality theory that is, our basic assumptions about which characteristics go together, and how people are likely to behave.

Handle Just as authors often assume pen

names, CB Radio enthusiasts use a 'Handle' partly to preserve anonymity, partly to reflect some kind of characteristic the CBer considers worthy of attention.

Hankey Committee Report on Television, 1943 Set up under the Coalition War Government in the UK, chaired by Lord Hankey, the committee was requested to 'prepare plans for the reinstatement and development of the television service after the War'. Hankey recommended a reopening on the 1939 basis of the 405-line system rather than wait for the development of any new, improved version. The Report was of the view that 'it is in the televising of actual events, the ability to give the viewer a front-row seat at almost every possible kind of exciting or memorable spectacle, that Television will perform its greatest service'. Hankey's general conclusion was 'that Television has come to stay . . .' See COMMISSIONS/COMMITTEES ON THE MEDIA.

Hard sell Where the advertiser goes straight for the consumer's jugular, cutting away the MYTH, the charm, the humour or the fantasy of the ADVERTISEMENT, and says bluntly, 'Buy this!' Hard sell usually indicates, on the part of the manufacturer, an impatience with his ad agency's artistry and subterfuges; or simply hard, cost-cutting times.

Harmonious interaction Fred Inglis uses this phrase in *The Imagery of Power: A Critique of Advertising* (UK: Heinemann, 1972) to describe the friendly and mutually supportive relationship between the media and the forces of ADVERTISING. This 'harmonious interaction' of advertising and editorial styles consistently reproduces and endorses the consumer's way of life, argues Inglis.

Hays Office In the US for three decades the Hays Office meant CENSORSHIP. In 1922 leading figures in the FILM industry formed Motion Picture Producers and Distributors of America Incorporated (MPPDA) to protect their interests against a range of would-be film censors in a climate that had produced Prohibition (Volstead Act, 1919). Will H. Hays, postmaster general to the Harding administration, was invited to become president.

In 1930 Martin Quigley, a Chicago publisher, and Father Lord, Society of Jesus, reframed the Hays Office studio recommendations of 1927, into a Production Code (The Hays Office Code) to meet the even more restrictive demands emanating from the recently formed Legion of Decency made up of leaders of the Roman Catholic church and other religious denominations.

A Production Code Administration was prised out of the MPPDA under the direction of Roman Catholic Joseph I. Breen who, between 1934 and the anti-trust decree of 1948, supervised 95% of films made in the US. Any film released without Breen's approval was liable to a $25,000 fine and condemnation by the Legion.

Political as well as moral attitudes and behaviour were subject to severe censorship. The Legion, for example, supported the Fascists in the Spanish Civil War and generally opposed any production with Leftward leanings. The Hays Office Code remained operative until 1966. See BROADCASTING STANDARDS COUNCIL.

H-certificate Category introduced by the BRITISH BOARD OF FILM CENSORS in 1930 to describe films dealing with the horrific or the supernatural and considered unsuitable for children. From 1951 the certificate was discontinued and films of this nature were included under the new X-certificate. See CERTIFICATION OF FILMS.

Hearsay See RUMOUR.

Hegemony The concept of hegemony owes much to the work of Italian political thinker Antonio Gramsci (1891-1937). A state of hegemony is achieved when a provisional alliance of certain social GROUPS exerts a CONSENSUS which makes the power of the dominant group appear both natural and legitimate.

Hegemony can, however, only be maintained by the won consent of the dominated. It is therefore, like consensus, subject to renegotiation and ongoing redefinition. Also, the consensus may be broken as the ideologies of the *subordinate* cannot always be accommodated. Institutions such as the mass media, the family, the education system and religion, play a key role in the shaping of people's awareness and consciousness and thus can be agents through which hegemony is constructed, exercised and maintained.

See IDEOLOGICAL STATE APPARATUSES; MEDIATION.

* Gramsci, A., *Selections from the Prison Notebooks* (UK: Lawrence & Wishart, 1971); Miliband, *The State in Capitalist Society* (UK: Weidenfeld & Nicholson, 1969).

Helical model of communication See DANCE'S HELICAL MODEL OF COMMUNICATION.

Helical scan See TELERECORDING.

Hermeneutics The science of interpretation or understanding. The word is taken from the Greek, *hermeneuein*, and derives from Hermes, messenger of the gods; it means to make things clear, to announce or unveil a MESSAGE. In FILM study, a hermeneutic code, or 'code of enigma', explains by one device or another the mysteries of the plot – the situation or predicament character find themselves in – and indicates the process of resolution.

Heterophily See HOMOPHILY.

HF Multipair cable Of limited BANDWIDTH, High Frequency Multipair is a simple form of transmission cable consisting of twisted pairs of wires, like those in the domestic TELEPHONE cable and capable of carrying four TV channels. See COAXIAL CABLE; OPTICAL FIBRE CABLE.

Hidden agenda When the underlying objective of an act of communication is different from that which is stated. See IMPRESSION MANAGEMENT.

Hidden needs For the marketer of consumer products or services, Vance Packhard in *The Hidden Persuaders* (UK: Penguin, 1960, latest edition 1981) cites eight 'hidden needs' which the adman can cater for. These are: emotional security; reassurance of worth; ego-gratification; creative outlets; love objects; a sense of power; a sense of roots; and immortality. See ADVERTISING; MASLOW'S HIERARCHY OF NEEDS.

Hierarchy Classification in graded subdivisions. The hierarchy of a company starts at the top with the chairperson or managing director; a social hierarchy is dominated by the ELITE classes who varyingly influence those CLASS divisions below them. In the media, the dominant hierarchy are the owners, top executives, major shareholders, boards of directors, etc. See CONGLOMERATES; ESTABLISHMENT; ORGANIZATIONAL CULTURES.

Highbrow Someone considered to be a member of the intellectual and cultural ELITE, whose tastes are, by definition, considered to be aesthetically superior to those of the majority, is deemed a *highbrow*. Highbrow tastes are limited to the few. The terms **middlebrow** and **lowbrow** are used to indicate a level of intellectual capacity or cultural appreciation judged against the standards of the highbrow elite.

High-definition TV 1982 saw the demonstration by Sony of Japan of 1000-line high-definition TV with picture quality indistinguishable from 35 mm FILM on a two-metre screen – this, 40 years after the UK government recommendation that the BBC start on such a project. With hi-def there is none of the old flicker visible; there is detail even in shadow. Developed by NHK of Japan, hi-def TV can, engineers claim, carry five times the information detail of a conventional screen. The format allows transmission of pictorial detail – patterns, designs – or print copy, opening up markets for the system in computer-aided design and publishing.

High fidelity See GRAMOPHONE.

High-speed photography One of the wonders of modern technology, but a preoccupation of photographers from the earliest pioneering days, the high-speed flash process slows down, or magnifies time: the splash of a drop of water, the trajectory of a bullet, can be reduced to SLOW MOTION that permits astonishing revelations. Foremost among developers of ultra-high-speed electronic flash photography as a tool of scientific analysis was the American Dr Harold Edgerton, inventor of the stroboscope. The term **stroboscopic photography**, or strobe photography, refers to pictures of single or multiple exposure taken by flashes of light from electrical discharges, permitting objects moving at their natural speeds to be observed in slow motion, the rate of the slow motion depending on the *frequency* of the strobe and object. When the flash frequency exactly equals that of the rotation or vibration, the object is illuminated in the same position during each cycle, and appears stationary.

Mechanical cameras such as the register-pin intermittent action camera are capable of 500 frames a second; for faster objects, there is the rotating prism camera at 1500 frames a second, slowing time down between 200 and 400 times. Even faster is the rotating mirror camera, capable of 10,000 pictures a second – a capacity which, however, is dwarfed by the image tube electronic camera which can take a million-million pictures a second.

In contrast to high-speed photography, **time-lapse photography,** by taking pictures at timed intervals of seconds, minutes, hours or days, speeds up, or telescopes time. In a few moments of FILM we can see the germination of a seed, the hatching of an egg or blow-fly maggots consuming a dead mouse. Audiences in the 1930s delighted in the time-lapse spectacle, in *Four Minutes to Brighton,* of travelling, via film, at 760 m.p.h. on the Brighton Belle. Apollo astronauts on the moon used time-lapse photography. Both high-speed and time-lapse phtography are employed most widely to answer two questions: how is it done, and what went wrong? See PHOTOGRAPHY, ORIGINS.

Historical revisionism Term addressed specifically to attempts in the USA and Europe to write out of history the genocide of the Third Reich of Adolph Hitler; to deny that any of the atrocities ever took place.

Hollywood Centre of the US film industry, located in California, providing maximum sunshine for outdoor shooting and some magnificent scenery. In 1908 *The Count of Monte Cristo,* begun in Chicago, was completed in California and the first Hollywood studio was set up in 1911. Within a year another 15 FILM companies had set up in business. The Hollywood studio system reached its peak in the 1930s. Its fortunes have since fluctuated, at first knocked sideways by the advent of TV, then restored by a simple philosophy of 'if you can't beat them, join them'.

Holography With the invention of the laser in 1960 an intriguing new form of three-dimensional photography – Holography – became possible. Though the theory originated with Dr Dennis Gabor as early as 1947, development was not possible until an intense source of 'coherent' light became available, which the laser supplied. Coherent light is light of 'pure' colour containing waves of a single frequency whose wave fronts all move in perfect step.

Derived from the Greek, 'holos', or whole, and 'gram', message, the **Hologram** is made without a lens by splitting a laser beam so that part of it is directed at the subject and part becomes a reference beam. When light reflected from the subject and light from the reference beam meet on the photographic plate, the wave fronts create interference patterns which contain all the visual information needed to construct a three-dimensional image of the subject, amazingly lifelike, and viewable from different angles. Recent developments have enabled Holograms to be made for viewing by ordinary white light.

Holography has proved a boon to the world of business. Machine-readable reflection holograms store digital information in hundreds of layers within the emulsion of a film or plastic card. The holographed data on a credit card (See SMART CARD), passport, security access card or ticket to a high-priced event, forming a three-dimensional pattern, can be read electronically, thus providing a formidable obstacle to counterfeiting.

Home Service Name of BBC Radio 4 founded in 1939 until the name-change in 1967. There was also the Light Programme (Radio 2) and the Third Programme (Radio 3).

* A. Briggs, *Sound and Vision: The History of Broadcasting in the United Kingdom,* vol. IV (UK: Oxford University Press, 1979)

Homo narrans See NARRATIVE PARADIGM.

Homophily Interacting individuals who share certain attributes – beliefs, VALUES, educational background, social status – are said to be **homophilous.** Communication is commonly believed to be closer when between people who are homophilous as they are more likely to share a common LANGUAGE level and pattern of MEANING. On the other hand, **Heterophily** refers to the degree to which interacting individuals differ in these attributes. Generally, heterophilic interaction is likely to cause some disturbance and confusion to the individuals concerned and thus more effort is required to make communication effective. The lack of a common language level and shared patterns of meaning which are likely to result in this situation may lead to many messages going unheeded. See CONGRUENCE THEORY.

Horse opera Nickname for the WESTERN film.

Hospital radio Founded in 1951. There are approximately 300 hospital RADIO services BROADCASTING music, quiz and chat shows, local news and even documentaries to 250,000 patients in some 80% of hospitals in the UK. Most of these are organized into the National Hospital Broadcasting Organization. Programmes are conveyed via cable from small studios into the bedside headphones of patients. See COMMUNITY RADIO: STUDENT RADIO.

Hot-line A direct TELEPHONE line open for instant communication between the leaders of different countries in cases of emergency.

Hot media, cold media Terms coined by Marshall MCLUHAN, author of *The Gutenberg Galaxy* (Canada: University of Toronto Press, 1962) and *Understanding Media* (UK: Routledge & Kegan Paul, 1964), and forming a basic tool of his analysis of the media. For McLuhan, 'hot' media extend one sense-mode with high-definition data. Examples of 'hot' media are RADIO and FILM. 'Cold' media provide, in contrast, low-definition data, requiring much more participation by the individual. Examples are TV, TELEPHONE and CARTOONS. As Ralph Berry queries in *Communication through the Mass Media* (UK: Edward Arnold, 1971), 'All this is highly controversial . . . for example, the "hot-cold" metaphor runs speedily into difficulties (is the living theatre significantly different in the front or the rear stalls?).'

Hunt Committee Report on Cable Expansion and Broadcasting Policy, 1982 Set up by the Conservative government, the three-man committee chaired by Lord Hunt, a former top civil servant, was required to report and make recommendations on the future of cable systems in the UK, in order to 'secure the benefits for the United Kingdom which cable technology can offer . . . in a way consistent with the wider public interest, in particular the safeguarding of public service broadcasting . . . .' In brief, the report, the result of a hurried investigation begun in March 1982 and finalized by September, recommended a future pattern of cable transmission systems marked by few regulations, many channels and as much ADVERTISING as operators could attract. The committee urged immediate expansion even before the proposed body for the supervision of FRANCHISES was created.

Pay-as-you-view TV was not given the green light by Hunt on the grounds that major national events, such as the Cup Final or Wimbledon, might be siphoned off from national access and be seen only by those on cable and able to pay. 'Cherry picking' – cabling just for the well-off suburbs of a city, for example – was also to be barred.

See CABLE TELEVISION.

Hyde Park of the Air The idea of giving access to BROADCASTING as open as Hyde Park Corner was given support by the BEVERIDGE COMMITTEE REPORT ON BROADCASTING, 1951 which considered very seriously the problems of 'controversy' on the air. Beveridge argued that debate on RADIO and TV needed to be conducted with a given set of rules; however, the Report acknowledged that there ought to be a public right of access to the air, especially in matters of religious controversy. They recommended a kind of 'Hyde Park of the Air' which would be slightly separate from the normal processes of BBC editorial control.

Hype A media hype is usually a massive publicity campaign or stunt for a series, a programme, a novel, a FILM, in which the whole paraphernalia of ADVERTISING is directed towards giving the new 'product' maximum media exposure before or during its appearance.

Hyphenized abridgement Herbert Marcuse uses this term in *One-Dimensional Man* (UK: Sphere Books, 1968) to describe the practice of the PRESS of concentrating information by bringing two or more descriptive facts together by using a hyphen. Thus: 'Georgia's highhanded-lowbrowed governor . . . had the stage set for one of his wild political rallies last week'. Marcuse argues, 'The governor, his function, his physical features and his political practices are fused together into one indivisible and immutable structure' by the press employing this device 'which in its natural innocence and immediacy, overwhelms the reader's mind. The structure leaves no space for distinction . . . it moves and lives only as a whole'.

Hyphenized abridgement, used repeatedly and assertively, 'imposes *images* while discouraging on the part of the reader, conceptualization; that is, it beats him/her with images, but impedes thinking; and thus the media define for us the terms in which we are permitted to think'. See EFFECTS OF MASS MEDIA; FRANKFURT SCHOOL OF THEORISTS; PSEUDO-CONTEXT; TABLOIDESE.

Hypodermic needle model of communication More a METAPHOR representing a view of the EFFECTS OF THE MASS MEDIA, the Hypodermic needle 'model' has formed a point of general reference in crediting the media with power over audiences. The basic assumption is that the mass media have a direct, immediate and influential effect upon audiences by 'injecting' information into the consciousness of the masses.

The audience is seen as impressionable and open to manipulation. Like other early models of communication flow from the media, it overlooks the possible effects of INTERVENING VARIABLES (IV) in the communication process and presents the masses as being unquestioning receptacles of media messages. This sense of the all-powerfulness of the media is a central feature of early MASS SOCIETY research. It is now regarded as crude and simplistic. See COMMERCIAL LAISSEZ-FAIRE MODEL OF (MEDIA) COMMUNICATION; COMMUNICATION MODELS; S-IV-R MODEL OF COMMUNICATION.

* D. McQuail, *Mass Communication Theory: An Introduction* (UK: Sage, 1987).

Hypothesis The first step of the research cycle is the formulation of an hypothesis. This will usually be based on an idea or hunch gained by the researcher from his/her own reading of earlier studies and/or from his/her own observations of society. Starting with this basic idea the researcher usually proposes a working hypothesis which will guide the research. The hypothesis proposes a relationship between certain social phenomena: for example, that people from a higher education background are more likely to read what is regarded as the quality PRESS.

Not all hypotheses are expressed as formal statements. Some can be a general collection of ideas about particular social phenomena. All hypotheses, though, must be capable of EMPIRICAL testing; that is, they must be capable of being proved or disproved by facts and argument. The hypothesis will determine the nature of the research design – the method of collecting the information which will prove or disprove the hypothesis.

Once this information has been collected and analysed the hypothesis is reviewed. It may be proved, disproved or amended. Indeed in many cases the original hypothesis may have been modified during the data collection stage of the research. Alternatively it may be decided that further evidence is required before any conclusion is reached. See MEDIA ANALYSIS.

Hypothesis of consonance See NEWS VALUES.

Ibid From the Latin, *ibidem,* meaning 'in the same place' or from the same source. Where, in a text, a reference to a book and its author has been made once, the use of the word *Ibid.* is an economical way of repeating the reference. Also, if a quotation is employed from a certain source, *Ibid.* means that a further quotation is from the same source.

Iconic Describes a SIGN which, in some way, resembles its object; looks like it, or sounds like it. Picture-writing is iconic, as is a map. ONOMATOPOEIA (word sounds that resemble real sounds) is iconic. In SEMIOLOGY/SEMIOTICS the iconic is one of three categories of sign defined by American philosopher C.S. Peirce (1834-1914). Where the iconic describes or resembles, an *Index* is connected with its object, like smoke to fire, while the SYMBOL has no resemblance or connection, and communicates MEANING only because people agree that it shall stand for what it does. A word is a symbol. The categories are not separate and distinct. One sign may be made up of all three categories.

* M. Blonsky, ed., *On Signs* (UK: Johns Hopkins University Press, 1985).

Iconoscope Name given to the first working electronic camera tube; developed by Vladimir Zworykin in the US (1931) and funded by the Radio Corporation of America (RCO).

Identification The degree to which people identify with and are influenced by characters, fictional or otherwise, in books, RADIO, films and TV has fascinated media analysts, especially in areas of behaviour where that identification might lead to anti-social activity such as violence. 'To identify with' has two common meanings: to participate in the situation of someone whose plight has caught one's sympathy; and to incorporate characteristics of an admired person into one's own identity by adopting that person's system of VALUES.

Identification is used in a more specific sense when we discuss the degree of influence persons, institutions and the media may have on others. In 'Processes of opinion change', *Public Opinion Quarterly,* 25 (1965), Herbert Kelman explores three basic processes of social influence with reference to opinion change and to communication. These are *compliance, identification and internalization.* The first position in this 'social influence theory' refers to the acceptance of influence in the hope of either receiving a reward or avoiding punishment. Identification in this sense occurs 'when an individual adopts behaviour derived from another person or a group because this behaviour is associated with a satisfying self-defining relationship to this person or group'. As with compliance, change or influence is reliant upon the external source and 'dependent on social support'. Internalization occurs when the proposed change, the influence, is fully believed in, accepted, taken fully on board, because the influenced person 'finds it useful for the solution of a problem or because it is congenial to his own orientation, or because it is demanded of his own values'.

Linked to the analysis of the extent to which identification takes place is the interest in *how* we identify – along lines of age, CLASS or gender. See EFFECTS OF THE MASS MEDIA.
* R. Frost and J. Stauffer, 'The effects of social class, gender and personality on physiological responses to film violence' in *Journal of Communication,* Spring, 1987; L. Taylor and B. Mullen, *Uninvited Guests: The Intimate Secrets of Television and Radio* (UK: Chatto & Windus, 1986).

Ideological state apparatuses This term derives from the work of the French philosopher, Louis Althusser. Ideological state apparatuses (ISAs) are those social institutions which, according to Althusser, help shape people's consciousnesses in a way that secures support for the IDEOLOGY of those who control the state, that is, the dominant ideology. Such institutions include education, the family, religion, the legal system, the party-political system and the mass media. The dominant ideology is thus represented as both natural and neutral. As a result it becomes almost unseen, taken-for-granted. See DOMINANT DIS-COURSE; ELITE; HEGEMONY; POWER ELITE.

Ideology An ideology is a system of ideas and beliefs about human conduct which has normally been simplified and manipulated in order to obtain popular support for certain actions, and which is usually emotive in its reference to social action. Karl Marx (1818–83) used the term to apply to any form of thought which underpins the social structure of a society and which consequently upholds the position of the ruling CLASS. French philosopher Louis Althusser (b. 1918), drawing on the work of Marx, sees ideology as being an unconscious set of VALUES and beliefs which provide frames for our thinking which help make sense of the world.

Ideology can often be found to be hiding (or hidden) under terms such as 'common sense' – the 'common sense view', which Marx would claim was merely the view of the ruling class translated by repeated usage through channels of communication into wisdom as apparently natural as fresh air – a process sometimes referred to as *mystification.* Within society there may be a variety of contending ideologies at play, representing different sets of social interests, each seeking to extend recognition and acceptance of its way of making sense of the world, its own capacity to give order and explain social existence. LANGUAGE itself may be seen not as a neutral MEDIUM but as ideological, thus in its use ensuring that ideology is present in all discourses.

Each may seek to become the dominant ideology and it can be argued that the capacity to make use of the channels of MASS COMMUNICATION is crucial to either achieving or maintaining this position. The use of the media in this respect is the focus of much media research and analysis.

German-British sociologist Karl Mannheim (1893–1947) in *Ideology and Utopia* (1936) distinguishes between ideas which defend existing interests, the STATUS QUO, which he terms *ideologies* and ideas which seek to change the social order, which he termed *utopias.* See CONSENSUS; CULTURE; CULTURAL APPARATUS; DISCOURSE; DOMINANT DISCOURSE; HEGEMONY; IDEOLOGICAL STATE APPARATUSES; MALE-AS-NORM.

Ideology of detachment See IMPARTIALITY.

Idiot salutations See PHATIC LANGUAGE.

Ido An international LANGUAGE devised by Louis Conturat in 1907. It was an offspring of the more famous ESPERANTO, and a simplification of it.

ILR Independent Local Radio, under the aegis of the IBA. See 'BROADCASTING IN THE 90S'; COMMERCIAL RADIO.

Image A likeness; a representation; a visualization. The term can have several meanings depending on the context in which it is used. It may refer to a visual representation of reality such as is seen in a photograph; it can also refer to a mental, imaginative conception of an individual, event, location or object as, for example, one conjures up an image of a character in a novel. The image does not merely reproduce, it interprets; it has added to it certain *meanings*. The writer, artist, architect, photographer and ADVERTISING image-maker all use assemblies of signs in order to represent or suggest states of mind, or abstractions. Van Dyck's equestrian portrait of Charles 1 shows the monarch on a noble steed against a background suffused with dramatic light. All the details of this painting converge to create an image of *kingship*, thus a process of symbolization has taken place.

The purpose of image-creation obviously varies, but all images are devised in order to evoke responses of one kind or another, usually emotional. Images often serve as psychological triggers effecting responses which are not always easy to articulate. Advertisements regale us with images of the good life; they play upon our perceived needs (See HIDDEN NEEDS; MASLOW'S HIERARCHY OF NEEDS). Image is also something we present of ourselves – our best face, the way we want the world to perceive us. Politicians work at their images more than most, and these are portrayed to fit in with the image appropriate to a public figure whose aim is to impress voters by his or her qualities of leadership and trustworthiness. Sometimes we talk of a person whose image 'has slipped', which seems to indicate the connection between image and performance (See IMPRESSION MANAGEMENT) and that it relates to an ideal. For the artist, whatever his or her MEDIUM, imagery is central to expression. It is a part of STYLE and a key to the construction of MEANING. See METAPHOR.

IMAX   Canadian FILM projection system developed in the 1970s, notable for the vastness of its screen for 70 mm film; first installed in the UK in 1983 at the newly opened National Museum of Photography, Film and Television in Bradford. The Bradford screen is 45 feet high and 62 feet wide. The whole IMAX system cost some £250,000. See OMNIMAX.

Immediacy   A prime NEWS VALUE in western newspaper, RADIO and TELEVISION news gathering and presentation. At the centre of decision-making and of news control is the time factor, usually related to the daily cycle. In his article 'Newsmen and their time machine', in *British Journal of Sociology* (September 1977), Philip Schlesinger points out that in industrialized societies an exceptional degree of precision of timing is necessary in our working lives. 'Especially noteworthy are those who operate communication and transport systems . . . Newsmen . . . are members of a stopwatch culture'.

Immediacy shapes and structures the approach to news gathering. The report of an event must be as close to the event as possible, and ideally the event should be reported as it happens. The pure type of immediacy would be the live broadcast. News, says Schlesinger, is 'hot' when it is most immediate. 'It is "cold"', and old, when it can no longer be used during the newsday in question'. Immediacy is not only a vital factor in the selection of a story for treatment; it also helps fashion that treatment. *Pace* is what counts in presentation, especially in TV news where the priority is to keep the audience 'hooked'.

The danger with such emphasis on immediacy is that news tends to be all foreground and little background, all events and too little context, all current happening and too little concentration on the historical and cultural background to such events. Schlesinger rounds off his article by saying that it is plausible to argue 'that the more we take note of news, the less we can be aware of what lies behind it'. See EFFECTS OF THE MASS MEDIA.

Impact of the mass media   See EFFECTS OF THE MASS MEDIA.

Impartiality   Just as Professor Stuart Hall doubts the existence, in media terms, of OBJECTIVITY, so Philip Schlesinger, in a remarkable study of the workings of BBC News, doubts the possibility of impartiality. Between 1972 and 1976, Schlesinger, now Head of the Division of Sociology at Thames Polytechnic, had a unique research opportunity to conduct in the newsrooms of Broadcasting House and the Television Centre, London, fieldwork which attempted 'to grasp how the world looks from the point of view of those studied' – the reporters, correspondents, editors and managing editors in the most prestigious media organization in the world. He interviewed over 120 BBC news staff and spent 90 days in observation. His findings were published in *Putting 'Reality' Together. BBC News* (UK: Constable, 1978; Methuen/University Paperback, with new Preface, 1987).

Several keywords framed the basic principles of news production: *balance, objectivity, responsibility, fairness,* freedom from *bias*; and these were, in the 'ordinary' discourse of newsmen' for the most part 'interchangeable'. They could be gathered under one banner, that of *impartiality*, what Schlesinger refers to as the central mediating factor in news processing at the BBC, 'the linchpin of the BBC's ideology'. Schlesinger found this a notion 'saturated with political and philosophical implications' and classifies the 'ideology of detachment' as in essence an example of 'latter-day Mannheimianism'. In *Ideology and Utopia* (UK: Routledge & Kegan Paul, 1936), Karl Mannheim explained how a 'socially unattached intelligentsia' could play a role in society which was *above* all conflict, capable of representing to society all relevant views. It is a theory which has regularly been condemned as an unrealistic dream but the doctrine has remained persistently attractive: by virtue of their education, argued Mannheim, the intellectuals, *déclassés*, are exposed to the 'influence of opposing tendencies in social reality'; thus theirs is the potential to improve social integration, to produce a new CONSENSUS by means of 'dynamic mediation'.

The theory implies that it is possible to view the world in a *value-free* way, and act accordingly. Schlesinger calls value-freedom 'a myth', yet one which in terms of the BBC's aspiration to impartiality, to being above the fray, 'is believed by those who propagate it' as well as being 'essential for public consumption'. Such beliefs, Schlesinger argues, 'anchor news production in the status quo'. What the BBC produces as news is 'structurally limited by the organization's place in Britain's social order' and the main consequence of that position is that 'the outputs of broadcasting are, in general, supportive of the existing social order'.

Imperialism in information systems See MEDIA IMPERIALISM.

Impression management Technique of self-presentation defined by Erving Goffman in *The Presentation of Self in Everyday Life* (US: Anchor, 1959; UK: Penguin, 1971). Because most social interaction requires instant judgements, alignments and behaviour, the individual must be able rapidly to convey impressions of him/herself to others, highlighting favourable aspects, concealing others. Goffman argues that impression management has the character of drama: all social ROLES, he believes, are, in a sense, *performances* in which it is important to set a scene and rehearse a role, and this means coordinating activities with others in the 'drama'. Thus we put up a *front,* 'that part of the individual's performance which regularly functions in a general and fixed fashion to define the situation for those who observe the performance'.

Our formal, public selves Goffman calls *front region* and our more informal, relaxed selves, *back region*. Indeed Goffman believes that all our roles depend upon the performer having a back region; equally all front region roles rely upon keeping the audience out of the back regions.

Teams as well as individuals operate in front and back regions: in a restaurant, for example, the front-stage conduct of the team of waiters and other staff subscribes to formal rules and rituals, even a *mystique*. Behind the scenes, however, the performers relax. The need to unify in sustaining an expected version of real-ity – of smartness, politeness, professionalism – gives way to a back-stage reality where individual differences can be freely aired without letting the team, or the performance, down.

Independent Television franchises See FRANCHISES FOR INDEPENDENT TELEVISION.

Index Short for **Index librorum prohibitorum,** a list of proscribed books. The Council of Trent, in attempting to turn the tide against the Protestant Reformation, drew up a set of rules about what Roman Catholics should, or rather should not, read. In accordance with these rules the *Index* was published by authority of Pope Paul IV in 1559. In its current form, the Index is a list not only of works prohibited in their entirety to the faithful but also of works not to be read unless or until they are corrected.

The **Index expurgatorius** or Expurgatory Index (1571), specifies passages to be expurgated in works otherwise permitted. Appropriately, the word has been used in the title of the UK magazine whose chief aim is to counter such repressions of information and expression, *Index on Censorship*.

Index as a sign See SIGN.

Indicators In INTERPERSONAL COMMUNICATION the means by which one communicator conveys his/her attitude and response to another – feelings of attraction or rejection, of evaluation or esteem of the other person. Proximity, for example, is an ideal indicator of liking (unless, of course, it becomes a GESTURE of threat or intimidation). Also important as indicators are frequent EYE CONTACT, body orientations and spontaneous gestures. See PROXEMICS; REGULATORS.

Inductive reasoning Involves the drawing of conclusions from collected observations and data – from evidence. The acceptability of the conclusions drawn depends upon whether or not the type and quantity of evidence can reasonably be said to support them. It is important to recognize how limited such conclusions may be. Someone unfamiliar with traffic observing the flow of traffic between 10.00 a.m. and 2.00 p.m. for one week, in a busy street, for example, may note that when the red traffic light is illuminated cars in front of the light stop. He/she may conclude that the illumination of the red traffic light caused the cars to stop, certainly at the times at which he/she was observing the traffic. The observer, however, could not reasonably draw conclusions about, for example, why this was the case or whether or not this occurred at times when he/she was not observing the traffic; that would require further investigation.

Deductive reasoning involves the application of an already accepted generalization or generalizations to an individual case. It is the reverse of inductive reasoning. Someone who has accepted, for example, that drinking too much alcohol before driving is dangerous might as a consequence regulate the intake of alcohol at a party if he/she were driving home – a decision based upon deductive reasoning. See EMPIRICAL; HYPOTHESIS.

Inferential structure In their book *Demonstrations and Communications* (UK: Penguin, 1970), J. Halloran, P. Elliot and G. Murdock describe the inferential structure of the news-gathering, news-presentation operation as '. . . a process of simplification and interpretation which structures the meaning given to the story around its original NEWS VALUE'. Past experience, standard practice, proven routines are constantly 'in gear': the fresh news event passes through the structure of inferences – clues, signals, generalizations, frames – into the finished product.

Inflection The patterns of alteration or modulation in the pitch of a person's voice.

Influence of the mass media See EFFECTS OF THE MASS MEDIA.

Informatics The organization of the equipment for the new generation of information services: the investment, research, manufacturing and marketing activities which result in a society being provided with the means to collect and distribute information. See INFORMATION TECHNOLOGY.

Information aggression Term used by Russian leader Mikhail Gorbachev in a speech in Moscow, February 1987, to an international audience; meaning how information is often used as an assault weapon to win political points.

Information gaps Several researchers have been interested in the inequality in the distribution of information among different GROUPS in societies. Such inequalities are mostly the result of educational or social CLASS differences with the advantage being enjoyed by the better-educated and those in the higher-status groups. The role of the mass media in creating, widening or narrowing information gaps has been the concern of a considerable amount of research. There will be differing kinds of gaps depending on the nature of the information.

Gaps may close or widen with time. It had been thought that the increasing flow of information from the mass media might help to decrease such gaps, but the evidence here is mixed. Whilst the media may have the potential to close gaps it seems that an advantage remains with those with most communication potential and new gaps open as old ones are closed.

Whilst information gaps may exist between groups within societies, the greatest inequalities seem to be those between more developed and the less developed societies. Most of the channels of global communication are controlled by the former. This means that not only have they the potential to acquire and disseminate more information, but that also they have the potential for considerable control of the flow and content of the information going to the less developed countries.

Information gaps can also be generated, reinforced or modified through patterns of INTERPERSONAL COMMUNICATION. See DIFFUSION; J-CURVE; MEDIA IMPERIALISM.

Information Society The Japanese were the first to apply the tag to this stage in the growth of the industrial era in which information is becoming the central and most significant 'commodity'. Through the development of computers and associated electronic systems, such aspects of national and international life as CLASS relationships, government, economics and diplomacy are being visualized as functions of information transfer. Indeed we are at the point when information and wealth are practically one and the same thing. With the development of satellite surveillance it is now possible for a country highly advanced in INFORMATICS, to know more about the topography of, say, a Third World country than that country's own government does. And information is power which crosses national boundaries with greater ease than invading armies.

Information is not only a commodity, but a social and cultural resource, raising questions of social allocation and control, with such associated problems as privacy, access, commercial privilege and public interest. The power game has moved into an information phase, argues Anthony Smith in *The Geopolitics of Information* (UK: Faber, 1980), with the industrial nations 'tooling up' for a vast process of rewiring society. 'A kind of scramble for media is under way,' Smith writes, 'on a scale similar to the first arms race of the post-war era.' See COMMODITIZATION OF INFORMATION; MEDIA IMPERIALISM.

Information technology (IT) Microelectronics plus computing plus telecommunications equals IT. Its formal definition is framed as follows in a UK Department of Industry publication (1981) for Information Technology Year (1982): 'The acquisition, processing, storage and dissemination of vocal, pictorial, textual and numerical information by a micro-electronics-based combination of computing and telecommunications.'

The booklet states that as many as 65% of our working population now earn their living in 'what may be broadly classified as information occupations', from banking to education, from defence to police, from manufacturing to transport and space exploration. The possibilities of IT are endless if there is the cash to pay for the hardware, the software and the service: laser beams carrying 30 channels of speech in digital form; cordless telephones; scanning devices which read the printed word out to the blind; telephones for the deaf; voice recognition; typewriters which read your typing back to you, and programmes which translate one LANGUAGE into another. See TECHNOLOGY OF THE MEDIA.

Information Technology Advisory Panel (ITAP) Report on Cable Systems See CABLE TELEVISION.

'Informization' of society The collecting, editing and distribution of information is now a key element in all economies. The term comes from a French governmental report by S. Nora and A. Minc, *L'Informatisation de la Societé* (Paris, 1978) and indicates how, more and more, governmental, economic and cultural processes have come to depend upon a set of companies, institutions and systems which make up the information sector. See CONGLOMERATES; INFORMATION SOCIETY; MEDIA IMPERIALISM.

Infra-red photography Permits the viewer to see what the eye cannot see, in what is known as the actinic infra-red range, and is used in aerial photography, astronomy, and medical and forensic photography. See HOLOGRAPHY; ULTRA-VIOLET/FLUORESCENT PHOTOGRAPHY.

Inheritance factor The TV programme which captures a viewer's attention paves the way for the programmes that follow it. Catch the viewer at 7.30 p.m. with *Eastenders* and he or she is likely to stay watching the same CHANNEL for the rest of the evening.

Some commentators have complained that because certain types of programmes enjoy greater popularity than others, each channel runs the same sort of programme in the same time slot, leading to an over-standardization of programme content and form. See FORMULA BROADCASTING; BUTTON APATHY; SCHEDULING.

Initial Teaching Alphabet (i.t.a.) System designed to teach the early stages of reading, consisting of 44 letters and code symbols; the intention of the i.t.a. is to give closer phonetic regularity than traditional spelling.

Inmarsat International Maritime Satellite Organization. By 1985 there were some 3500 ships using the Inmarsat communications NETWORK. Both TELEX and TELEPHONE calls are bounced off geostationary satellites. The service has been such a success that Inmarsat has plans to provide international air travellers with full telecom facilities from their aircraft seat. See CELLULAR RADIO.

Innovation An innovation is an idea, practice or object perceived as new by individuals or GROUPS. Much research has been conducted into discovering the role of communication processes in achieving the DIFFUSION, rejection or adoption, and INTEGRATION of innovations.

Inoculation effect In the processes of persuasion, a relative immunity in an audience may be induced by 'inoculation' prior to a concerted exercise in persuasion: if an audience is forewarned about an attempt to persuade it, when that attempt occurs, they are more capable of defence against influence.

Insert shot In FILM, close-up inserted into a dramatic scene, usually for the purpose of giving the audience a view of what the character on the screen is seeing, such as a newspaper headline, the title of a book, a cigarette, a letter, etc. See SHOT.

Institution The term institution is generally applied to patterns of behaviour which are established, approved and usually of some permanence. Such patterns of behaviour are normally rational and conscious. The term can be applied to both the abtract (e.g. religion) and the concrete (e.g. media organizations) concept of an institution. The patterns of behaviour to which this term is applied can vary, from simple routine acts to large complexes of standardized procedures governing social relationships in a large section of the population.

All institutions embody a particular complex of NORMS, VALUES, ROLES and role structures. They also, often, evolve relationships with other institutions. FUNCTIONALIST analysis tends to represent institutions as performing the functions essential to the maintenance of society and views them as being mutually sustaining. Recent research has, however, pointed to the relative autonomy of most institutions and to the often conflicting goals to be found within them. Much research into the mass media has concentrated upon their corporate role as major social institutions; upon their norms, values and relationships with other major social institutions.

Insult signals Generally defined as those signals which are *always* insulting, no matter what the context in which the signal has been made; though these do vary substantially between nationality and nationality. Such signals may communicate disinterest, boredom, superiority, contempt, impatience, rejection and mockery. **Dirt signals** appear to be universal and refer to human and animal waste products on the basis, presumably, of: cleanliness – good; filth – bad. Picking the nose with forefinger and thumb in Syria means 'Go to blazes' while in the UK a GESTURE of derision is to pull an imaginary lavatory chain at the same time as holding the nose. In Greece, pushing the flat of the palm towards another's face is the ultimate insult signal. Called the *moutza,* the signal represents a thrusting of filth into the opponent's face, and has ancient roots (See RELIC GESTURES).

Beyond the insult signal is the **Threat signal,**

an attempt to intimidate without, necessarily, recourse to blows. Threat signals are mostly violence substitutes rather than prologues to violence, because such signals are checked, held back and distance maintained between threatener and threatened. Also, such signals are often redirected – to the insulter's own body, such as mock strangulation.

Of **Obscene signals**, the phallic-displaying gesture is as old as civilized man. The Romans for example referred to the middle finger as the impudent and obscene finger. The more expressive forearm jerk is common throughout the western world and is employed particularly in France, Italy and Spain as a threatening insult by one male towards another; however, in the UK, the signal tends to be more a crude sexual comment than a direct insult. It is the V-Sign, with palm facing the communicator, which is the most potent gestural insult in Britain along with its single-finger variant. See NON-VERBAL BEHAVIOUR: REPERTOIRE.

* D. Morris, *Manwatching: A Field Guide to Human Behaviour* (UK: Jonathan Cape, 1977).

Integration New ideas and behaviour vary in the degree to which they are incorporated – to which they are integrated – into the continuing operations and way of life of members of a SOCIAL SYSTEM or sub-system. The term **communication integration** is used to describe the degree to which the members/units of a social system are interconnected by INTERPERSONAL COMMUNICATION channels.

In-tel-sat Acronym for International Telecommunications Satellite (Consortium), an organization of over 70 member nations formed to control and promote work in global communications by means of satellites. See SATELLITE TRANSMISSION.

Intensity Some news stories receive much more concentrated, more intense, coverage by the media than others, and tend to dominate or stifle competing stories. Intensity, if appropriate in terms of timing, and if given the promise of FREQUENCY, abetted by CONSISTENCY of coverage, equals *influence,* at least in the sense of making audiences aware.

General elections provide useful illustrations of the intensity of media coverage. National attention is focused on the event (usually more on personalities than ISSUES) and the legitimacy of the event is given substance and flavour. In contrast, local elections derive neither substance nor flavour from the media, who largely ignore them; and grassroots democracy rather takes a belly-flop. See EFFECTS OF THE MASS MEDIA; NEWS VALUES.

Interaction The reciprocal action and communication, verbal or non-verbal, between two or more individuals, or two or more social GROUPS.

Interactive television Process by which TV viewers are enabled, through TELEPHONE link or cable and computer terminal, to respond to programmes and to questions put to them by programme companies.

This mode of instant FEEDBACK has immense potential and the social, political and cultural ISSUES are far-reaching. First, only those able to afford the necessary press-button equipment will be able to register a 'vote' or opinion. Unlike the absolute secrecy of the ballot box, that vote is *recordable;* that is, computers will be able to bank the response patterns of individuals and GROUPS.

The almost obsessive use of opinion polls in recent years will be accelerated by interactive TV: instant referendums on vital matters could become standard practice; even more intensely than at present, TV would be the central focus of election campaigns – what has been termed *electronic democracy* will have come of age.

The case *for* interactive TV is that it has potential for a more regular and sustained consultation process between the public and those who sell to them, offer them services, or govern them and thus can engender a greater sense of involvement in decision-making.

Interception of Communications Act, 1985 A London antique dealer, Mr James Malone, charged the British government with unlawful PHONE-TAPPING in a case which was heard by the European Court of Rights. On 2 August 1984 the Court found in his favour, declaring that UK law covering interception was 'Obscure and open to differing interpretations'. A White Paper outlining the Government's response to the Euro court's finding was published in February 1985 and the Interception of Communications Act was on the Statute book by July. 'Intentional interception' became punishable by a maximum of two years imprisonment and a £2000 fine. However, the Act exempts official interception from prosecution provided that the Government and its agencies adhere to a set of administrative practices – in essence, the obtaining of warrants before interceptions can be made. Prevention and detection of 'serious crime' are the criteria for warrant-issue to the police and customs and excise. 'Interests of national security' suffice for an MI5 warrant.

The European Court ruled that a system of redress be instituted for anyone subject to a phone-tap. The Act ignores the ruling: Section 9 declares inadmissable any evidence which 'tends to suggest' that a government official has been directly involved in tapping, whether lawful or not.

Inter-cultural invasion (and the mass media) In recent years several media researchers have sought to assess the degree, if any, to which the mass media in developing countries have reflected the VALUES of economically dominant countries like the US and as a result have undermined traditional values – a process which J.O. Boyd-Barrett in 'Cultural dependency and the mass media', in M. Gurevitch, T. Bennett, J. Curran, and J. Woollacott, eds., *Culture, Society and the Media,* (UK: Methuen, 1982), calls 'Inter-cultural invasion'.

The focus for concern has been the use of the media in aiding modernization by helping to undermine those traditional values felt inimical to western style economic development and in producing a *cultural* dependency which could be said to reflect the *economic* and *political* dependency on the west. Researchers have pointed to the extent of ownership of national media by international interests, international ADVERTISING corporations and the sale of Western European and US, TV programmes to developing countries. Concern is now focused upon the effects of 'global' television, which may result from SATELLITE TRANSMISSION. See MEDIA IMPERIALISM.

Interights An international human rights law centre, based in London, whose primary function is to provide advice on human rights law and procedure, and to help individuals and non-governmental organizations in bringing cases before tribunals such as the European Commission and Court of Human Rights. Interights supports civil liberties lawyers in defending victims of human rights abuse.

Interior monologue See STREAM OF CONSCIOUSNESS.

Internalization See IDENTIFICATION.

International Broadcasting Trust Comprises over 60 member organizations – development agencies, churches, environmental GROUPS, trade unions, educational bodies, race and immigration bodies – whose common concern is to use TV as a means of promoting greater discussion in the UK about its relationships with developing countries and the world community. The intention is that the programmes will be an educational resource as well as informative to the general public, and the Trust publishes and distributes literature to enable educational groups using the programmes to follow up the ISSUES raised in greater depth. The Trust was formally established as an educational charity on 2 July 1982 and its launch programme was *Lucky You, Lucky Me* shown on CHANNEL FOUR in November 1982, in which Jonathan Dimbleby took a critical look at public and mass media attitudes to the developing countries.

International Commission for the Study of Communication Problems – Report, 1980 See MACBRIDE COMMISSION.

International Federation of Journalists (IFJ) Organization whose testament is that 'the promotion of a new world order of infor-mation is first and foremost the business of journalists and the trade unions and not of states, governments or any pressure group of whatever kind'. The IFJ is made up of chiefly western journalists and was formed to monitor and counteract moves through Unesco to 'impose', through governments, a NEW WORLD INFORMATION ORDER. See MACBRIDE COMMISSION; MEDIA IMPERIALISM; WORLD PRESS FREEDOM COMMITTEE.

International Programme for the Development of Communication IPDC See MACBRIDE COMMISSION; MEDIA IMPERIALISM; NEW WORLD INFORMATION ORDER.

Interpersonal communication Describes any mode of communication, verbal or non-verbal, between two or more people. While the term MEDIO COMMUNICATION has often been used to specify interpersonal communication at a greater than face-to-face distance, such as when the communication is by letter or TELEPHONE, it is most useful to keep the definition as wide and unprescriptive as possible. The reader is referred to the following main entries: COMMUNICATION; COMMUNICATION, NON-VERBAL; DECODE; ENCODE; GESTURE; GROUPS; INTRAPERSONAL COMMUNICATION; KINESICS; LANGUAGE (Collective entry); MEANING; PROXEMICS; ROLES; TOUCH. *See also:* APACHE SILENCE; BARNLUND'S TRANSACTIONAL MODEL OF COMMUNICATION, 1970; BARRIER SIGNALS; BATON SIGNALS; CENTRALITY; CHANNEL; CIVIL INATTENTION; CLIQUE; CLOTHING SIGNALS; COCKTAIL PARTY PROBLEM; CODES; COMMUNICATION, FUNCTIONS; CONFRONTATION DRESSING; CONGRUENCE THEORY; CONSUMPTION BEHAVIOUR; COSMOPOLITE AND LOCALITE CHANNELS; CUT-OFF; DEFENSIBLE SPACE; DEFENSIVE COMMUNICATION; DIFFERENTIAL PERCEPTION; DIFFUSION; DISCOURSE; DISEMBODIMENT; DISQUALIFYING COMMUNICATION; DISSONANCE; DYAD; ENCOMPASSING SITUATION; ETHOS; EUPHEMISM; EYE CONTACT; FEEDBACK; GENDER SIGNALS; GSR; HOMOPHILY; HETEROPHILY; IMPRESSION MANAGEMENT; INDICATORS; INSULT SIGNALS; INTEGRATION; INTERACTION; INTERVENING VARIABLES; LANGUE AND PAROLE; LAW OF THE TOTAL SITUATION; LEVELLING, SHARPENING, ASSIMILATION; LOOKING BEHAVIOUR; MESSAGE; METASIGNALS; NETWORK; NOISE; NON-VERBAL BEHAVIOUR; REPERTOIRE; NORMS; OPINION LEADER; OVERHEARING; PARA-SOCIAL INTERACTION; PERSONAL SPACE; PHATIC LANGUAGE; POSTULATES OF COMMUNICATION; POSTURAL ECHO; PRAGMATICS; PRINCIPLE OF LEAST EFFORT; PRIVATE CUES; PUBLIC CUES; REGULATORS; RELIC GESTURES; RUMOUR; SALUTATION DISPLAY; SHORTFALL SIGNALS; SIGNIFICANT OTHERS; SIGNIFICANT SYMBOLIZERS; SLIDER; SOCIODRAMA; SOCIOMETRICS; SPATIAL ZONES; TELEPATHY; TIE-SIGNS; ZONES.

Interpretant C.S. Peirce (1839–1914), generally

regarded as the founder of the American strand of SEMIOLOGY/SEMIOTICS, used the word *interpretant* in his model defining the nature of a SIGN, which 'addresses somebody, that is, it creates in the mind of that person an equivalent sign, or perhaps a more developed sign. The sign which it creates I call the *interpretant* of the first sign. The sign stands for something, *its object*' (from J. Zeman, 'Pierce's theory of signs' in T. Sebeok ed; *A Perfusion of Signs;* US: Indiana University Press, 1977).

The *interpretant,* then, is a mental concept produced both by the sign itself and by the user's experience of the object. Peirce's sign and interpretant find a parallel in the *signifier* and *signified* of the father of the European strand of semiology, Swiss linguist Ferdinand de Saussure (1857–1913).

Intersubjectivity This term is used by Tim O'Sullivan, John Hartley, Danny Saunders and John Fiske in *Key Concepts in Communication* (UK: Methuen, 1983) to refer to those aspects of an individual's reactions to a MESSAGE which he or she shares with members of the CULTURE or SUB-CULTURE to which he or she belongs. The connotative and ideological orders of the meaning of signs are usually shared as they stem from cultural forces. See CONNOTATION; IDEOLOGY.

Intervening variables (IV) Those influences which come between the encoder, the MESSAGE and the decoder are referred to as *intervening variables,* mediating factors which influence the way a message is perceived and the nature and degree of its impact. Time of day, mood, state of health can all constitute intervening variables.

More importantly family, friends, peer GROUPS, respected persons, opinion leaders, etc. are capable of significant MEDIATION between what we are told and what we accept, believe or reject. Whilst people may act as intervening variables between media messages and audience, the media may also be intervening variables between people: the TV socializes the child as do parents. It also 'comes between them' in the sense that it can stop interaction, modify it, improve it, re-channelize it (not to mention the DISSONANCE it might cause in a family when, for example, it provokes controversy). See S-IV-R MODEL OF COMMUNICATION.

Interviews Though there are many forms of interview and many different reasons for conducting them, the common goal is that of gaining more information from and understanding of other people, through a planned process of questions and answers. PRESS and TELEVISION journalists use interviews as a means of collecting information and opinions. Interviews can be used to provide entertainment as in chat shows; they are the most common means of selecting people for jobs or students for courses; they are a major method of data collection in the social sciences.

The kinds of questions widely used in interviews are: (1) *open* questions; these are broad, usually unstructured and often simply introduce the topic under discussion in a way that allows the interviewee a good deal of freedom in answering; (2) *closed* questions; these are restrictive, offering a fairly narrow range of answers from which the interviewee must choose; (3) *primary* questions; these introduce the subject or each new aspect of the subject under discussion; (4) *subsidiary* or *secondary* questions; these follow up the answers to primary questions; (5) *neutral* questions; these do not suggest any preferred response and (6) *leading* questions which suggest a preferred response and are not normally used in research interviews.

Intimacy at a distance See PARA-SOCIAL INTERACTION.

Intrapersonal communication That which takes place within ourselves: our inner monologues; our reflection upon ourselves, upon our relationships with others and with our environment. What goes on inside our heads (or hearts) is conditioned and controlled by our *self-view* and that self-view has emerged from a vast complex of past and present influences – on the view we perceive others holding about us, on our past achievements and failures, on memory-banks of good, bad and neutral actions and impressions.

Our concept of self *interacts* with our view of the world. Having been formed by experience, it is shaped and modified by subsequent experience, though rarely straightforwardly. The psychologist, for example, speaks of the *extravert* personality and the *introvert* personality. On the face of it, the extravert is characterized by a confidence in public *performance* which may indicate inner assurance, while the introvert may demonstrate a public shyness or guardedness reflective of inner uncertainty. However, the outer confidence may well be a *role,* as in a play or performance, which may conceal an altogether different inner image or performance. The so-called introvert, on the other hand, may, through the richness or assurance of inner resources, have opted out of public role playing, or selected the role of introvert as a public defence mechanism.

Arising from both inner and outer stimuli, intrapersonal communication is a convergence, a coming-together, of both. A piece of music stirs in us, perhaps, previous memories; these memories – of people or places – may join with immediate impressions of events to create an ongoing DISCOURSE, between ourselves in the past – our former selves – and our selves, perceiving and perceived, in the present.

Through intrapersonal communication we come to terms (or fail to come to terms) with ourselves and with others. Through it we create bridges or battlements; we make connections or we sever them; we open ourselves up or we establish self-defences.

Most of us, it is important to note, are, as it were, on our own side. We use intrapersonal communication as a means of self-assurance, of confidence-building or confidence-maintenance as well as self-discovery (or indeed self-delusion). It is what makes us unique.

* G. Burton and R. Dimbleby, *Between Ourselves* (UK: Edward Arnold, 1988).

Iras Infra-red astronomy satellite; a cooperative venture by the US, Holland and the UK, Iras was launched in 1983 from California into polar orbit 560 miles above the earth, circling the earth every 103 minutes. It sent back data a thousand times more detailed than any previously obtained by astronomers, including evidence of an embryo planet system in the Vega nebula. Iras ran for a 100 days longer than expected, shutting down on 25 November, having furnished enough data to keep researchers occupied for several years.

Issues Those social, cultural, economic or political concerns or ideas which are, at any given time, considered important, and which are the source of debate, controversy or conflict. What is an issue for one social GROUP may not be considered such by another. Environmental issues have arguably grown out of middle CLASS concern, in particular among the younger, often college-educated members of that class.

Of vital interest to the student of communications are such questions as: how are issues disseminated? Why do some issues 'make it' to the national forum of debate while others fall by the wayside? What are the characteristics of a 'successful' issue? What prolongs an issue? What factors, other than the resolution of the issue, are involved in the decline of an issue? And, running through all these questions, what role do the processes of communication play in the definition, shaping and promoting of issues?

The media are, of course, themselves an issue, like all institutions wielding power and influence and the issues involving the role of the media in society are meat and drink for the student of communication. This has been given due acknowledgment in communication and media study syllabuses. Among the many issues of current interest involving the media are: CENSORSHIP; media ownership and control, including the role of CONGLOMERATES in world wide media activity; the part played by the media in the REINFORCEMENT of the STATUS QUO in society; in SOCIALIZATION; in their claim to represent the so-called FOURTH ESTATE; in policing the boundaries of social and political dissent and in being largely unquestioning advocates of the capitalist consumer-orientated society. See DEVIANCE AMPLIFICATION; EFFECTS OF THE MASS MEDIA; LABELLING PROCESS; McCOMBS and SHAW AGENDA SETTING MODEL OF MEDIA EFFECTS, 1976; MEDIA CONTROL; MAINSTREAMING; MEDIA IMPERIALISM; NEWS VALUES.

ITV Code See VIOLENCE ON TV: CODES OF PRACTICE.

J-Curve One focus of communications research has been the part played by personal contact in the diffusion – the spread – of information about news events featured in the mass media. The assassination of President Kennedy in 1963 and the speedy diffusion of the news of the event gave an impetus to this research. The J-Curve arose from the conclusions of B.S. Greenberg and stems mainly from his work on the Kennedy assassination when he investigated the first sources of knowledge about 18 different news events. It represents the relationship between the overall extent of awareness people have of such an event and the proportion of those learning of it through interpersonal sources.

Greenberg argues that news events can be divided into three GROUPS as regards the manner of their diffusion and the involvement of personal contact in it.

Type 1 events are important to the few people who may be affected by them but are of little concern to the general public. Such events, though reported in the media, will be most generally diffused by personal contact – the announcement of an engagement, for example.

Type 2 events such as those in typical main news stories are generally regarded as important and command the attention of a large number of people. News of such events is not likely to be passed on as information through personal contact, although they may be discussed as it will be taken for granted that most people will either know of such news or that it is not of vital interest to them. An example here might be an earthquake in another country.

Type 3 events are dramatic, important and of very wide interest. Such events, like the assassination of President Kennedy, get speedy and detailed coverage from the media. They also mobilize interpersonal sources and the proportion of those who learn of the events from personal sources will be considerably higher than for type 2 news items. Such events are, however, rare and are usually related to crisis situations. In the case of the Kennedy assassination, Greenberg and Parker found

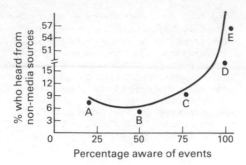

J-curve of news diffusion

that the extent and speed of diffusion was incredible: 99.8% of the US population knew of the event within five hours of its occurrence. About 50% of people first heard about it through personal sources and of these a fairly high proportion were strangers – revealing the degree of which people departed from established communication patterns.

By plotting the proportion of people eventually aware of all types of events against the proportion who heard about them first from personal contacts, it was possible to group them into five categories and the line joining these five categories was J-shaped as shown in the diagram above.

A is in type 1, B, C, D are in type 2 and E is in type 3. It can be seen that the size of the total audience increases progressively but the proportion of those receiving information from interpersonal sources does not; the proportion is higher for some of type 1 than for type 2 but highest for type 3.

Jakobson's model of communication, 1958 A linguist, Roman Jakobson is concerned with notions of By MEANING and of the internal structure of MESSAGES. His model is a double one, involving the constitutive factors in an act of communication; each of these factors is then locked on to the function it performs. Thus the constitutive factors are:

	Context	
Addresser	Message	Addressee
	Contact	
	Code	

The functions form an identically structured model:

	Referential	
	(Reality orientation of message)	
Emotive	Poetic	Conative
(Expressive)	Phatic	(Effect of a
	Metalingual	message on
		addressee)

Phatic here refers to the function of keeping the channels of communication open and Metalingual is the function of actually identifying the communication code which is being used. See COMMUNICATION MODELS; REDUNDANCY.

Janis's Law See GROUPTHINK.

Jargon The specialist speech of GROUPS of people with common identity – of religion, science, medicine, art, trade, profession, political party, etc. We can have educational jargon, cricket jargon, sociological jargon – that is, the in-LANGUAGE of people with specialist knowledge or interest. For those creating and operating jargon, it is a useful and vital means of communicating quickly between expert and expert. For those outside, jargon appears to be an unnecessarily complicated alternative to plain speaking, and a barrier to good communication. Without the growth of jargon words and expressions in Communication and Media Studies, this dictionary would not have been deemed necessary.

Jingoism Extreme and uncritical form of national patriotism. The word derives from G.W. Hunt's song, written at the time of the Russo-Turkish War (1877–78) when anti-Russian feeling in the UK was running high and Disraeli ordered the Mediterranean fleet to Constantinople: 'We don't want to fight, but by Jingo if we do/ We've got the ships, we've got the men, and got the money too.' The Falklands War of 1982 stirred up similar sentiments in Britain's popular PRESS which used LANGUAGE as declamatory and as sensational as anything employed during the Boer War, the two World Wars or the British invasion of Suez (1956). From the *Sun* ('The paper that supports our boys'): '74 Days That Shook the World!', 'Lions Who Did The Impossible – By land, sea and air, our boys never faltered in their fight against tyranny' and, on the front page, in three-inch high type, 'We've Won!' (15 July).

Johari Window The term Johari Window is derived from the first names of those who devised the model – Joseph Luft and Harrington Ingram. Effective interaction depends largely on the degree of and growth of understanding between the individuals concerned. Luft's theory of the Johari Window expounded in his work entitled *Of Human Interaction* (US: National Press Books, 1969), is a useful way in which to look at such factors of INTERPERSONAL COMMUNICATION as SELF-DISCLOSURE and FEEDBACK and the way these may influence our SELF-CONCEPT. The model, shown below, represents a way of analysing the self.

The *free area* represents the public self: information about yourself that is known to

Solicits feedback →

	Things I know	Things I don't know
Things they know	Free Area	Blind Area
Things they don't know	Hidden Area	Unknown Area

Discloses or gives feedback ↓

The Johari window

you and to others, such as your gender or race. There is a free and open exchange of information in this area.

The *blind area* contains information about yourself which is not known to you but which is known to others, such as any irritating mannerisms you might have.

The *hidden area* contains things you know about yourself but wish to keep hidden from others, such as your lack of confidence in certain situations. You normally take action to protect this area from the scrutiny of others.

The *unknown area* contains information that neither you nor others are fully conscious of but which might still be influencing your behaviour – unconscious fears, for example.

The model can be used to analyse many aspects of interpersonal behaviour. Through interpersonal communication we can come to understand ourselves better and increase the size of the free area and decrease the size of the other three. For example, self-disclosure can reduce the hidden area and increase the free area and thus enhance communication with others. Feedback from others has the potential to reduce the blind area, although possibly at some cost to SELF-ESTEEM, and further increase the free area. The degree to which we may be willing to make such changes to the relative size of the areas will of course vary with the situation and relationship. Generally speaking the greater the free area in any given situation, the easier the interaction.

Joint Committee on Censorship of the Theatre See LORD CHAMBERLAIN.

Journalese A manner of writing which employs ready-made phrases and formulas and which breeds its own short-cut LANGUAGE and clichés, rarely without some catchy word-

rhythm: 'Tory, Tory, Hallelujah' proclaimed the *Daily Express* in 1982; in 1900, their headlines were equally ringing: 'The Boers' Last Grip Loosened'. The aim is to squeeze out the most dramatic expression with the minimum use of words. The higher the pressure on space, the more pronounced the journalese. See TABLOIDESE.

Jump cutting In films, switching abruptly from one scene to another to make a dramatic point. See MONTAGE; SHOT.

Katz and Lazarsfeld's two-step flow model of mass communication and personal influence See ONE-STEP, TWO-STEP, MULTI-STEP FLOW MODELS OF COMMUNICATION.

Key-word outline A skeletal set of notes, based upon key-words or phrases, and used to remind a speaker of the content of his or her speech.

Kineme A segment or fraction of a whole communicative GESTURE; a kinetic parallel to a PHONEME (element of verbal LANGUAGE). The term was invented by Ray Birdwhistell. In *Kinesics and Context* (US: University of Philadelphia, 1970), Birdwhistell draws up a vocabulary of 60 kinemes which he found in the gestural/postural/expressive movements of American subjects. He maintains that these kinemes combine to form large units *(kinemorphs)* on the analogy of *morphemes* (or words). An example would be waving a fist or prodding the air with a finger while at the same time smiling or looking angry. See KINESICS.

Kinescope recording Technique of recording on FILM pictures originating in a TV camera.

Kinesics The study of communication through GESTURE, posture and body movement. In *Communication* (UK: Open University, Block 3, Units 7–10, 1975), the OU course team loosely classify *Kinesics* under five headings: (1) *Information* (indicating, for example, welcome or 'keep away'). (2) *Communication markers* (head and body movements to give emphasis to a spoken MESSAGE). (3) *Emotional state* (as expression of feeling). (4) *Expression of self* (in the way you sit or walk or hold yourself). (5) *Expression of relationship* (revealing attitude to others by how close you stand to someone, how you angle, tilt, shift your body in relationship to others or by the way hair or clothes are touched, a tie adjusted). See COMMUNICATION, NON-VERBAL; NON-VERBAL BEHAVIOUR: REPERTOIRE; PROXEMICS; TOUCH.

* R. Birdwhistell, *Kinesics and Context* (US: University of Philadelphia, 1970).

Kinetoscope Early form of FILM projection invented in 1887 by Thomas Alva Edison (1847–1931) and his assistant K.L. Dickson. On 14 April 1894, the first Kinetoscope Parlor was opened on Broadway, New York. The Kinetoscope was a wooden cabinet furnished with a peep-slit and an inspection lens through which a single person could view the endless loop of CELLULOID film which passed below it. It was driven by a small electric motor and illuminated by an electric lamp. Edison's lasting contribution to cinematography was his use of celluloid film 35 mm wide, with four perforations for each picture – a practice that has continued to this day. See CINEMATOGRAPHY, ORIGINS.

KISS rule The most important rule in all report writing says G. Wells in *How to Communicate* (UK: McGraw-Hill, 1978) is Keep It Short and Simple (KISS). And it is not, he believes, 'such a bad idea in other walks of life either'.

'Kite' co-orientation approach See McCOMBS AND SHAW AGENDA SETTING MODEL OF MEDIA EFFECTS, 1976.

Kuleshov effect Lev Kuleshov (1899–1970) was in at the sunrise of Russian cinema. He was FILM designer, film maker and film theorist. In 1920 he was given a workshop to study film methods with a group of students. His *Kuleshov effect,* demonstrated in 1922, proved how, by altering the juxtaposition of film images, their significance, for the audience, could be changed.

In 1929 he wrote 'The content of the shot in itself is not so important as the joining of two shots of different content and the method of their connection and their alternation.'

An experiment, aimed at proving his theory, showed a close-up of an actor playing a prisoner. This is linked to two different shots representing what the prisoner sees: first a bowl of soup, then the open door of freedom. Audiences were convinced that the expression on the man's face was different in each instance, though it was the same piece of film. See MONTAGE; SHOT.

Label libel A McLUHANISM. Marshall McLuhan, (1911–80) media guru of the 1960s, wrote of the way that the mass media stick labels on people, trap them in STEREOTYPES, typecast them, pigeon-hole them to the point that such generalizations become invidious and thus a mode of DEFAMATION

Labelling Process (and the media) Howard Becker in a classic study, *The Outsiders: Studies in the Sociology of Deviancy* (US: Free Press, 1963), analyses the process by which certain social actions or ideas and those who perform or express them come to be defined as DEVIANT; and which he calls 'the labelling process': 'The deviant is one to whom the label has successfully been applied; deviant behaviour is behaviour that people so label.'

Becker's work highlights the role that powerful social GROUPS and individuals play in defining the limits of acceptable and unacceptable behaviour, through the labelling process. He argues that certain groups within society, MORAL ENTREPRENEURS, are particularly able to shape, via the mass media, new images of deviancy and new definitions of social problems. See CRISIS DEFINITION; ISSUES.

LAN Local Area Network, a system of centralizing and coordinating the myriad forms of INFORMATION TECHNOLOGY equipment used in business; knitting together the items of office machinery which most companies have gathered piecemeal – TELEX, WORD PROCESSING, computers, VIEWDATA processes, document FACSIMILE machines, telephones. An alternative unifying system is PABX, private automatic branch exchange.

Landsat Remote-sensing satellite built and first launched by the US in 1972, with an 'open skies' policy of providing crucial data to the nations of the world; in particular to assist poor and developing countries. Landsat has been of enormous value in the detailed surveying of land surface conditions. See ANSAT; SATELLITE TRANSMISSION.

Language See APACHE SILENCE; ARBITRARINESS; BRAILLE; CENSORSHIP; CODES; COLLOQUIALISM; COMMUNICATION, ANIMAL; COMMUNICATION, NON-VERBAL; COMPETENCE; COMPUTER LANGUAGE; CONNOTATION; CULTURAL MODES; CULTURE; DEEP STRUCURE; DESIGN FEATURES; DIACHRONIC LINGUISTICS; DISCOURSE; DISPLACEMENT; DUAL-AUDIO TV; ELABORATED AND RESTRICTED CODES; EMOTIVE LANGUAGE; ESPERANTO; EUPHEMISM; EYE CONTACT; GESTUNO; GESTURE; GRAPHOLOGY; HOMOPHILY; IDO; INDICATORS; JARGON; JOURNALESE; LANGUAGE AND THOUGHT; LANGUE AND PAROLE; LEXIS; LINGUISTICS; MALE-AS-NORM; MEANING; METAPHOR; METONYMY; MILITARY METAPHOR; MORPHOLOGY; MULTI-ACTUALITY; NEOLOGISM; NEWSPEAK; NUKESPEAK; ONOMATOPOEIC; OPENNESS; PARADIGM; PARA-LINGUISTICS; PERSONAL IDIOM; PHATIC LANGUAGE; PHEREMONES; PHONEME; PHONETICS; PIDGIN ENGLISH; POSTULATES OF COMMUNICATION; PRAGMATICS; PROFANE LANGUAGE; PROSODIC SIGNALS; PROXEMICS; RECEIVED PRONUNCIATION; RAPID FADING; REDUNDANCY; REGISTER; REGULATORS; RHETORIC; SAPIR-WHORF HYPOTHESIS; SEMANTICITY; SEMANTICS; SHORTHAND; SIGN; SIGNIFICATION; SIGNIFICS; SLANG; STREAM OF CONSCIOUSNESS; STRUCTURALISM; SUMMITESE; TABOO; TABLOIDESE; 10-CODES; TOUCH; TRADITIONAL TRANSMISSION; VOLAPÜK.

Langue and Parole In his *Cours de Linguistique Générale* (1916), published after his death, Ferdinand de Saussure (1857–1914) defined *La langue,* or LANGUAGE, as a system, while *La parole* represented the actual manifestations of language in speech and writing. The former he conceived as an 'institution', a set of interpersonal rules and NORMS; the latter, events or instances, taking their MEANING from, or giving meaning to, the system.

* De Saussure, *Course in General Linguistics* (English translation; UK: Fontana/Collins, 1974).

Laser printer While a scanner translates the printed word into digital CODES for computer storage and distribution, the laser printer reverses the processes, turning the digital code back into verbal and graphic form. As an alternative to the laser beam, a liquid crystal display (LCD) strip may be used. This should eventually prove more reliable than laser printers, which have more moving parts.

LaserVision The disc alternative to the VIDEO tape, it works like a record player but with a laser beam instead of a stylus. Devised and marketed by Philips Electronics, the system has considerably higher fidelity in picture reproduction and sound than the tape system. Its disadvantage is tht LaserVision cannot be used for personal recording. Introduced into the UK in 1982, Laser Vision was given impetus as a viable alternative to VIDEO tape with the arrival of COMPACT DISC, whose excellence of sound made it a serious rival to the GRAMOPHONE record. New developments in the creation of CDVs (Compact Disc Videos), combining high fidelity sound with LaserVision-quality pictures, crowned a startling decade of electronic wizardry.

See INTERACTIVE VIDEO.

Lasswell's model of communication, 1948 A questioning device rather than an actual model of the communication process, Harold Lasswell's five-point approach to the analysis of the mass media has nevertheless given enduring service. It remains a useful first step in interpreting the transmission and reception of messages.

In 'The structure and function of communication in society' in L. Bryson, ed., *The Communication of Ideas* (US: Harper & Row, 1948) Lasswell suggests that in order to arrive at a due understanding of the MEANING systems of MASS COMMUNICATION the following sequence of questions might be put:

Who
Says *what*
In which *channel*
To *whom*
With what *effect?*

Assuming that the last question would include the notion of FEEDBACK, Lasswell's model could still do with an additional question – In what *context* (social, economic, cultural, political, aesthetic) is the communication process taking place? Also Lasswell makes no provision for INTERVENING VARIABLES, those mediating factors which have impact on the ways in which messages are received and responded to. It is useful to compare Lasswell's list to the verbal version of GERBNER'S MODEL OF COMMUNICATION, 1956. In 'Towards a general model of communication' in *Audio-Visual Communication Review*, 4 (1956), George Gerbner offers the following formula:

1 Someone
2 perceives an event
3 and reacts
4 in a situation
5 through some means
6 to make available materials
7 in some form
8 and context
9 conveying content
10 with some consequence.

See COMMUNICATION MODELS.

Law of minimal effects Point of view that the media have little or no effect in forming or modifying the attitude of audiences. See EFFECTS OF THE MASS MEDIA.

Law of the Total Situation British psychiatrist Henry Harris broaches this 'law' in *The Group Approach to Leadership* (UK: Routledge & Kegan Paul, 1949). The total situation of communication has to be borne in mind if an act of communication is to be successful and DISSONANCE avoided. What is varyingly deemed 'error of judgement', 'a communication breakdown' or a 'personality disturbance' arises from one form or another of *communicative negligence*, the nature of which Harris explores.

A person who is unable to respond to the total situation as a result of being insensitive to, or blind to, critical cues from the environment; or distorts verbal or non-verbal cues from another person; or fails to revise inappropriate assumptions regarding time and place, may find it difficult if not impossible to construct meanings that will permit him/her to function in productive ways. It is common experience that, in both interpersonal and mass communicative environments, an insensitivity to or misreading of cues within the total situation isolates and often alienates a speaker from his/her 'audience'. See BARNLUND'S TRANSACTIONAL MODEL OF COMMUNICATION.

Leadership Leaders can generally be defined as individuals within GROUPS or organizations who have influence, who provide focus, coordination and direction for the activities of the group. It may be argued that the purpose of leadership is to enable the group to function effectively and achieve its goals although in practice leadership may not always have this effect. Leadership may be and often is invested in one person but it can also be shared. Leaders may be emergent or appointed. An emergent leader is one who comes to acquire the role of leader through the process of group INTERACTION. He or she may, for example, be the person with the best ideas or communication skills. An appointed leader is one who is formally selected; leaders in work situations are often appointed to their position.

A considerable amount of research has been conducted with the aim of trying to ascertain the qualities and interpersonal skills required for effective leadership and the type of leadership needed for the optimum performance of groups or organizations. An early perspective was the *trait* approach to leadership which argues that individuals who become leaders have certain personality traits or characteristics enabling them to cope well with leadership. The suggestion is that leaders are born, not made. However, this approach has been widely criticized for being simplistic and lacking in any hard evidence to substantiate its claims.

Another approach examines the varying *styles* of leadership which may be adopted and the characteristics of each style. An example here would be represented by the work of Robert Likert. In *The Human Organization*, (US: McGraw-Hill, 1967), Likert identifies four main styles of leadership: *Autocratic, Persuasive, Consultative* and *Democratic*. Research into leadership styles tends to point towards the democratic leadership style as being superior to the others. However, the *situational* approach to leadership argues that different styles of leadership will be appropriate to different situations. Examples of key situational factors identified as determining suitable leadership styles include the nature of the task, the characteristics of the group and the organizational CULTURE. The *functional* approach to leadership focuses on identifying the behaviour needed from leaders so that particular groups and organizations may achieve their goals. The implication here is that individuals can improve their leadership abilities. One point all approaches are agreed on is that a good leader has to be a good communicator.

Leaks A time-honoured way in which governments disseminate information, often through 'sources close to' the president or the prime minister; a way of authority manipulating the media. Leaks can always be denied. Sometimes, of course, leaks are genuine, that is they are true divulgences of information which those in authority would wish to be withheld. Here, those close to the centres of power, perhaps disagreeing with decisions about to be made or affronted at the potential mismanagement of power, disclose information with the intention of causing embarrassment and, through publicity, a change of policy. See DEEP THROAT; SECRECY.

Learnability See DESIGN FEATURES.

Legislation See CINEMA LEGISLATION; BROADCASTING LEGISLATION.

Levelling, sharpening, assimilation In *The Psychology of Rumor* (US: Henry Holt, 1947), G.W. Allport and L. Postman classified these three processes which, in terms of the creation of RUMOUR, shape the form of the final MESSAGE: **levelling** is the stage in which certain important facts of a story are omitted; **sharpening** is when special emphasis is placed upon certain facts, and **assimilation** is when certain facts are incorporated into the available frame of reference.

Lexis Linguist's term to describe the vocabulary of a LANGUAGE: a unit of vocabulary is generally referred to as a **lexical** item or **lexeme**. A complete inventory of the lexical items of a language constitutes a dictionary, a **lexicon**. **Lexicography** is the overall study of the vocabulary of language, including its history.

Libel A written accusation; any malicious, defamatory publication or statement. The spoken equivalent of libel is SLANDER. Both constitute DEFAMATION and the law in the UK may impose heavy fines on those proved to have injured someone's good name. However, it is not possible to obtain legal aid in order to take, for example, a newspaper to court for libel.

Light Programme One of three BBC RADIO channels until the introduction of Radio 1 in 1967, and a change of names for the rest: Light became Radio 2, HOME SERVICE Radio 4 and THIRD PROGRAMME Radio 3. The Light Programme, for general entertainment radio, was created in the year the 2nd World War ended, 1945.

* A. Briggs, *Sound and Vision: The History of Broadcasting in the United Kingdom*, Vol. IV (UK: Oxford University Press, 1979).

Lighting cameraman In a FILM crew, the lighting cameraman or woman is responsible for the pictorial composition of the film IMAGE as well as the arrangements for lighting.

Lindup Committee Report on Data Protection, 1978 See DATA PROTECTION.

Linguistics The scientific study of LANGUAGE; a field that has seen remarkable expansion and diversification in the 20th c. particularly since the 1960s. **Diachronic** or **historical linguistics** investigates how language use has changed over time; **Synchronic linguistics** is concerned with the *state* of language at any given point in time; **General linguistics** seeks to establish principles for the study of all languages; **Descriptive linguistics** is concerned with the analysis of the characteristics of specific languages; **Contrastive linguistics** explores the contrasts between different languages or families of languages while **Comparative linguistics** concentrates on common characteristics. Among a profusion of other linguistics-related studies are *anthropological linguistics, biolinguistics, psycholin-*

guistics and *sociolinguistics*. See PARADIGM; SEMIOLOGY/SEMIOTICS; STRUCTURALISM.

* D. Crystal, *What is Linguistics?* (UK: Edward Arnold, 1974, 4th edition, 1985).

Linotype printing Invented in 1896 by German immigrant to Baltimore, US, Ottmar Mergenthaler. The operator uses a keyboard similar to that of a TYPEWRITER. As each key is depressed a brass matrix for that particular letter drops into place. When the line is complete, the row of matrices is placed over a mould and the line of type is cast, the molten lead alloy setting almost at once. See MONOTYPE PRINTING; PRINTING.

Lip sync Synchronization between mouth movement and the words on the FILM soundtrack.

Lithography PRINTING from stone, slate or a substitute such as zinc or aluminium, with greasy ink; invented in 1798 by Alois Senefelder.

Little masterpieces lasting one minute Watching a reel of British TV commercials, Italian FILM director Federico Fellini (b. 1920) gave them the ultimate compliment: 'How can these people produce such little masterpieces lasting one minute?' See ADVERTISING.

Little Red Schoolbook In the same year as the OZ TRIAL, 1971, Richard Handyside was taken to court for his publication *The Little Red Schoolbook*, which had originated in Denmark in 1969. Handyside's whole stock of books was sequestered by the police, and the book was successfully prosecuted under the Obscene Publications Act of 1959. The subject matter concerned religious education, homework, teachers' foibles, pupils' complaints, school rules, corporal punishment, streaming, sex and drugs.

See CENSORSHIP; SECTION 28.

Living newspaper A form of political PROPAGANDA drama which uses topical material and journalistic techniques in the handling of current political, cultural and social ISSUES. Usually comprises short sketches on stage, or in FILM, of a satirical nature. The form originated with the Red Army of the Soviet Union during the Revolution (1917). In the US the Federal Theater Project created a Living Newspaper Unit in 1935; around the same time the living newspaper was promoted in the UK by the Unity Theatre in St Pancras, London. It was a left-wing amateur group and specialized in what was termed 'agitational' drama. See AGIT-PROP.

Lloyd Committee Report, 1967 Following a decision by the secretary of state for education and science, Anthony Crosland, in 1965, a committee under Lord Lloyd of Hampstead was set up to enquire into the need for a National Film School in the UK. The committee's report, *National Film School*, Department of Education and Science, HMSO Code Number 27-404, recommended that a FILM school be established at the earliest possible moment and that it should provide professional training in film-making for those showing outstanding promise as film-makers. SEE NATIONAL FILM AND TELEVISION SCHOOL.

Lobbying A process in which individuals or GROUPS seek to influence those in power. Literally, the *lobby* is the passage through which MPs pass to record their votes in Parliament. Lobbying includes any device to persuade other people to give an issue their support.

Lobby Practice A book of rules of conduct written by, and abided by, parliamentary Lobby correspondents who operate from offices in the House of Commons and whose access to the centres of power is highly prized. The lobby system in the British House of Commons goes as far back as 1886. Correspondents meet daily at Downing Street, the home of the prime minister, and weekly on Thursdays in the Commons for a briefing by the PM's PRESS secretary.

The system has been subjected to considerable criticism on the grounds of its SECRECY, alleged cosiness and danger of collusion between government and privileged lobby correspondents. It has been varyingly called 'an instrument of closed government' and the 'real cancer of British journalism'. At the heart of the criticism is the fact that the lobby correspondents receive no more information than government wishes them to know; if they break the rules of Lobby Practice they know their privileges will be withdrawn.

Localite channel of communication See COSMOPOLITE AND LOCALITE CHANNELS.

Longford Committee Report on Pornography, 1972 An unofficial enquiry chaired by Lord Longford arising from a debate in the House of Lords on PORNOGRAPHY, 21 April 1971, where Longford called attention to what he considered to be mounting public concern over the great expansion of pornographic, or near pornographic, material. Among members of the enquiry were novelist Kingsley Amis, disc-jockey Jimmy Savile, the Archbishop of York, Lord Shawcross (see SHAWCROSS REPORT) and the deputy editor of the *Sunday Telegraph*, Peregrine Worsthorne.

Denying that they were 'prudes or kill-joys' the committee expressed a firm belief that, in D.H. Lawrence's stark phrase, pornography 'does the dirt on sex'. The Report – *Pornography: The Longford Report* (UK: Coronet Books, 1972) declared its antipathy to pornography 'precisely because we are *for* a loving, pleasurable and satisfying sexual expression and experience as a means of enhancing the lives of men and women', and the view that 'Some liberties have to be limited if other liberties are to be enjoyed.'

The Longford enquiry was conducted amid a blaze of publicity at a time when the conflict between free expression and control was very much in the headlines (see OZ TRIAL). Perhaps above all things, the Longford Report was concerned to protect children but its desire to translate that concern into extensive legislation would, critics believed, have restrictive effects far beyond the actual dangers posed by pornography.

See BROADCASTING STANDARDS COUNCIL; CENSORSHIP; WILLIAMS COMMITTEE REPORT ON OBSCENITY AND FILM CENSORSHIP.

Looking behaviour See CIVIL INATTENTION; EYE CONTACT.

Loony Leftism In the 1980s in the UK a mythology was created by local and national newspapers about the policies of Labour-led councils, particularly those in Greater London. 'Loony' became the catchword whenever councils such as Hackney, Haringay or Islington were mentioned; and the accusation arose from rumours that were simply untrue. For example, The *Daily Star* printed a headline story declaring that the Hackney council, in its attempt to stamp out racism and racist LANGUAGE in the borough, had banned the singing of 'Baa, Baa, Blacksheep' in playschools. Hackney had never considered banning the nursery rhyme; however, newspapers throughout the country and in the rest of the world picked on this example of 'loony Leftism'. Once in print, the story gained momentum and credence. Even Labour MPs took on board the Loony Left slogan.

A study of this campaign of DISINFORMATION was conducted by the Goldsmith's College Media Research Group and the findings summarized in an Open Space TELEVISION programme on BBC 2 (March 1988). The researchers found no substance in PRESS allegations, yet these allegations had far-reaching effects: they coloured popular perceptions of Labour-run councils; they created out of local authority leaders a set of FOLK DEVILS and managed to sever them from their natural supporters – members of their own party and of the public they were attempting to serve; and they softened the ground for central government in its onslaught on local government, particularly Metropolitan boroughs.

See EFFECTS OF THE MASS MEDIA; HEGEMONY; MYTH; SECTION 28.

Lord Chamberlain Until they were abolished in 1968 the powers of the Lord Chamberlain to censor plays in the British theatre went as far back as the reign of James I, though such powers were not defined by statute until 1737. All plays, except those performed by theatre clubs, were obliged to obtain a licence from the Lord Chamberlain's office. Each script was vetted for bad LANGUAGE, subversive ideas and any criticism of monarchy, parliament, the church, etc. In 1967 a Joint Committee on Censorship of the Theatre was set up by government. This recommended freedom for the stage 'subject to the overriding requirements of the criminal law' and that managements and dramatists should be protected from 'frivolous or arbitrary' prosecutions. These recommendations formed the basis of Labour MP George Strauss's private member's bill which became law, liberating the theatre from the Lord Chamberlain in the Theatres Act of September 1968.

Lord Vigour & Venom Nickname given to himself by Lord Northcliffe (1865–1922), one of the most powerful and intrusive PRESS BARONS.

Lowbrow See HIGHBROW.

LP See GRAMOPHONE.

MacBride Commission International Commission for the Study of Communication Problems under the chairmanship of Sean MacBride, former secretary general of the International Commission of Jurists, to hear, distil and report on evidence submitted with regard to media information interaction between the Western and Third World countries. In particular, the Commission was to report on the impact of western media technology, and the subsequent flow of western-orientated information, upon developing nations.

Set up by Unesco in 1978 with a committee of 'fifteen wise men and one woman', including Colombian novelist Gabriel Garcia Marquez and Canadian media guru Marshall McLuhan, the Commission produced a 484 page report in 1980. This urged a strengthening of Third World independence in the field of information gathering and transmission and measures to defend national cultures against the formidable one-way flow of information and entertainment from western capitalist nations, chiefly the US.

Successor to MacBride is the International Program for the Development of Communication (IPDC), coordinated by an intergovernmental council comprising representatives of 35 member states, elected by the General Conference of Unesco. See MEDIA IMPERIALISM.

Machinery of representation In modern societies, the various forms of mass media have been named the 'machinery of representation' by Professor Stuart Hall in his chapter on Media power and class power in *Bending Reality: The State of the Media* (UK: Pluto Press, 1986), edited by James Curran, Jake Ecclestone, Giles Oakley and Alan Richardson. Hall writes of the 'whole process of reporting and construction' through which reality is translated into media forms – forms which the audience is expected to recognize as reality. Yet reality, argues Hall, is not simply transcribed in 'great unassimilated lumps through our daily dose of newspapers or our nightly diet of television': 'They *all* work using language – words, text, pictures, still or moving; combining in different ways through the practices and techniques of selection, editing, montage, design, layout, format, linkage, narrative, openings, closures – to represent the world to us'. The media exercise 'the power to represent the world in certain ways. And because there are many different and conflicting ways in which meaning about the world can be constructed, it matters profoundly what and who gets represented, *what* and *who* regularly and routinely gets left out; and *how* things, people, events, relationships are represented'. See HEGEMONY; MEANING; PREFERRED READING; POWER ELITE.

Magic system See ADVERTISING.

Magnetic tape recording Magnetic tape was invented as early as 1898 by Valdemar Poulsen in Denmark. Its possibilities were ignored for decades until developed and used by the Germans during the 2nd World War (1939–45). The impact on RADIO and FILM technology was profound.

Main distribution frame (MDF) In TELEPHONE technology, exchange equipment which sorts incoming customer lines into numerical order.

Mainstreamers See ADVERTISING: MAINSTREAMERS, ASPIRERS, SUCCEEDERS AND REFORMERS.

Mainstreaming Professor George Gerbner and a team of researchers at the Annenberg School of Communications, University of Pennsylvania, have conducted a massive and ongoing research project throughout the 1980s on the impact of TELEVISION on cultural attitudes and attitude formation. A process is identified which Gerbner calls *mainstreaming*, whereby television creates a coming-together, a convergence of attitude among viewers. In their article, 'The "Mainstreaming" of America: Violence Profile No. 11' in *Journal of Communication* (Summer, 1980), Gerbner, Larry Gross, Michael Morgan and Nancy Signorielli write, 'In particular, heavy viewing may serve to cultivate beliefs of otherwise disparate and divergent groups towards a more homogeneous "mainstream" view'. The authors' opinion is that TV's images 'cultivate the dominant tendencies of our culture's beliefs, ideologies, and world views' and that the 'size' of an 'effect' is far less critical 'than the direction of its steady contribution'.

The light viewer is more likely to hold divergent views and the heavy viewer more convergent views: 'For heavy viewers, television virtually monopolizes and subsumes other sources of information, ideas and consciousness'. Convergence in this sense is to the world *as shown on television*. Returning to this theme in an article for the American magazine *Et cetera* (Spring, 1987), Gerbner writes, in 'Television's Populist Brew: The Three Bs', 'The most striking political difference between light and heavy viewers in most groups is the collapse of the liberal position as the one most likely to diverge from and challenge traditional assumptions.

The three Bs referred to in Gerbner's article are the processes by which television brings about mainstreaming. First, television *b*lurs traditional social distinctions; second, it *b*lends otherwise divergent GROUPS into the mainstream and thirdly *b*ends 'the mainstream in the direction of the medium's interests in profit, populist politics, and power'.

See EFFECTS OF THE MASS MEDIA; MEAN WORLD SYNDROME; RESONANCE; SUPRA-IDEOLOGY OF TELEVISION; SHOWBUSINESS, AGE OF.

Male-as-norm In her introduction to *Man Made Language* (UK: Routledge & Kegan Paul, 1980) Dale Spender says 'One semantic rule which we can see in operation in the language is that of the male-as-norm. At the onset it may appear to be a relatively innocuous rule for classifying the objects and events of the world, but closer examination exposes it as one of the most pervasive and pernicious rules that has been encoded.' The rules of society are manmade and so, Spender eloquently argues, is the LANGUAGE we use – the 'edification of male supremacy'. Other terms used for male-as-norm in relation to language are *Androcentralism* (male centred) and *masculist*, as well as *patriarchal*.

Maletzke's model of the mass communication process, 1963 What is so useful about the model constructed by G. Maletzke and presented in *The Psychology of Mass Communications* (West Germany: Verlag Hans Bredow-Institut, 1963) is the comprehensiveness of the factors operating upon the participants in the mass communication process and at the same time of the complex interaction of such factors.

The self-image of the communicator corresponds with that of the receiver: both act upon and are influenced by the MESSAGE which is itself constrained by the dictates of the MEDIUM chosen. To add to the complexity, the message is influenced by the communicator's IMAGE of the receiver and the receiver's image of the communicator. Maltezke's is a model suggesting that in the communication process many shoulders are being looked over: the more shoulders, the more compromises, the more adjustments.

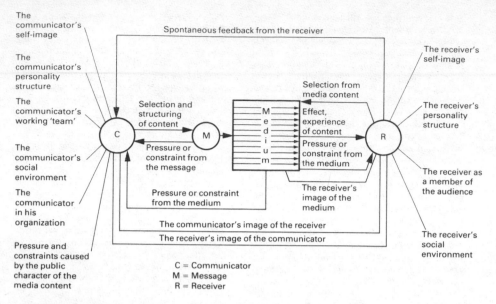

The communicator's self-image

The communicator's personality structure

The communicator's working 'team'

The communicator's social environment

The communicator in his organization

Pressure and constraints caused by the public character of the media content

Spontaneous feedback from the receiver

Selection and structuring of content

Pressure or constraint from the message

Pressure or constraint from the medium

Selection from media content

Effect, experience of content

Pressure or constraint from the medium

The receiver's image of the medium

The communicator's image of the receiver

The receiver's image of the communicator

The receiver's self-image

The receiver's personality structure

The receiver as a member of the audience

The receiver's social environment

C = Communicator
M = Message
R = Receiver

Maletzke's model of the mass communication process, 1963

Thus not only is the communicator taking into due regard the medium and the nature of AUDIENCE, and perceiving these things through the filter of self-image and personality structure, he or she is also keenly responsive to other factors – the communication team, with its own special set of values (See NEWS VALUES) and professional practices. Beyond the team, there is the organization which in turn has to look over its shoulder towards government or the general public (See IMPARTIALITY).

Just as the communicator is a member of a team within an organizational environment, so the receiver is part of a larger context of reception: he or she is subject to influences other than the media message. Those influences may start in the living room of a family home, and the influencers might be the viewer's or reader's family, but there are contextual influences beyond that – in the pub, at work, in the community.

Maletzke's model provides students of the media with a structure for analysis. By its complexity, by suggesting an almost limitless interaction of variables, it also indicates the enormous difficulty faced by research into the EFFECTS OF THE MASS MEDIA. As Denis McQuail and Sven Windahl say in *Communication Models for the study of mass communication* (UK: Longman, 1986 edition), 'This complexity is, no doubt, an important reason why mass communication research has been fairly unsuccessful in explaining and predicting outcomes of the mass communication process'. See COMMUNICATION MODELS.

Manufacture of consent See CONSENT, MANUFACTURE OF.

March of Time Famous US NEWSREEL series of the 1930s, and a classic example of media interaction. Roy Larsen, one of Henry Luce's aides on *Time* magazine, had arranged to have items from the magazine broadcast on RADIO, and these newscasts became so popular among listeners that they were developed into a NETWORK programme, *The March of Time*. One attraction was that the programme dramatized the news; actors played 'memorable scenes from the news of the week'.

In 1934, Louis de Rochemont, under Larsen's supervision, adapted the radio format to FILM which, after early uncertainties, made a notable impact. The monthly film panoramas of American and international events alerted the public to the growing menace of Fascism. They carried an Academy award winning report on life inside Nazi Germany (1938) and an even more powerful one on refugees. In 1935, 432 US cinemas were showing the *March of Time*, with its famous end-of-programme words, 'Time . . . marches on.' and by 1939 the number had trebled. The series continued till 1953. See DOCUMENTARY.

Marginality See DISPLACEMENT EFFECT.

Marine Broadcasting (Offences) Act, 1965 Forbade illegal BROADCASTING and also made it an offence to supply illegal broadcasters with ADVERTISING. Effectively killed off PIRATE RADIO in and around the UK. See COMMERCIAL RADIO.

Marxist (mode of media analysis) Focuses

on social conflict which is seen as being essentially derived from the mode of production in capitalist societies. Karl Marx argued that the CULTURE – and communication process – of a capitalist society reflects the NORMS and VALUES of that section of the community which owns the means of production: out of the dominant CLASS springs the dominant IDEOLOGY which the media serve to disseminate and reinforce in the 'disguise' of CONSENSUS.

Marxist analysts have employed three main strategies of research (also used by other, non-Marxist commentators): *structuralist, political/economic* and *culturalist*. The structuralist approach examines the ideology embodied in media content, concentrating on 'text' and the source of the ideology. The political/economic approach investigates the location of media power within economic processes, and the structure of media production. The culturalist approach commences from the standpoint that all societies are made up of a rich variety of group cultures, but seeks to indicate that some GROUPS – therefore some cultures – receive a disproportionate representation in the media in the process of shaping and defining consensus and obscuring the roots of genuine conflict. See FUNCTIONALIST/SOCIAL ACTION (MODES OF MEDIA ANALYSIS).

Maslow's hierarchy of needs According to Abraham Maslow in his highly influential book, *Motivation and Personality* (US: Harper & Row, 1954), human behaviour reflects a range of basic needs which form a hierarchy. 'For the man who is extremely and dangerously hungry,' writes Maslow, 'no other interests exist but food.' When that need is satisfied, 'new (and still higher) needs emerge'. In what he terms a holistic-dynamic theory of MOTIVATION, Maslow cites the following basic needs: *physiological*; *safety* needs; *belongingness* and *loving* needs; *esteem* needs and the need for *self-actualization*. Among the physiological needs are food, water, sleep and sex. Safety needs include security, stability, protection, freedom from fear, from anxiety and from chaos; the need for structure, order, law, limits; the preference for the familiar over the unfamiliar, the known rather than the unknown; for religion.

Maslow writes that the threat of chaos or humiliation can be expected in most human beings 'to produce a regression from any higher needs to the prepotent safety needs', so that a common, almost expectable reaction, is the easier acceptance of dictatorship or of military rule' and this is 'most true of those living near the safety line'. Such people are 'particularly disturbed by threats to authority, to legality, and to the representatives of the law' (See MAINSTREAMING).

Belongingness and loving needs include the

'deeply animal tendency to herd, to flock, to join, to belong'.

Maslow's highest-order need is self-actualization, where a person seeks and finds fulfilment; 'A musician must make music, an artist must paint' if they are ultimately to be at peace with themselves'. 'What a man *can* be, he *must* be'. The term itself was coined by Kurt Goldstein in *The Organism* (US: American Book, 1939), and means in Maslow's words, 'to become everything that one is capable of becoming'. Maslow argues that the fulfilment of needs depends on essential preconditions, obviously, at the physiological level, the availability of food and water, but at the higher levels such conditions as 'freedom to speak, freedom to do what one wishes so long as no harm is done to others, freedom to express oneself, freedom to investigate and seek for information, freedom to defend oneself'. In Maslow's view 'Secrecy, censorship, dishonesty, blocking of communication threatens *all* the basic needs'.

An essential part of the process of self-actualization is the desire to know and to understand, 'to systematize, to organize, to analyse, to look for relations and meanings, to construct a system of values' and these aspects too tend towards a hierarchy: to know leads us to want to understand. Within this frame too are *aesthetic* needs. Maslow speaks of some individuals who 'get sick (in special ways) from ugliness, and are cured by beautiful surroundings'.

The hierarchy as cited by Maslow is dynamic and capable of reversal. Some people for example may go for esteem before love (though at the same time these may 'seek self-assertion for the sake of love rather than self-esteem itself'). There are artists who put creation before all else; there is the psychopathic personality suffering from a permanent loss of the love needs; and there is the potential reversal caused by the undervaluing of a long-satisfied need: 'Thus a man who has given up his job rather than lose his self-respect, and who then starves for six months or so, may be willing to take his job back even at the price of losing his self-respect.'

The hierarchy is at its most reversible in situations involving 'ideals, high social standards, high values, and the like. With such values people become martyrs'. Torture victims who defy their oppressors also confound Maslow's hierarchy. It is also acknowledged by Maslow that human behaviour is prompted by *multiple* motivations. It would be theoretically possible, he says, 'to analyse a single act of an individual and see in it the expression of his physiological needs, his safety needs, his love needs, his esteem needs, and self-actualization'. Equally, not all behaviour is motivated; and motivation must also be considered in the light of the 'external field', the pressures placed upon people to react in certain ways. See SELF-CONCEPT; VALUES.

Mass communication Term describes institutionalized forms of public MESSAGE production and dissemination, operating on a large scale, involving a considerable division of labour in their production processes and functioning through complex mediations of print, FILM, recording tape and photography. J. Corner and J. Hawthorn point out in *Communication Studies: an introductory reader* (UK: Edward Arnold, 1980) that 'mass communications are *industrial* activities, produced within large organizations whose policies and professional routines are located within the political, economic and legal structures of the societies in which they operate'. Mass communication systems are deeply involved in the process of *culture production*. See CULTIVATION; CULTURAL APPARATUS; MASS COMMUNICATIONS: SEVEN CHARACTERISTICS.

* J. Tunstall, *The Media in Britain* (UK: Constable, 1983); D. McQuail, *Mass Communication Theory: An Introduction* (UK: Sage, 2nd edition, 1987).

Mass communications: seven characteristics In *Towards a Sociology of Mass Communications* (UK: Collier-Macmillan, 1969), D. McQuail poses the following features of mass communications: (1) They normally require complex formal organizations. (2) They are directed towards large audiences. (3) They are *public* – the content is open to all and the distribution is relatively unstructured and informal. (4) Audiences are heterogeneous – of many different kinds – in composition; people living under widely different conditions in widely differing cultures. (5) The mass media can establish simultaneous contact with very large numbers of people at a distance from the source, and widely separated from one another. (6) The relationship between communicator and audience is addressed by persons known only in their public role as communicators. (7) The audience for mass communications is 'collectively unique to modern society'. It is an 'aggregate of individuals united by a common focus of interest, engaging in an identical form of behaviour, and open to activation towards common ends', yet the individuals involved 'are unknown to each other, have only a restricted amount of interaction, do not orient their actions to each other and are only loosely organized or lacking in organization'.

Massification However large the population, it is made up of individuals. Massification – a US term – is the process by which the population is regarded as, and treated as, a lumpen mass with similar if not identical tastes and atti-

tudes. Massification serves as an excuse by society's privileged and ELITE to regard the mass as 'only capable' of benefiting from ART, education, information, entertainment if it is presented in its simplest, most unchallenging form. Massification only makes headway when large numbers of people accept the image of themselves as projected by the purveyors of *mass culture*. See ADVERTISING; PUBLIC SERVICE BROADCASTING; MASS SOCIETY.

* A. Swingewood, *The Myth of Mass Culture* (UK: Macmillan, 1977).

Mass manipulative model of (media) communication See COMMERCIAL LAISSEZ-FAIRE MODEL OF (MEDIA) COMMUNICATION.

Mass media See MASS COMMUNICATION.

Mass media effects See EFFECTS OF THE MASS MEDIA.

Mass Observation An organization founded in 1937 by Charles Madge and Tom Harrisson, with the purpose of furthering the scientific study of human behaviour in the UK. Large numbers of volunteer observers were used, recruited through advertisements in the national PRESS. At one time it is estimated that there were over 1000 such volunteers. The object of Mass Observation was ultimately the 'observation of everyone by everyone, including themselves'.

Data that has been collected is to be found in the Tom Harrisson Mass Observation Archives in the University of Sussex. See MEDIA ANALYSIS.

Mass society Term applied to those modern western-type societies, particularly the US, in which many or most major social institutions are organized to deal with people in *aggregate* and in which the similarities between people's attitudes and behaviour tend to be viewed as more important than their differences. The central concern of mass society theorists is the impact of large-scale social organization on individual freedom and the relationships between the individual, the community and society.

See ALIENATION; ANOMIE; FRANKFURT SCHOOL OF THEORISTS; MASSIFICATION; POPULISM.

Mathematical theory of communication See SHANNON AND WEAVER MODEL OF COMMUNICATION, 1949.

Max Headroom The first male computer-generated TELEVISION personality; followed by Roxscene, the first female. *The Max Headroom Show* on CHANNEL 4 won the Royal Television Society's Original Programme Award in 1986.

McCombs and Shaw agenda-setting model of media effects, 1976 The process and effects of AGENDA SETTING have been a central interest for media research and study. Two important contributions to our understanding of agenda-setting theory have been articles by M.E. McCombs and D.L. Shaw – 'The agenda setting function of mass media' in *Public Opinion Quarterly*, 36 (1972) and 'Structuring the "Unseen Environment" ' in the *Journal of Communication* (Spring, 1976). Shaw followed these up with 'Agenda setting and mass communication theory' in the *Gazette* XXV, 2 (1979). In their 1976 publication, the authors write, 'Audiences not only learn about public issues and other matters through the media, they also learn how much importance to attach to an issue or topic from the emphasis the mass media place upon it. For example, in reflecting what candidates are saying during a campaign, the mass media apparently determine the important issues. In other words, the mass media set the "agenda" of the campaign'. Thus in the view of McCombs and Shaw, the media are highly influential in shaping our perceptions of the world: 'This ability to affect cognitive change among individuals is one of the most important aspects of the power of mass communication' (See EFFECTS OF THE MASS MEDIA).

As the model indicates, there is a direct correlation between the amount of media exposure of X (the issue) and the degree to which the public sees X as being important. Some writers have been critical of this model for oversimplifying the process of media influence. It takes no account of influences *other* than the media in setting personal agendas in relation to public ISSUES (See INTERVENING VARIABLES (IV); ONE-STEP, TWO-STEP, MULTI-STEP FLOW MODELS OF COMMUNICATION; SIGNIFICANT OTHERS). Another problem with the McCombs and Shaw model is highlighted by Denis McQuail and Sven Windahl in *Communication Models for*

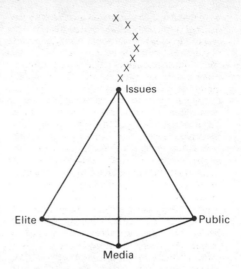

McQuail and Windahl's 'dual role' model

the study of mass communications (UK: Longman, 1986 edition). They identify not one but a range of agendas: 'We can speak of the agendas of individuals and groups or we can speak of the agendas of institutions – political parties and governments. There is an important distinction between the notion of setting personal agendas by communication directly to the public and setting an institutional agenda by influencing the politicians and decision makers.'

Issues	Differential media attention	Consequent public perception of issues
X_1		X_1
X_2		X_2
X_3		X_3
X_4		X_4
X_5		X_5
X_6		X_6

McCombs and Shaw's agenda-setting model of media effects, 1976

McQuail and Windahl perceive here a dual role for the media, influencing public opinion and influencing the ELITE: 'In reality there is a continuous interaction between elite proposals and public views, with the media acting as carrier as well as source.' What has been termed a 'co-orientation approach' (by J.M. McLeod and S.H. Chaffee in 'Interpersonal approaches to communication research' in *American Behavioural Scientist*, 16, 1973) is cited by McQuail and Windahl in the following kite-shaped model deriving from NEWCOMB'S ABX MODEL OF COMMUNICATION, 1953.

A third criticism of McComb's and Shaw's model relates to the actual intentions of the media: do they initiate and select the issues which they go on to amplify; climb aboard a 'bandwagon' of nascent public interest or respond chiefly to the promptings of the POWER ELITE? See CONSENT, MANUFACTURE OF; MAINSTREAMING; MEAN WORLD SYNDROME; NOELLE-NEUMANN'S SPIRAL OF SILENCE MODEL OF PUBLIC OPINION, 1974.

McGregor Commission Report on the Press, 1977 Under the chairmanship of Professor O.R. McGregor, the Royal Commission produced an interim report in 1976. Concerned about the shaky finances of newspapers, the Commission proposed that the State should give interest relief on loans which papers would need if they were to modernize their printing methods and cut costs. Like so many inspired ideas emerging from royal commissions, the proposal got nowhere. In its final report (1977), the Commission recognized the anti-Labour bias in most of the nation's PRESS: 'We have no doubt that over most of this century, the press had treated the beliefs and activities of the Labour movement with hostility.'

The matter was one of concern but McGregor rejected the idea of a launch fund to help new newspapers – to achieve balance politically – 'because we are opposed to the element of Government involvement in the press which would arise over the allocation of such a fund'. McGregor suggested that if the Left was sufficiently concerned about Right-wing bias in the press, the TUC might consider initiating a paper of the left (like the old *Daily Herald*). The Commission's philosophy was clear (though a minority report dissented): 'Our firm belief is that the press should be left free to be partisan and restrained as at present by the law and the voluntary system of a Press Council . . .' The Commission recommended that the PRESS COUNCIL be strengthened, its influence increased; that, for example, its lay members be equal in number to its press representation. This recommendation was accepted, though the Council demurred at other advice. See COMMISSIONS/COMMITTEES ON THE MEDIA.

McGuffin FILM director Alfred Hitchcock (1899–1980) was fond of using this expression to describe any device or element of plot which captures the attention and interest of the audience, but which is intended to be, and acknowledged to be, merely a means to an end: an amiable red herring. Hitch himself described the *McGuffin* as 'that which spies are after (in films) but the audience don't care'.

McLuhanism The archpriest of media analysis in the late 1960s was the Canadian professor, **Marshall McLuhan** (1911–80), creator of the Centre for Media Studies in Toronto. His headline-catching assertions and prophesies about the effect of the new media, particularly TV, on society as we know it were aided and abetted by inspired phrase-making. Described by Northrop Fry as a 'manic depressive rollercoaster of publicity', McLuhan foretold the annihilation of the printed word by the electronic media, yet his books sold (and were read) in thousands.

The most quoted McLuhanism is his phrase, the MEDIUM IS THE MESSAGE, used as the heading of chapter 1 in *Understanding the Media* (UK: Routledge & Kegan Paul, 1964). McLuhan was convinced that with electronic transmission, especially TV, content was everywhere swamped by process. Equally he was concerned at the irresistible cultural spread which RADIO, TV and FILM made possible throughout the world, turning it into a *global village*. Radio he called the *Tribal Drum*, photography was the *Brothel-without-walls*, TV the *Timid Giant*, the motorcar the *Mechanical Bride*.

Perhaps McLuhan's most valuable analysis is to be found in his examination of the impact of printing on civilization in *The Gutenberg Galaxy: The Making of Typographic Man* (UK: Routledge & Kegan Paul, 1962). See HOT MEDIA, COLD MEDIA.

McNelly's model of news flow, 1959 An improvement upon WHITE'S GATEKEEPER MODEL, 1950. In 'Intermediary communicators in the international news' in *Journalism Quarterly*, 36 (1959), J.T. McNelly identifies several intermediary stages through which a news item passes from event to presentation in mass communication form. The author follows the progress of a newsworthy event (E) taken up by a foreign correspondent (C1) and then passed through several agencies where the report of E is shaped and shortened (rather like the game of Chinese Whispers, though, hopefully, not with the same hilarious results):

McNelly illustrates a very complex process of MEDIATION which continues beyond the production/presentation stage when readers or viewers pass on the news to others by word of mouth. What the model does not do is address the criteria for news selection, the NEWS VALUES which operate the operators of the gatekeeping process.

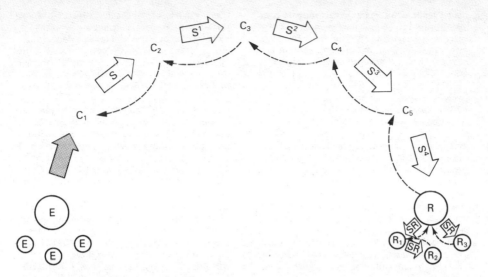

McNelly's model of intermediary communicators in news flow, showing news passing different 'gatekeepers' (after McNelly 1959)
Key to symbols in diagram:
E = Newsworthy event
C_1 = Foreign agency correspondent
C_2 = Regional bureau editor
C_3 = Agency central bureau or deskman
C_4 = National or regional home bureau editor
C_5 = Telegraph editor or radio or TV news editor
S, S^1, S^2, etc. = The report in a succession of altered (shortened) forms
R = Receiver
R_1, R_2, etc. = Family members, friends, associates, etc.
S – R = Story as modified by word of mouth transmission
Dotted line = feedback

McNelly's model of news flow, 1959

See GALTUNG and RUGE'S MODEL OF SELECTIVE GATEKEEPING, 1965.

Mean world syndrome It is argued by commentators such as the American media analyst George Gerbner that the more people watch TELEVISION, the more likely they will consider that out there is a 'mean world'. On the small screen, CONTENT ANALYSIS tells us, crime rages about ten times more often than in real life. On TV in America – and it is little different in the UK – 55% of prime-time characters are involved in violent confrontations once a week. Heavy viewers, according to Gerbner in a series of published analyses since 1980, overestimate the statistical chance of violence in their own lives (see RESONANCE) and consequently harbour a heightened mistrust of strangers. See EFFECTS OF THE MASS MEDIA; MAINSTREAMING.

Meaning In communication terms, a dynamic interaction between reader/viewer/listener etc. and the MESSAGE. As J. Fiske puts it in *Introducing Communication Studies* (UK: Methuen, 1982), 'A reader is constituted by his socio-cultural experience and thus he is the channel through which message and culture interact. This is meaning.' When we say something is 'a question of semantics', we are referring to the hazardous nature of actually pinning down, with any exactitude, the meaning of what a person says or has written. The word 'freedom' on some lips has quite a different CONNOTATION than if expressed by others.

There is a ready tendency to consider words as actually the embodiment of the meaning they attempt to describe; in fact they are approximations. Just as paper money has no intrinsic value, words have no intrinsic meaning: rather they are accredited with value or meaning by common consent. Like currency, word-meanings are subject to devaluation and manipulation. Ultimately you can paper the walls with debased currency; debased LANGUAGE becomes a weapon *against* meaning.

There is a prevalent – and understandable – assumption that an act or work of communication has to mean *something*. Thus a bemused spectator in front of, say, a work of abstract ART, might declare, 'But what does it mean?' The short answer is that our spectator is unfamiliar with (or resistant to) the nature of the DISCOURSE which has, in the first instance, taken place between the artist, his/her MEDIUM and his/her environment (in place and time). Unless the spectator can 'tune in' to the signals – the CODES – operated by the artist, unless the spectator can recognize that a discourse is actually taking place, then the art he or she witnesses – for him or her, not necessarily anyone else – is meaningless. On the other hand, the spectator might instinctively warm to a work of art – be attracted by its colour, shape, texture – and still be at a loss to grasp its meaning. In this case, common ground between artist, work of art and spectator has been found. Communication has begun, and so, arguably, has meaning.

Meaning, obviously, has to be worked at. The codes or practices of specific communicative discourses have to be recognized and eventually understood, and the relationship between speaker/writer/artist/musician actor/dancer, etc. and the forms and conventions of the chosen medium of communication responded to – preferably sympathetically and with EMPATHY.

Meaning can be said to be in a perpetual state of re-working or re-negotiation. The artist's meaning may never be the spectator's meaning; but meaning is the property of neither. Indeed to regard meaning as something universally determinable and fixed is to create MYTH and to deal in PROPAGANDA. See DEEP STRUCTURE; NEWSPEAK; PARADIGM; SEMIOLOGY/SEMIOTICS; TRANSACTION.

Meaning systems See DOMINANT, SUBORDINATE, RADICAL.

Media analysis See FUNCTIONALIST/MARXIST/SOCIAL ACTION (MODES OF MEDIA ANALYSIS).

Media control Four categories of media control are generally recognized: Authoritarian; Paternal; Commercial and Democratic. They can apply to an individual communications system, such as ownership of a newspaper, or to a state pattern of control. The first indicates a total monopoly of the means of communication and control over what is expressed. The second is what Raymond Williams in *Communications* (UK: Pelican, 1966) terms 'authoritarianism with a conscience', that is, authority with VALUES and purposes beyond those concerning the maintenance of its own power. The third relates to control by market forces: anything can be said provided that you can afford to say it and that you can say it profitably.

Democratic control is the rarest category, implying active involvement in decisions by the workforce and, indeed, the readership or audience. Control works at different levels – at the *operational* level (editors, producers, etc.), at the *allocative* level (of funds, personnel, etc.) and at the *external* level (government, advertisers, consumers).

Trends in media control have been towards greater concentration of ownership; towards ownership by CONGLOMERATE organizations and subsequently a series of over-diversifying control NETWORKS in which international finance has fingers in practically every communications pie, from newspapers to cinema, from records to satellites. Running parallel with these trends has been the development of multi-marketing of media products – books, films, TV series, VIDEO cassettes – with such products being packaged for world-wide consumption; audience maximization, and therefore profit maximization being the most important driving force. See NORMATIVE THEORIES OF MASS MEDIA.

* J. Tunstall, *The Media in Britain* (UK: Constable, 1983); D. McQuail, *Mass Communication: An Introduction* (UK: Sage, 2nd edition, 1987).

Mediacy Term first given public prominence at the 1983 British Association conference by Michael Weiss and Carol Lorac of the Communication and Social Skills Project at Brighton Polytechnic. Deemed as important, in the education curriculum of the future, as literacy and numeracy are today, mediacy is defined by Weiss and Lorac as 'the ability to understand and manipulate recorded sound and vision. Information technology and video are the machinery of mediacy: its pen and paper.'

Media effects See EFFECTS OF THE MASS MEDIA.

Media: hot and cold See HOT MEDIA, COLD MEDIA.

Media images These are the 'truths' or some would say STEREOTYPES – most certainly *conventions* – which the media operate in the definition and redefinition of CONSENSUS and by which they define, and sometimes police, the normative contours of society. As a considerable amount of our knowledge of others comes to us at second hand, through the media, the images the media use provide us with benchmarks or points of reference. Consensus is regularly defined by the media's concentration on DEVIANCE from consensus. Equally, the media stand forth as WATCHDOGS of the 'moral constituency' of society as Howard S. Becker puts it in *Outsiders: Studies in the Sociology of Deviance* (US: Free Press, 1963); and it is their images, repeated, dramatized, often expressed in panic terms, which provide the major source of current information in society. See EFFECTS

OF THE MASS MEDIA; FOLK DEVILS; MAINSTREAM-ING; MEAN WORLD SYNDROME; MORAL ENTREPRE-NEURS; MORAL PANIC.

Media imperialism Term used to describe the role western capitalist media play in dominating Third World developing countries through communication systems. Crucial to the notion of media imperialism is the understanding of the relationship between economic, territorial, cultural and informational factors. In the age of western economic colonialism in the 19th c. the flow of information was a vital process of growth and reinforcement. Where the trade went, so followed developing media practice and technology, reflecting the VALUES and assumptions of those who owned and manned the service.

As developing countries reached independence much concern was felt at the degree of penetration by western media. In 1972, the General Conference of Unesco drew attention to the way the media of the richer sections of the world were a means towards 'the domination of world public opinion or a source of moral and cultural pollution'. Since then the movement towards a NEW WORLD INFORMATION ORDER has grown in vigour and strength. In 1973, in Algiers, a meeting of heads of state of non-aligned countries agreed to take concerted action to promote a fairer, more balanced exchange of information among themselves and release themselves from dependence upon the experts of the richer nations, demanding the 'reorganization of existing communication channels which are the legacy of the colonial past . . .'. By 1978, the Unesco General Council agreed its new *Declaration on Mass Media* emphasizing the 'balanced' aspect of a concept of information based on the principle of 'free and balanced flow'.

Developing countries have long held a heartfelt belief that western agencies only report the bad news of what happens in their countries and that this bad news – based upon what Anthony Smith in his book *The Geopolitics of Information* (UK: Faber, 1980) terms 'aberrational' criteria for news selection – causes serious harm, especially when such countries are in need of western financial support and investment.

The contradiction implicit in the goal of 'free and balanced flow' of information is evident. As Anthony Smith points out, 'Free flow enhances freedom only between equals.' There is little sign of developing countries being able to compete with the massive advantages which still lie with the west, the US and UK in particular, in the import and export of information and entertainment. The growth of SATELLITE TRANSMISSION is considered likely to deepen that divide. See INTER-CULTURAL INVASION;

INTERNATIONAL FEDERATION OF JOURNALISTS MACBRIDE COMMISSION; NON-ALIGNED NEWS POOL; TALLOIRES DECLARATION; WORLD PRESS FREEDOM COMMITTEE.

Media research centres See RESEARCH CENTRES.

Media studies Three phases of the communication process have traditionally made up the 'meat' of media studies: source system, MESSAGE system and receiver system. Later work has seen the concentration also upon the *context* of the message process – social, cultural, aesthetic, political and economic. A contemporary troika of study aspects might be: structure, process and change. See SEMIOLOGY/SEMIOTICS.

Media technology See TECHNOLOGY OF THE MEDIA.

Mediation Between an event and the reporting or broadcasting of it to an audience, *mediation* occurs, that is, a process of interpretation – shaping, selecting, editing, emphasizing, de-emphasizing – according to the PERCEPTIONS, expectations and previous experience of those involved in the reporting of the event; and in accordance with the requirements and characteristics of the means of reporting. Between the *event* of a car accident or a murder and the *report* of such an event a whole series of **intermediating** actions take place. The event is translated into words or pictures; it is processed according to the demands of the MEDIUM – for headlines, for good pictures – and pressures such as time, space and contending messages.

Even when, in INTERPERSONAL COMMUNICATION, A communicates a message to B which B conveys to C, a process of mediation inevitably takes place: B may rephrase the message, give parts of it prominence and understate other parts, supplement or distort the information.

Mediation is inescapable: much of our knowledge of life and the world comes to us at second hand, through the mediation of PRESS and TV; our perceptions of events are coloured by the perceptions, preoccupations, VALUES, of the **mediators**.

However, the *construct* of events is far from a monopoly of the mass media; it is further **mediated**, and the process modified or altered altogether, by those around us who exert influence – friends, relatives, work colleagues etc. – and other so-called INTERVENING VARIABLES such as personal mood, time of day or state of health. See S-IV-R MODEL OF COMMUNICATION.

Medio communication That mode of communication between direct, face-to-face address and MASS COMMUNICATION; into this classification comes communication by letter or TELEPHONE.

Medium The physical or technical means of converting a communication MESSAGE into a signal capable of being transmitted along a given CHANNEL. TV for example is a medium which employs the channels of vision and sound. John Fiske in *Introduction to Communication Studies* UK: Methuen, 1982), divides media into three categories: (1) The **presentational media**: the voice, face, body; the spoken word, GESTURE; where the medium is actually the communicator. (2) **Representational media**: books, paintings, photographs, etc., using cultural and aesthetic conventions 'to create a "text" of some sort'; they become independent of the communicator, being *works* of communication (whereas presentational media are *acts* of communication). (3) **Mechanical media** TELEPHONE, RADIO, TV, FILM, etc., and they are transmitters of 1 and 2.

The properties of the medium determine the range of CODES which it can transmit; and considerably affect the nature of the message and its reception.

Medium is the message One of the classic quotes of media literature and perhaps the best-known of Marshall MCLUHAN (1911–80). *The medium is the message* is the first chapter heading in *Understanding Media: the Extensions of Man* (UK: Routledge & Kegan Paul, 1964). *What* is said, McLuhan believes, is deeply conditioned by the MEDIUM through which it is said. The particular attributes of any medium help to determine the MEANING of the communication, and no medium is neutral.

Message That which an act, or work, of communication is *about*. For purposes of definition and analysis it is sometimes necessary to treat the message as something separable from the *process* of communication; but ultimately a message can only meaningfully be examined in the context of other elements all of which are interlinked and interacting.

It is important to distinguish between the actual signal which carries the message and the message itself: a wink is a signal but what is its message? The answer depends on many factors – for example, who is winking, to whom and in what context? While message–signals, in the form of visual or aural CODES may be sent, the message may well not be understood. Thus an ambiguous smile may represent the signal that a message is being conveyed, but the receiver may fail to understand the message while recognizing the signal.

The message may draw its initial shape or purpose from the Sender or Communicator: it will be similarly influenced by the nature of the MEDIUM in which it is sent. The Receiver of a message may be close at hand, in sight of the Communicator, or some distance away. If the message involves INTRAPERSONAL COMMUNICATION, the Communicator and the Receiver may be one and the same. Both the signal and the intended message may encounter NOISE – that is, physical or psychological interference which

will affect its meaningfulness. The message may elicit FEEDBACK which will further modify the message and indeed create a new communication situation and new signals and messages.

Denis McQuail in *Communication* (UK: Longman, 1975) writes that the simplest way of regarding human communication is 'to consider it as the sending from one person to another of meaningful messages'. We can rarely if ever be certain of how other people will interpret our signals, or whether we will 'get our message across'; thus the message sent may be quite different from the message received, and while we think we are communicating a single message we may, unconsciously, be putting across all sorts of other messages too.

We are selecting in and selecting out a barrage of message-carrying signals all the time. We give attention to them if we are *motivated* to do so. Thus a teacher's signals and messages may run into a thicket of difficulties: he/she is boring, has just offended the class in some way, they are distracted by the basketball match outside or Wallace on the back row has just let off a stink bomb.

The effectiveness of a message depends, at a basic, instrumental level, on the weight it carries in competition with other signals and messages but equally it depends upon the significance attached to it by the receivers. This in turn depends upon the 'set' or preparedness, of the receivers for the Sender/Message/Medium. The message of a satirical cartoon, for example, might be completely lost if the reader knows nothing about the particular circumstances to which the cartoon refers. Even a knowledge of the facts may not be enough to facilitate the intended interpretation, because this may only occur if the reader shares the social, political or cultural VALUES of the cartoonist. The CHANNEL too may affect interpretation. The fact that, say, an anti-Tory cartoon appears in the *Guardian* gives rise to a host of contextual meanings which would be modified at the very least if the same cartoon appeared in the *Daily Mail*. In short, whether we 'get our message across' depends partly upon the context in which it is received; and the values, attitudes, perceptions and knowledge of the receiver at a crucial part of that context. See INTERVENING VARIABLES.

Metalingual function of communication See JAKOBSON'S MODEL OF COMMUNICATION, 1958.

Metaphor A figure of speech or a visual device which works by transporting qualities from one plane of reality to another: 'the camel is the ship of the desert'; 'life for Mary was a bed of roses'. Without metaphor there would be no scope for the development of either visual or verbal LANGUAGE; it would remain clinical and colourless; indeed as R. Ridout and C. Witting say in *The Facts of English* (UK: Pan Books,

1976), 'the metaphor is the life-blood of our language, for without it no new idea could be expressed, no new thing named, without the intervention of a completely fresh word'.

The danger with metaphors is that they can quickly descend to the unthinking banality of the cliché without actually losing their power to impress or convince. They can impede new thinking. The trade unions remain, in many minds, highwaymen holding the passengers of the national stagecoach to ransom. It is a harmful metaphor for it substitutes a STEREOTYPE between reality and image. Equally, the metaphor once invented may be manipulated: in ADVERTISING menthol cigarettes have long been linked by advertisers with fresh air and flowing streams – though nothing could be more inapt. Yet the metaphor holds: truth is disarmed by the dishonest metaphor.

At least it may be said that advertisers are constantly in pursuit of new metaphors, or new versions of old metaphors. The PRESS generally seems to be more content to exploit the **military metaphor** and by doing so to demonstrate dependence upon conflict as a prime source of news and feature content.

All newspapers, serious and popular, use the military metaphor in all sorts of topic areas, but chiefly in politics, commerce and sport. Even where peace is being referred to, the military metaphor is in action: 'War Breaks out over Classroom Peace Plans'. Press LANGUAGE is riddled with the bombast of conflict – things are axed, chopped, smashed, slashed; knives are constantly out; prime ministers stick to their guns, oppositions are routed.

The so-called **mixed metaphor** contains in one statement two or more ineptly linked images: 'Lame ducks will be barking up the wrong tree if they think government is going to bail them out every time profits take a hammering.' See EUPHEMISM; METONYMY; RHETORIC.

Metasignals A metasignal is a signal that makes a comment about a signal, or a set of signals: it directs us to the accurate MEANING of the signals. For example, two people appear to exchange blows: is the fight real or make-believe? Their smiling faces form the metasignal which indicates that, at least on the surface, what we are seeing is a play-fight.

Body posture is among the chief metasignals. Equally, uniform serves effectively in this capacity. We react differently to the policeman in uniform than we might to the same person in off-duty jeans and tee-shirt. Desmond Morris in *Manwatching: A Field Guide to Human Behaviour* (UK: Jonathan Cape, 1977) says that 'In a sense the whole world of entertainment presents a non-stop Metasignal, in the form of the proscenium arch around the stage of a theatre, or the edge of the cinema or TV screen.' Audiences, he believes, can tolerate – and gain entertainment from – films and plays featuring dollops of death and mayhem because of the metasignals which indicate 'this isn't real'. Morris argues that though the actors may aim at maximum reality in their dark deeds, 'no matter how convincing they are, we still carry at the back of our minds (even as we gasp when the knife plunges home) the Metasignal of the "edge" of their stage.'

Methodology The study of methods used in conducting research within the social and natural sciences. Methods commonly used in the field of communication and media studies include CONTENT ANALYSIS, INTERVIEWS, QUESTIONNAIRES, and PARTICIPANT OBSERVATION.

Metonymy A figure of speech in which the thing meant is represented by something which is an attribute of the original. For example, 'The *stage* (acting profession) is furious with the government over the imposition of 15% VAT on Britain's theatres.' When we talk of the newspaper business, we refer to the PRESS – something that stands for the whole. As far as images are concerned, the metonym is a selection of one of those available to represent the whole; and from that selection flows our interpretation or understanding of the whole. Thus the selection of a piece of FILM of young people lounging at a street corner, or pickets in combat with the police, acts as the 'trigger of meaning' for the way the teenager or the striker is defined. For this reason, metonyms are powerful conveyors of reality, indeed so powerful that they can come to be accepted as actually *being* reality, the way things really are.

The selection of the image to serve as a metonym does not of course take place arbitrarily or in a vacuum. It is conditioned by NEWS VALUES and MYTH, that is, the dominant beliefs, cultural interpretations and explanations of reality which have come to have common currency. Pickets struggling with the police clearly fulfil a dominant myth about striking pickets; and the dominant myth is the criterion for selecting one image rather than another (for example, of peaceful, orderly pickets). Metonym and myth, therefore, are powerful agents in exploiting the 'truth factor', so it is essential to bear in mind that they are approximations and very often simulations: that is, 'constructed truth'.

Microfiche See MICROFORMS.

Microforms Photographic film usually 16, 35 or 105 mm wide is used with microforms for the storage, retrieval and display of information and images. The first two widths are generally roll-film in format and loaded into plastic cartridges or cassettes. The 105 mm width is usually cut into lengths of 148 mm to produce flat microform or **micro-fiche**. A fiche contains a mass of information reduced between 18 and 48 times. Microforms save space and cost, combining in one MEDIUM the ability to store and display data. It is now possible to scan the pages of *The Times* going all the way back to its origin in 1785.

Microforms have found increasing use as part of computer-based information systems. It is now possible to summon information on microform from data 'libraries' and screen it on video display units.

*P. Zorkoczy, *Information Technology: An Introduction* (UK: Pitman, 1982).

Micro-myth, macro-myth Philip Schlesinger in *Putting 'Reality' Together. BBC News* (UK: Constable, 1978; Methuen/University Paperback, 1987) examines the BBC news machine at work, and identifies what in his view are two myths entertained by those who work in BBC news: the micro-myth that production staff are permitted autonomy within the organization; the macro-myth, that the BBC is an independent organization, largely socially unattached. See IMPARTIALITY.

Microwaves In telecommunications, RADIO signals used for high-capacity SATELLITE TRANSMISSION.

Microwriter Or microwriter WORD PROCESSOR; a computerized piece of apparatus less than half the size of a TYPEWRITER with a five-key board. Combinations of the five keys permit the operator to 'type' in messages which are displayed and stored in the microwriter's memory. Text can be edited before the apparatus is plugged into an electronic typewriter or printer; or the MESSAGE transferred to a TV screen, audio cassette or computer.

Mid-Atlantic solution Term used by Stuart Hood in *Hood on Television* (UK: Pluto Press, 1980) to describe the creation of entertainment projects with a 'mid-Atlantic' tone – that is with characteristics enabling material to be shown with equal acceptance in the US and UK. In Hood's view this solution has tended to be slick but undistinguished, bearing all the marks of unhappy editorial compromise.

Middlebrow See HIGHBROW.

Milieu The social environment of the individual, GROUP, CULTURE or nation.

Military metaphor See METAPHOR.

Mime A mode of entertainment in which the actor or actress uses bodily movement, GESTURE and facial expression alone to communicate with the audience. French actor Marcel Marceau (b. 1923) is perhaps the most notable exponent of the art.

Minders Newspaper reporters who double up as bodyguards to people who have important news stories and who have, usually, signed exclusive rights to the reporters' paper. The minders keep their subject incommunicado while the story is put together, or the 'true confessions' *ghosted*.

Minimal cinema Mode of extremely simplified realism, typified by the work of such directors as Robert Bresson (b. 1907) or Carl Dreyer

(1889–1968); using the fewest possible elements within the code of the MEDIUM. A single, unbroken shot of an upturned box, a face, without movement or distancing would be typical characteristics of a FILM made in the minimal cinema STYLE.

Minneapolis City Council enquiry into pornography See PORNOGRAPHY.

Minority Report of Mr Selwyn Lloyd This was attached to the majority BEVERIDGE COMMITTEE REPORT ON BROADCASTING, 1950, and, contrary to Beveridge who supported a continued monopoly of BROADCASTING for the BBC, argued that independent – and commercial – competition would be a good thing. Author of the Minority Report was Conservative MP Selwyn Lloyd who produced a scheme for a Commission for British Broadcasting to be set up which would licence a number of rival broadcasting stations. Lloyd wrote, 'Having considered these arguments put forward by the BBC on behalf of monopoly, I am of the opinion that independent competition will be healthy for broadcasting.' His view had considerable support in the Tory party and in the business world: commercial broadcasting in the UK was on the horizon. See MONOPOLY, FOUR SCANDALS OF; COMMERCIAL RADIO; COMMERCIAL TELEVISION.

Miracle of Fleet Street Description by Lord Northcliffe (1865–1922) of the redoubtable *Daily Herald* (1912–64), a sometimes swashbuckling radical paper which, despite having a substantial circulation and vast readership, received little ADVERTISING as a result partly of its left-wing views but perhaps more importantly because its insistence on thorough reporting of political ISSUES appealed, at that time, more generally to male readers. When other national popular papers were priced at one penny, the *Daily Herald* was forced to charge two pence. Yet it lost very little in circulation, due to the energy and leadership of its greatest editor, George Lansbury, MP (1859–1940).

The *Herald* was the first newspaper in the world to reach a circulation of two million – in mid-1933 – though it was soon overtaken by Beaverbrook's *Daily Express*. By the time the *Herald* had reached its peak circulation of 2.1 million in 1947, the *Daily Mirror* and *Daily Express* were pushing four million and by 1960, sales had tumbled to 1.6 million. The *Herald* struggled on until 14 September 1964. See PRESS.

Misspeaks A US media term for bloomers committed by important persons addressing the PRESS or TV. In the UK, the word 'gaffe' has the same meaning.

Mix In FILM making a gradual transition between two shots where one dissolves into another. It is a soft fade, often used to denote the passage of time. See MONTAGE; SHOT; WIPE.

Mixing In FILM making, the process of re-recording all original dialogue, music and sound effects on to a single master sound track. See SYNCHRONOUS SOUND.

Model In social science research, a model is a tentative description of what a social process, say the communication process, or system might be like. It is a tool of explanation and analysis – very often in diagrammatic form – which attempts to show how the various elements of a situation being studied relate to each other. Models are not statements of reality; only after much further research and testing would the model be considered viable. It could then develop into a theory.

The term can also refer to a familiar process or object which is used as a point of reference when an attempt to explain the unknown is being made. An analogy is made showing the similarities between the phenomenon to be explained and one which is well known i.e. the model.

Additionally, a model can be a person whose behaviour others wish to imitate, on whom they wish to *model* themselves. The desire to model oneself on other persons is particularly strong in one's teenage years; the mass media play a significant role in presenting teenagers with a variety of such models. See COMMUNICATION MODELS; HYPOTHESIS; IDENTIFICATION.

Modem Device for converting analogue signals to digital signals and from digital to analogue. Modem is short for *mod*ulator/*dem*odulator.

Models of communication See COMMUNICATION MODELS.

Modes of media analysis See FUNCTIONALIST/MARXIST/SOCIAL ACTION (MODES OF MEDIA ANALYSIS).

Modulation The process of imprinting information such as speech or data, on to high frequency carrier waves, for example RADIO or light waves, usually by varying their amplitude (AM) or frequency (FM).

Monofunctional In a media sense, the term ascribing to a work – of literature, RADIO, FILM, TV – a single function; for example, to entertain. Research findings over the years have seriously challenged assumptions that particular forms of content are monofunctional. Adults declare a considerable interest in news programmes, yet functional studies have shown that for many viewers, the primary function of news is not informational. The news broadcast is, apparently, more closely related to habit; and it also affords the individual feelings of security and of social contact. See EFFECTS OF THE MEDIA.

Monomorphic opinion leadership See OPINION LEADER.

Monopoly, four scandals of According to the BEVERIDGE COMMITTEE REPORT ON BROADCASTING, 1950, these were 'bureaucracy, complacency, favouritism and inefficiency', indicators which the Committee saw in the performance of the BBC as monopoly-holder of British airwaves. Nevertheless, Beveridge recommended the Corporation's licence be renewed because the alternative, US-style commercial TV, promised a system which was considered to be much worse. See COMMERCIAL RADIO; COMMERCIAL TELEVISION; MINORITY REPORT OF MR SELWYN LLOYD.

Monotype printing Invented in 1889 by American Tolbert Lanston. The machine is in two parts. The first, operated by the keyboard, punches coded holes into a paper tape; the second has the tape fed into it and the code controls the casting operation. In monotype casting, unlike LINOTYPE PRINTING, every letter and space is cast separately.

Monroe motivated sequence Five-step sequence advocated by American Professor Alan Monroe in *Principles of Speech Communication* by Douglas Ehninger, Bruce E. Cronbach and Monroe (USA: Scott, Foresman, 1984) for use in organizing speeches, especially those with an intent to persuade. First stage, *Attention*, commanding and maintaining audience attention by some eye or ear-catching device (such as a lively story, anecdote or dramatic set of statistics). Second, *Need*, in which the speech is made to appear relevant to audience needs. These needs are than met in step three of the sequence, *Satisfaction*, where solutions are proposed and examined. The speaker then proceeds to *Visualization*, where the audience is persuaded to see more clearly how the speaker's information or ideas will help them. Finally, *Action*, a plea for response, for the taking-up of the speaker's points.

Montage From the French, 'monter', to assemble; the process of cutting up FILM and arranging – editing – it into the screened sequence. Sergei Eisenstein (1898–1948) explained montage as putting together camera shots which, in combination, made a greater impact than did the sum of the parts – a creative juxtaposition. Separate elements combine to produce a new MEANING. Montage is the synthesis which gives film its unique character.

Montage is used as a *narrative* device and an *expressive* device, the one concerned with sequencing, ensuring the smooth continuity of action, the other with the intention of producing a particular effect by the clash, comparison or contrast of two or more images, often symbolic or metaphoric in meaning. This use of montage is often compared with collage in art in that it draws attention to itself as an exercise in construction: it says, Look at me as film, not reality. See ALIENATION EFFECT; KULESHOV EFFECT; SHOT.

Moog synthesizer A synthesizer is a machine which generates and processes sounds electronically in real time; a *Moog* synthesizer is the version invented by Robert Moog (b. 1934) and originally manufactured by his own R.A. Moog Company in New York. Synthesizers permit the direct creation of sounds so that all properties – such as pitch, amplitude, reverberation or modulation – are controlled automatically. They can produce a great variety of sounds, considerably surpassing the scope of mechanical instruments, though at the same time resembling the sounds made by conventional musical instruments.

Moral entrepreneurs Howard Becker first used this term in *Outsiders: Studies in the Sociology of Deviance* (US: Free Press, 1963) to describe those members of the community who take upon themselves the role of watchdog, vigilant against alleged attempts to subvert public morals. Such individuals often try, sometimes with success, to use the media to gain public support for their views. The letters columns of the various newspapers can be a particular vehicle for the expression of their views. Such entrepreneurs can play an important role in the development of a MORAL PANIC. See 'CLEAN UP TV' MOVEMENT.

Moral panic Individuals and social GROUPS can by their activities emerge as a focus for outrage expressed by influential members of society who perceive these activities as seriously subverting the MORES and interests of the dominant CULTURE. Such reactions are, says Stanley Cohen in *Folk Devils and Moral Panics* (UK: MacGibbon & Kee, 1972), disseminated by the mass media usually in an hysterical, stylized, and stereotypical manner thus engendering a sense of moral panic. Dick Hebdige argues in *Subculture: the Meaning of Style* (UK: Methuen, 1979), that media coverage of the emergence of the PUNK YOUTH CULTURE, for example, displayed all the classic symptoms of a moral panic.

Mores Those social rules concerning acceptable behaviour which it is considered wrong to break. Such rules play an important part in the maintenance of social order and cohesion; consequently breaches of mores usually meet with the imposition of sanctions by society – formally through laws, informally through, for example, social rejection.

Some mores are particular to a specific society, others can be found in most societies. A majority of societies respects the sanctity of human life, though this is varyingly weighed against the sanctity of social order. Also, within a society different social GROUPS may have different mores. Traditionally it is against the unwritten law of school life for pupils to tell tales to teacher. The sanction against those who do may be their temporary isolation or ejection from the group – or reprisals after school.

Mores may often prescribe both the tone and content of communication. Differences in sexual mores, for example, underpin many of the arguments about the dissemination of PORNOGRAPHY.

Morphology Study of the structure or forms of words, traditionally distinguished from SYN-TAX which deals with the rules governing the combination of words in sentences. Generally morphology divides into two fields: the study of inflections and of word-formation. See LANGUAGE.

Morse Code Devised by Samuel Morse (1791–1872), American artist and sculptor, and one of the great pioneers of TELEGRAPHY, the Morse Code is a binary code made up of dots and dashes to represent letters of the alphabet, numbers 0 to 9 and punctuation marks. By 1838 Morse had developed his code using from one to four bits (binary digits) to encode letters of the alphabet, five bits for each number and six bits for punctuation. Thus A = · –; the number one = · – – – –; a question mark = · · – – · · while the vital SOS (Save Our Souls) = · · · – – – · · ·

Subsequently modified to suit newer operations, the Morse Code – now the International Morse Code – continues in use.

MOS It is claimed that in the early days of cinema German technicians in Hollywood spoke of shooting FILM 'mit out sound'; thus – believe if it you will – MOS is silent filming.

Motivation Ernest R. Hilgard, Richard C. Atkinson and Rita L. Atkinson in *Introduction to Psychology* (US: Harcourt Brace Jovanovich, 1975) define motivation as 'A general term referring to the regulation of need-satisfying and goal-seeking behaviour'. The sources of motivation are varied and complex. There is general agreement that motivation arises from the desire to satisfy many needs, but there are different theories about the nature of such needs and the relative importance attached by different individuals to them.

The concept of motivation is relevant to several areas of communication and media studies. Motivation theories, for example, can help to provide a range of ideas about why people want to communicate. Of relevance here is William Schutz's theory of interpersonal needs. Schutz, in his book entitled *The Interpersonal World* (US: Science and Behaviour Books, 1966), identifies three basic interpersonal needs which he argues underlie most interpersonal behaviour: the need for *inclusion*, the need for *control* and the need for *affection*. These then are the needs one might wish to have satisfied in INTERPERSONAL COMMUNICATION. Situations in which others satisfy one or more of your needs are likely to be valued; those situations in which your needs are not met may well be avoided.

Another example of the use made of the concept of motivation is in the consideration of why and how people might be influenced or persuaded to act in certain ways, by certain messages. Much effort is expended in the ADVERTISING and public relations industries trying to devise strategies for selling products, services or people, by appealing to what are thought to be the motivations of the general public.

Scc HIDDEN NEEDS; MASLOW'S HIERARCHY OF NEEDS; MOTIVATION RESEARCH (MR).

Motivation research (MR) The post-2nd World War period saw a boom in the US in studies which sought to understand the social psychology of audience exposure to ADVERTISING. What influences people to purchase? How can such influences be transformed into a reliable system by the advertiser? In his classic analysis of the US world of advertising, *The Hidden Persuaders* (UK: Longmans, Green, 1957; Penguin, 1960, revised and reprinted, 1981), Vance Packard describes a range of HIDDEN NEEDS identified by motivation research for the advertiser to satisfy. These include emotional security, reassurance of worth and what Packard terms ego gratification.

MR has sharpened and sophisticated its tools of measurement over the years. We now have the pupilometer to measure respondents' eye movements and the degree of 'stopping power' of the adverts under scrutiny. There are machines which offer voice-pitch analysis; machines to tabulate brain waves. Not only is psychology wheeled into action in the service of MR but so are the findings of psycholinguists, who study the mental processes governing the learning and use of language. See MEDIA ANALYSIS.

Motivation theory See MASLOW'S HIERARCHY OF NEEDS.

Mr Gate American media analyst David Manning White in 1950 investigated the process of GATE KEEPING by studying the editing selections by a copy-editor – 'Mr Gate' – from the (then) three major American NEWS AGENCIES on a 30,000-circulation daily newspaper in the midwest. 'Mr Gate' in one week used 1,297 column inches – about one-tenth of the 11,910 column inches supplied. 'Mr Gate' confessed to a few prejudices which might well cause him to put items on the SPIKE (reject them), and to a preference: 'I go for human interest stories in a big way'; but White also perceived how important the pressure of time was on the selection process. The nearer the next edition of the newspaper came, the stronger in NEWS VALUE a story had to be not to be rejected. See WHITE'S GATEKEEPER MODEL, 1950.

Multi-actuality The MEANING of communication signs – LANGUAGE – is not fixed but subject to differing interpretations according to context. The term originated with Valentin Volosinov in *Marxism and the Philosophy of Language* (US: Seminar Press, 1973; first published in Russian, 1929–30) who argued that the prevailing meaning of a word or expression – such as democracy or freedom, for example – works towards the suppression of multi-actuality, except in terms of 'social crises or revolutionary changes'. In other words, the dominant HIERARCHY will strive to impose its own meaning – *one* meaning as opposed to many. Signs, therefore, Volosinov believes, may become the 'arena for the class struggle' as the dominant group of interpreters of meaning strive to eradicate alternative meanings. See HEGEMONY; IDEOLOGY; METAPHOR.

Multipair cable See HF MULTIPAIR CABLE.

Multiplane Walt Disney (1901–66) used this word to explain an innovation in the process of ANIMATION, illustrated in *Fantasia* (1940). Instead of building up a drawing by laying 'cells' one directly on top of the other, an illusion of depth was achieved by a space being left between the CELLULOID images of foreground, background and principal figures.

Multiple image A number of images printed beside each other on the same FILM frame, often showing different camera angles of the same action, or separate actions. Abel Gance (1889–1981) used this device with stunning effect in his masterpiece of 1926, *Napoleon*. A well known modern example of the use of multiple image is Norman Jewison's *The Thomas Crown Affair* (1968).

Multiplexing Technique used to transmit a large number of TELEPHONE conversations through one cable or RADIO path simultaneously. See PHONE-TAPPING.

Multiplier effect Where CULTURE as a commodity – usually in the form of films and TV programmes – exported to other countries, opens up markets for other goods. James Monaco in 'Images and sounds as cultural commodities' in *Sight & Sound*, Autumn 1980, quotes American professor Dallas Smythe: 'The distribution of television programs around the world from the United States . . . has the double purpose of making money for itself and serving as the front runner for the industry of the country which produced it. It is a form of advertisement; it is like the battleships, gunboats, which used to show the flag . . .' See MEDIA IMPERIALISM.

Musical – film musical Essentially the invention and hallmark of the US, and of Broadway, New York, in particular. Though *The Jazz Singer* (1927) was not by any means the first FILM to be accompanied by music, it is nevertheless classified as the first film musical as well as the 'talkie' which made the break-through for SYNCHRONOUS SOUND. The first all-talking, all-singing, all-dancing film was *The Broadway Melody* (1929). Colour in musicals was used with earliest success in *The Wizard of Oz* (1939).

The hey-day of the musical stretched glitteringly from the 1930s to the end of the 1950s when vastly increased production costs and the decline in mass audiences made musicals uneconomical. They were replaced in their extravagance with musical stories such as *Oklahoma!* (1955), *West Side Story* (1961) and *My Fair Lady* (1965), with *The Sound of Music* (1965) capping all at the box-office. Imitations failed, though *Cabaret* (1972) proved that old forms and old patterns could be creatively extended.

Mystification See HEGEMONY.

Myth The generally accepted meaning of myth is of a fictitious (primitive) tale usually involving supernatural characters embodying some popular idea concerning natural or historical phenomena, often symbolizing virtues or other timeless qualities. In everyday parlance, a myth is something invented, not true. For analysts of the communication process, myth has more specific connotations. Myth is an interpretation of the way things are; a justification, a 'charter' as Bronislaw Malinowski (1884–1942) put it. For Claude Lévi-Strauss (b. 1908) myth is a force generated to overcome contradictions. Either way, at the heart of myth is IDEOLOGY, chiefly the value-system of those at the top of society.

The French philosopher Roland Barthes (1915–80) ascribes myth to the second order of SIGNIFICATION, that is, CONNOTATION, but connotation with a very special task – to distort, to become a charter, yes, but also an *alibi*. The way Barthes defines it, myth is a weapon of the bourgeoisie which it uses to regenerate its cultural dominance.

In *Mythologies* (UK: Paladin, 1973), Barthes writes, 'Myth does not deny things, on the contrary, its function is to talk about them; simply, it purifies them, it makes them innocent, it gives them a natural and eternal justification, it gives them a clarity which is not that of an explanation but that of a statement of fact'. Myth defines 'eternal verities' which may neither be eternal nor verities. And myth acts economically, 'it abolishes the complexity of human acts, it gives them the simplicity of essences, it does away with all the dialectics, without any going back beyond what is immediately visible, it organizes a world which is without contradictions because it is without depth, a world wide open and wallowing in the evident, it establishes a blissful clarity: things appear to mean something by themselves.'

Statistically, Barthes believes, myth is on the political Right, and one of its chief inspirations is *order*, its communication mode, RHETORIC. See SEMIOLOGY/SEMIOTICS.

* J. Cuffer, *Barthes* (UK: Fontana, 1983).

Narcoticizing dysfunction One of the chief social consequences of the mass media upon AUDIENCES, in the view of P.H. Lazarsfeld and R. Merton in 'Communication, taste and social action' in L. Bryson ed., *The Communication of Ideas* (US: Harper & Row, 1948). This rather awful sounding affliction, of first being subdued, or 'drugged', and then put out of action by exposure to the media, comes about, believe the authors, because audiences are reduced to 'mass apathy' by a heroic effort to keep up with the vast amount of information placed before them. 'Mass communications may be included among the most respectable and efficient of social narcotics . . . increasing dosages of mass communications may be inadvertently transforming the energies of men from active participation into passive knowledge.' See EFFECTS OF THE MASS MEDIA; USES AND GRATIFICATIONS THEORY; MAINSTREAMING.

Narration In, for example, a TELEVISION documentary what the narrator or the voice-over tells the AUDIENCE helps structure both programme and response. Narration is the intermediary between 'raw information' and the ordered discourse or TEXT. In his monograph *Television Discourse and History* (UK: British Film Institute, 1980), Colin McArthur argues that the 'central ideological function of narration is to confer *authority* on, and to elide *contradictions* in, the discourse'. Narration, therefore, serves to identify and help further an ideological base.

Narration is as much a technical convenience as an ideological mechanism. It is a time-saver; permits summary; allows for efficient transition; it is custom-built for an expensive, time-conscious MEDIUM. Given creative independence, many programme producers have reduced the dominance of narrative or done away with it altogether, as much as possible letting the world 'speak for itself' by using sound and vision without comment; allowing camera and microphone to eavesdrop on activities free from a framing narrative. Of course the process of MEDIATION is ultimately unavoidable – cameras have to be set up in one place or another; pointed in one direction rather than another; decisions have to be made about long-shot and close-up and finally the FILM has to be edited: even without a narrator, a story has been told; reality has been reconstructed. See NARRATIVE PARADIGM; SYMBOLIC CONVERGENCE THEORY.

Narrative paradigm Theory that sees people as essentially storytellers, defining humankind as *homo narrans*. A substantial section of the Autumn 1985 edition of the *Journal of Communication* was devoted to an analysis, by a variety of contributors, of the notion that if storytelling is central to human discourse and INTERACTION, then the paradigm provides an important METAPHOR for communications research which has its own story – its own narrative-base – rooted in beliefs about truth and falsehood, fact and fiction and the nature of reason.

Walter R. Fisher, Professor of Communication Arts and Sciences at the University of Southern California, in 'The narrative paradigm: in the beginning', believes that rationality in humans is determined by the nature of persons as narrative beings, by 'their inherent awareness of *narrative probability*, what constitutes a coherent story, and their constant habit of testing *narrative fidelity*, whether the stories they experience ring true with stories they know in their lives'. He goes on, 'the world is a set of stories which must be chosen among to live the good life in a process of continual recreation.'

The narrative paradigm differs from *dramatism*, or the 'dramatic paradigm' which sees humans as playing parts – prescribed ROLES – in scripts provided by existing situations, cultural patterns, institutions.

In the same issue of the *Journal*, Thomas B. Farrell, in 'Narrative in natural discourse: on conversation and rhetoric', offers a cautious qualification: 'The question, bluntly put, is whether we can be actors in and authors of the same unfinished story without doing damage to the one indispensable outcome of successful narrative: character.' Rather than narrative being the 'primary art form of everyday life', Farrell opts for RHETORIC and conversation. See SYMBOLIC CONVERGENCE THEORY; THEORIES AND CONCEPTS OF COMMUNICATION.

Narrowcasting As contrasted with *broad*casting; JARGON word to describe the process whereby advertisers, programme makers, VIDEO marketeers and producers aim at specialized-interest audiences, from gardening to golf, from astonomy to cookery; or at special *levels* of AUDIENCE distinguished by, for example, social CLASS, education or spending power.

Nasties See VIDEO-NASTIES.

National Film and Television School (UK) The LLOYD COMMITTEE REPORT, 1967, had recommended that a National Film School should be established to provide professional training.

Located at Beaconsfield Studios, working under the authority of the Films Act, 1970 and funded by a direct grant from the Treasury on the Arts Vote, in association with the Office of Arts and Libraries, the National Film and Television School has produced many graduates who have made notable contributions to British cinema and TELEVISION, among them Nicholas Broomfield whose *Soldier Girls* (1981) won the the Prix Italia for DOCUMENTARY (in 1982), David Anderson whose *Dreamland Express* won a British Academy Award for Best Animation Film, 1982, and Michael

Radford whose *Another Time, Another Place* won critical acclaim in 1983. Perhaps the most distinguished of all the Film School's alumni is the Scotsman, Bill Forsyth (*Gregory's Girl*, 1981, *Local Hero*, 1983 and *Comfort and Joy*, 1984).

National Film Archive Founded in May 1935, the NFA is the largest division of the BRITISH FILM INSTITUTE, employing over 130 staff, Its role is to acquire, preserve and make available for study a collection of films and TV programmes of all kinds exhibited or transmitted in the UK from any source and of any nationality, but with particular emphasis on British productions, which may have lasting value as works of art, examples of FILM or TV history or as valuable records of past and present contemporary behaviour. The Archive contains over 80,000 titles, going back as early as 1895.

National Viewers' and Listeners' Association (NVLA) See 'CLEAN UP TV' MOVEMENT.

Naturalistic illusion (of television) The visual qualities of TV can lead to the assumption that it is merely a window on the world, showing life as it really is. Stuart Hall in 'The rediscovery of "ideology" ', in M. Gurevitch, T. Bennett, J. Curran, and J. Woollacott, eds., *Culture, Society and the Media* (UK: Methuen, 1982), refers to this phenomenon as the 'naturalistic illusion'. TV programmes are in fact the result of considerable planning and research.

Elaborate procedures of framing, editing and the matching of images with dialogue have to be undertaken in order to present an exposition. During these procedures decisions are taken which may significantly affect the finished presentation. Different impressions can be given, for example, of a demonstration depending upon when or where the FILM is taken and how it is edited.

Stuart Hood, in *Hood on Television* (UK: Pluto Press, 1980) also argues that TV transforms reality: every programme about a real event or occasion is 'a reinvention not a reflection of reality'.

Needle time The amount of time permitted by arrangement with the organizations representing performers – orchestras, instrumentalists, bands, soloists – and the record companies, for recorded music on BROADCASTING channels.

Needs See MASLOW'S HIERARCHY OF NEEDS.

Negative frequency See FREQUENCY.

Negative news See NEWS VALUES.

Negotiated code See DOMINANT, SUBORDINATE, RADICAL.

Neologism The invention or usage of a new word, or giving an old word a new MEANING, such as 'viewer' from the French 'voyeur' to indicate someone who views other people's sometimes illicit activities. Examples: summit conference; hi-fi; motel; tailback; motorcade; pot.

Neorealism The Greek word 'neos' means 'new' or young. The term was used by Umberto Barbaro in 1943 in praise of films in France such as those made by the team of Marcel Carné (b. 1909) and screenwriter Jacques Prévert (1900–77) (See FILM NOIR). The sombre down-to-earthness of such films as *Le Jour se Lève* (1939) was an inspiration for post-war Italian Neorealists such as Roberto Rossellini (1906–77), Vittorio de Sica (1901–74) and Luchino Visconti (1906–76). Their themes portrayed rural and urban poverty, their tone that of anger and bitterness at a world of poverty and injustice.

Network Channels of communication which are interconnected are termed networks, to be found in all communication in which numbers of people are involved, such as GROUPS and organizations. Basically a communication network consists of linked dyads in which the *receiver* in one DYAD is the *source* in the next. Such networks will vary in size and not all members of the network will necessarily have equal access to information or participation. A *communication structure* is a network in which some channels are systematically neglected. Generally speaking the greater the number of links between members, and the closer the distance between them, the more likely it is that information is distributed equally; assuming all members communicate through all the links at their disposal. In a network with a high level of CENTRALITY it is likely that some members will possess more information than others. Communication networks may take several forms, such as the two illustrated here.

Networks may vary as to the ease with which individual members can be isolated from fellow members and some networks will suffer more than others from the removal of a member or a link. If a member or link is missing from a *chain* network, for example, the effect is likely to be more serious than if either were missing from a *circle* network. A network may also spawn a sub-network: a sub-network can be said to exist when the number of links between certain members is greater than the number of links between these members and others.

The term network is used in BROADCASTING to describe the pattern of connection of the broadcasting stations of a broadcasting company or companies. Such a connection allows the simultaneous broadcast of the same programme. **To network** a programme means to broadcast it to the widest number of TV/RADIO stations both within one network and in other networks. In the US, the term is used more specifically: the Networks are those companies which commission programmes and programme series.

Newcomb's ABX model of communication, 1953 In contrast to the linear structure of the SHANNON AND WEAVER MODEL OF COMMUNICATION, 1949, T.H. Newcomb's model is triangular in shape, and is the first to introduce as a factor the role of communication in a society or a social relationship.

A and B are communicators and X is the situation or social *context* in which the communication takes place. Both the individuals are orientated to each other and to X, and communication is conceived of as the process which supports this orientational structure. Symmetry or balance is maintained between the three elements by the transmission of information about any change in circumstance or relationship, thus allowing adjustment to take place.

For Newcomb, the process of communication is one of the interdependent factors maintaining *equilibrium*, or as Newcomb himself puts it in 'An approach to the study of communicative acts' in *Psychological Review*, 60

Chain

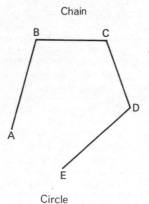

Circle

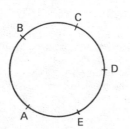

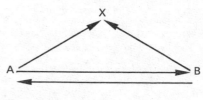

Newcomb's ABX model

(1953) 'communication among human beings performs the essential functions of enabling two or more individuals to maintain simultaneous orientation to each other *and* towards objects of an external environment.' See COMMUNICATION MODELS; CONGRUENCE THEORY; McCOMBS and SHAW AGENDA SETTING MODEL OF MEDIA EFFECTS, 1976; WESLEY AND MACLEAN'S MODEL OF COMMUNICATION.

New International Information Order See NEW WORLD INFORMATION ORDER.

New Populism See MAINSTREAMING.

New Wave In the year 1959–60 an astonishing 67 new directors made their FILM debut in France: this was the *nouvelle vague* as Françoise Giroud described it. At the crest of the wave were critics writing for the film magazine *Cahiers du Cinéma*, including François Truffaut (1932–84), Jean-Luc Godard (b. 1930) and Claude Chabrol (b. 1930). Their films were made cheaply, often with unknown actors, improvisation, hand-held cameras, location shooting and without huge teams of technicians.

The New Wave were always a loose-knit grouping of individual directors, and it was individualism – the belief in the film director as *auteur* – which was their common characteristic. They reacted against the studio product and produced films of extraordinary richness and variety.

Others in the Wave have been Alain Resnais, Chris Marker, Eric Rohmer, Jacques Rivette, Louis Malle, Roger Vadim and Agnès Varda.

New World Information Order Unesco-sponsored campaign to counter MEDIA IMPERIALISM by creating an information order that gives a more balanced view of developing countries than has been generally presented by western capitalist PRESS coverage. The intentions of Unesco, with its International Programme for the Development of Communication (IPDC), have been interpreted as a means of exerting greater national control over access to and use of information. This, allege the critics of the Programme, would constitute a dangerous form of CENSORSHIP.

In 1981 the US Congress directed the Reagan administration to withdraw its contribution to Unesco – a quarter of its budget – if measures were taken to restrict the free flow of information. The US withdrew effectively from UNESCO on 31 December, 1984 and was joined in its move by the UK. See INTERNATIONAL FEDERATION OF JOURNALISTS; MACBRIDE COMMISSION; NON-ALIGNED NEWS POOL; TALLOIRES DECLARATION; WORLD PRESS FREEDOM COMMITTEE.

News agencies 'The invention of the news agency', writes Anthony Smith in *The Geopolitics of Information* (UK: Faber, 1980) 'was the most important single development in the newspaper industry in the early 1800s, apart from the rotary press.' The early agencies – Reuter, Havas and Wolff – carved up the world into spheres of activity in much the same way as imperialist nations parcelled out Third World territories between them.

In 1869 the major agencies signed an Agency Alliance Treaty. Reuter was 'granted' the British Empire and the whole of the Far East; Havas – a French agency – was granted Italy, Spain, France and the Portuguese empire and the Germany-based Wolff received Austria, Scandinavia and Russia. America was awarded jointly to Havas and Reuter.

The five agencies today which supply international news in bulk are: the Associated Press (AP), United Press International (UPI), Reuters, Agence France-Presse and the Soviet Union's Tass. They have all emerged from the imperial and post-imperial competition of the last century by which, as Anthony Smith says, 'the great powers tried to spread their news networks throughout the area of their economic and political suzerainty'. These agencies today have almost 50,000 offices spread round the world. The four western agencies send out between them some 34m words a day and claim to service nine tenths of the world's newspapers, RADIO and TV stations. The AP alone estimates that it reaches a third of the world every day.

There are more than 120 agencies throughout the world, though the location-balance of these and the big four is not evenly spread. For example, taking the world agencies together, including Tass, 34% of their correspondents are kept in the US, 28% in Europe (East and West), 17% in Asia and Australia, 11% in Latin America, 6% in the Middle East and 4% in Africa (1980 figures). AP collects only 1% of its revenue from the Third World, though it spends 5% of its revenue on collecting information from there. See MEDIA IMPERIALISM, NEW WORLD INFORMATION ORDER; NON-ALIGNED NEWS POOL.

* O. Boyd – Barrett, *The International News Agencies* (UK: Constable, 1980).

News consensus See CONSISTENCY.

News frameworks Consist of a shared set of assumptions by reporters and editors about what is newsworthy. These assumptions influence the selection of items for investigation and reporting and to some extent how they will be presented. This set of assumptions also enables journalists and editors to relate news items to an image of society in order to give them MEANING. Thus the framework can provide a 'ready reckoner' for constructing as well as selecting news which allows deadlines to be met. See NEWS VALUES.

News-literate Term used by John Hartley in *Understanding News* (UK: Methuen, 1982) to describe the ability of a reader, listener or viewer to comprehend the NORMS, CODES and conventions of news programmes; to intelligently scan the news, 'recognize its familiar cast of characters and events' and to be able to spontaneously 'interpret the world at large in terms of the codes we have learnt from the news'. See NEWS VALUES.

News management Refers to the tactics employed by those – usually in government or important positions in society – who wish to shape the news to their own advantage, or to control events in such a way as to win favourable publicity. See CULTURAL APPARATUS; ELITE; NEWS VALUES.

Newspapers, origins The earliest newspapers in Britain were far more internationalist in outlook and interest than they tend to be today. The reason for this was the extensive CENSORSHIP of home news by monarch and council. As early as the 17th c. there was the co-called *Relation*, the publication of a single news story, usually related long after the events. The *Coranto* served to join individual Relations into a continuity, though still not appearing regularly. The *Diurnall* was a step forward, providing a weekly account of occurrences over several days. Like the others before it, the *Mercury* appeared in book-like form, but bore more prominently the individual stamp of writers and tended to be more immediate and more diverse. During the Civil War (1642–46) Mercuries appeared in great abundance, even on Sundays.

Contemporaneous with the *Mercury* was the *Intelligencer*, usually more formal, aspiring to be 'official'. A notable example was *The Publick Intelligencer* published with the blessing of Protector Oliver Cromwell. Indeed the street journalism of all kinds which emerged in the heady days of the English Civil War laid the basis for the popular journalism we recognize today. In the 20 years between 1640 and the restoration of the monarchy under Charles II, 30,000 news publications and pamphlets emerged in London alone.

The date usually cited for London's first regular daily paper is 1702. The intention of Samuel Buckley's *Daily Courant* was 'to give news, give it daily and impartially', and it continued for 6000 editions. By 1750 London had five daily papers, six thrice-weeklies, five weeklies and several other periodicals, all amounting to a circulation of 100,000 copies a week.

The Stamp Act of 1712 heralded over a century of increasing concern on the part of the authorities about the proliferation and influence of newspapers. Government agents reported on the contents of newspapers and there was a bristling array of laws to use against the PRESS, such as seditious libel and profana-tion. Of dubious legality but considerable effectiveness was the general warrant enabling arrests and seizures of unnamed persons to be made by the King's Messengers, practically at their discretion. Though general warrants were no longer legal after 1766, the STAMP DUTY and other TAXES ON KNOWLEDGE were burgeoning until the middle of the 19th c. when massive and sustained press and popular pressure led to the reduction and eventual abolition of the duties.

New technology, the growth of ADVERTISING and a more literate general public contributed to a massive expansion of newspapers in the latter half of the 19th c. In 1821 there had been 267 newspapers, including weeklies, in the UK and by 1861, 1,102. Newspaper trains which began running in 1876 meant that the London papers could reach all parts of the country, while TELEGRAPHY speeded news, increasingly provided by the NEWS AGENCIES (Paul Julius Reuter opened his London office in 1851). By 1880 London had 18 dailies; in the English provinces there were 96 dailies, four in Wales, 21 in Scotland and 17 in Ireland.

The most dramatic example of the rise in the popularity of newspapers was the boom in Sunday papers, whose audience, writes Anthony Smith in *The Newspaper: An International History* (UK: Thames & Hudson, 1979) 'came increasingly to consist of the newly literate who could not afford six papers a week and were interested in non-political news. The Sunday journals traded in horrible murders, ghastly seductions and lurid rapes, but they were combined with a distinct brand of radicalism.' Edward Lloyd's *Weekly News*, founded in 1842, was the first periodical to reach a circulation of a million, leaving the highest selling daily paper, *The Daily Telegraph*, with a 200,000 circulation, well behind.

The pattern for the future was set: new technology facilitated (and made economically necessary) massive print runs; journalism targeted itself for vast readerships; advertising became more and more the staple financial support of the press; ownership rested with very rich individuals or joint stock companies; readership patterns hardened along lines of social CLASS – and competition became increasingly desperate. See ELECTRONIC NEWSPAPER; NORTHCLIFFE REVOLUTION; PHOTOJOURNALISM; PRESS BARONS.

Newspeak As opposed to Oldspeak in George Orwell's novel *Nineteen Eighty-Four* (1949), where private thought and individual LANGUAGE were crimes against the totalitarian state of Oceania, and where the TV screen could actually hear what viewers were saying and see whether they were indulging in one of the worst of all crimes – private reading. Guardian of Newspeak – the official language divested of all superfluities by the MEANING defined by the State – was the Ministry of Truth (which, incidentally, had a sub-section called *Pornsoc*).

Orwell's Appendix to the novel, *The Principles of Newspeak*, explains that Newspeak was 'not only to provide a medium of expression for the world-view and mental habits proper to the devotees of Ingsoc (English Socialism), but to make all other modes of thought impossible'. Though the word 'free' would be retained in Newspeak, its meaning applied in the sense of 'This dog is free from lice'. See NUKESPEAK.

News production in broadcasting; central features See IMPARTIALITY.

Newsreel The Lumière brothers fathered newsreel FILM at the birth of the cinema, from 1895, but the first regular newsreel, *Pathé Journal*, began in 1908, and French influence upon news on film was considerable for many years.

The 1st World War (1914–18) gave impetus to newsreel especially in Germany, and with the Revolution in Russia (1917) PROPAGANDA-newsreel (see AGITPROP) was regarded by the Communist government as being of vital importance in the war for hearts and minds. Dziga Vertov's *Kino-Pravda* newsreel series ran from 1922 to 1925.

Companies in the US were the first to add sound to newsreels and in the UK *British Movietone* was the first to adopt sound (1928). In the 1930s the outstanding newsreel in the US was the MARCH OF TIME series. News on TV eventually put an end to cinema newsreels. See CINEMATOGRAPHY, ORIGINS; DOCUMENTARY.

News values According to the former editor of *The Sunday Times* and *The Times*, Harold Evans, in his book *The Practice of Journalism* (UK: Heinemann, 1963), 'News is people'. Long-time journalist Denis MacShane in *Using the Media* (UK: Pluto Press, 1979) sums up what journalists are on the look out for with five tenets: conflict; hardship and danger to the community; the unusual (oddity, novelty); scandal; and individualism. He quotes Lord Northcliffe (1869–1922), one of the original PRESS BARONS, who once declared, 'News is what somebody somewhere wants to suppress; all the rest is advertising.' Stuart Hood in *Hood on Television* (UK: Pluto Press, 1980), refers to *news sense* as 'the ability to judge the language and attitudes permissible within the opinion-forming organization of our society', well within CONSENSUS thinking.

One of the most succinct explanations of news values is that of Johan Galtung and Mari Ruge in 'Structuring and selecting news' in S. Cohen and J. Young, eds., *The Manufacture of News* (UK: Constable, 1973). Events will be more likely to be reported if they fulfil any, some or several of the following criteria: (1) *Frequency*: if the event takes a time approximate to the FREQUENCY of the MEDIUM. A mur-

der, for example, is more newsworthy than the slow progress of a Third World country. (2) *Amplitude*: the bigger, the better, the more dramatic – the greater is the likelihood of the story achieving what the authors call 'threshold value'. (3) *Unambiguity*: the more clear-cut, uncomplicated the events, the more they will be noticed and reported. (4) *Familiarity*: that which is ethnocentric, of cultural proximity, and that which is *relevant*; so things close to home matter most, unless things close to home are affected by far away events.

(5) *Correspondence*: that is, the degree to which the events meet with our expectations, our predictions, even. In this case, say Galtung and Ruge, 'news' is actually 'olds'. They term this the 'hypothesis of consonance' – that which is familiar is registered, that which is unfamiliar is less likely to be registered. (6) *Surprise*: this forms an antidote in terms of criteria to (4) and (5), and works to the benefit of *good* news: 'Events have to be unexpected or rare, or preferably both, to become good news.' (7) *Continuity*: that which has been defined as news – which has hit the headlines – will continue to be newsworthy even if amplitude is reduced. (8) *Composition*: the need for a 'balance' in a news-spread leads the producer or editor to feed in contrasting elements – some home news if the predominant stories have been foreign; a little good news if the news has generally been gloomy.

Galtung and Ruge draw the following generalizations: the more events concern ELITE nations or elite people, the more events can be seen in personal terms and the more *negative* the event is in its consequences, the greater is the likelihood of selection. Consequently, once a news item has been selected, what makes it newsworthy will be accentuated (the authors call this stage 'Distortion'). *Selection* and distortion will, it is argued, take place at all steps in the chain from event to reader ('Replication').

Although Galtung and Ruge's study deals only with newspaper content, Jeremy Tunstall in *Journalists at work* (UK: Constable, 1971), referring to the Galtung and Ruge article which had first been published in the *Journal of International Peace Research* (1965), adapts the scheme to TV news values. He itemizes four points of difference: (1) In TV the visual is given pre-eminence. The possession of new FILM will often increase the prominence given to a news story. (2) News items which include film of 'our own reporters' interviewing or commentating on a story are preferred. (3) TV makes use of a small fraction of the *number* of stories the newspapers carry, and even major TV items are short compared with newspaper coverage. (4) There is preference for 'hard' stories or actuality on TV news. See GALTUNG and RUGE'S MODEL OF SELECTIVE GATEKEEPING, 1965; IMMEDIACY; IMPARTIALITY.

* J. Hartley, *Understanding News* (UK: Methuen, 1982); M. Harrison, *TV News: Whose Bias?* (UK: Policy Journals, 1985).

Nickelodeon An early and primitive form of cinema, of immense popularity in the US by 1905, usually consisting of a long, narrow room furnished with wooden bench seats and very basic equipment for FILM projection; frequently converted from a shop or store. The term is thought to have been used by showman John P. Harris, combining the Greek for theatre with the SLANG expression for the five cents charged for admission. The English equivalent was the *penny gaf*. Soon the Nickelodeon gave way to the more stately film-houses. In 1913, Mitchell L. Mark bought the Strand Theatre, a 3000-seater on Broadway, New York, and set in motion a fashion for neo-Baroque splendour. The movies had moved up market.

Much later, the jukebox got referred to as the nickelodeon; a translation in MEANING testified in the post-2nd World War hit song, 'Put another nickel in/In the Nickelodeon . . .'

Noelle-Neumann's spiral of silence model of public opinion, 1974 In her paper, 'The spiral of silence: a theory of public opinion' published in the *Journal of Communication*, 24 (1974), German professor of communications research Elisabeth Noelle-Neumann examines the interplay between three communicative factors: the mass media, INTERPERSONAL COMMUNICATION and an individual's PERCEPTION of his or her own standpoint in relation to others in society. The model is based upon the belief that people are uneasy – suffer

DISSONANCE – if they feel themselves to be *isolates* with regard to general opinion and attitude: that they are the odd one out. In response to a situation, we tend to ask, what do other people think; what is the majority or dominant opinion?

A person may find 'that the views he holds are losing ground; the more this appears to be so, the more uncertain he will become of himself, and the less he will be inclined to express his opinion'. This is the spiral of silence:

The dominant view which the mass media express (see ELITE; HEGEMONY; POWER ELITE) exerts pressure to conform, to step into line; and the more this view is expressed, the more the dominant view is reinforced; the more dominant it appears, the more difficult it becomes to hold a contrary view. In a sense, Noelle-Neumann's model is a spiral within a spiral, the one an assertion, the other a withdrawal into a silence as the assertion grows stronger. In particular, note the arrows at the right hand side of the model. In relation to others around them, those holding 'different' opinions and ATTITUDES grow more and more isolated. Thus a spiral of silence on the part of individual members of the public reflect the spiral of dominance represented by the media.

Professor Noelle-Neumann's definition of public opinion is that 'which can be voiced in public without fear of sanctions and upon which action in public can be based . . . voicing opposite opinions, or acting in public accordingly, incurs the danger of isolation'. The model prompts the query whether the public merely holds back from expressing diverging or contrary views, but continues to

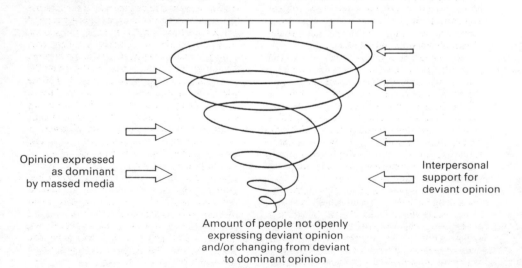

Opinion expressed as dominant by massed media

Interpersonal support for deviant opinion

Amount of people not openly expressing deviant opinion and/or changing from deviant to dominant opinion

Noelle-Neumann's spiral of silence model of public opinion, 1974

hold them, or whether attitudes have actually been changed as a result of dominant media voices.

See COMMUNICATION MODELS.

Noise Impedance or barrier between the sending and receiving of communication signals. C.E. Shannon and W. Weaver in *The Mathematical Theory of Communication* (US: University of Illinois Press, 1949) posit two levels of noise problems: level A, **engineering noise** and, at the higher level B, **semantic noise**. Level A is physical and technical and is defined as any distortion of MEANING occurring in the communication process which is not intended by the source, but which affects the reception of the MESSAGE carrying signals and their clarity. The semantic level is 'noise' or impedance in terms of CODES – linguistic, personal, psychological, cultural, etc. See COMMUNICATION MODELS.

Non-Aligned News Pool World-wide, non-profit-making news agency brought into existence by a decision of the Fifth Non-Aligned Summit Conference in Colombo, August 1976. 85 nations undertook to share information from their respective news gathering agencies with the aim of achieving greater balance in the reporting of events and development in non-aligned countries. The News Pool has been useful, but its potential has been limited by the competition offered by major NEWS AGENCIES and by the political situation in many countries where governments censor the free flow of information. See MEDIA IMPERIALISM.

Non-verbal behaviour: repertoire A useful classification scheme for the repertoire of non-verbal behaviour is suggested by American authors Paul Ekman and Wallace V. Friesen in 'The repertoire of nonverbal behaviour: categories, origins, usage and coding' in *Semiotica* 1 (1969). Their five categories of non-verbal movement are: emblem, illustrators, affect displays, regulators and adaptors.

Emblems are non-verbal behaviours which directly suggest specific words or phrases, usually without vocal accompaniment. Thus the beckoning first finger is the emblem for 'Come here'. Emblems are short-cut communication signals useful in many ways, especially where verbal communication is difficult or inappropriate, for example when a person is thumbing a lift.

Illustrators accompany and reinforce verbal messages – the nod of the head, a supportive smile, leaning forward to show interest, sketching something in the air with finger or hand, to give a point emphasis or clarity. Illustrators tend to be less culture-specific than emblems.

Affect displays are movements of the face and body which hold emotional MEANING: disappointment, rage, happiness, hopefulness, shock, etc., indeed our whole *body language* constitutes affect displays.

For Ekman and Friesen, *regulators* are non-verbal actions which monitor and control the communication of another individual. These can take the form of encouragement of the other person to go on speaking, to explain more fully, to quicken up, slow down, or get to the point. Here we use nods, smiles, grunts, ah-ha's; we shake our heads, we glance away, blink, pucker lips. Equally we can employ regulators in a negative sense by using non-verbal behaviours to discourage the other person from talking.

Adaptors are generally habitual behaviours used to make a person feel more at ease in communication interactions: twisting a lock of hair, scratching, stroking (the hair, the chin, etc.), wringing hands, turning a ring round the finger, fiddling with jewellery, playing with matches – actions which are more private than public and are likely to undergo some modification when the private action extends into a public domain. See COMMUNICATION, NON-VERBAL; GESTURE; PROXEMICS.

Non-verbal communication See COMMUNICATION, NON-VERBAL.

Normative theories of mass media Building on an early work by American media analysts G.F. Siebert, T. Peterson and W. Schramm, *Four Theories of the Press* (US: University of Illinois Press, 1956), Denis McQuail posits six normative theories of the mass media. In *Mass Communication Theory: An Introduction* (UK: Sage, 1983), McQuail lists (1) Authoritarian Theory; (2) Free Press Theory; (3) Social Responsibility Theory; (4) Soviet Media Theory; (5) Development Media Theory and (6) Democratic-Participant Theory.

By normative, we mean how the media *should* be, what is to be expected of them rather than what necessarily happens in practice; and it is out of the political, cultural and economic CONTEXT that the normative principles arise. Central to the normative theory is the way the media 'behave' in relation to the state, and the dominant expectations that the state has of the role of the media. The Authoritarian Theory thus appertains in a state in which PRESS or BROADCASTING freedoms not only do not exist but are not considered – by those in power, or those who support them in power – desirable even as ideals. The underlying principles of Authoritarian Theory are that the media should do nothing to undermine established authority; that they should be subordinate to that authority and that they should avoid giving offence to majority or dominant moral or political VALUES. Under such a theory, CENSORSHIP is justifiable and to offend against the reigning CONSENSUS of values is considered, potentially, a criminal offence.

What Siebert *et al.* call 'Libertarian theory' McQuail terms the Free Press Theory, which is considered the chief legitimating principle for the print media in liberal democracies. Free and public expression is, implies this theory, the best way to arrive at the truth and expose error. It is a principle enshrined in the First Amendment of the American Constitution. This states that 'Congress shall make no law . . . abridging the freedom of speech of the press'. McQuail's analysis of this principle in practice is well worth noting, for he asks searching questions about *whose* freedom; about monopoly tendencies; about the close identification of notions of freedom with profit and private ownership.

The Social Responsibility Theory believes in freedom so long as it is harnessed to responsibility. Independence is desirable only so long as it is reconcileable with an obligation to society. In this sense, the media are perceived as fulfilling a role of public stewardship. They are the watchdogs of the common good against government or private abuse of power or corruption. There is an emphasis on neutrality and balance; most of all, a belief in media *accountability* to society.

Soviet Media Theory derives from the postulates of Marx, Engels and Lenin. Here, the media should serve the interests of the socialist state, the state being an embodiment of all the members of a classless society. Because the media are *of* the people, they belong *to* the people. In practice, of course, they belong to the people's LEADERSHIP. The tasks of media are to socialize the people into desirable NORMS as defined in Marxist doctrine; to educate, inform, motivate and mobilize in the aims and aspirations of a socialist society. Thus a 'free' media in the sense that it is free to call into question those aims and aspirations would be an unacceptable contradiction of its perceived function; hence the justification of media control and censorship.

Development Media Theory has arisen out of special needs in the Third World developing nations (See MACBRIDE COMMISSION; MEDIA IMPERIALISM; NEW WORLD INFORMATION ORDER). This theory eschews BAD NEWS theory and favours positive reporting on the grounds that for developing nations, often struggling for economic survival in competition with western industrialized countries, reporting of disasters and setbacks can substantially injure the process of nation building. Development Media Theory favours media content that opposes dependency and foreign domination; that supports autonomy and cultural identity; that accepts and carries out positive development tasks in line with nationally established policies. Freedom should be allowed within the parameters of a nation's economic and cultural priorities and development needs.

The most recent addition to the body of normative theory is Democratic-Participant Media Theory, several of whose tenets are to be found among those of the other theories mentioned here. McQuail says of the theory, 'There is a mixture of theoretical elements, including libertarianism, utopianism, socialism, egalitarianism, localism'. Individual rights of access, of citizen and minority GROUPS, to the media are important constituents of the theory – the right *to* communicate; to be served by the media according to a more democratic determination of need. Thus the theory opposes the concentration of ownership and rejects the role of AUDIENCE as tame receiver. Media should be answerable, free of government or big-business intervention, small-scale, interactive and participative (See CAMPAIGN FOR PRESS AND BROADCASTING FREEDOM; COMMUNITY RADIO; RIGHT OF REPLY). The emphasis is upon the needs and aspirations of the receiver rather than, say, with the Free Press Theory, where the rights of the media themselves stand paramount. While querying whether the Democratic-Participant Media Theory actually *is* an independent theory, McQuail decides that it deserves its separate identity because it challenges reigning theories and offers a positive stimulus towards new forms of media institution. See COMMUNICATION MODELS.

Norms Shared expectations or standards of behaviour within a particular social group or society. Any type of established group will have norms, both peculiar to itself and shared with the wider community. Of those norms widely accepted in a society, some will operate on a high, some on a low CONSENSUS. Any individual's perception and interpretation of experience will be influenced by the norms of the social GROUPS and society to which he/she belongs. Individuals generally take such norms for granted. Communication between individuals likewise reflects certain norms, such as those of grammar and style of writing or norms of conduct which guide social INTERACTION.

Norms arise from such interaction between various individuals and social groups. Once developed, they are passed on through SOCIALIZATION to new members. Norms are not static: they are subject to renegotiation. They play a significant part in maintaining the social position of particular groups and individuals and constitute an influential agent of informal social control.

The media, as agents of communication and socialization, are in a position to both reinforce general societal norms and express the norms of certain social groups. In addition, the media have the potential to *shape* EXPECTATIONS of behaviour, particularly with regard to individuals or groups with whom the viewer, listener or reader is unfamiliar. It is this potential that has aroused considerable research interest. See CULTURE; MALE-AS-NORM; VALUES.

Northcliffe revolution New schooling in the late 19th c. in the UK following the Foster Education Act of 1870 created a rapidly expanding readership of literature and news; Alfred Charles William Harmsworth (1865–1922), later Lord Northcliffe, perhaps the most dynamic and extraordinary of the PRESS BARONS built a PRESS empire on the new flood-tide of literacy. Creator of the *Daily Mail* (1896) and the *Daily Mirror* (1903), Northcliffe combined a marked 'popular-educator' emphasis with a marketing sense which was energetic, imaginative, daring and ruthless. Northcliffe represents the fundamental shift towards the exploitation of, and increasing dependence upon, ADVERTISING as a means of newspaper finance.

Publicity was everything. Rivalry between papers, in terms of sensation-seeking and attention-grabbing stunts resembled – as it continues to do today – the Battle of the Titans. Raymond Williams in *The Long Revolution* (UK: Chatto & Windus, 1961) says, 'The true "Northcliffe Revolution" is less an innovation in actual journalism than a radical change in the economic basis of newspapers, tied to the new kind of advertising.'

By 1908 Northcliffe's press empire included the *Mail*, the *Mirror*, *The Times*, two Sunday papers (*Observer* and *Dispatch*) and an evening paper (*News*) plus a host of periodicals such as *Tit-Bits* and *Answers* (whose circulation had leapt from 12,000 at its inception to 352,000 two years later).

Though the so-called Northcliffe revolution was chiefly characterized by the employment of new technology, the drive for mass circulations and the wholesale reliance on advertising as the prime source of press revenue, the 'flavour' of that revolution must not be overlooked – that is, the STYLE and content emanating from the Press Barons themselves. J. Curran and J. Seaton in *Power Without Responsibility: The Press and Broadcasting in Britain* (UK: Methuen 1985; 3rd ed. Routledge, 1988), write 'Northcliffe and Beaverbrook shaped the entire content of their favourite papers, including their lay-out.' When *The Times* changed the place in the paper of the weather report, Northcliffe raged: '. . . if it's moved again, whoever does it is fired.' Curran and Seaton speak of how the personal tastes of the Barons influenced the popular journalism of the time: 'Northcliffe had a lifelong obsession with torture and death: he even kept an aquarium containing a goldfish and a pike, with a dividing partition, which he would lift up when he was in need of diversion'. He told staff of the *Daily Mail* to find 'one murder a day'.

Meddling with the content by newspaper proprietors was not, of course, new. It had gone on throughout the 19th c., but then interference had focused mainly upon political matters. What was different with Northcliffe and his ilk was that the new proprietors meddled in *everything*. See NEWSPAPERS, ORIGINS.

Nukespeak A play on George Orwell's NEWSPEAK, and associated in MEANING in that it constitutes a EUPHEMISM, something very nasty dressed up in sweet-flavoured, neutralizing LANGUAGE. Nuclear destruction is so horrible a prospect, and nuclear weaponry so much an integral element of western capitalism, that it has become necessary for the namers of names to disarm our fears with titles such as Trident, Cruise, Polaris, Skybolt, Jupiter and Thor. Nukespeak mystifies or renders homely: the uranium bomb which detonated over Hiroshima was called 'Little Boy'; the plutonium bomb dropped on Nagasaki was 'Fat Man'.

* C. Aubrey, ed., *Nukespeak: The Media and the Bomb* (UK: Comedia, 1982).

NVC See COMMUNICATION, NON-VERBAL (NVC)

Object See SIGN.

Objectics In their book *Understanding and Sharing: An Introduction to Speech Communication* (US: Brown, 1979, reprinted 1985), authors Judy Cornelia Pearson, Paul Edward Nelson and Donald Yoder, define Objectics, or object LANGUAGE, as the study of 'clothing, adornments, hairstyles, cosmetics and other artefacts that we carry with us or possess. Object language conveys information about our age, sex, status, role, personality, relationships with groups and with other people, psychological and emotional state, self-concept, and the physical climate in which we live'. See COMMUNICATION, NON-VERBAL (NVC); SELF-CONCEPT.

Objectivity Professor Stuart Hall has expressed the view that objectivity, 'like impartiality, is an operational fiction' (in 'Media power: the double bind', *Journal of Communication*, Autumn 1984). In examining the media, analysts encounter the Famous Five: balance, CONSENSUS, IMPARTIALITY and objectivity, upon which all good reporting and BROADCASTING is said to be based. The questions arising from this precept are: balance between what and what? (for example, between the case for and the case against Apartheid); consensus among whom? Impartiality in what sense? Objectivity in whose eyes? Considering the complex processes of MEDIATION between an event and its report in media form, is it possible to have value-free information?

'All edited or manipulated symbolic reality,' says Hall, 'is impregnated with values, viewpoints, implicit theorizings, common-sense assumptions.' When there are differences between what is objective and what is not, whose opinion wins the day? Hall says of consensus that it is 'structured dominance', that is, the prevailing definition usually rests with the POWER ELITE, the 'power-ideology complex' in any society whose control of and influence upon the media gives them a greater say in the definitions of objectivity. See CULTURAL APPARATUS; DIFFERENTIAL PERCEPTION; ELITE; HEGEMONY; MACHINERY OF REPRESENTATION.

Obscene signals See INSULT SIGNALS.

Obscenity and film censorship See WILLIAMS COMMITTEE REPORT ON OBSCENITY AND FILM CENSORSHIP, 1979.

Obsolescence Generally, anything passing out of date or out of use. In a communications sense, it refers to the link between social habits and media-using habits. The cinema, for example, for several decades of its history, was a social habit, a family ritual; cinemagoing was part of the fabric of social activity for a large percentage of the population. However, after the 2nd World War (1939–45), cinema-going declined as society found other gratifications for social and personal needs. Thus obsolescence can be defined as the abandoning of formerly institutionalized modes of conduct related to some established cultural activity.

OCR Optical character reading, or recognition. A means of feeding information into a WORD PROCESSOR without keying it in. A page of type is fed through a machine (OCR) which photographs the text and transmits an electronic signal to the memory of the word processor. Any text changes can be made at the keyboard.

Odorama Yet another attempt to make the cinema a total experience. The audience is provided with special cards which, at a given signal on the screen, have to be scratched – and the subsequent smell savoured. See CINERAMA; 3-D.

Oeuvre French for 'work', generally the complete works of an artist, writer, composer, etc. The word refers to the work of the mind as well as of hand and eye. Thus we may refer to the *oeuvre* of Pablo Picasso (1891–1973) and mean not only the items of his work – paintings, sculpture, pottery – but, by implication, the nature or character of that work. See OPUS.

Official Secrets Act Born in a spy scare during the Agadir crisis of 1911, reinforced in 1920 during the Troubles in Ireland, given its present formidable form as war broke out in 1939, the Act censors information – access to it, and expression of it – which might be of use to the nation's enemies. It is easier to define what the Act does not cover rather than what it does. Without question, it is the single most comprehensive weapon of CENSORSHIP with regard to the activities of government in the UK, and has few parallels in the 'Free' world.

In January 1988 Conservative MP Richard Shepherd introduced a private member's bill into the House of Commons designed to reform Section 2 of the Act. Shepherd's Protection of Official Information Bill, while confirming present provisions protecting defence and natural security secrets, would have reduced the catch-all powers exercised by government under Section 2. Ministers would no longer have the exclusive right to decide that disclosure of information would damage the national interest. The government proved adamant: secrets were government business. A three-line whip was placed on the vote – at which more than 70 Tory MPs refused to vote as instructed. The bill was killed by a narrow majority of 37. Tory rebel MP and former Prime Minister Edward Heath called it a 'tarnished victory'.

In June of the same year, the government White Paper, *Reform of Section 2 of the* Official Secrets Act, 1911, was published, with the declared intention of trimming the areas defined as secret under Section 2 and clarifying what constitutes a breach of secrecy. Home Secretary Douglas Hurd claimed a 'liberalizing' of the law. However, critics, including MPs on both sides of the House, judged the new provisions to be potentially more draconian than the ones they were to replace. In particular, the White Paper rejects *public interest defence*, even in cases where the information concerns corruption or other forms of criminality. Brian Raymond, solicitor to civil servant Clive Ponting who was unsuccessfully prosecuted under the Act for revealing information about the sinking of the *Belgrano* during the Falklands War, said 'The obliteration of the public interest defence. . . amounts to a licence to cover up Government wrongdoing.' See D-NOTICES; SECRECY; SPYCATCHER AFFAIR.

'Oh Calcutta!' Homonym (word of similar sound but different MEANING) for the French, 'Oh! quel cul t'as', and the title of a 'revue with music' sponsored by drama critic Kenneth Tynan in London in 1970, and source of much displeasure among the censorious. Hailed at its New York opening in 1969 as containing 'nudity and sex unlimited' and 'the kind of show to give pornography a dirty name', *Oh Calcutta!* contained 'ballet' which could also be defined as communal striptease and sketches which included an American wife-swapping extravaganza. The voice of righteous protest (as well as the sound of cashflow at the box-office) was resounding, from the Dowager Lady Birdwood and Mary Whitehouse in particular. The Director of Public Prosecutions decided not to bring a court case against the show and when Lady Birdwood tried for a private prosecution the then Attorney-General, Sir Peter Rawlinson, refused permission. See CENSORSHIP; GAY NEWS: THE LOVE THAT DARED TO SPEAK ITS NAME; LITTLE RED SCHOOL BOOK; OZ TRIAL; PORNOGRAPHY.

Oligopolization Oligarchy is government by a small exclusive CLASS or GROUP; in media terms, *oligopolization* is the process of communication systems falling into the hands a small exclusive group of owners or corporations.

Omnimax Spectator-surrounding FILM projection technique developed, like IMAX, in Canada from a system invented by an Australian, Ron James. Though there are several Omnimax screens in North America, the first in Europe – and the largest screen in the world – operates at the 55 hectare Paris exhibition complex, Cité des Sciences et de L'Industrie at Porte La Villette, which opened in 1986.

La Géode offers a projection screen covering 10,000 square feet and surrounds the spectators with a complete hemisphere, exceeding the normal field of vision. Like Imax, Omnimax uses 70mm film which passes through the camera horizontally producing a 5×7 cm film image – approximately nine times the image area on ordinary cinema film. Camera and projector use a 25mm fish-eye lens with a scope of 172 degrees. A massive light source is required to project such a gigantic picture and Omnimax has a 15 kw water-cooled xenon lamp. See TECHNOLOGY OF THE MEDIA.

One-step, two-step, multi-step flow models of communication Basically these are refinements of the HYPODERMIC NEEDLE MODEL OF COMMUNICATION. The one-step model denies the role of the OPINION LEADER in the flow of communication and presents the view that the mass media communicate directly to a mass audience. There is no suggestion, however, that the messages reach all receivers equally or that they have the same effect on each individual in the audience. The model takes into account the influence of an individual's perception, memory and SELECTIVE EXPOSURE on his/her particular interpretation of a message. SALIENCE – or the factor of prominence – is also considered to be an important variable in the model.

A study conducted by Paul Lazarsfeld and others of the 1940 presidential election in the US threw doubt on the validity of the **one-step** theory. Reporting in *The People's Choice* (US: Duell, Sloan & Pearce, 1944), the authors found little evidence of the direct influence of the media; indeed people seemed more influenced by face-to-face contact with others. Lazarsfeld and his fellow researchers suggested that the flow of communication to the individual is often directed through an opinion leader who plays a vital role in both spreading and interpreting the information. They thus proposed a **two-step model** of communication flow which later research has found to be generally useful. In highlighting the importance of the *social context* of the receiver in the process of the interpretation of mass communication messages this model differs significantly from earlier ones. It presents the mass audience as being composed of interacting and responsive individuals rather than of the socially isolated, passive atoms of earlier MASS SOCIETY theories.

The **multi-step model** is a development of the other two, allowing for the sequential relaying of a MESSAGE. It is not specific about the number of steps there will be in the relaying process nor does it specify that messages must originate from a source and then pass straight through the agencies of the mass media. The model suggests a variable number of relays in the communication process and that the receivers may receive the message at various stages along the relay NETWORK. The exact number of steps in the process depends upon the following: (1) the intentions of the source; (2) the availability of the mass media; (3) the extent of audience exposure to agencies of communication; (4) the nature of the message; (5) the importance of the message to the audience.

The model has often been used in recent research. Its advantage is that it allows the researcher to account for different variables in different communication situations. See COMMUNICATION MODELS.

Onomatopoeia Words which imitate actual sounds are *onomatopoeic*, such as *bang, thud, crackle, hiss, quack* and *twitter*. They are mostly invented words. The first ever attempts at spoken LANGUAGE were very probably onomatopoeic and such words continue to be invented, not a few of them (*zap*, for example) starting life in COMICS and CARTOONS.

Open, closed texts Italian semiologist Umberto Eco has made this useful separation between texts which are varyingly shaped – to permit little interpretation on the part of audience (*closed* texts) or allow plenty of room for interpretation (*open* texts). A work of art – a poem, a painting, a piece of sculpture, for example – would represent an open text in that the intention of the writer, painter or sculptor is to express ideas or feelings which may be interpreted in different ways and at different levels.

The open text invites a sense of participation in the reader or viewer and the interaction which occurs between creator, creation and audience is one in which 'right answers' are less important than the possibility of a *proactive* response; and this may be subject to flux in differing instances and at varying times. PROPAGANDA would constitute closed text in that there is a rigorously PREFERRED READING: the decoder is expected to receive the MESSAGE, and register its MEANING as intended by the communicator. Any divergence from acceptance would, to quote another term of Eco's, represent ABERRANT DECODING. See ANCHORAGE.

Open College Following in the footsteps of the OPEN UNIVERSITY, the Open College addresses itself to those in the population of the UK wishing to further their education in their own time, using *distance learning* approaches – correspondence units linked with BROADCASTING on RADIO and TELEVISION. The Open College's first broadcast was on 21 September 1987. The College's aim is to assist in the improvement of the UK's economic performance using open learning to widen access to training in a range of skills necessary for the changing world of work.

Openness One of the most important DESIGN FEATURES of human LANGUAGE, posited by US linguist Charles Hockett *Openness*, or productivity, writes Hockett in 'The origin of speech', *Scientific American*, 203 (1960), is 'the capacity to say things that have never been said or heard before and yet can be understood by other speakers of the language.'

Opera omnia Latin for 'All his works', the term denotes a total ban on an author's writings imposed by the Roman Catholic *Index Librorum Prohibitorum,* first issued in 1559. A few such prohibited writers have been David Hume, Emile Zola, Jean-Paul Sartre and Alberto Moravia. See CENSORSHIP; INDEX.

Operational code Phrase employed by Nathan C. Leites in *The Operational Code of the Politburo* (US: McGraw-Hill, 1951), meaning the basic assumptions and directives underlying the communications of political ELITES. See CODES.

Opinion leader Someone able to influence informally other individuals' attitudes and/or behaviour in a desired way with relative frequency. He/she is a type of informal leader. Opinion leadership is earned and maintained by the individual's technical competence, sociability and conformity to the NORMS of the SOCIAL SYSTEM. When such leaders are compared to their followers several characteristics are of note: opinion leaders are more exposed to all forms of external communication; more COSMOPOLITE; of a higher social status; and more innovative. Opinion leaders are widely thought to play a vital role in the spreading of new ideas, VALUES and beliefs.

An opinion leader whose range of influence is limited to one specific topic exercises **Monomorphic opinion leadership**. This type of leadership is thought to be typical of modern, industrial societies as the complex technological base of such societies results in a sophisticated DIVISION OF LABOUR and considerable specialization of ROLES. An opinion leader whose influence covers a wide range of topics exercises **Polymorphic opinion leadership**. This is generally thought to be more common in traditional societies. A respected, elderly member of a village, for example, might be consulted on a variety of matters ranging from marriage problems to methods of harvesting.

Opinion poll The increasing reportage of opinion poll findings after the 1945 general election in the UK was a noticeable innovation in the media's coverage of political ISSUES, and in particular in its coverage of election campaigns. Typically, such a poll is designed to illustrate 'public opinion' on a topical issue and consists of a breakdown of responses, from a SAMPLE to pre-set questions. During election campaigns polls are used primarily for forecasting the results. Some researchers, notably Colin Seymour-Ure in *The Political Impact of the Mass Media* (UK: Constable, 1974) have expressed the view that polls may also *influence* the outcome of a campaign, especially when their findings are well publicized. The publication of poll findings is also thought to influence opinions on specific political issues, particularly if the findings suggest a CONSENSUS of opinion.

Oppositional code See DOMINANT, SUBORDINATE, RADICAL.

Optical fibre cable See FIBRE OPTIC TECHNOLOGY.

Optical-storage technology See MICROFORMS.

Opus Latin for 'work', a term most often applied to musical compositions in order of their creation (e.g. Beethoven's 9th Symphony is Opus 125). The practice began in the early 17th c. In the case of Corelli (1653–1713), Vivaldi (CIRCA 1676–1741) and others, opus numbers applied not to single compositions but to collections of work, such as sonatas. The exception to the *Opus* numeration is Mozart (1756–91) whose works are tabulated with the letter K. At Mozart's death, his works, as far as chronological numbering was concerned, were in disorder. Botanist and mineralogist Ludwig von Köchel (1800–77) took in hand the numeration of Mozart's compositions. His listings have since carried K or KV (V meaning *Verzeichnis*, list). Modern composers usually adopt single-work numeration. A *magnum opus* is a masterwork; and *Op. Post.* indicates a work published after the creator's death. See OEUVRE; OPERA OMNIA.

Oracle The Independent Broadcasting Authority's version of CEEFAX. See TELETEXT.

Oral culture An oral CULTURE or SUB-CULTURE is one in which essentially most communication is by word of mouth. Pictures may also be used as a supplement but reading and writing play a minor role in the communication process.

Organization cultures In examining the NORMS, VALUES and practices of business organizations in his *Understanding Organizations* (UK: Penguin, 1976), C.B. Handy identifies four forms of organizational CULTURE which affect the nature or 'profile' of the organization and its patterns of communication. These are: (1) The **power culture**. This depends upon a central power source, with 'rays of power and influence' (and communication) spreading out from a central figure. An example of such a culture is the self-made business person running his/her own company. Without such a 'spider', the web structure of the culture would collapse.

(2) The **role culture**. This is the classic bureaucracy, its model like a Greek temple, with the leadership – directors, governors, etc. represented by the pediment, the various organizational departments, the pillars of the temple and the workers at the base. Here, plainly, the communication process, following lines of authority, is vertical and chiefly one-way.

(3) The **task culture**. This is a skills or ability orientated culture in which *what* an employee is capable of doing is more important than *who* he/she is in terms of position or role. The model is net-shaped, made up of interdependent strands; leadership is exchangeable according to the task in hand. This so-called *matrix* structure is characterized by very flexible channels of communication, horizontal rather than vertical in direction, and is responsive to change.

(4) The **person culture**. In terms of business organizations the rarest of the four. Here the organization exists only to serve the individuals within it. The model is of a cluster, a galaxy of individual stars, without hierarchical structures, constantly interchanging in form. As Handy says, 'Clearly not many organizations can exist with this sort of culture, since organizations tend to have objectives over and above the collective objectives of those who comprise them.' In its purest form, the *kibbutz* (small egalitarian Israeli community) is an example of the person culture. The *factors* Handy cites as influencing organization cultures are: history and ownership; size; technology; goals and objectives; the environment and the people.

Orthophonic recording See GRAMOPHONE.

Out of band BROADCASTING stations using other stations' areas of the wavelength spectrum are 'out of band'; poachers, usually, on Short Wave; or jammers of the air waves.

Out-take Piece of FILM which is not actually used in the completed version.

Overhearing Kurt H. Wolff in *The Sociology of Georg Simmel* (US: Free Press, 1950) uses this expression to describe how recipients of messages may proceed, usually below the level of awareness, to select certain parts for special attention, often distorting them, while at the same time overlooking ('overhearing') other parts entirely. In short, the human organism perceives to a considerable degree what it wants to perceive. See DIFFERENTIAL PERCEPTION; PERCEPTION; SELECTIVE EXPOSURE.

Overkill signals See SHORTFALL SIGNALS.

Oz Trial The longest-ever obscenity trial in the UK, lasting 26 days in the summer of 1971, centred on the *Oz School Kids Issue* (*Oz* 28). The three editors, Richard Neville, Felix Dennis and Jim Anderson were eventually acquitted on the most serious charge – that of conspiring to corrupt the morals of children, but a majority of ten to one of the trial jury found *Oz* guilty of publishing an obscene article, sending such articles through the post and having such articles for profit and gain.

Oz Publications Ink Ltd, received a total fine of £1000 with £1250 costs. Neville got a 15-month jail sentence and a recommendation that he be deported (he was Australian). Anderson received 12 months and Dennis nine.

See CENSORSHIP; GAY NEWS: THE LOVE THAT DARED TO SPEAK ITS NAME; LITTLE RED SCHOOL-BOOK; 'OH CALCUTTA!'; SPYCATCHER CASE.

PABX Private Automatic Branch Exchange; a British Telecom system for the coordination and integration of office TELEPHONE traffic. The original PBX (Private Branch Exchange) comprised a system of up to 9000 phones belonging to a single business or organization, installed on one location or to be employed on a set of locations. The additional *automatic* element means that personnel in the organization can dial their own out-going calls while the local exchange merely directs in-coming calls. However, with the more advanced DID (Direct In-Dialling) in-coming calls can be directed automatically to any extension phone in the system. See SYSTEM X.

Packaging The STYLE and the framework within which TV programmes are presented on our screens: good-looking announcers or interviewers, titling, music, the tailoring of programmes to suitable lengths, indeed any form of image-making for a media product. The word gives emphasis to the connection between the manufacture and sale of goods and the making and presentation of media products. Stuart Hood in *Hood on Television* (UK: Pluto Press, 1980) refers to TV announcers as the 'sales people of the air'.

Paget-Gorman Sign System An aid to teaching deaf children devised by Sir Richard Paget and further developed by Pierre Gorman and Lady Paget in the 1960s. It presents an exact, grammatical *signed* representation of spoken

English and bears no relation to traditional sign LANGUAGE. The System provides a good basis for reading development, though its drawback is that it is an invented system and most of the signs are not ones which the adult deaf use.

Paparazzo Aggressive, prying and often unscrupulous freelance photographer who specializes in taking pictures of celebrities; pursuing them wherever they go, armed with thick skin and zoom lenses. The word is an Italian – Calabrian – surname. It was suggested by writer Ennio Flaiano as a name for a character in Federico Fellini's *La Dolce Vita* (The Sweet Life), made in 1960, a FILM which made famous, indeed notorious, Rome's Via Veneto, symbol of the high-life, big spending, glamour – which in turn drew the famous, especially film stars, to sit at the pavement cafés, and let life simulate art. At the risk of an occasional black eye or broken nose, the Paparazzo snapped indiscreet moments and sold these to a willing PRESS. Today the Paparazzo haunts royalty – with even longer lenses.

Paper of the man on the knife-board of the omnibus Title claimed from 1835 onwards by the *Daily Telegraph* which, for 40 years, was to lead the expansion of the daily PRESS. The knife-board was a seat running along the top of the old form of bus, on which was to be found, presumably, the archetype – the MODEL – of the ordinary man or Mr Average. In later decades, the man on the knife-board became the one on the famous 'Clapham omnibus' to whose balanced judgement and common sense politicians often referred – and occasionally continue to refer – when seeking to prove the support for their policies of the SILENT MAJORITY. The 'down-to-earth' *Telegraph* had, by 1860, a circulation of 140,000, by 1880, 250,000 and by 1890, 300,000. 'What we want,' Levy, the paper's publisher, used to tell new entrants, 'is a human note.'

Paradigm (paradigmic) In LINGUISTICS, describes the set of relationships a linguistic unit – such as a letter or a word – has with other units in a specific context. The word is applicable in all SIGN systems, verbal, numerical, musical, etc. The alphabet is a paradigm, or set of signs, from which a choice is made to formulate the MESSAGE. A **syntagm** is a combination of the chosen signs, a chain that amounts to MEANING. In LANGUAGE we can describe the vocabulary we use as **paradigmic,** and the sentence that vocabulary is formed into, **syntagmic.**

All messages, therefore, involve *selection* from a paradigm and *combination* into a syntagm. All the units in a paradigm must share characteristics that determine the membership of that paradigm, thus letters in the alphabetic paradigm, numbers in the numerical paradigm, notes in the musical paradigm. Each unit within the paradigm must be clearly differentiable from other units; it must be characterized by *distinctive features*. Just as the paradigm is governed by shared characteristics and distinctive features, the syntagm is determined by rules or conventions by which the combination of paradigms is made – rules of grammar and SYNTAX or, in music, rules of harmony. See SEMIOLOGY/SEMIOTICS.

Para-linguistics The study of aspects of vocal communication other than actual words – what is communicated for example by stress, rhythm, tone and quality of voice; by whispering, shouting, sighing, grunting, etc.

Para-proxemics Term used to classify the way TV handles the space between people in its programmes, echoing and simulating the real-life use of space (see PROXEMICS) by individuals – for example, the close-up, medium range and distance camera shots paralleling the SPATIAL ZONES of intimate, personal and social space. Joshua Meyrowitz in 'Television and interpersonal behavior: codes of perception and response' in G. Gumpert and R. Cathcart, eds., *Inter/Media: Interpersonal Communication in a Media World* (US/UK: Oxford University Press, 1979) writes, 'the way in which a person is framed' [by the TV camera] may suggest an interpersonal distance between that person and the viewer.' Distance, in fact, shapes viewer response, with the TV screen becoming 'a kind of "extended retina" for the viewer'.

Para-social identification See PARA-SOCIAL INTERACTION.

Para-social interaction The illusion, contributed to both by the performer and the audience in mass media communication, especially RADIO, TV and FILM, of an *interpersonal relationship* existing between them, free of MEDIATION. Characters (or persona) on air or film, actual or fictional, are often cited as being more 'real' to audiences than the real people they know.

In 'Mass communication and para-social interaction: observation on intimacy at a distance', *Journal of Psychiatry*, 19 (1956), D. Horton and R.R. Wohl write, 'The persona offers, above all, a continuing relationship. His appearance is a regular and dependable event, to be counted on, planned for, and integrated into the routines of daily life' and may be considered by his audience as 'a friend, counsellor, comforter, and model', but unlike all those real people around him, the persona is *changeless*. 'Typically, there are no challenges to a spectator's self . . . that cannot be met comfortably.'

Arguably the strongest relationship or interaction is that between audiences and fictitious characters, especially those in long-running series such as BBC Radio's *The Archers* or *Coronation Street* from Granada TV. Indeed, on occasion, what happens in these series, though entirely fictional, becomes a matter for national attention. Half the nation grieved – and a great many protested most passionately – when Grace Archer was burnt to death; and when that beloved villain of SOAP OPERA, JR of *Dallas* was shot, the incident was reported on BBC News. See BIBLIOTHERAPY.

Parallel processing Our visual capacity allows us to process many images simultaneously – in parallel; to record both foreground and background actions. In contrast, speech capacity depends upon *serial processing*: we hear one word or phrase at a time and process it before proceeding to subsequent data.

Parental Guidance (PG) See CERTIFICATION OF FILMS.

Participant observation Some research evidence is collected by the researcher becoming a member of the group or social situation under observation. The researcher participates fully in the situation and those being observed may be unaware that he/she is a researcher. The advantage of this method of data collection is that the greater involvement of the researcher may facilitate an increased insight into and greater understanding of the behaviour being investigated.

Partisan An adherent of a particular party or cause. The term is also used to describe actions as well as allegiances. Within media studies, much research has focused upon the political partisanship of the PRESS and TV companies, that is, upon the degree to which they may support one or other political party or faction, and colour their political coverage accordingly. If such coverage gives space to the views of two factions or parties it is generally described as being **bi-partisan**; if its tone is one of general disinterest, of being above party politics, it is described as being **anti-partisan.** Partisan perspectives may not, though, permeate political coverage only; they may pervade media presentations generally. See EFFECTS OF THE MASS MEDIA.

Passivity A long and widely held view of mass audiences is that they are lumpen, unreflective and essentially passive. There is no evidence for this, though assumptions carry weight, and are reflected in content selection and approach, regardless of evidence. The PILKINGTON REPORT 1962 indicated a crude view of audience response particularly to TV programmes, and it is difficult not to believe that *some* programmers regard their audiences as fields of turnips.

Modern media commentators insist on the diversity of response of audiences. J. Curran and J. Seaton in *Power Without Responsibility* (UK: Methuen, 1985; Routledge & Kegan Paul, 1988) believe 'The public is not a passive empty box merely waiting to be filled with the injunctions of advertisers. How people react to what they see is determined by their class, age and the beliefs they already hold.' See AUDIENCE RESEARCH; EFFECTS OF THE MASS MEDIA.

Pauper press See UNDERGROUND PRESS.

Peacock Report, 1985 Under the chairmanship of Professor Alan Peacock, the Report of the Committee on Financing the BBC held back from recommending ADVERTISING as a form of revenue for the corporation, but suggested that Radio 1, Radio 2 and the BBC's local radio NETWORK be hived off to independent commercial control – advice which was not promptly taken up by government (See RADIO: BROADCASTING IN THE 90s). Though the BBC appeared to have been reprieved from the imposition of TV advertising, the underlying commitment of the Report was to 'consumer sovereignty'. The Peacock Report concludes with the statement that if the Committee 'had to summarize the conclusion by one slogan . . . it would be direct consumer choice rather than the continuation of the licence fee'.

'Pencil of Nature' Title of the first book ever illustrated with photographs, published in England in 1844, the work of William Henry Fox Talbot (1800–77), inventor of the CALOTYPE process of photo-printing. The range of photographs pasted into *The Pencil of Nature* was extraordinary and included intimate, informal studies of Talbot's household at his home, Laycock Abbey. See PHOTOGRAPHY, ORIGINS.

Perception The process of becoming aware and making sense of the stimuli received from our environment by the senses: sight, hearing, smell, taste, and TOUCH. Perception is selective. We are surrounded by many sensations but we tend to direct our attention to only a few of these. Our decision as to what to attend to can be influenced by environmental and personal factors: for example, *environmental* factors can include the intensity, size, motion or novelty of the stimuli whilst *personal* factors can include present needs and drives, physiological features, past experiences and learning – perceptual set – and personality. The influence of personal factors explains why individuals may pay attention to different stimuli, to different messages or parts of a MESSAGE.

See ATTITUDES; BELIEFS; CULTURE; DIFFERENTIAL PERCEPTION; EMPATHY; EXPECTATIONS; FIRST IMPRESSIONS; HALO EFFECT; LABELLING PROCESS (AND THE MEDIA); MALE-AS-NORM; MORES; MOTIVATION; NORMS; PROJECTION; SAPIR-

WHORF HYPOTHESIS; SELECTIVE EXPOSURE; SELF-CONCEPT; SELF-FULFILLING PROPHECY; STEREOTYPE; SUB-CULTURE; VALUES.

Periodicity Describes the time-scale of the schedules of news organizations; thus a daily newspaper has a 24-hour periodicity. The more the time-scale of a potential item of news coincides with the periodicity of the news organization, the more likely it is that the story will 'make the headlines'. Graham Murdock in 'Political deviance: the press presentation of a militant mass demonstration' in S. Cohen and J. Young, eds., *The Manufacture of News* (UK: Constable, 1973), speaks of the 'event-orientation' of the daily newspaper – information which can be gathered, processed and dramatized within a 24-hour cycle (such as assassinations, clashes with the police, the speeches of politicians) stands a better chance of breaking through the news threshold than news which is gradual and undramatic. See NEWS VALUES.

Persistence of vision The realization that the eye retains an image for a split second after the object has passed gave birth to the cinema. The principle was first illustrated, and proved marketable, with toys of the 19th c. such as the THAUMATROPE – a disc with images on each side; when the disc was spun round the images merged into a single action. The ZOETROPE was a drum with illustrations of figures inside which, when spun round, conveyed the impression of movement. See CINEMATOGRAPHY, ORIGINS.

Personal idiom Or idiosyncratic LANGUAGE; occurring in interpersonal relationships; serves the function of building relationship cohesiveness. Results of research into the use of personal idiom were published in an article 'Couples' personal idioms: exploring intimate talk' in the *Journal of Communication* (Winter, 1981) by Robert Hopper, Mark L. Knapp and Lorel Scott. Such idioms, they found, take the form of a range of idiomatic exchanges: partner nicknames; expressions of affection; labels for others outside the relationship; for use in confrontations; to deal with requests and routines; sexual references and EUPHEMISMS; sexual invitations and teasing insults (or 'kidding').

Personalization One of the chief conventions of media reportage. Where a potential news item can be personalized it has a greater chance of being included than if it is difficult to translate into personality terms. The preference is for ELITE personalities. See NEWS VALUES.

Personal space That which every individual feels easy in and which, if encroached upon, causes anxiety, tension or resistance. Personal space is fluid, and mobile, whereas **territorial space** tends to be stationary. S. Lyman and M. Scott in 'Territoriality: a neglected social dimension' in *Social Problems*, 15 (1967) refer to personal space as 'the most private and inviolate of territories belonging to an individual'. See PROXEMICS.

Phatic (language) Derives from the Greek, 'phasis', utterance; a term finding its modern CONNOTATION in the phrase '**phatic communion**' coined by anthropologist Bronislaw Malinowski (1884–1942), meaning that part of communication which is used for establishing an atmosphere or maintaining social contact rather than for exchanging information or ideas. Phatic words and phrases have been called 'idiot salutations' and, when they comprise dialogue, 'two-stroke conversations'. Comments about the weather, enquiries about health, everyday exchanges, including nods, smiles, waves, are part of the phatic communion essential for 'oiling' or maintaining channels of communication.

Phatic LANGUAGE is central to human relationships; its significance can be best noted by its absence: you give a cheery 'Hello' to a friend passing in the street to be greeted by stony silence; you halt your car to permit another motorist to go ahead of you, and he/she does not acknowledge your GESTURE. . . The response to such phatic neglect can be considerable. See JAKOBSON'S MODEL OF COMMUNICATION.

Phoneme The smallest unit in the sound system of a LANGUAGE. Each language can be shown to operate with a relatively small number of phonemes, some having as few as 15, others as many as 50. **Phonemics** is the study of the basic sounds of language.

Phone-tapping Practised by most governments, though invariably they deny it. In the UK phone-tapping is the responsibility of British Telecom. According to articles written by Duncan Campbell for the *New Statesman* in 1980, the monitoring service operates 24 hours a day with a capacity to tap 1000 telephone lines simultaneously (See 'Big Buzby is watching you', NS, 1 February 1980). New technology, such as SYSTEM X, has made phone-tapping a potential tool for mass surveillance. See CENSORSHIP; INTERCEPTION OF COMMUNICATIONS ACT, 1985; PRIVACY; TELEPHONE PREFERENCE SCHEME (TPS).

* P. Fitzgerald and M. Leopold, *Stranger on the Line, The Secret History of Phone Tapping* (UK: Bodley Head, 1987).

Phonetics The science of human sound-making, especially sounds used in speech. Phonetics includes the study of articulation, acoustics or perception of speech, and the properties of specific languages.

Phonodisc First-ever VIDEO recording, developed by John Logie Baird (1888–1946) in 1928. This was a 10 inch 78 rpm record, in every way similar to the acoustic discs already being produced for conventional sound recording. Despite its novelty, the Phonodisc, coming so early in the age of the development of TV, failed to succeed commercially.

Phonograph See GRAMOPHONE.

Phonology A branch of LINGUISTICS which studies the sound systems of languages. Its aim is to demonstrate the patterns of distinctive sound in spoken LANGUAGE and to make as general statements as possible about the nature of sound systems in languages throughout the world.

Photography, aerial. See AERIAL PHOTO-GRAPHY.

Photography, origins Joseph Nicéphore Niépce (1765–1833) and his brother Claude, officers in the French army and navy, were the first to fix images of the CAMERA OBSCURA by chemical means in 1793, though the light sensitivity of silver nitrate had been known and written about as early as 1727 when Johann Heinrich Schulze, professor of anatomy at the University of Altdorf, published a paper indicating that the darkening of silver salts was due not to heat but to light.

1826 is generally recognized as the year in which the first photographic image was captured. Joseph Niépce's reproduction of a roof-top scene, on a pewter plate, he called Héliographie – sun drawing. In 1830 he teamed up with Louis Daguerre (1789–1851) theatrical designer and co-inventor of the DIORAMA. The death of Niépce three years later left Daguerre to lead the field in France. He discovered that an almost invisible latent image could be developed using mercury vapour, thus reducing exposure time from around eight hours to between 20 and 30 minutes.

His DAGUERROTYPE was taken up by the French government in 1839, and elicited from Paul Delaroche the immortal line, 'From today, painting is dead!' In the UK astronomer Sir John Herschel (1792–1871) read a paper 'On the Art of Photography' to the Royal Society, accompanied by 23 photographs. He was the first to use the verb *to photograph* and the adjective *photographic*, in 1840 to identify *negative* and *positive* and 20 years later to use the term *snap-shot*.

William Henry Fox Talbot (1800–77) won fame and fortune with his CALOTYPE (1841), the true technical base of photography because, unlike the Daguerrotype, its negative/positive principle made possible the making of prints from the original photographs. The inventions and discoveries which followed helped to improve the effectiveness of the photographic process. Frederick Scott Archer's *collodion* or wet-plate process, details of which were published in 1851, greatly increased sensitivity;

the use of gelatine silver bromide emulsion, invented in 1871 by Dr Richard Leach Maddox, and later improved upon by John Burgess, Richard Kennett and Charles Bennett, proved a considerable advance on the collodion method, and ushered in the modern era of factory-produced photographic material, freeing the photographer from the necessity of preparing his/her own plates.

CELLULOID was invented by Alexander Parkes in 1861 and roll film made from celluloid was produced by the Eastman Company in the US from 1889. By 1902, Eastman, manufacturers of Kodak, were producing between 80% and 90% of the world's output. Very swiftly photography became the hobby of the man in the street. Every tenth person in the UK – four million people – was estimated to own a camera by 1900.

Colour film photography hit many technical snags in its development. A colour screen process was patented as early as 1904 by the Lumière brothers. They commercially introduced their Autochrome plates in 1907 when good panchromatic emulsion was available. However, exposure was about 40 times longer than that for black and white film. Modern methods based on multiple-layer film and coupling components were simultaneously introduced by Kodak and Agfa. In 1935, Kodachrome, created by two American amateurs, Leopold Godowsky and Leopold Mannes, was marketed, a year ahead of Agfacolor. In both, transparencies were obtained suitable for projection as well as reproduction. Electronic flash was invented in 1931 by Harold E. Egerton. See CAMERA, ORIGINS; FILMLESS CAMERA; HIGH-SPEED PHOTOGRAPHY; PHOTOMONTAGE; PHOTO-JOURNALISM; TIME-LAPSE PHOTOGRAPHY.

Photogravure Engraving by photography, for purposes of PRINTING, was invented by Englishman William Henry Fox Talbot (1800–77) in 1852. It was not until 1947 that the first machine to do a complete typesetting job by means of photography was invented.

Photo-journalism Despite the popularity of photography among the general public, the PRESS were curiously slow to realize the possibilities of photographs. The *Daily Mirror* was first in the field in the UK at the turn of the 20th c., but the use of photographs did not become commonplace till the end of the 1st World War (1914–18). In June 1919, the New York *Illustrated Daily News* at last fully acknowledged a vital means of communication – 39 years after the feasibility of printing a half-tone block (reproducing light and shade by dots of different sizes and densities) alongside type had been demonstrated by Stephen H. Horgan in the New York *Daily Graphic*. Even during the 1st World War (1914–18) press photographs were rare, and photo-reportage in the modern sense only began in the mid-1920s with the introduction of the Ermanox camera and ultra-rapid plates.

Among the fathers of modern photo-journalism were Erich Saloman (1886–1944), Felix H. Man and Wolfgang Weber. With a camera hidden in his top hat, Arthur Barrett secretly took court photographs of the suffragettes and, in February 1928, Saloman took sensational pictures of a Coburg murder trial. Man pioneered the *picture story* in, for example, *A Day in the Life of Mussolini*, 1934, and it was Man who founded *Weekly Illustrated* in the same year. He became chief photographer for *Picture Post*, founded 1938, a position he held until 1945.

Photo-journalism was given increasing status over the years by many outstanding photographers: Henri Cartier-Bresson (b. 1908) photo-reported visits to Spain (1933) and Mexico (1934); Robert Capra (1913–54) won undying fame with his war photography, especially his pictures taken during the Spanish Civil War; Bill Brandt (1905–1983) photographed the English at Home (1936) while Margaret Bowke-White, in *You Have Seen Their Faces* (1937) portrayed the conditions in the South of the US, in particular the negro chain-gangs.

Suppression of the photo-reportage of Bert Hardy from the Korean War by the proprietors of *Picture Post* led to the resignation of the magazine's outstanding editor, Tom Hopkinson.

Talented, fearless and concerned photo-journalists continue to the present, even in the age of TV and the closure of photo-papers. Donald McCullin (b. 1935) has photo-reported war, oppression, hardship and carnage all over the world in a vast array of unforgettable images. He was, incidentally, one of the photographers *not* given permission by the Ministry of Defence to cover the Falklands War (1982).

In *A Concise History of Photography* (UK: Thames & Hudson, 1965), Helmet and Alison Gernsheim write, 'No other medium can bring life and reality so close as does photography and it is in the fields of reportage and documentation that photography's most important contribution lies in modern times.' Not the least of its achievements, photography and photo-journalism have proved powerful agents in the awakening of social conscience. See DOCUMENTARY.

Photomontage Process of mounting, superimposing, one photograph on top of another; a method almost as old as photography itself. The dadaists and surrealists experimented with Photomontage to produce visionary pictures. Laslo Moholy-Nagy (1895–1946) combined several picture components in the production of a new work and termed his approach 'photoplastics'. Malik of Berlin were the first publishers to use photomontage for book jackets. Most extensively, the process has been employed in ADVERTISING.

Photonics Light-based technology under development in the late 1980s, promising to make the computer run hundreds of times faster than is possible employing the silicon chip. As up to a million components have been concentrated on to one chip, a survival limit is reached, for passing too many electric currents through the same wire on the chip results in seizure. Photonics promises an answer, employing beams of light which can pass through each other. A single beam can be split into 25 channels of information, equivalent to using the same number of separate wires.

Photoresist Process by which the minute but precise printed circuits of microelectronic chips are produced by photographic etching.

Phototypesetting Method that bypasses the traditional metal type stage of print production by PRINTING type photographically from an optical or electric store of individual characters. Though the first photocomposing machine was created as early as 1894, it was not until it could be 'manned' by computers, in the 1960s, that the process became widespread. Modern typesetting allows operators to lay out pages on VDUs. This means that the same person can enter copy, make up the pages, check errors; then, one touch of a button and a high-quality proof is produced.

Picture postcards German Heinrich von Stephan is generally considered to have thought up the idea of a postcard, in 1865, though Emmanuel Hermann ran him close, persuading the director-general of the Austrian Post to issue the first government postcard, in 1869. It was called a 'Correspondence Card'. In 1870 the first government postcard was issued in the UK; 70 m such cards were sold in the first year. The US government followed suit in 1872.

Since then the picture postcard has provided a treasure house for the analysis of contemporary interests and attitudes: art, fashion, new technology, warfare, royalty, exploration, history, travel; ideas of patriotism and Empire, of family, entertainment, comedy, etc. The title *Mail art* has been given to a practice widespread in the late 1970s and 1980s of artists exchanging visual ideas by postcard. During the same period the postcard became popular in a propagandist role, especially among protest groups of the Left. A classic piece of PHOTOMONTAGE in postcard form is Peter Kennard's version of the Constable painting, *The Haywain*, in which the artist has superimposed cruise missiles on the 19th c. rural tranquillity of Suffolk. Such cards use CARTOONS, photographs, photo-graffiti and quotations.

Inevitably cards of past ages have become collectors' items; the word *Deltiology* (from the Greek, *deltion*, small picture) was coined by American Randall Rhoades for picture postcard collecting and study. See CIGARETTE CARDS; POSTERS.

Pidgin English In trading and doing business with the English in the far east, the Chinese and other peoples such as Malays communicated in a very basic, utilitarian mode of half-English. *Pidgin* is a Chinese corruption of the word 'business'. Chiefly, Pidgin English is made up of mispronounced English words with certain native grammatical constructions.

Pilkington Committee Report on Broadcasting, 1962 Set up under the chairmanship of Sir Harry Pilkington in 1960, the Committee's chief concern in a 297-page strongly worded deposition, was the nation's cultural and intellectual life and the effect upon these of BROADCASTING now that COMMERCIAL TELEVISION had been on the scene since 1954: 'Our conclusion,' declared the Committee, 'is that triviality is a natural vice of television, and that where it prevails it operates to lower general standards of enjoyment and understanding.'

The BBC emerged unscathed, and not a little praised, from the Committee Report: 'The BBC knows good broadcasting and by and large they are providing it.' The 'villian' of the scenario was ITV. So dissatisfied with ITV programmes were the Committee that one of their recommendations (never put into practice) was that the IBA take on responsibility for the planning of programmes.

Pilkington expressed disquiet at the portrayal of physical violence in TV programmes and of a 'comprehensive carelessness about moral standards generally'. 'From the representations which have been put to us, this is the underlying cause of the disquiet about television: the belief, deeply felt, that the way television has portrayed human behaviour and treated moral issues has already done something and will in time do much to worsen the moral climate of the country.'

Most of the recommendations of Pilkington were ignored. Only minor recommendations made any immediate progress – the right to party political broadcasts was extended; ADVERTISING magazines disappeared. Yet the Report did have its effect. It gave the BBC, staggering from the impact of ITV competition, a shot in the arm. And it was through Pilkington that the BBC was the first to receive a second channel (BBC 2, 1964); ITV should receive such a channel, Pilkington recommended, only when it had been reformed.

John Whale in *The Politics of the Media* (UK: Fontana, 1977) says Pilkington 'aimed at large effects and missed them'. Nevertheless, Pilkington established a set of judgemental criteria, albeit elitist-cultural, which have formed a rallying point ever since for broadcasting reformers. See COMMISSIONS/COMMITTEES ON THE MEDIA.

Pilot study A preliminary testing or 'experimental experiment' in which the researcher seeks to try out a new idea, system or approach; to determine whether an intended study is feasible, to clarify assumptions and improve instruments of measurement.

Pirate radio The monopoly of RADIO BROADCASTING held in the UK by the BBC was colourfully challenged in the 1960s by 'pirate' stations BROADCASTING from ancient forts and ships anchored in the North Sea. They played nonstop popular music, collected ADVERTISING revenues, paid no royalties on the music they played and thus made substantial profits. In 1964, Radio Caroline, from a ship called Caroline, took the air on 28 March, one of a long line of Pirates. Ronan O'Rahilly, founder of Caroline, received over 20,000 letters in the first 10 days of broadcasting. The Duke of Bedford was the first advertiser, for Woburn Abbey – an advertisement that brought in 4,500 people the next day.

By the end of 1965 some 15 million listeners were tuning in regularly to pirate radio, and the pirates were making a lot of money – until the Labour Government put paid to existing and further development with the Marine etc. Broadcasting (Offences) Act which became law in 1967.

They appealed to a generation of teenagers – an audience the BBC later tried to win over with the creation of Radio One. War on the pirates was initially conducted in the Council of Europe which drew up The European Agreement for the Prevention of Broadcasts transmitted outside National Territories, which member states signed in Strasbourg in 1965 and which the UK government presented to Parliament in the same year.

Among sections of the broadcasting and political establishment there was fear that the pirates might not only undermine existing systems of broadcasting but have an 'undesirable' cultural and even political impact. The Labour government's Marine Broadcasting (Offences) Act made it an offence to direct broadcasts into the UK which were unlicensed and made it an offence to buy advertising time on illegal channels. With the apparent defeat of the pirates, and the dismantling of their stations, there was clearly a gap to be filled in the pattern of official broadcasting services. At the end of 1966 the Labour government issued a White Paper containing proposals which opened the way for the creation of Radio One.

That was not the end of Pirate radio. A widespread enthusiasm for radio broadcasting independent of the DUOPOLY was sustained through the 1970s, and in the 1980s pirates began popping up all over – making illegal broadcasts from unlicensed transmitters in woodlands, on hilltops, in back bedrooms, in garages or even on the move. Pirate *television* made its appearance by 1986, with Network 21, broadcasting to over 50,000 viewers throughout London, screening half-hour programmes on Fridays at midnight, thus bringing upon it the wrath of the Department of Trade and the full weight of the law. See 'BROADCASTING IN THE '90s': GOVERNMENT WHITE PAPER, 1988; CB – CITIZENS' BAND RADIO; COMMERCIAL RADIO; COMMUNITY RADIO; RADIO: BROADCASTING IN THE '90s.

Pistolgraph See CAMERA, ORIGINS.

Pitch The highness of lowness of a speaker's voice. Technically, pitch is the frequency of sound made by the vocal cords.

Pitman shorthand See SHORTHAND.

Plagiarism From the Latin, 'plagiarius', kidnapper; the act of stealing from others their thoughts or their writings and claiming them for one's own.

Play theory of mass communication In *The Play Theory of Mass Communication* (US: University of Chicago Press, 1967), William Stephenson counters those who speak of the harmful EFFECTS OF THE MASS MEDIA by arguing that first and foremost the media serve audiences as play-experiences. Even newspapers, says Stephenson, are read for pleasure rather than information and enlightenment. He sees the media as 'a buffer against conditions which would otherwise be anxiety producing'. The media provide *communication-pleasure*. Stephenson argues that what is most required by people within a national CULTURE is something for everyone to talk about. For him mass communication 'should serve two purposes. It should suggest how best to maximize the communication-pleasure in the world. It should also show how far autonomy for the individual can be achieved in spite of the weight of social controls against him.' See THEORIES OF COMMUNICATION.

Pluralism The view that modern industrial societies have populations which are increasingly heterogeneous – that is, different in kind – divided by such factors as ethnic, religious, regional and CLASS differences. Such heterogeneity, it is argued, will progressively produce a diversity of VALUES, NORMS, interests, and so on within such societies and a plurality of GROUPS to compete for power and influence within society. Power is seen, therefore, as being increasingly diffuse in terms of its distribution within these societies. This perspective is not without its critics. Some groups are likely to have more power than others and will be in a better position to impose their perspectives, values, and so on upon other groups. As far as the field of media studies is concerned, the recent concentration in the ownership of the PRESS throws some doubt on the degree to which power is becoming more diffuse in its distribution. See ELITE; SOCIAL ACTION (MODE OF MEDIA ANALYSIS).

Pluralist Many modes, many alternatives; in media terms, *diversity* – of ownership, STYLE, content and standpoint. A pluralist society is one in which there are many choices and many interpretations of MEANING.

Politics of accommodation (in the media) Potential conflict between various individuals and GROUPS within media corporations and between these corporations and a central social authority is seen by some commentators to be *mediated* by what Tom Burns in *The BBC: Public Institution and Private World* (UK: Macmillan, 1977) calls a 'politics of accommodation'. This is a *negotiated compromise* in which notions such as professional standards and the public interest are used as trading pieces. Negotiations of this type can be conducted at several levels: between the professionals and the management, between one corporation and another and between a corporation and the government. Margaret Gallagher argues in 'Negotiation of control in media organizations and occupations' in M. Gurevitch, T. Bennett, J. Curran and J. Woollacott, *Culture, Society and the Media* (UK: Methuen, 1982), that within this accommodation the amount and limits of control of the various groups and individuals are in constant negotiation. Trade-offs range from the everyday compromises over, say, the amount of bad LANGUAGE allowed in a broadcast script to the long-term and politically significant. In an article 'The future of broadcasting in Britain', *New Statesman*, 20 October, 1972, Hugh Greene states that the relatively muted stance of the BBC's director-general, John Reith, during the General Strike of 1926 'made it possible for his successors to be much more firm and uncompromising when they faced the anger of governments about the BBC's treatment of such crises as Suez'. See CONSENSUS; ELITE; ESTABLISHMENT; MEDIA CONTROL; MEDIATION.

Polymorphic opinion leadership See OPINION LEADER.

Polysemic Ambiguous, able to generate many different meanings. A primary, self-set task of the media is to counter the polysemic by presenting ISSUES in simplified, cut-and-dried forms (see STEREOTYPE). *Unambiguity* is classified by commentators as an important NEWS VALUE. As John Hartley says in *Under-*

standing News (UK: Methuen, 1982), 'Events don't have to be simple necessarily (though that helps), but the range of possible meaning must be limited.'

Poor Man's Guardian Perhaps the most influential radical newspaper in Britain during the 19th c., edited by Bronterre O'Brien, published by Henry Hetherington. It appeared between 1831 and 1835, and was described by George Jacob Holyoake, a campaigner against the TAXES ON KNOWLEDGE levied by government on the PRESS, as 'the first messenger of popular and political intelligence which reached the working classes'. Other radical papers of this turbulent period, were Richard Carlile's *Gauntlet* (1833–34), Robert Owen's *Crisis* (1832–34), James Watson's *Working Man's Friend* (1832–33) and Fergus O'Connor's *Northern Star* (1837–52), principal organ of the Chartist movement. See STAMP DUTY; UNDERGROUND PRESS.

Population (statistical) See SAMPLING.

Populism According to MASS SOCIETY theorists one of the distinguishing features of a mass society is its **populist** nature. Legitimacy is given to those persons, ideas or actions which are thought to best express the popular will or meet the most widely shared EXPECTATIONS. One result is, such theorists claim, that a premium is placed upon the capacity of those in leadership positions, to both create and placate popular opinion. The mass media tend to be seen as the agents through which such leaders control and exploit the masses.
* W. Kornhauser, *The Politics of Mass Society* (US: Free Press, 1959).

Pornography Word originates from the Greek, 'writing of harlots'. Two sorts of pornography are usually differentiated, *erotica* – concentrating on physical aspects of heterosexual activity; and *exotica* – focusing on abnormal or deviationist sexual activity. Attitudes to pornography reflect a society's permissiveness, its current 'tolerance threshold' and also cast a light on prevailing social VALUES.

Tolerance of pornography only makes sense if there is no *felt* risk; if pornography is thought to be linked with the abuse of women and children and the degradation of human relationships and family life, pornography will be fought against whether the link is proven or not. In any case, pornography itself often makes the link between sexuality and violence: *hard porn* is, by general definition, a DISCOURSE in violence which, at the very least, poses examples of possible behaviour. Of interest and concern is the indisputable fact that in many countries, including the UK, pornography is big business. Civic concern about the possible link between porn and violence was registered by the Minneapolis City Council in 1983. Exhaustive public hearings took place to provide a basis of information

for a decision whether or not to add pornography as a 'discrimination against women' to existing civil rights legislation. The transcript of the Minneapolis hearings was published in 1988. Quoting evidence from academic and clinical research on the effect of pornography on ordinary men, the report stated that, exposed to pornography, men become desensitized; they see themselves more likely to commit rape, less likely to respond sympathetically to women who are victims of rape or more likely to be lenient in their response to men who commit rape. According to the Minneapolis transcript, pornography which portrays women enjoying rape or violence or humiliation is most damaging.

As a result of the hearings the City Council passed a civil rights law enabling women victims of pornography to bring civil rights actions against the pornographers. However, the law was vetoed by the mayor and never implemented. A similar situation arose in Indianapolis where pornographers claimed they were being denied their constitutional right to free speech (Under the First Amendment). Thus, in the courts, free speech took precedence over women's equality and safety from violence. See CENSORSHIP; DESENSITIZATION; STEREOTYPE; VIDEO NASTIES; WILLIAMS COMMITTEE REPORT ON OBSCENITY AND FILM CENSORSHIP, 1979.
* Dworkin, A. *Pornography: Men Possessing Women* (UK: Women's Press, 1981). N.M. Malamud and E.M. Donnerstein, eds., *Pornography and Sexual Aggression* (US: Academic Press, 1984); D. Zillman and J. Bryant, 'Pornography, sexual callousness and the trivialization of rape' in *Journal of Communication*, Autumn, 1982. *'Pornography and Sexual Violence' Evidence of the Links* (UK: Every woman Magazine 1988).

Postcards See PICTURE POSTCARDS.

Posters Printed posters have had a short but vivid history, dating from the 1870s when the perfection of techniques in colour LITHOGRAPHY first made mass production possible. Posters have been described as the art gallery of the street and indeed the form has appealed to many artists, such as Henri Toulouse-Lautrec (1864–1901), members of the art nouveau movement and the graphic designers of the bauhaus and the de stijl group. Posters have served every mode of PROPAGANDA – social, political, religious, commercial. The arresting clarity of their images, combined with words used dramatically, emotively, humorously have often continued to impress long after the ideas, events or products they relate to have faded from attention.

So immediate and memorable are posters, and so widely recognized, that they have formed a regular inspiration for serious artists: imitated, reproduced, turned into cult objects, transmuted into other meanings. Many different uses have been made, for example, of Alfred Leete's famous poster (1914) 'Your Country Needs You', whose straight-eyed sergeant-major, with sweeping moustache, points out towards the audience, offering a formidable challenge to all those who have not yet volunteered for the Great War.

In peacetime, between elections, ADVERTISING dominates the poster contents of the billboards – sometimes with bold, witty and memorable images such as the Guinness adverts. Yet posters come into their own in time of protest or revolution. Some of the finest posters were designed and printed during and after the Russian Revolution of 1917, while the Spanish Civil War (1936–38) stimulated the production of hundreds of hard-hitting, passionate and often tragic images.

* J. Barnicoat, *A Concise History of Posters* (UK: Thames & Hudson, 1972).

Post-synchronization Or *dubbing*. In FILM making, the process of adding new or altered dialogue in the original language to the sound track of a film after it has been shot. See SYNCHRONOUS SOUND.

Postulates of communication To define the fundamental *attributes* of the communication process is possibly a more fruitful area of analysis than struggling for an all-embracing and acceptable *definition* of communication. C.D. Mortensen in *Communication: the Study of Human Interaction* (US: McGraw-Hill, 1972), poses a single, basic postulate, that 'Communication occurs whenever persons attribute significance to message-related behaviour'; and then follows this up with five secondary postulates. These are: (1) Communication is *dynamic*. (2) Communication is *irreversible*. (3) Communication is *proactive* (as opposed to *re*active). Mortensen says here, 'The notion of man as a detached bystander, an objective and dispassionate reader of the environment, is nothing more than a convenient artefact. Among living creatures man is the most spectacular example of an agent who amplifies his environment.' We are *shapers*, not mere recipients. (4) Communication is *interactive*. (5) Communication is *contextual*. See COMMUNICATION MODELS; THEORIES AND CONCEPTS OF COMMUNICATION.

Postural echo Occurs when people – friends, lovers, etc. – unconsciously imitate or 'echo' each other's GESTURES and postures; this Desmond Morris in *Manwatching: A Field Guide to Human Behaviour* (UK: Jonathan Cape, 1977) describes as 'part of a natural body display of companionship'. He writes, 'Because acting in unison spells equal-status friendship, it can be used by dominant individuals to put subordinates at their ease.' See TIE-SIGNS.

Power One of the best known definitions of power is that of Max Weber (1864–1920) who defined it as 'the probability that one actor within a social relationship will be in a position to carry out his own will despite resistance, regardless of the basis on which this probability rests'. Power is something which people exercise over each other. A concept closely related to that of power is *influence*, a term often used to describe the exercise of power. C.B. Handy in *Understanding Organizations* (UK: Penguin, 1976) describes the relationship between power and influence thus: 'Influence is the process whereby A modifies the attitudes and behaviour of B. Power is that which enables him to do it.'

Power can be exercised at many levels and to varying degrees: some GROUPS or individuals may be seen as being powerful within society generally, whilst others may only be able to exercise power in very specific situations. Power and power relationships provide an important focus for analysis of mass, organizational, group, interpersonal or intrapersonal communication.

The analysis of the exercise of power gives rise to many areas of investigation including the identification of power bases, of factors which predispose individuals to be influenced, of the various methods of influence, of the effect of social or societal context upon the influence process and of the qualitative difference which might exist in the degree to which individuals may be influenced. See EFFECTS OF THE MASS MEDIA; ELITE.

Power elite Term used by C. Wright Mills in his seminal analysis *Power, Politics and People* (US: Oxford University Press, 1963) to describe those members of a society who combine social and political privilege with power and influence. See CULTURAL APPARATUS; ELITE; HEGEMONY.

Power value In researching the rating given by US children to the kind of jobs and professions portrayed on TV, M. De Fleur in 1964 found a large majority valuing most in an occupation its capacity to exert *power* over others. De Fleur constructed an 'index of power' by which he could give each job portrayed on TV a power value which reflected the proportion of dominant acts to submissive ones.

* M. De Fleur 'Occupational roles as portrayed on television', *Public Opinion Quarterly*, vol. 28.

Pragmatics The study of LANGUAGE from the viewpoint of the user, especially the choices he/she makes, the constraints he/she meets with in employing language in social situations, and the effects the use of this language has upon others in the communication situation.

Preferred reading Stuart Hall poses this concept in 'The determination of news photographs' in S. Cohen and J. Young, eds., *The Manufacture of News* (UK: Constable, 1973). Here the preferred reading of a photograph – preferred, that is, by the transmitter of the photograph – is one, Hall believes, which guides us to an interpretation that lies within the traditional social, political and cultural VALUES of the time, symbolizing and reinforced by the interests of the dominant HIERARCHY. The framing, cropping, captioning and juxtaposition of the photograph with text all serve to close off the reader from lateral, or independent, interpretations of the photograph; from ABERRANT DECODING of the MESSAGE. Thus CLOSURE is achieved. The term has come to be applied to message systems generally. See DOMINANT, SUBORDINATE, RADICAL.

Prejudice Ernest R. Hilgard, Richard C. Hilgard and Rita L. Hilgard in *Introduction to Psychology* (US: Harcourt Brace Jovanovich, 1975) define prejudice as 'an attitude that is firmly fixed, not open to free and rational discussion and resistant to change'. Such an attitude may be directed towards ideas, objects, situations or people and may be positive or negative. Prejudice is arguably of greatest concern when it is negative and directed towards other people. In this instance prejudice is often accompanied by negative stereotypes of its targets. The targets of prejudice tend to be those who are the relatively powerless members of GROUPS, organizations, or societies as well as those who are perceived as being deviant. It is of course possible to be both. The term *discrimination* is normally used to describe the acting out of prejudice.

See DEVIANCE; LABELLING PROCESS (AND THE MEDIA); NORMS; STEREOTYPE.

Presidentialism Colin Seymour-Ure in *The Political Impact of Mass Media* (UK: Constable, 1974), comments that since the introduction of TV coverage of political events – particularly elections – political campaigning in the UK has become increasingly similar in style to that of the US. Manifestations of this trend are an increasing concentration of attention upon the party leader and the need for such a person to perform well on TV. The party leader's *command* of TV coverage raises the possibility of him/her dominating a campaign the way an American presidential candidate does; hence the term 'presidentialism' to describe the trend.

Press See NEWSPAPERS, ORIGINS; NEWS VALUES; NORTHCLIFFE REVOLUTION; PRESS BARONS; UNDERGROUND PRESS. *See also:* ARTILLERY OF THE PRESS; BY-LINE; CHEQUEBOOK JOURNALISM; CONGLOMERATES; DEVELOPMENTAL NEWS; DISINFORMATION; FOLK DEVILS; FOURTEEN-DAY RULE; FOURTH ESTATE; FREQUENCY; HARMONIOUS INTERACTION; HEGEMONY; JINGOISM; LOBBY PRACTICE; MCGREGOR COMMISSION REPORT ON THE PRESS, 1977; MEDIATION; MILITARY METAPHOR; MR GATE; NEWS AGENCIES; NEWS FRAMEWORKS; NEWS-LITERATE; NEW WORLD INFORMATION ORDER; NON-ALIGNED NEWS POOL; OZ TRIAL; PAPARAZZO. PAPER OF THE MAN ON THE KNIFE-BOARD OF THE OMNIBUS; PERIODICITY; PHOTO-JOURNALISM; PHOTO-TYPESETTING; POOR MAN'S GUARDIAN; PRESS CONFERENCE; PRESS COUNCIL; PRESS, FOUR THEORIES OF; PRINT UNIONS; RHETORIC; RIGHT OF REPLY; ROSS COMMISSION REPORT ON THE PRESS, 1949; SHAWCROSS COMMISSION REPORT ON THE PRESS, 1962; SHOCK ISSUES; SHOTGUN APPROACH (TO NEWS COVERAGE); SIGNIFICATION SPIRAL; SILENT MAJORITY; SPIKE; SPOILER; STAMP DUTY; STATUS QUO; STEREOTYPE; TABLOIDESE; TALLOIRES DECLARATION, 1981; TAXES ON KNOWLEDGE; TERRORISM AS COMMUNICATION; THESIS JOURNALISM; TOKENISM; VICTIM FUNDS; WATCHDOGS; WATERGATE; WESTMINSTER VIEW; WORLD PRESS FREEDOM COMMITTEE; YELLOW JOURNALISM; ZINOVIEV LETTER 1924.

Press barons As early as 1884 Scots-American steel magnate Andrew Carnegie headed a syndicate which controlled eight daily papers and ten weeklies. Edward Lloyd owned the mass circulation *Daily Chronicle* and the blockbuster Sunday paper, *Lloyd's Weekly*, the first periodical to sell a million copies. As the costs of founding and running newspapers grew, leaving ownership a privilege of none but the very rich, or joint stock companies, the trend towards chain ownership accelerated.

By 1921, Lord Northcliffe (1865-1922) controlled *The Times*, the *Daily Mail*, the *Weekly Despatch* (later a Sunday paper) and the *London Evening News*. His brother Harold, later Lord Rothermere, controlled the *Daily Mirror*, the *Sunday Pictorial*, the *Daily Record* and several other papers. Together they owned the large magazine group Amalgamated Press while brother number three, Sir Lester Harmsworth, owned a string of papers in the south-west of England. Between them these baronial brothers owned papers with an aggregate circulation of over six million. Though controlling only a modest four papers – one of which, the *Daily Express*, led all its competitors in the late 1930s – Lord Beaverbrook (1879–1964) reached a joint circulation of 4.1 million by 1937.

Regional newspaper chains displayed similar baronialist tendencies. The Berry brothers, Lords Camrose and Kemsley, pushed their tally from four daily and Sunday papers in 1921 to 20 daily and Sunday papers by the outbreak of the 2nd World War in 1939. As newspapers fell into fewer hands, circulation expanded dramatically. Between 1920 and 1939 the circulation of national dailies went from 5.4 m to 10.6 m while Sunday paper circulation rose from 13.5 m to 16 m.

Though the leading Sunday paper owners, Kemsley, Beaverbrook and Camrose, controlled 59% of national sales in 1937, it was 8% less than the control exercised in 1910 by lesser-known barons, Dalzil, Riddell and Lloyd.

Equally the control exercised over daily circulation in 1937 by Rothermere, Beaverbrook and Cadbury fell 7% below that exercised by Pearson, Cadbury and Northcliffe in 1910. As James Curran and Jean Seaton say in *Power Without Responsibility* (UK: Routledge & Kegan Paul, 1988), 'The press magnates' hegemony over the press was, in fact, waning during the period celebrated for their ascendancy.'

Almost to a man, the press barons were autocratic, eccentric and immensely ambitious, exerting far-reaching editorial control and involving themselves minutely in the day-to-day running of a newspaper business. Competition was savage and unrelenting. It was necessary for the press barons to attract readership with special offers, life insurance, attention-catching competitions, and to fill their pages with stories their readers were interested in – which meant, as a *News Chronicle* survey of readers' responses in 1933 indicated, more stories about accidents, crime, divorce and human interest (and less 'serious' matters such as politics and world events).

Politics were important, but profits came first. In fact the British political establishment viewed the press barons with dislike and suspicion, for they were not so easily 'bought' or persuaded as their predecessors had been. Of course this did not stop them meddling in politics. Between 1919 and 1922 Rothermere and Northcliffe put all their PRESS backing behind policies advocating public spending cuts. Their Anti-Waste League won three parliamentary by-elections in 1921.

Beaverbrook and Rothermere formed the United Empire Party in 1930 aimed at creating a tariff wall around the British Empire, and an election victory was achieved on the issue at Paddington in October 1930. Prime Minister Stanley Baldwin fought back – on the issue of who rules, government or press? – and won the Westminster St George's by-election comfortably.

During the 1930s Rothermere's papers the *Daily Mirror* and *Daily Mail* supported the British Union of Fascists for a brief period and were rabidly anti-Red. The record of press persuasion on single ISSUES is, however, less significant than the longer-term influence the popular press had at this time. According to Curran and Seaton this demonstrated itself in 'the consolidation of public opinion, particularly amongst the middle class, against change': 'The papers controlled by the press barons conjured up imaginary folk devils that served to strengthen commitment to dominant political norms and to unite the centre and the right against a common enemy', that is, socialism and Marxism; the so-called 'Red peril'. (See FOLK DEVILS).

Patriotism, a deep emotional attachment to Empire, ill-concealed racialism, hatred of foreigners, these – along with their inveterate anti-socialism – characterized the 'voice' of press baronage in the inter-war years.

The post-war period saw new styles of press leadership as the one-product newspaper tycoons gave way to multi-marketing trends, conglomerate ownership and more self-effacing, though no less far-reaching control. However, the 1980s have not been without baronialism in the old style. Australian Rupert Murdoch owns *The Times, Sunday Times, The Sun, Today* and *The News of the World* along with powerful newspapers in the US and Australia. In addition, Murdoch has control of FILM studios and TELEVISION stations in the US and his media interests in Britain include Sky Television. A rival baron emerged in the mid-1980s: Robert Maxwell acquired the Mirror group, the *Daily Mirror* becoming, in the words of journalist John Pilger, 'something approaching a family album.' (See Pilger's remarkable book on the life and times of a journalist, *Heroes*, published in paperback by Pan, 1986). See CONGLOMERATES; MEDIA CONTROL; NEWSPAPERS, ORIGINS.

Press commissions See COMMISSIONS/COMMITTEES ON THE MEDIA.

Press conference The use of PRESS conferences was established in the UK by the Labour Party during the 1959 election campaign. They are held when public figures, often leading politicians, wish to relay a particular MESSAGE to the general public and to use the press as a MEDIUM for it. Such conferences have become a particular feature of general elections campaigns since the late 1960s and they are now covered on TV as well as in the press. They do facilitate an economic and efficient media coverage of such campaigns. Most importantly, press conferences are a mechanism by which the agenda can be established of ISSUES on which the campaign will be fought. See AGENDA SETTING; PRESIDENTIALISM.

Press Council Watchdog body of the UK press, created out of recommendations made in the ROSS COMMISSION REPORT ON THE PRESS, 1949, reconstructed to include 20% lay membership in 1963. While the Council has done some good work in attempting to uphold professional and ethical standards in the PRESS, it remains without real power and influence in many important areas. A body set up and financed by the newspaper industry itself, the Council has been likened to 'a eunuch, impotent in the face of the crime and crumpet brigade, able only to adjudicate, unable to enforce its writ' (Tom Baistow, *Guardian*, 23 August 1982).

The activities of the Press Council were subjected over a two-year period to a consumer survey by an independent committee set up by the Campaign for Press Freedom (now the CAMPAIGN FOR PRESS AND BROADCASTING FREE-DOM), culminating in the report by Geoffrey Robertson *People Against the Press* (UK: Quartet Books, 1983). 'A remarkable picture emerged' writes Robertson 'of the response of complainants to the Council's action on their behalf, 'of a complaints commission whose procedures seemed to give more cause for complaint than the conduct of the newspapers it was investigating.' See CHEQUEBOOK JOURNALISM; RIGHT OF REPLY.

Press, four theories of So termed by F.S. Siebert, T. Peterson and W. Schramm in *Four Theories of the Press* (US: University of Illinois Press, 1956), these are the *libertarian, communist, authoritarian* and *social responsibility* traditions. See NORMATIVE THEORIES OF THE MEDIA.

Pressure groups Also known as interest groups or lobbies, pressure groups aim to influence central and local government and its actions in certain, limited areas of policy. They do not usually seek formal political office although some pressure groups do sponsor individual MPs – the National Union of Mineworkers, for example. Pressure groups can be usefully divided into two main types: those which act to protect their members' interests and those which are concerned to promote a cause which they believe will be in the general interests of society.

Pressure groups vary not only in the focus of their concern but more crucially in the degree of influence they have. In some cases a government may consult relevant pressure groups before introducing or amending legislation or policies and some groups enjoy relatively easy access to government.

To be successful, pressure groups need well-planned strategies of communication, or CAMPAIGNS. The methods used here vary but include letter-writing, gaining INTERVIEWS on local or national RADIO, using radio 'phone-in' slots, the distribution of literature, advertisements, demonstrations and, if possible, gaining TELEVISION coverage. The mass media clearly play an important role in attempts to gain widespread public support. See LOBBYING.

Prestel See VIEWDATA.

Prevarication See DESIGN FEATURES.

Primacy, the law of The view that whichever side of a case or argument is presented first will have greater impact on an audience than anything which follows. F.H. Lund is considered to have been the first to advance this theory in 'The psychology of belief' in the *Journal of Abnormal and Social Psychology* (1925). There are those, however, who espouse the law of *recency*, asserting that that which is most recent is the more likely to have greatest impact and retention. Primacy puts its faith in first impressions, recency in last impressions; both are marginal factors in the real context of debate where *who* goes first or last, and *what* is said first or last, in what *situation* and by what *means*, are more fundamental criteria.

Primary groups See GROUPS.

Principle of least effort Posed by G.K. Zipf in *Human Behavior and the Principle of Least Effort* (US: Addison-Wesley, 1949). Zipf believed that the human communicator minimizes wherever possible the 'probable average rate of work required' in any given situation. This Zipf describes as *effort*. The communicator needs to be understood but his/her desire, Zipf argues, is to be brief. For a full explanation, see Colin Cherry's *On Human Communication* (US: MIT Press, 1966), Chapter 3, 'On signs, language, and communication'.

Printing The system of printing used by John of Gutenberg in the 15th c., and still widely practised today, works by the application of ink, and subsequently paper, to a raised surface. This is known as *relief printing*. Other methods are *planographic* and *intaglio* or *gravure*. With the former, the design to be printed and its background are in one flat surface; in intaglio printing the part to be printed is etched or cut into the plate – the exact reverse of relief printing.

Bavarian actor/playwright Alois Senefelder in 1798 found that some kinds of stone absorb both oil and water. He drew on the stone with a greasy crayon and then dampened the stone which absorbed the water only where there was no crayon design. He then made an ink of wax, soap and lampblack which stuck to the crayon and came off on paper, producing a print. *Lithography* from the Greek 'lithos', stone, was born. Today zinc or aluminium sheets are used and the design to be printed is applied to the plates by a photographic process.

Off-set lithography, the main process of planographic printing employed today, came about as a result of an accident by American printer Ira W. Rubel who had allowed the rubber covering of the impress cylinder to become inked. He discovered that the perfect impression it transferred to the sheet of paper was of better quality than that produced by direct contact with the plate. The first patent for a system of printing using *photocomposition* was taken out by William Friese-Greene in 1895, though typesetting by photography was not in commercial use till the early 1950s. Modern photocomposition is computer-controlled. See COLD-TYPE TECHNOLOGY; CYLINDER PRESS; LASER PRINTING; LINOTYPE PRINTING; MONOTYPE PRINTING.

Print unions In the UK, print workers are represented by four unions: the National Graphical Association (NGA) for the highly skilled composing room and foundry areas of the newspaper business; the National Society of Operative Printers, Graphical and Media Personnel (NATSOPA) for printing room and clerical staff; the Society of Graphical and Allied Trades (SOGAT) for paper handlers and publishing and distribution workers; and for process workers who make blocks for illustrations, the Society of Lithographic Artists, Designers and Engravers (SLADE). On the ownership/management side of newspapers there is the National Proprietors Association (NPA) formed in 1906. For journalists, the chief trade union is the National Union of Journalists (NUJ).

Privacy An ISSUE of rapidly growing importance in the 1980s and whose survival might be at risk in the 1990s is the privacy of the individual – his or her private space. With the advent of the computer, immense amounts of data about a person are retrievable at the touch of a button. With advances in TELEPHONE technology and electronic bugging it is no longer possible to be confident that our phones are not tapped. Developments such as SYSTEM X have made PHONE-TAPPING easier, swifter and practically impossible to detect.

In their book *Stranger on the Line: The Secret History of Phone Tapping* (UK: Bodley Head, 1987), Patrick Fitzgerald and Mark Leopold examine the inadequacy of legal protection of citizens against government and other agencies 'accessing' into people's homes via phone-tap or bugging devices (See INTERCEPTION OF COMMUNICATIONS ACT, 1985). They conclude that unless British society evolves 'ways of controlling covert surveillance by the state, we will run the risk of becoming a society with no private space, anywhere.'

Changes in the welfare state in the 1980s moved in the direction of increased central control and direction allied with escalating demands for more and more information.

See CENSORSHIP; DATA PROTECTION ACT, 1984; SECRECY; TELEPHONE PREFERENCE SCHEME (TPS).
* D. Campbell and S. Connor, *On The Record: Surveillance, Computers & Privacy . . . The Inside Story* (UK: Michael Joseph, 1986).

Privacy transformation See DATA PROTECTION.

Private cues See BARNLUND'S TRANSACTIONAL MODEL OF COMMUNICATION.

Pro-con, Con-pro In capturing the attention of an audience, is it best to put good news, or good points (pro) before the bad (con), or after them? Researchers have indicated that pro-con generally works best. See PRIMACY, THE LAW OF.

Profane language The Latin derivation of profane is *pro fana*, meaning outside the temple. Profanity referred to anyone refusing to be initiated into the ways of the temple, thus showing a contempt for that which is sacred.

Profane LANGUAGE takes three main forms: religious, excretory or sexual; and the questions asked about such language are, why do people use profanities and what are the effects upon listeners – upon AUDIENCE – of the use of profanity?

J.D. Rothwell in 'Verbal obscenity: time for second thoughts' in *Western Speech*, 35 (1971) listed five reasons for using profane language: (1) to create attention; (2) to discredit someone or something; (3) to provoke confrontations; (4) to provide a type of CATHARSIS or emotional release for the user and (5) to establish interpersonal IDENTIFICATION. Profanity depends for its impact on who is actually using it and in what circumstances.

In 'The effects of three type of profane language in persuasion messages' in the *Journal of Communication* (December 1973) Robert N. Bostrom, John R. Baseheart and Charles M. Rossiter Jr write of research which indicates that where profanity is used, greater attitude change can be expected to occur if the communicator is female, in any of the three categories (religious, excretory, sexual). Bostrom *et al.* also reach the general conclusion that profanity has a detrimental effect on the perceived credibility of the communicator.

Programme flow 'In all developed broadcasting systems,' writes Raymond Williams in *Television: Technology and Cultural Form* (UK: Fontana, 1974), 'the characteristic organization, and therefore the characteristic experience, is one of sequence or flow.' Williams believes that flow is a chief principle of programming; the process of organizing a pattern of programmes each one leading on to the next; each one being a 'tempter' for the audience to stay tuned to a particular CHANNEL. Programme boundaries, says Williams, are constantly being obscured by advertisements and/or trailers for other programmes, to counteract the itchy finger on the remote control button, and the much-feared viewer indulence in ZAPPING.

Project Mercury See SATELLITE TRANSMISSION.

Project work In *Case Studies and Projects in Communication* (UK: Methuen, 1982), Neil McKeown writes of project work that it 'allows you much more freedom than you normally have in the real world, or on traditional academic courses. You can work on your own, or chose to work with student colleagues who share your interests.' Projects offer opportunities for wide and varied research, not only in libraries but in the community, and the fruits of that work can take the form of films, slide-tape shows, RADIO programmes, VIDEO and exhibitions as well as written reports.

McKeown tells his A-Level readers that project work 'is going to involve your development as a ''social being'' more than most traditional types of classroom learning'. You go out and meet people; sometimes you share their working lives; you have to persuade strangers that your requests for information and help are deserving of the time and effort they may give you. You will need a constant flow of FEED-BACK in the preparatory process, and courage to go on when lines of enquiry vanish into cul-de-sacs. The *Project* in the AEB A-Level in Communication Studies is submitted in the second year of the course. It counts for 30% of the overall final mark and includes an oral. See Chapter 5 in McKeown.

Projection A throwing outwards or forwards; term commonly used within several areas of communication and media studies. The ability to project oneself is an important communication skill. Here projection has been achieved when a person, in giving a talk, making a speech or acting a part on stage has reached the whole audience both with words and his/her personality. Voice, posture, EYE CONTACT, facial expression, GESTURE combine in creating effective projection.

The term can be used in a psychological sense: when people tend to project certain of their motives for behaviour, in particular those which cannot be gratified or which are regarded as unacceptable, onto other people; that is, to assume that these others share the same motives. We may be more inclined to make such assumptions about those we like and perceive as being similar to ourselves. Clearly projection can lead to errors in PERCEP-TION and to misunderstandings in the communication process.

Projection of pictures A German Jesuit, Athanasius Kircher (1601-80), professor of mathematics at the Collegio Romano in Rome, is generally thought to be the first person to project a picture on to a screen. His apparatus was crude but effective, containing all the essentials – a source of light with a reflector behind it and a lens in front, a painted glass slide and a screen. Kircher's astonished audience spoke of black magic. Undaunted, the inventor published a description of his findings. The projection of moving pictures was first demonstrated by Baron Von Uchatius (1811-81) in 1853. He used a rotating glass slide, a rotating shutter and a fixed lens. An improved version contained a rotating light source, fixed slides and a series of slightly inclined lenses whose optical axes met on the centre of the screen. See CINEMATOGRAPHY, ORIGINS.

Prolefeed The rubbishy entertainment and spurious news piped to the proletariat by the Party in George Orwell's novel *Nineteen Eighty-Four* (1949).

Propaganda Usually deliberate manipulation by means of SYMBOLS (words, gestures, images, flags, monuments, music, etc.) of other people's thoughts, behaviour, attitudes and beliefs. The word originates with the Roman Catholic Congregation for the Propagation of the Faith, a committee of cardinals in charge of missionary activities of the church since 1622. See ADVERTISING; BRAIN-WASHING; EFFECTS OF THE MASS MEDIA; LOBBY-ING; RHETORIC.

Propinquity A significant determinant of group membership, propinquity is liking through proximity; when people are close together physically there is a strain towards amicability which aids group formation, more reliably than with physically distant persons. See GROUPS.

Prosodic signals Timing, pitch and stress of utterances to convey MEANING.

Proxemics The study of the way people approach others or keep their distance from others; the analysis of what we do with space as a dimension of non-verbal communication (See COMMUNICATION, NON-VERBAL). There appear to be definite features that mark the distance people observe between each other in communication situations. Within three feet is intimate; up to about eight feet is personal; over that distance is semi-public or social. The proximity between communicators differs, obviously, according to the nature of the MESSAGE and varies between cultures, classes and nations. The personal but not intimate distance of Arabs, for example, can be as little as 18 inches - intimidating for an English listener. Middle CLASS distances tend, it has been found, to be slightly greater than those maintained between working-class communicators. Proxemics extends to the way we allocate space to those extensions of ourselves - rooms, houses, towns, cities - and the manner in which we occupy those extensions. See DEFENSIBLE SPACE; PARA-PROXEMICS.

* E.T. Hall, *The Hidden Dimension: Man's Use of Space in Public and Private* (UK: Bodley Head, 1966); A. Fry, *Safe Space* (UK: J.M. Dent, 1987).

PR: Public relations In *Advertising as Communication* (UK: Methuen, 1982), Gillian Dyer cites the aim of PR as being 'to promote positive and favourable images of people or firms in public life, without actually appearing to do so'. Most companies have PR departments dedicated to creating and sustaining a good image with the general public. PR has also grown big in the service of politicians and political parties. As Dyer says, 'The "publicity boys" rehearse politicians before they go in front of the camera . . . they stage-manage walkabouts . . . kissing babies, all for the benefit of the mass media. Politicans and campaigns are marketed like soap.' In winning the 1979, 1983 and 1987 general elections in the UK,

Margaret Thatcher and the Conservative Party owed not a little to the PR work of Saatchi and Saatchi. The Labour Party in 1983 and 1987 also used an ADVERTISING agency to promulgate the party's image to the public.

Pseudo-context In his sharply critical assessment of the impact of TELEVISION on society, in *Amusing Ourselves to Death* (UK: Methuen, 1986), American author and communications professor Neil Postman says of a pseudo-context that it is 'a structure invented to give fragmented and irrelevant information a seeming use'. However, the pseudo-context offers us no useful function for the information in terms of action, problem-solving or change. TV is the culprit in this fragmenting process. All that is left for what Postman calls the 'decontextualization of fact' by the non-print media, particularly TV, is to amuse. All knowledge, having been fragmented, is reduced to a trivial pursuit. See EFFECTS OF THE MASS MEDIA.

PSI Para-social identification; that is, members of an audience associate with fictitious characters as portrayed in the media, or with well known personalities whom they regularly 'meet' through the MEDIATION of RADIO, TV, etc. See PARA-SOCIAL INTERACTION.

Psychology This discipline seeks to explore the way in which individual behaviours are linked together to form a 'personality'. Its focus is upon the experience and behaviour of the individual, upon the individual's reaction to certain physiological and/or social conditions.

Some areas of *social* psychology are concerned with the behaviour of individuals in small GROUPS or crowds; here there is some overlap between this discipline and that of SOCIOLOGY.

Public communication Term used to describe all forms of spoken address involving a speaker and an AUDIENCE. In *Understanding and Sharing: An Introduction to Speech Communication* (US: Brown, 1985), Judy Cornelia Pearson and Paul Edward Nelson define public communication as 'a transaction in which people simultaneously give and receive MEANING from each other'.

Public cues See BARNLUND'S TRANSACTIONAL MODEL OF COMMUNICATION, 1970.

Public opinion See NOELLE-NEUMANN'S SPIRAL OF SILENCE MODEL OF PUBLIC OPINION, 1974.

Public radio Term used in Australia to refer to COMMUNITY RADIO.

Public relations See PR: PUBLIC RELATIONS.

Public service broadcasting Writing in the *Observer* (5 December 1982), John Birt, director of programmes for LWT and how head of news and current affairs with the BBC claimed that public service BROADCASTING was 'one of the greatest British inventions and achieve-ments of this century'. The term refers to any broadcasting system whose first duty is to a public within a democracy, serving to inform, educate and entertain, and not serving to fulfil the requirements of commercial interests. From the initiation of RADIO BROADCASTING in the UK, the principle of public service and answerability to parliament was enshrined in legislation and manifested in the BBC, whose monopoly continued until the introduction of COMMERCIAL TELEVISION. Even then, the Independent TV Authority (later the IBA) was – and is – subject to rigorous criteria of public broadcasting.

John Birt's article was written at a moment in the evolution of broadcasting in the UK when commercial interests, as represented by the onset of CABLE TRANSMISSION and following the HUNT COMMITTEE REPORT ON CABLE TELEVISION, 1982, posed a substantial future threat to the broadcasting NORMS and practices that have made Britain's broadcasting system respected throughout the world. See 'BROADCASTING IN THE 90s': GOVERNMENT WHITE PAPER, 1988.

Pulitzer Prize for journalism American award created by Joseph Pulitzer, Hungarian-born newspaper proprietor and rival of William Randolph Hearst (model for Orson Welles' FILM *Citizen Kane*, 1943). Along with Pulitzers for journalism, there are prizes for music and literature. Originating in 1947, the Pulitzer prizes are awarded annually.

Punk Youth SUB-CULTURE which came to public attention in the UK during the summer of 1976. The name Punk is derived from Punk Rock, a musical STYLE developed between the early and mid-1970s in the US and UK. The style of this sub-culture, much influenced by the art school and by conceptual art, was designed to shock. Hair was worn shaved close to the head and dyed in startling colours. Dress was based on the themes of bondage and sexuality. Outfits were made from everyday items which normally served a different function, especially those associated with waste such as dustbin liners and toilet chains. Its members were drawn largely from the lower middle class and the working class. Some sociologists such as Mike Brake in *The Sociology of Youth Culture and Youth Subcultures*, (UK: Routledge & Kegan Paul, 1980) see Punk style as an expression of the rejection of a society which offers an increasing number of young people no jobs and few prospects. The lyrics of Punk Rock often articulate a sense of bitterness and outrage as well as the spirit of anarchism, and political protest.

The spectacular style of dress and the unconventional behaviour of some Punk musicians ensured that the Punks received considerable media attention. See YOUTH CULTURE.

Quadrophony See GRAMOPHONE.

Quadruplex technique See TELERECORDING.

Qube See INTERACTIVE TELEVISION.

Questionnaires A popular method of data collection, a questionnaire basically consists of a series of questions designed to obtain factual information and/or information about people's attitudes, VALUES, opinions, or BELIEFS about a particular subject or issue. A questionnaire can also be constructed so as to contain questions about a *range* of topics or ISSUES. They are regularly used as a tool of market research; and are central to AUDIENCE RESEARCH. Questionnaires may be conducted in a variety of ways: for example, face-to-face with the researcher reading out the questions to the respondent and filling in the responses for him or her. Alternatively a written questionnaire may be sent out and returned through the post. The best way must be chosen for the job in hand. Each has its strengths and limitations: postal questionnaires are relatively easy to distribute but the response rate is often low.

It is not usually possible to give a questionnaire to all those who make up the group in which you are interested and so questionnaires are normally given to a sample (see SAMPLING); care needs to be taken to ensure that the sample represents the total population, that is the total number of people in that group, in all significant respects.

Questionnaires are useful for gathering large amounts of data but may be less useful for investigating an issue in depth; here PARTICIPANT OBSERVATION or INTERVIEWS may be more useful. Further, constructing an unambiguous, unbiased and productive questionnaire is not easy – nor is the impartial analysis of the responses collected.

Quotas Limits placed upon the import of foreign printing, FILM and broadcast material to protect indigenous, home-grown media products. Quotas are immensely difficult to establish and sustain and, with the modern shift of emphasis from producers to consumers (through the availability of VIDEO, CABLE TRANSMISSION and SATELLITE TRANSMISSION) import controls will be even less effective. For quotas to work, it would be necessary to rival the attraction-value of the materials available – cheap, packaged, of proven success with audiences. See MEDIA IMPERIALISM.

Quota sample See SAMPLING.

QWERTY Arrangement of letters on the traditional TYPEWRITER keyboard, devised in 1873 to overcome jamming problems on the world's first production machine, a Remington.

Radcliffe Committee Report, 1967 See D-NOTICES.

Radical press See UNDERGROUND PRESS.

Radio See RADIO BROADCASTING; WIRELESS TELEGRAPHY; RADIO DRAMA; BBC RADIO IN THE NINETIES; CELLULAR RADIO; CB – CITIZENS' BAND RADIO; COMMERCIAL RADIO; COMMUNITY RADIO; DOCUMENTARY; FEDERAL RADIO COMMISSION; FOURTEEN-DAY RULE; HOME SERVICE; HOSPITAL RADIO; ILR; LIGHT PROGRAMME; MARCH OF TIME; NETWORK; PIRATE RADIO; RADIO BALLADS; RADIO: BROADCASTING IN THE 90s; RADIO DATA SYSTEM; RADIO HAM; RADIO JUKEBOXES; RADIO 1, RADIO 2, RADIO 3, RADIO 4; SYNCHRONOUS SOUND; THIRD PROGRAMME; 'WAR OF THE WORLDS'; WIRELESS TELEGRAPH ACT, 1964.

Radio ballads Form of musical DOCUMENTARY inspired by RADIO producer Charles Parker, and compiled by folk-singers Ewan McColl and Peggy Seeger, beginning in 1958 with *The Ballad of John Axon*. The introduction of high-quality portable taperecorders to the BBC enabled Parker and his team to create new patterns of vocal sound, interlaced with sound effects (real, not studio-simulated) which served as an 'impressionistic' means of describing the lives and work of ordinary people. John Axon was a train driver, killed in a crash, and the nature of his life was recreated in ballad and recollection. *Singing the Fishing* (1960), taking for its theme the hard life of the North Sea fisherman, won the Italia Press award. The BBC withdrew financial support from this pioneering team in 1964. See RADIO DRAMA.

Radio broadcasting The 1st World War (1914–18) had given impetus to the development of RADIO for military purposes, and the training of wireless operators. Visionaries of the age saw the possibility of wireless programmes as an exciting extension of wireless messages – a 'household utility' which would create a world of sound, of voices and music; that would annihilate distance and offer undreamed-of opportunities for CULTURE, entertainment and information. With the ending of the war, crystal sets tuned in by their 'cat's whisker' became immensely popular. The valve – called the 'magic lantern of radio' – developed between 1904 and 1914, soon usurped the place of the crystal.

The first 'broadcast' of music and speech was made by an American R.A. Fissenden in 1906. The American Radio and Research Company was BROADCASTING concerts twice and three times a week as early as 1916, though KDKA of Pittsburg won the earliest renown as a pioneer in the field (on air, 1920).

A ban imposed on 'amateur' radio in Britain at the outbreak of the 1st World War was not lifted until 1919, but in February 1920 the

Marconi Company in the UK began broadcasting from WRITTLE, Chelmsford, though later in the year the Post Office withdrew permission for these broadcasts. However, on 14 February 1922 the first regular broadcasting service in Britain was again beamed from Writtle, organized by the Experimental Section of the Designs Department of Marconi. Their London station, 2LO, began broadcasting on 11 May of the same year.

The Post Office, faced with nearly 100 applications from manufacturers who wanted to set up broadcasting stations, and realizing the need to have some sort of control of the airways, proposed a consortium of companies to centralize broadcasting activity: the British Broadcasting Company was born, and John REITH was appointed its managing director (See BBC, ORIGINS). The BBC, set up by Royal Charter, came into existence 1 January 1927 and was to hold a monopoly of broadcasting in the UK until COMMERCIAL RADIO was legalized in the SOUND BROADCASTING ACT 1972.

From its beginning, radio broadcasting in the US was financed by ADVERTISING; from its beginning, radio broadcasting in the UK was free of advertising; the one was predominantly local, the other a national public service and eventually a national institution. No study of the evolution of broadcasting in the UK can avoid also being an analysis of the philosophy, vision and practices of the BBC's Managing director and later director general John (later Sir John) Reith. Varyingly called the Napoleon of Broadcasting, and Prospero, the all-powerful magician, Reith disliked politics and politicians, viewed commerce with disdain (and commercialism with contempt). He forged a definition of PUBLIC SERVICE BROADCASTING that dominated broadcasting – both radio and TV – for generations and, even in the age of the dispersal of control, affects us still.

Radio news readers wore dinner jackets and bow ties to read the news, a symbol of the aloofness and distancing characteristic of Reith and much of the output of the BBC. There was even a Pronunciation Committee. Yet the Corporation resisted criticisms from the popular PRESS that its tastes were too elitist. It was to give drama and classical music – as well as many other forms of music – a new stature and a new popularity. Equally, there was room for developing the special potentials of radio – in outside broadcasts, drama DOCUMENTARY, discussion programmes, and fireside talks.

The greatest fear of the broadcasters was – and continues to be – of government interference. Reith's caution was as monumental as the extent of his control. His desire to render the BBC beyond political reproach led to the Corporation often censoring itself so as to be one

step ahead of being censored. The risks to the BBC were not imagined. During the General Strike of 1926 Winston Churchill wanted the government to commandeer the Corporation, a move Reith managed to resist – but at a price: during the strike no representative of organized labour was permitted to broadcast, and the Leader of the Opposition, Ramsay MacDonald, was also banned.

* A. Briggs, *The History of Broadcasting in the United Kingdom* (UK: Oxford University Press, four volumes, 1961, 1965 and, volumes 3 and 4, 1979); A. Crisell, *Understanding Radio* (UK: Methuen, 1986).

Radio: broadcasting in the 90s Conservative government Home Secretary Douglas Hurd announced proposals for changes in British RADIO BROADCASTING in January 1988. The BBC would continue to provide PUBLIC SERVICE BROADCASTING as a backcloth to changes in the independent sector; provision would be made for three new national commercial stations, each offering a diverse and varied programme service; several hundred new local and community radio stations would be permitted to take to the airwaves. There would be a new Radio Authority to licence all non-BBC radio.

The wasteful practice of broadcasting the same programmes on different frequencies would be halted and, in Hurd's own words, there would be 'a light touch system of regulation for independent national, local and community stations alike'. National commercial radio NETWORKS would be allocated by competitive tender 'but any applicant will first have to pass a test of diversity before financial bids are compared'.

Radio Data System Electronic process enabling RADIO listeners to have press-button access to the programme of their choice. The radio of the future will not only have buttons for pre-tuned stations, but a digital display to indicate which station is being listened to. In addition, the set will locate the best signal for any particular station.

Radio drama The first ever RADIO play was Richard Hughes's *Danger* (1923), about a couple trapped in a mine, but the play which appears to have had the most substantial impact as a work in a new MEDIUM was Reginald Berkeley's *The White Château*, broadcast by the BBC to an audience of over 12 m on Armistice Day, 1925 and telling an extremely harrowing story of the trench-war. Since that time hundreds of writers have been given a start in their professional lives by radio, one of whose many virtues is cheapness: today, a 30-minute radio play requires one day's studio time; an hour-long play, two days. The radio playwright need not concern him/herself with the massive costs of scene-changes; there is little need to keep costs down by writing plays for two people and an armchair. The whole world of time and space is at the writer's command.

Most importantly, there is the awaiting *imagination* of the listener. The best radio plays take the listener on a journey into his/her imagination, where the play is given its own unique setting, the characters a unique appearance – all with the help of voices, sound effects and silence; an art form, as the poet W.H. Auden once said, which is 'not spoiled by any collision with visual reality'.

Radio drama possesses the characteristic of intimacy – it has made the interior monologue, the soliloquy, a dramatic device perhaps more convincingly acceptable than on the stage; at the same time, because its stage is contained by no proscenium arch or screen-frame, because its 'stage-set' is actually the mind of the listener, radio also lends itself successfully to epic drama: Shakespeare is marvellous on radio.

Among writers who took an early and serious interest in radio as a serious art form was the Irish poet Louis MacNeice (1907–65). His verse plays broadcast during and after the 2nd World War, such as *The Story of My Death* (1943) and *The Dark Tower* (1946) impressively explored the potential of radio, while in 1953 another poet, Welshman Dylan Thomas (1914–53), within a few months of his death, gave to the world one of the best known and most loved plays for radio, *Under Milk Wood*. The play was first broadcast on 25 January 1954, with a distinguished all-Welsh cast and produced by Douglas Cleverdon.

For 30 years Val Gielgud as Head of Radio Drama at the BBC guided the evolution of the radio play, himself producing and writing. Throughout its history, radio drama has witnessed a strong tradition of able producers – such as Cleverdon, Lancelot Sieveking, Donald McWinnie and Alfred Bradley – nurturing writers who later became famous: Harold Pinter, Stan Barstow, Giles Cooper, Allan Prior, Alun Owen, William Trevor, Henry Livings, Peter Terson, Alan Plater, David Rudkin and Tom Stoppard.

Despite its creative potential, radio as a dramatic medium has acquired less *status*, and been paid less attention than other – more glamorous – media; and less than it deserves. However, the BBC continues to broadcast between 200 and 300 radio plays a year, classical drama as well as new works. See TELEVISION DRAMA.

Radio ham Commonplace name applied to licensed amateur RADIO operators. These enthusiasts are interested in the technology and operation of radio equipment and they operate on specified frequencies set aside for their use by the government. In order to obtain a transmitting licence from the Home Office, radio hams have to pass an examination. However, more frequencies and higher transmitting powers are then available to them than on CB-CITIZENS' BAND RADIO.

Radio jukeboxes Phrase used in a BBC publication *Local Radio in the Public Interest* (1966) to describe the nature of RADIO BROADCASTING as typified by American local stations. The BBC urged that local radio should become, instead of one more jukebox service of endless light music, a forum for the cultural life of the community. See COMMUNITY RADIO.

Radio Luxembourg See COMMERCIAL RADIO.

Radio Normandy See COMMERCIAL RADIO.

Radio Northsea PIRATE RADIO station which began BROADCASTING off the coast of Essex immediately prior to the General Election of 1970. Mindful of the Labour Government's antipathy to COMMERCIAL RADIO and the Conservatives' support for it, Radio Northsea broadcast pro-Tory PROPAGANDA at an election in which the 18–21 age group were voting for the first time.

Many constituencies in London and the south-east were marginal seats and a swing of only 1% was needed to change the result. Labour lost the election; in the constituencies nearest Radio Northsea, the swing against Labour was greatest. At the Royal Opening of Parliament on 2 July 1970, the Queen's Speech confirmed that legislation would be introduced for local radio stations 'under the general supervision of an independent broadcasting authority'.

Radio 1, Radio 2, Radio 3, Radio 4 The four RADIO channels of the BBC have broadcast in their present form since 1967. Prior to that there was the HOME SERVICE catering for news, plays, magazine programmes; the LIGHT PROGRAMME largely for popular music and entertainment and the THIRD PROGRAMME, a minority CHANNEL serving the world of classical music and literature. During the 1960s PIRATE RADIO invaded the airwaves with pop music which drew large audiences, especially among teenagers. The MARINE BROADCASTING (OFFENCES) ACT, 1967 made such stations illegal. It was realized that there was a considerable audience for popular music now not being catered for. BBC's *Radio 1* was created to meet the new demand.

Radio 2 took on a similar if not identical role to that of the Light Programme, *Radio 3* that of the Third and *Radio 4* that of the Home Service. See BROADCASTING; RADIO: BROADCASTING IN THE 90s.

Random sample See SAMPLING.

Rapid fading One of US linguist Charles Hockett's 16 DESIGN FEATURES of human LANGUAGE described in publications which appeared in the 1960s. The term refers to the way in which speech sounds fade rapidly in contrast with, for example, communication by letter or smell. They do not 'linger for reception at the hearer's convenience', writes Hockett in 'The origin of speech', *Scientific American*, 203 (1960).

Rate In relation to vocal delivery – of a talk or speech – the speed at which words are spoken, usually between 125 and 190 per minute.

Ratings Audience ratings are taken regularly by both the BBC and the independent TV companies in an attempt to ascertain which programmes attract the largest audiences. High ratings are often considered to be of particular importance to the independent broadcasting companies as they rely for finance on selling ADVERTISING space and such space is priced in accordance with the size of the audience likely to be watching at that time. Ratings can, however, only give an approximation of the number of people watching a particular programme; they cannot indicate the extent to which such a programme is liked, the degree to which it is being seriously watched, or the potential demand for certain types of programme. For these reasons some media commentators have argued that ratings should not be taken as a serious reflection of public taste, or inhibit the development and screening of more creative and intellectually demanding programmes. See AUDIENCE RESEARCH; SCHEDULING.

Reaction shot When a person is being interviewed on TELEVISION there are regular in-cuts where the viewer is offered a glimpse of the reactions of the reporter or interviewer – nodding, smiling, acknowledging. When interviews take place on location rather than in the studio, such reaction shots are usually filmed separately and edited in later. See SHOT.

Received pronunciation (RP) That mode of pronunciation in English which is free of regional accent and aspires to a generally accepted standard; derives from the speech of the court and of public schools; traditionally the 'vocal sign' of the educated person, adopted as the norm for BBC broadcasters, and eventually being termed 'BBC English'. RP no longer has the prestigious status or the dominance it once had. Regional accents have been 'in' since the 1960s, though RP has retained a substantial foothold in national BROADCASTING.

Receiver See SENDER/RECEIVER.

Recency effect See FIRST IMPRESSIONS; PRIMACY, LAW OF.

Record player See GRAMOPHONE.

Redundancy In communication terms, that which is conventional or predictable in any MESSAGE. Its opposite is **Entropy**, that which is unexpected and surprising, of low predictability. John Fiske in *Introduction to Communication Studies* (UK: Methuen, 1982) says 'The English language is about 50% **redun-**

dant. This means we can delete about 50% of any utterance and still have a usable language capable of transmitting understandable messages.' Redundancy is established through frequent use until it becomes a CONVENTION, both technical, in terms of correctness, and social, in terms of general acceptability. It is essential if the MEANING of messages is to have wide currency and be 'on wave-length' with the CODES and reference tables of the receiver.

The **Entropic** challenges these codes and reference tables with novelty – new expression, new thought, overturning predictability and probability. The art of the AVANT-GARDE is entropic; at least in its initial phase, it speaks in a LANGUAGE the general public find difficult to understand, and often provocative. Of course the shock of the new passes: yesterday's outrage is today's fashion, yesterday's entropy is today's redundancy. A scan of the popular arts reveals their reliance on the conventional forms and practice which make up redundancy – the predictable rhymes and metres of pop songs, for example, the repetitive refrains of folks songs. Fiske writes, 'Redundancy is generally a force for the status quo and against change. Entropy is less comfortable, more stimulating, more shocking perhaps, but harder to communicate effectively.' See PHATIC LANGUAGE.

Reference a term which refers to the mental image produced by a SIGN or SYMBOL and by the experience the individual has of its REFERENT.

Referent The actual object, entity in the external world to which a SIGN or linguistic expression **refers**. The referent of the word *table* is the object 'table'.

Reflective-projective theory of broadcasting and mass communication Posed by Lee Loevinger in 'The ambiguous mirror: the reflective-projective theory of broadcasting and mass communication' in G. Gumpert and R. Cathcart, eds., *Inter/Media: Interpersonal Communication in a Media World* (US/UK: Oxford University Press, 1979). Loevinger states 'that mass communications are best understood as mirrors of society that reflect an ambiguous image in which each observer projects or sees his own vision of himself and society.' The media reflect images of society but not of the individual.

'While the mirror can pick out points and aspects of society, it cannot create a culture or project an image that does not reflect something already existing in some form in society.' BROADCASTING can clarify or distort images of society; it can focus broadly or narrowly. According to the theory, the media 'are most unlikely to become instruments of social reform or great public enlightenment'. Thus violence on TV reflects the existence of and tolerance of violence in society.

Loevinger emphasizes the point that the image is perceived *individually* by each member of the media audience who projects or sees in the media his/her own visions or images: 'broadcasting is an electronic mirror reflecting an ambiguous image of its environment in which the audience sees its vision of society.' See THEORIES AND CONCEPTS OF COMMUNICATION.

Reflexiveness See DESIGN FEATURES.

Reformers See ADVERTISING: MAINSTREAMERS, ASPIRERS, SUCCEEDERS AND REFORMERS.

Refutation The employment of counter-arguments, evidence and proof to dispute the arguments of another person. Strictly speaking, to disprove allegations.

Register Term describing the compass of a voice or instrument, the range of sound tones produced in a particular manner. The soprano and the bass sing in different *registers*. The word also describes the structures of LANGUAGE used in varying social contexts: its levels of vocabulary, sentence construction, tones and inflexions. Thus the register adopted by an infant school teacher in his/her class will differ from the register selected for the staff room, just as a scientist will adjust his/her register between conversations held with scientific colleagues and with casual acquaintances in the local pub. In PRINTING, register refers to the exact adjustment of position, as of colours in a picture, or letterpress on opposite sides of the page.

Regulators Means by which the flow of INTERPERSONAL COMMUNICATION is regulated – checked, slowed, speeded up, acknowledged, etc. Regulators can be both verbal (such as 'What's that again?') or non-verbal, such as head nodding, EYE CONTACT or avoidance, shifting body positions, the punctuation of communication by hand movements or the raising of eyebrows. See INDICATORS; NON-VERBAL BEHAVIOUR: REPERTOIRE.

Reinforcement There has been much argument over the role of the mass media in reinforcing, in underpinning, certain social and political VALUES and structures. Considerable attention has been given to two areas: the media's portrayal of violence and the role of the mass media in political communications.

There are those who claim that the frequent incidence of violence in the media has contributed to an alleged increase in acts of violence in society. Research evidence, however, gives few clear pointers as to the nature or extent of any media influence. One school of thought rejects the notion that the media directly encourage violent behaviour in all viewers but argues that the media violence may reinforce already existing tendencies to violence in some viewers. This position is not without its critics. James Halloran in an essay entitled 'The effects of the media portrayal of violence and aggression' in J. Tunstall, ed., *Media Sociol-*ogy (UK, Constable, 1970), points to several research projects which have indicated that the media may play a more direct and general role in the shaping the audience's attitude towards violence.

P.F. Lazarsfeld, B. Berelson and H. Gaudet in a classic study of the effects of political communication by the mass media on voting behaviour, *The People's Choice* (US: Columbia University Press, 1948), comment that the media's main effect is to reinforce existing political preferences. The notions of *selective perception*, SELECTIVE EXPOSURE and *selective recall* are used to explain how the same output can reinforce the diverse views, values and beliefs of a mass audience. It is suggested that the audiences, rather than being passive receptacles for media output, select from the output those messages which are in accordance with their own prior dispositions and give attention to these. If, for example, a particular programme is likely to offer little reinforcement individuals operate the mechanism of selective exposure: they do not watch it.

More recent research has tended to challenge such findings. Some commentators have emphasized the importance of AGENDA SETTING to a political campaign; others have made important modifications to the reinforcement doctrine. Jay Blumler and Denis McQuail in 'The audience for election television', also in Tunstall (1970), argue from the results of their analysis of the 1964 British general election that whilst some individuals seek, consciously, reinforcement of their own ideas and beliefs when choosing which political communication they will expose themselves to, others will use such communication for guidance. If, then, as some commentators argue, political communication by the mass media tends to reflect the political ideas of certain GROUPS rather than others, it obviously will play a much more active role in shaping political attitudes than was thought by early researchers. Indeed at a time when many researchers are pointing to the increased volatility of voting behaviour it may be that political communication by the mass media will be of increasing significance.

The close links between media organizations and other dominant social and political institutions have led researchers to investigate the degree to which the mass media reinforce prevailing social and political hierarchies. Michael Tracey in *The Production of Political Television* (UK: Routledge & Kegan Paul, 1978) argues that as regards BROADCASTING the relationship between the media and dominant institutions tends to be complex and to have been characterized by 'alternate moments of apparent autonomy and real subjection'. Tracey further argues that constraints on the media tend to function indirectly. Researchers analysing the media's treatment of women have noted the way the media reinforce the traditional, limited role of women in society. In this respect the media would appear by and large to back up the patriarchalism of contemporary British social and political hierarchies. See EFFECTS OF THE MASS MEDIA: POLITICS OF ACCOMMODATION (IN THE MEDIA).

Reithian Attitudes to BROADCASTING as typified by the first Director General of the BBC, Sir John **Reith**, who dominated the rise of broadcasting in the UK like a colossus. Dour, high-principled, autocratic, paternalist and a Scottish Presbyterian to boot, Reith was appointed General Manager of the newly formed British Broadcasting Company in December 1922. 'Some might call it luck,' writes Ronald Blythe in *The Age of Illusion: England in the Twenties and Thirties 1919–40* (UK: Penguin, 1964), 'he called it Providence. The microphone was born and John Reith was there to suckle it, to guide its infant lispings, to wean it from the pap of the first years, to train it, lecture it, cherish it, and protect it from the tycoons, sometimes to spank it, but finally to see it take its place authoritatively among the most ancient institutions in the country. And all in less than a decade.'

Reith's philosophy was that broadcasting was a heaven-sent opportunity to educate and enlighten the people in the ways of quality, and that 'giving the people what they wanted' was the way to perdition. This 'Tsar of Savoy Hill' as the PRESS called him, believed 'in the medicinal effects of education – a cultural dictatorship' said the *New Statesman* on Armistice Day, 1933. Though George Lansbury MP said of Reith, 'I have always felt that Sir John Reith would have made a very excellent Hitler for this country', Clement Attlee saw advantages: 'He puts up a splendid resistance to vested interests of all kinds.' Elitist, imperious and sabbatarian, Reith nevertheless created in the BBC an organization resistant to commercialism, favouring the arts, serious debate and notions of public responsibility. Reith strove for IMPARTIALITY but never achieved balance: coverage of Royal activities in the 1920s and 1930s was not in any way matched by coverage of the activities of the Labour Movement and the unions and, during the General Strike of 1926, the BBC remained strictly 'neutral': it stayed silent. Reith, the Napoleon of Broadcasting, as Colonel Moore Brabazon called him, resigned as 'DG' (Director General), as his own staff spoke of him, in 1937. See BBC, ORIGINS; PUBLIC SERVICE BROADCASTING.

Relativism In his study *Forms of Intellectual and Ethical Development in the College Years: A Scheme*, (US: Holt, Rinehart & Winston, 1968), W.G. Perry proposes a scheme of intellectual and ethical development which is parti-cularly concerned with the manner in which individuals hold attitudes, VALUES and beliefs and their ability to modify them in the light of new information and experience. Perry argues that in the process of ethical and intellectual development a person progresses from **Dualism** through *Relativism* to **Commitment**.

Dualism is characterized by a rigid, 'black or white' attitude to knowledge, values and beliefs. At this stage, individuals tend to see information or actions narrowly as being right or wrong, without qualification. A **relativistic** perspective acknowledges that there are numerous and conflicting interpretations of knowledge, values and beliefs, that people see things differently, and that there is rightly uncertainty as to which views are correct; further, it appreciates that what is or is not perceived as correct varies with particular circumstances and the background of various individuals and that the onus is upon each individual to decide which, if any, interpretations to accept.

The later stage, of **commitment** comes with the decision to internalize a particular standpoint. Such commitment will then influence how an individual reacts to life experiences and forms part of an individual code by which he/she will try to live.

Relic gestures Those physical *gestures* which have outlived their original situation, yet continue to be used to effect even though their derivation is no longer obvious or explicable. Such gestures survive not only from historical past but from a human's infantile past. For example, the rocking to and fro of disaster victims in the face of intolerable grief.

Repertoire of non-verbal behaviour See NON-VERBAL BEHAVIOUR: REPERTOIRE.

Representation The process by which SIGNS and SYMBOLS are made to convey certain meanings; the term representation also refers to the signs and symbols which claim to stand for, which represent, some aspect of reality, that is to the products of representation. Representations are an essential feature of social life; they allow us to communicate and make sense of our surroundings. As such they and the process of representation can become weapons of social conflict and ideological differences as much as elements of social cohesion. The ideological role of representing and representations is a focus for media research; an example here being research concerned with the representation of women in the media.

Representation, machinery of See MACHINERY OF REPRESENTATION.

Representative sample See SAMPLING.

Repressive use of the media See EMANCIPATORY USE OF THE MEDIA.

Research centres (into the media) In the UK there are centres of research into CULTURE and the media at the universities of Birmingham, Glasgow, Leeds, Leicester, London and Sheffield. At Birmingham there is the Centre for Contemporary Cultural Studies; at Glasgow the GLASGOW UNIVERSITY MEDIA GROUP; at Leeds the Centre for Television Research; at Leicester the Centre for Mass Communication at London, the Goldsmith's Media Research Group and at Sheffield the Centre for English Cultural Tradition and Language.

Resonance Term used by George Gerbner and fellow researchers at the Annenberg School of Communications, University of Pennsylvania, Philadelphia, to describe a condition experienced by TELEVISION viewers when what they see matches their expectations. If what they see confirms their vision of the world, of reality, that vision *resonates*. It is reinforced. More, for in 'The "mainstreaming" of America: violence profile no. 11' (*Journal of Communication*, Summer 1980) Gerbner, Larry Gross, Michael Morgan and Nancy Signorielli state that where TV reality and a person's experience or PERCEPTION of reality are in alignment, 'the combination may result in a coherent and powerful "double dose" of the television message.' For example, city dwellers living in centres of high crime will find TV's violent imagery congruent with their experience. 'These people receive a "double dose" of messages that the world is violent, and consequently show the strongest associations between viewing and fear.' See EFFECTS OF THE MASS MEDIA; MAINSTREAMING; MEAN WORLD SYNDROME.

Response Reaction to a stimulus or stimuli which may or may not result in observable behaviour. In the context of communication and media studies, the term usually refers to an individual or audience's reaction to messages received. See AUDIENCE.

Restricted code See ELABORATED AND RESTRICTED CODES.

Revisionism See HISTORICAL REVISIONISM.

Rhetoric Traditionally, the theory and practice of eloquence, whether spoken or written; the use of LANGUAGE so as to persuade others. The word is almost always used today as a term of criticism: rhetoric is the STYLE in which barefaced persuasion – politicking – is used. It is emotive; it belongs to speeches and while it is very often resounding it is rarely eloquent because it trades in empty phrases and endless repetitions. It is essentially REDUNDANT in that it tells supporters what they already know and antagonists what they know and don't want to hear. Rhetoric is the stock-in-trade of the PRESS, and of the popular press in particular. Practically every front-page headline is rhetorical in that it is soaked through with the ideological attitudes of the newspaper, not the least the belief in what sells newspapers, what commands attention, what readers want to be told.

Indeed it might be said that one of the prime functions the popular press sets itself is to translate actuality into rhetoric: complex ISSUES are translated into the simplifying mode of MYTH, of Us and Them, Militant and Moderate, Order and Disorder, Black and White, Management and Unions, Dries and Wets. See NEWS VALUES.

Rhyming slang See SLANG.

Right of reply A long-established practice in continental countries, the right of reply in the UK press has been argued for long, hard and generally unsuccessfully. Such a right would require newspaper editors to publish within a given time the replies of individuals or organizations who allege serious PRESS misrepresentation, or face a special court and a fine if found to be in error. It is argued that such a right would act as a deterrent to editorial bias and unethical practices. Newspapers *do* publish apologies but these are usually for printing factual errors which might land them with LIBEL actions.

The PRESS COUNCIL receives, considers and often acts upon complaints but it has no power to force newspapers to apologize or retract statements. The late 1980s saw an increase in support among MPs for Right of Reply legislation. Tony Worthington's private member's bill on the right of reply received an unopposed second reading in February 1989, but was adjourned at Report stage in April before its third Reading. See CAMPAIGN FOR PRESS AND BROADCASTING FREEDOM.

Riley and Riley model of mass communication, 1959 John W. Riley Jr and Matilda White Riley in 'Mass communication and the social system', in R.K. Merton, L. Broom and L.S. Cottrell Jr, eds., *Sociology Today: Problems and Prospects* (US: Basic Books, 1959; Harper Torch Books, vol. 2, 1965) pose a model in which the process of communication is an integral part of the SOCIAL SYSTEM.

For Riley and Riley, both the Communicator (C) and the Recipient (R) are affected in the MESSAGE process of sending, receiving, reciprocating, by the three social orders: the primary group or GROUPS of which C and R are members; the larger social structure, that is the immediate community – social, cultural, industrial – to which they belong, and the overall social system. All of these are in dynamic interaction, with messages flowing multi-directionally. See figure overleaf.

The mass media audience Riley and Riley perceive as being neither impassive nor isolated but 'a composite of recipients who are related to one another, and whose responses are

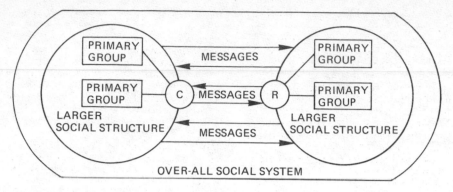

Riley and Riley model of mass communication, 1959

patterned in terms of these relationships'. See COMMUNICATION MODELS; NETWORK.

Ritual, rites of passage A ritual can be seen as a carefully constructed act of communication, a focused organization of SYMBOLS, loaded with a range of meanings significant for the individuals or social GROUPS concerned. Some rituals involve a great deal of ceremonial activity whilst those of everyday life may be fairly simple. Rituals can be religious or secular. They operate to give individuals or groups a sense of collective identity and security.

Rites of passage is a term used to refer to those rituals which mark transition from one status, stage or state to another either by the whole community or, more commonly, by individuals. The ceremonies which mark such changes provide a symbolic confirmation of the change of social identity involved – a wedding ceremony would be an example of one such ceremony.

Roles A social role consists of the expected behaviour associated with a particular social position. Thus the social position of a 'journalist' identifies a body of behaviours expected of a journalist, that is the role of the journalist in society. Role is a relational term. People play roles within a context in which other people are also playing roles. Roles within society or a social group carry with them responsibilities, obligations and rights. There is some evidence that the role a person or GROUP occupies within a given social context can influence the pattern of communication adopted. Basil Bernstein, for example, argues in 'Social class, language and socialization' in P.P. Giglioli, ed., *Language and Social Context*, (UK: Penguin, 1972) that selective access to the Elaborated LANGUAGE code may well result from the fact that there is selective access to the social roles which require its use (see ELABORATED AND RESTRICTED CODES).

Behaviour identified with a role is not neces-

sarily rigidly prescribed. Through INTERACTION with others, individuals can change the expectations which determine a particular role. To some extent roles can be *negotiated* within a social context; within small, informal groups roles are often arrived at through interaction alone. An individual usually performs several roles, such as teacher, wife, daughter, mother, friend and neighbour. This multiplicity of roles tends to generate problems of conflicting demands, known as **role strain**. The individual may often have to adjust his/her communication pattern – non-verbal as well as verbal – to suit each particular role. Role strain occurs when our communication patterns cut across each other; when unexpected encounters take place between people from different role situations or, more seriously, when the role is deeply unnatural to us – an apparent denial of 'true' self.

The concept of role is used not only to describe the position of individuals within a social structure but also that of groups or organizations. In this sense commentators write of the role – or roles – of the mass media in society; hence the so-claimed role of the PRESS as WATCHDOGS, defenders of the public good.
*E. Goffman, *The Presentation of Self in Everyday Life* (UK: Penguin, 1959).

Roll film The first roll FILM for use in cameras was introduced by A.J. Melhuish and J.B. Spencer in 1854, though roll film cameras were not marketed until the Kodak of 1888.

Ross Commission Report on the Press, 1949 Under the chairmanship of Sir David Ross, the Commission followed from an initial debate on the PRESS in the House of Commons. It worked for two years before producing its report (1949). Ross's main conclusions were that there was nothing approaching a monopoly of ownership of the UK press, and that the existing concentration of ownership was not so great as to prejudice the free expression of opinion or the accurate presentation of news.

However, Ross was not so optimistic about standards of quality and OBJECTIVITY: 'all the popular papers and certain of the quality fall short of the standards achieved by the best, either through excessive partisanship or through distortion for the sake of news values.' The Report proposed the formation of a General Council of the Press to encourage the growth of public responsibility and public service on the part of journalists.

It took four years for the newspaper industry to respond positively to this proposal. The Council, later named the PRESS COUNCIL (1964), made its first pronouncement in July 1953 concerning a *Daily Mirror* poll on whether Princess Margaret should marry her father's equerry, Group Captain Peter Townsend. See COMMISSIONS/COMMITTEES ON THE MEDIA.

Rostrum camera In TV, a FILM camera fixed in position over a table and used to take still photographs.

Rotary press See CYLINDER PRESS.

Royal Commissions on the media See COMMISSIONS/COMMITTEES ON THE MEDIA.

Rumour Indirect and unsubstantiated information; hearsay; transmitted along informal channels by word of mouth. Rumour has the following characteristic features: it can rarely if ever be traced back to its origin; it can spread (almost) at the speed of light; it will only spread if the rumour has the momentum of credibility (even if this credibility is only the size of a pinch of salt), and it thrives in close-knit communities which have either no regular or formal channels of communication or channels which are inefficient or not recognized as important.

A process of MEDIATION occurs at most or all points of telling, the original narrative being exaggerated and usually decorated with envy, spite or resentment. Good news rarely travels as quickly as bad news. In organizations, rumour often circulates most strongly in subcultures of those people generally well down in the HIERARCHY and who tend to be last in the queue when information is passed through formal channels.

The only antidote to rumour is efficient, full and open, participative communication, with strong lines of horizontal as well as vertical communication. The impact of rumour is rarely beneficial; in the main, rumour is corrosive of relationships, fuels suspicion and bad feeling. Its favourite habitat is a communication vacuum. One dubious compensation is that the subjects, or 'victims', of rumour are generally the last to hear of it; unless, of course, they started the rumour themselves. See INTERPERSONAL COMMUNICATION; LEVEL-

LING, SHARPENING, ASSIMILATION; LOONY LEFTISM.

Running story See SPOT NEWS.

Rushes In FILM-making, prints of 'takes' that are made immediately after a day's shooting; these are examined by the film team, led by the director, before the next day's shooting. Produced at a 'rush' from negative, they are also known as 'dailies'.

Salad When the FILM jams, and piles up, inside a movie camera or equally in a projector, it is often referred to as a *salad*; a *concertina* might be as descriptive.

Salience All messages are not given equal attention by the receiver; some messages, or parts of a MESSAGE, appear more prominent, more **salient**, to the receiver. This predisposition towards certain messages, or parts of a message, can be the result of a complex of factors such as life experience, attitudes, VALUES and interests. There has been considerable research into the role of the media in the formation of salience, particularly in the field of current affairs. The focus of investigation here is the extent to which extensive media coverage of certain ISSUES leads the audience to perceive those issues as being politically significant. See AGENDA SETTING; McCOMBS AND SHAW AGENDA SETTING MODEL OF MEDIA EFFECTS, 1976.

Salutation display Means by which we demonstrate that we wish someone well, or at the very least do not ostensibly wish them harm – greetings when we meet and when we part company. Salutation display varies according to such factors as the nature of our relationship with the greeted person, the context of the encounter and the length of prior separation. See GESTURE; SHORTFALL SIGNALS.

Samizdat Russian, meaning 'self-published', a secret publication, circulated by hand, usually printed on a duplicator or simply on a TYPEWRITER with carbon copies, by dissident writers, at great personal risk of reprisals by the authorities. Samizdat literature expresses views contrary to those of the state, in argument, criticism, poetry, novels and plays. *The First Circle* (1968) by Russian novelist Alexander Solzhenitsyn (b. 1918) began life in Samizdat. The word **Tamizdat** describes work produced by Russians in the west, published there and then smuggled into the Soviet Union. *Dr Zhivago* (1957) by Boris Pasternak (1890–1960) is an example of this. See GLASNOST; TYPEWRITER CULTURE.

Sampling A statistical method of selecting a group for analysis, from a larger social group known as the *population*, the statistical term for all those persons, events or entities that are relevant to the subject of the enquiry. The aim of sampling is to be able to use what is discovered about the **sample** group as a basis for inference about the behaviour of the population. The reliability of such inferences depends upon how far the sample is representative of the population. A **representative sample** is constructed in such a way that it contains members of various significant categories and classifications in the same proportion as they appear in the population.

Not all samples are representative, or *quota* samples: random sampling techniques are also used. A **random sample** is selected in such a way that every member of the population has an equal chance of being chosen. Such a sample is used when it is felt that the population is not divided into particularly significant categories or classifications.

Saniel Pedwar Cymru   See s4c.

Sapir-Whorf hypothesis   Developed by two notable linguists, Edward Sapir (1884–1939) and Benjamin Lee Whorf (1897–1941). Succinctly stated, it proposes that ways of thinking and patterns of CULTURE (and also to some extent social structure), are determined by the structure of the LANGUAGE used in a particular culture. An individual's or group's thought and DISCOURSE about life generally can only be expressed in language and are thus constrained by the language structure available.

Satellite Business Systems (SBS)   Company formed by IBM, Comsat (the US Communications Satellite Company) and Action Life Insurance Company, to offer large corporations the chance to send all of their messages – letters, invoices, computer data and TELEX and TELEPHONE services – by satellite to small ground stations situated on the premises of the companies concerned. The potential for SBS is world-wide, cutting across existing information-transfer systems, offering cheaper and more efficient services than many of those available in nation states.

Satellite transmission   There are three main types of satellite: (1) weather and observational satellites; (2) communications satellites and (3) space probes. Sputnik in 1957 was the first observational satellite; *Telstar*, in 1962, the first communications satellite. Working off solar-powered batteries, satellites have equipment for monitoring the conditions in and around themselves and sending data back to earth for control purposes. Also, they carry reception equipment for control signals from earth for correction of orbital travel etc. Satellites orbiting the earth have generally given way to geo-stationary operation, that is satellites stationed some 23,000 miles out in space at a constant altitude and keeping pace with the revolutions of the earth.

Signals from ground stations are beamed to the geo-stationary communications satellites and reflected by them to receiving stations which then relay the signals by cable for recording or transmission, or to receiving 'dishes' or antennae. Most communications satellites receive and transmit simultaneously from a number of earth stations. A notable pioneer was *INTELSAT 1V-A*, launched on 1 February 1976 as primary satellite of the International Telecommunications Satellite Organization with a capacity of 6000 circuits plus two TV channels.

TV pictures were first transmitted via satellite on 10 July 1962 when *Telstar* was launched at Cape Canaveral, US, and circled the earth every 157.8 minutes, enabling live TV pictures transmitted from Andover, Maine, to be received at Goonhilly Down, Cornwall and in Brittany (11 July). In 1964 the unmanned *Syncom* relayed pictures of the Olympic Games from Tokyo. The first commercial communications satellite was *Early Bird* which marked the beginning of regular TV transmission via satellite (2 May 1965).

The UK franchise for a three-transponder direct-broadcast satellite (DBS) was granted in 1986, with a start date of 1990. After financial and investment doubts which led to early backers – such as the BBC – withdrawing from DBS plans, the contract for Britain's first two DBS channels was awarded to British Satellite Broadcasting (BSB). Rupert Murdoch's Sky Satellite arrived ahead of BSB, beginning programme transmission in the UK in March 1989.

Viewer demand for more and more channels to be piped into the home has been arguably less of a consideration than the pressure from the British aerospace and electronics industry with their eyes on world markets for satellite technology estimated to be worth billions of pounds in the 1990s. The transmission of TELEPHONE communications by satellite is also big business. British Telecom's Madley earth station near Hereford, for example, which came into operation in 1981, transmits and receives 6000 telephone calls at once, while at the same time BROADCASTING on its two TV channels to 40 countries across the world, via *INTELSAT*. Six bowls at Madley, costing £50m will complement British Telecom's other earth station at Goonhilly.

1981 marked the end of monopoly rights in telecommunications transmission in the UK following the Conservative government's British Telecommunications Act of October 1981, giving the secretary of state sweeping powers to license competition. A consortium of Cable & Wireless, British Petroleum (BP) and Barclay's Merchant Bank, formed Project Mercury which was granted a 25 year licence to set up and run alternative long-distance telecommunications networks, including satellite communication, for business users. See

AMSATS; TECHNOLOGY OF THE MEDIA.

Scanner Mobile control room used in outside TV broadcasts.

Scheduling Process by which programmes or types of programme are 'timetabled' in order to attract maximum audiences, and to keep them attracted in the face of competition from rival programmes. The aim of the programme scheduler is to minimize the danger of audiences switching off, or even worse, over. Michael Pilsworth in ' "An imperfect art" – TV scheduling in Britain' in *Sight and Sound*, Autumn 1980, describes the 'art' as building 'towards a climax, the audience peak, little by little as the evening progresses. Peaks and troughs are to be avoided'. Low-appeal programmes are usually placed against weak opposition, or they are 'hammocked', that is, placed in between 'bankers', trusting to the INHERITANCE FACTOR. Conversely there is the so-called 'pre-echo' effect where anticipation of a really popular programme can induce viewers to switch on earlier – and thus watch a programme with less popular appeal.

In the UK constraints on free scheduling are rigorous, more rigorous, in fact, for commercial programmes than for the BBC. The IBA has laid down a complex set of rules to which ITV schedulers must adhere: overseas imports must not exceed 14%, averaged over six months; no more than seven feature films a week may be shown and there have to be two hours of serious programmes a week in peak time, including one peak time hour allocated to DOCUMENTARY.

Scheduling techniques assume a high degree of passivity on the part of an audience, and might be said seriously to underestimate audience potential for variety and challenge. Competitive scheduling above all reduces the range of choice open to the viewer simply by making risk-taking more difficult.

The UK government White Paper, 'BROADCASTING IN THE 90s: *Competition, Choice and Quality*', published in 1988, significantly cites competition as its paramount principle, and this will dictate future programme schedules.

Schema (plural, schemata). A schema is basically a framework or pattern, stored in the memory, which preserves and organizes information about some event or concept. The framework may be expanded as new information about the event or concept is acquired. It is argued by several researchers concerned with learning and memory, that existing schemata affect our PERCEPTION of new information and that there is a tendency for us to try and fit new information into our existing frameworks – at least initially.

Schemata themselves can form cross-linkages to provide a wider mental or conceptual map of an area of knowledge or experience. This perspective on the way in which we receive and process information has important implications for the analysis of the way in which we send and receive messages in the communication process.

Schramm's models of communication, 1954 Wilbur Schramm built on the SHANNON AND WEAVER MODEL OF COMMUNICATION, 1949

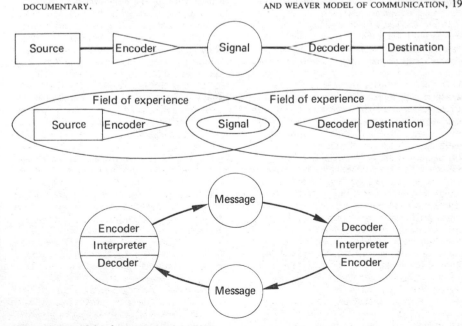

Schramm's models of communication, 1954

(The Mathematical Theory of Communication), but was more interested in mass communication than in the technology of communication transmission. In 'How communication works' in W. Schramm, ed., *The Process and Effects of Mass Communication* (US: University of Illinois Press, 1954) the author poses three models (see figure).

Shannon and Weaver's 'Transmitter' and 'Receiver' become 'ENCODER' and 'DECODER', and their essentially linear model is restructured in Schramm's second model to demonstrate the overlapping, interactive nature of the communication process and the importance of what the Encoder and Decoder bring with them to the communication situation, their 'Field of Experience'; where that field of experience overlaps is the signal. Schramm's third model emphasizes FEEDBACK, and in doing so points up the *circularity* of the communication process. See COMMUNICATION MODELS.

Schüfftan process A means by which life-size action is filmed in combination with models or artwork using an angled mirror; named after its inventor, FILM cameraman Eugene Schüfftan, and used as early as 1927 in Fritz Lang's *Metropolis*.

Secondary groups See GROUPS.

Secondary viewing Term describing the circumstances in which TV viewing forms an accompaniment to other activities such as homework and reading.

Secrecy In a *Guardian* review, 'Whitehall secrets farce' of David Hooper's *Official Secrets: The Use and Abuse of the Act* (UK: Secker, 1987), former civil servant Clive Ponting writes that secrecy 'is deeply embedded in the British political and administrative structure and the ethos of the ruling class. We desperately need a democratic revolution and a massive increase in government accountability'. In the 1980s in Britain secrecy became a way of government perhaps even more intensely than in the past. But it is selective secrecy. Ponting himself was unsuccessfully prosecuted for divulging information about the sinking of the Belgrano during the Falklands War (1982). His argument in defence was that he had a public duty which in certain circumstances should always override confidentiality. However, he states that when ministers rather than their servants 'leaked' damaging information, 'instead of the police the Cabinet Secretary was called in to conduct a discreet enquiry and the Attorney-General handed out immunity from prosecution.' 'In 75 years,' says Ponting, 'not a single Minister or ex-Minister has ever been prosecuted despite the most flagrant breaches of the law.'

See CENSORSHIP; ELITE; HEGEMONY; OFFICIAL SECRETS ACT; SPYCATCHER CASE; ZIRCON AFFAIR.

Section 28 Local government legislation introduced by the Tory government in 1988 included a clause – section 28 – banning the 'promotion of homosexuality' by local authorities.

Selective exposure Individuals have a tendency to attend to, **expose** themselves to, messages that are consistent with their existing attitudes and beliefs. Equally they practise *selective perception* – reading messages in accordance with their existing attitudes. Thus they may either ignore or misinterpret those messages, or parts of a MESSAGE, which conflict with or are dissimilar to held attitudes and expectations. Sometimes also referred to as *selective negligence*. See DIFFERENTIAL PERCEPTION; DISSONANCE; REINFORCEMENT.

Self-actualization See MASLOW'S HIERARCHY OF NEEDS.

Self-concept A person's self-concept is the total view that person has of him or herself. It includes such elements as an individual's PERCEPTION of his or her character, body image, abilities, emotions, qualities and relationships with others. The self-concept is commonly seen as being composed of the self-image and self-esteem. The self-image can be seen as the descriptive part of the self-concept. It is the picture we have of ourselves. Self-esteem, on the other hand is the evaluative part – it is how we feel about ourselves.

The self-image can be further divided into three elements: the self as I think I am, the self as I think others see me and the self I would like to be (the ideal self-image). Discrepancies between the ideal self-image and the self as I think I am can result in a low level of self-esteem as our self-esteem is usually based on our perceived successes and failures in life. Other people are clearly very influential in shaping any individual's conception of self, as in part an individual's self-concept depends upon his/her perception of the ideas others have about him/her. Individuals also attempt to influence the ideas others have, through controlling the impressions they create in self-presentation. The FEEDBACK received from self-presentation enables the individual both to evaluate and shape his/her self-image. Paul Watzlawick, Janet Helmick Beavin and Don. D. Jackson have suggested in *Pragmatics of Human Communication: A Study of Interactional Patterns, Pathologies and Paradoxes* (US: W.W. Norton, 1967), that others respond to us in three distinct ways and that these include *confirmation, rejection* and *disconfirmation*. Confirmation takes place when others affirm our self view; rejection when others do not treat us in a manner consistent with our self-view and disconfirmation when others fail to respond to our view of self or when others respond in a neutral manner.

Messages concerning the self abound in the content of INTERPERSONAL COMMUNICATION, whilst INTRAPERSONAL COMMUNICATION also plays a vital role not only in the generation of ideas about ourselves, some of which we may incorporate into the self which we present to others for FEEDBACK, but also in the decoding and evaluating of messages which receive from others and in deciding whether to or how to act on them.

How we see outselves affects the way we communicate. If, for example, we see ourselves as popular and sociable we are likely to be confident and outgoing in our communication with others. Excessive concern over self-esteem can lead to self-consciousness. People who are self-conscious are often shy, easily embarrassed and anxious in the presence of other people.

It should be remembered that the self-concept is not fixed but subject to continuing modification and change; it can change according to the situations we are in, the people we are with and over time.

See ASSERTIVENESS TRAINING; DEVIANCE AMPLIFICATION; JOHARI WINDOW: LABELLING PROCESS (AND THE MEDIA) SELF-FULFILLING PROPHECY.

* G.E. and M.T. Myers, *The Dynamics of Human Communication*, (US: McGraw-Hill, 1985).

Self-disclosure statements, verbal and non-verbal, that we make intentionally about ourselves which give others previously unknown information. See JOHARI WINDOW.

Self-disclosure is based on honest, open INTERACTION between people. Usually when we self-disclose to others, they reciprocate and in this way a deeper understanding and relationship may develop. Of course we have to make careful choices in the first place about those to whom we will self-disclose, at what rate, to what extent, on what topics and in what situations. Self-disclosure involves an element of risk; an error of choice, for example if we self-disclose too much too soon in a relationship, may result in a rebuff.

Through self-disclosure we not only learn more about others but also more about ourselves in that others' disclosures can contain views about ourselves. It is also a means by which we can come to terms with the positive and negative aspects of our self-image.

Self-fulfilling prophecy This effect occurs when the act of predicting that certain behaviour will take place helps cause that behaviour to occur and the prediction or prophecy is fulfilled. The expectations people have of an individual's behaviour can, if communicated to the individual, help create a situation in which the individual conforms to the expectations and fulfils the prophecy. There is a clear link between LABELLING and the self-fulfilling prophecy effect in that the act of applying a label can be the first step in ensuring a self-fulfilling prophecy.

The effect may be found particularly in situations where individuals have differing amounts of POWER and where one or more individuals are involved in the evaluating of others.

Clearly the messages contained in INTERPERSONAL and MASS COMMUNICATION may often carry labels and thus have the potential for triggering self-fulfilling prophecy effects, but it is largely through INTRAPERSONAL COMMUNICATION that an individual decides whether or not to conform to the expectations of others. Further, the self-fulfilling prophecy effect is only one of many influences on our behaviour and it may not be relevant in all cases. See DEVIANCE AMPLIFICATION; LABELLING PROCESS (AND THE MEDIA); SELF-CONCEPT.

Self-image See SELF-CONCEPT.

Selsdon Committee Report on Television 1935 The task of Lord Selsdon's Committee was 'to consider the development of Television and advise the Post Master General on the relative merits of several systems and on the conditions under which any public television should be provided'. The Report recommended that the BBC be made the initiating body, and that the cost of TV broadcasting be borne from the revenue derived from the existing 10 shilling RADIO licence fee. See COMMISSIONS/COMMITTEES ON THE MEDIA.

Semantic differential The analysis of *semantic differential* is one of three traditional EMPIRICAL methods of measuring audience response to the media, the others being CONTENT ANALYSIS and the investigation of uses and gratifications. In exploring SEMANTIC – or MEANING – differentials, analysts concentrate on people's attitudes, feelings and emotions towards certain concepts and VALUES as actuated by media performance. The values under scrutiny are presented in preliminary form by words or statements. These are then selected and expressed as binarily opposed concepts (Offensive – Not Offensive, for example) on a five or seven point scale. Binary opposition is the most extreme form of significant difference possible. A SAMPLE audience, or selected group, is tested on the scale or scales, and the results averaged. The method was given currency by Charles Osgood in *The Measurement of Meaning* (US: University of Illinois Press, 1967).

Semanticity That feature of LANGUAGE which has MEANING; the combination of sounds that make up a word which is associated with some aspect of our world. *Semanticity* is one of 16 DESIGN FEATURES of human language posited by US linguist Charles Hockett.

Semantics A major branch of LINGUISTICS in which the MEANING of LANGUAGE is analysed. The study of the origins of the form and meaning of words is *Etymology*, a branch of Semantics. The critical point about the study of Semantics is that it is an exploration of change – how the context of usage, historical, social, cultural, etc. – alters the meanings of words and expressions used. When King James II observed that the new St Paul's Cathedral was *amusing*, *awful* and *artificial* he did not intend to be derogatory about Sir Christopher Wren's masterpiece; rather he *meant* that it was 'pleasing, awe-inspiring, and skilfully achieved'.

The differences are, of course, far from merely evolutionary. What, for example, is the meaning of the word *equality*? Its definition is modified by the perceptions and VALUES of all those who use it, and the situation in which it is used. As Simeon Potter points out in *Our Language* (UK: Penguin, 1950), 'Men frequently find themselves at cross-purposes with one another because they persist in using words in different senses. Their long arguments emit more heat than light because their conceptions of the point at issue, whether Marxism, democracy, capitalism, the good life, western civilization, culture, art, internationalism, freedom of the individual, equality of opportunity, redistribution of wealth, social security, progress, or what not, are by no means identical. From heedless sloth, or sheer lack of intelligence men do not trouble to clarify their conceptions.' Semantics, therefore, must lie at the heart of any serious study of communication processes. See SEMANTIC DIFFERENTIAL.

Semiology/Semiotics Word derives from the Greek, 'semeion', sign, and Semiology is the general science of sign systems and their role in the construction and reconstruction of MEANING. All social life, indeed every facet of social practice, is mediated by LANGUAGE – conceived as a system of signs and representations, arranged by CODES and articulated through various discourses. Sign systems, believes the Semiologist, have no fixed meaning. The perception of the sign system rests upon the social context of the participants and the interaction between them.

Semiology examines the SIGN itself, the codes or systems into which the signs are organized and the CULTURE within which these codes and signs operate. The primary focus of Semiology is upon the text, thus differentiating such an approach from the *process* models of communication which regard the text – the MESSAGE – as only one element of several in the communication process. For example, the

Semiologist prefers the term 'reader' (even of a painting, photograph or FILM) to receiver because it implies a greater degree of activity, and that the process of reading is socially and culturally conditioned. The reader helps to create the meaning and significance of the text by bringing to it his/her experience, VALUES and emotional responses.

There is special emphasis on the link between the 'reading' and the IDEOLOGY of the reader. 'Wherever a sign is present,' writes V.N. Volosinov in *Marxism and the Philosophy of Language* (US: Seminar, 1973), 'ideology is present too. Everything ideological possesses a semiotic value'; or as Umberto Eco says, 'Semiology shows us the universe of ideologies arranged in codes and sub-codes within the universe of signs' (in 'Articulations of the cinematic code' in *Cinematics* 1, undated).

The theories of Swiss linguist Ferdinand de Saussure (1857–1913) provided the foundation stone of Semiology. His lectures, *Cours de Linguistique Générale* (1916) were published after his death by two pupils, Charles Bally and Albert Sechehaye. De Saussure set out to demonstrate that speech is not merely a linear sequence like beads on a string but a *system* and a *structure* where points on the string relate to other points on the string in various ways (the so-called *syntagmic* structure) and operate in a network of relationships with other possible points which could substitute for it (the *paradigmic* structure).

The American logician and philosopher C.S. Peirce (1834–1914) approached the structure of language with a wider-angle lens, conceiving semiotics (the term preferred in the US) as being an interdisciplinary science in which sign systems manifested in structures and levels could be analysed from philosophical, psychological and sociological as well as linguistic points of view.

Peirce and other philosophers such as Charles Morris and Rudolph Carnap saw the field as divisible into three areas: SEMANTICS, the study of the links between linguistic expressions and the objects in the world to which they refer or which they describe; SYNTACTICS, the study of the relation of these expressions to each other; and PRAGMATICS, the study of the dependence of the meaning of these expressions on their users (including the social context in which they are used).

The terminology of Semiology/Semiotics is complex and daunting, but the names Peirce gave to his categories are worth quoting here: the sign he called an ICON resembles the object it wishes to describe, like a photograph; an *index* establishes a direct link between the sign and its object (smoke is an index to fire); finally, the SYMBOL where there is neither connection nor resemblance between sign and object. A symbol communicates only because there is agreement among people that it shall stand for what it does (words are symbols).

Semiology has come to apply, as a system of analysis, to every aspect of communication. There is practically nothing which is not a sign capable of meaning, or SIGNIFICATION. The work of the French philosopher Roland Barthes (1915–80) has exercised particular influence on our understanding of areas such as music, eating, clothes and dance was well as language. See PARADIGM; MYTH.

Semiotics See SEMIOLOGY/SEMIOTICS.

Sender/receiver General terms often used in linear models of communication to denote the beginning and end of the communication process. Tim O'Sullivan, John Hartley, Danny Saunders and John Fiske in *Key Concepts of Communication* (UK: Methuen, 1983), draw some comparisons between the usage of these terms and others marking the same positions in the communication process.

Research with a technical or process-centred orientation tends to employ the terms *transmitter* and *receiver* to mark these key positions in the communication process, as is the case for example in the SHANNON–WEAVER MODEL OF COMMUNICATION, 1949.

The terms *encoder* and *decoder* imply that communication involves coding processes and they are commonly used in research analysing such processes; an example here is SCHRAMM'S MODELS OF COMMUNICATION, 1954.

Addresser and *Adressee* are the terms used in JAKOBSON'S MODEL OF COMMUNICATION, 1958 and they imply that certain modes of address are appropriate to each position.

The terms *author* and *reader* tend to be used in the semiotic school of thought. Research here concentrates on the TEXT and the process by which its MEANING is generated. In this process the reader, as well as the author, is accorded an active role through, for example, the personal and cultural experiences he or she brings to the reading of the text. The author may and often will, in constructing the text, try to guide the reader towards a PREFERRED READING, a preferred interpretation, but cannot actually determine exactly how the reader will interpret the text. See DECODE; ENCODE; SEMIOLOGY/SEMIOTICS.

Sensitization The process by which the media can alert the public, and specific social GROUPS, to the fact that certain social actions are taking place, or to the possibility that certain social actions might take place. Stanley Cohen, for example, concludes in 'Sensitization: the case of the Mods and Rockers', in S. Cohen and J. Young, eds. *The Manufacture of News: Deviance, Social Problems and the Mass Media*, (UK: Constable, 1973) that media coverage of the Bank Holiday activities of the mods and

rockers gangs, at certain southern holiday resorts in the mid-1960s, played a significant role in 'Reinforcing and magnifying a predisposition to expect trouble: "Something's going to happen." '

Cohen argues that once this perception had been established there was a tendency to interpret new, similar incidents in the same manner and fairly trivial events, normally overlooked, received media attention. Thus, 'Through the process of sensitization, incidents which would not have been defined as unusual or worthy of attention . . . acquired a new meaning.' In this particular case sensitization was the first step in a process of media coverage which, Cohen argues, significantly affected the course of real events. See LOONY LEFTISM; MEDIA IMAGES.

Serial processing See PARALLEL PROCESSING.

Set A state of mental expectancy which is grounded in pre-formed ideas about some future event. The impact of a MESSAGE is always influenced, to some extent, by the mental set of the receiver.

Seven characteristics of mass communications See MASS COMMUNICATIONS, SEVEN CHARACTERISTICS.

S4C The Welsh counterpart of CHANNEL FOUR – *Saniel Pedwar Cymru*. Approximately half the channel's output is in Welsh to serve the 500,000 Welsh-speakers in Wales, 40% of whom were soon tuned in to *Pobol y Cwm*, the channel's first SOAP OPERA.

Shadow-mask tubes The shadow-mask cathode ray tube was devised in the 1950s by the American RCA company and is the basis of COLOUR TV reception. A metal shadow mask is fitted in front of a screen of red, green and blue phosphor dots, allowing sharp monochrome definition and concurrently decoding colour for the colour receiver. The shadow-mask tube was improved in the 1970s. The Mullard 20AX tube needed less correction than its predecessors and the 45AX required no adjustment at all, and provided for a flatter, squarer screen.

Shadowing See COCKTAIL PARTY PROBLEM.

Shannon and Weaver model of communication, 1949 Developed by C.E. Shannon and W. Weaver to assist the construction of a mathematical theory of communication which could be applied in a wide variety of information transfer situations, whether by humans, machines or other systems. It is essentially a linear, process-centred model. (See below)

Shannon and Weaver were engineers working for the Bell Telephone Laboratories in the US and their objective was to ensure maximum efficiency of the *channels* of communication, in their case TELEPHONE cable and RADIO wave. However, in *Mathematical Theory of Communication* (US: University of Illinois Press, 1949), they claim for their theory a much wider

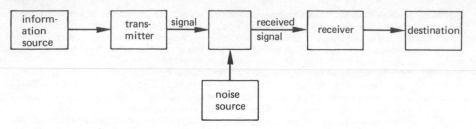

Shannon and Weaver model of communication, 1949

application to human communication than solely the technical one. Within the framework of their model of transmission, the authors identify three levels of problems in the analysis of communication. Level A (technical), Level B (semantic – the MEANING as emanating from the Transmitter's mode of address) and Level C (effectiveness in terms of reception or understanding on the part of the Receiver). Shannon and Weaver's model was constructed mainly to tackle Level A problems, and the assumption seems to be that to sort out the technical problems by improving ENCODING will, almost automatically, lead to improvements at Levels B and C.

In the Shannon and Weaver model, no provision has been made for FEEDBACK and the fact that feedback modifies both the MESSAGE and the communication situation; nor is there any acknowledgment of the importance of *context* – social, political, cultural – in influencing all stages of the communication process. Nevertheless, the Shannon and Weaver model arguably gave birth to what has come to be termed Communication Studies. See CHANNEL CAPACITY; COMMUNICATION STUDIES; CYBERNETICS: REDUNDANCY.

Shawcross Commission Report on the Press, 1962 The five-member Commission chaired by Lord Shawcross, lawyer and former Labour minister, declared that the real enemy of good-quality newspapers was competition; and competition threatened diversity. 'Within any class of competitive newspapers', said the Report, 'the economies of large-scale operation provide a natural tendency for a newspaper which already has a large circulation to flourish, and to attract still more readers, whilst a newspaper which has a small circulation is likely to be in difficulties.' Like the ROSS COMMISSION REPORT, Shawcross offered no radical solution to the problems his Committee had delineated, trusting, as Ross had done, in the free market, albeit reluctantly: 'there is no acceptable legislative or fiscal way of regulating the competitive and economic forces so as to ensure a sufficient diversity of newspapers.'

The Report put forward an idea for a press amalgamations court which should scrutinize proposed mergers of all daily or Sunday papers with sales over three million, and to give the go-ahead only if the court considered such mergers to be no threat to public interest. In 1965 the Monopolies Commission was created by the Labour Government under Harold Wilson, by means of the Monopolies and Mergers Act, which ruled that ISSUES were to be decided by government, not the courts.

Shawcross also successfully recommended the strengthening of the PRESS COUNCIL: a year later, in January 1964, a lay chairman (retired judge, Lord Devlin) was appointed; five lay members out of 25 became the rule, and the title of General Council of the Press was changed to Press Council. See COMMISSIONS/COMMITTEES ON THE MEDIA.

Shock issues Those social ISSUES about which it is considered most people are sensitive: madness, for example; and which are prone to being treated in a sensational manner by both the PRESS and TV in order to obtain the attention of the audience. Thus concern has often been expressed that the serious dimensions of such issues may be overlooked. See TABLOIDESE.

Shortfall signals In interpersonal contact, a shortfall signal is, for example, a smile of greeting that disappears too soon; in other words, it fails to carry conviction as a true smile of greeting. In the main, shortfall signals consist of simulated warmth in salutation. The evasive glance, the pulled-away glance, the frozen smile, the smile of mouth without eyes – all of these and many more are INDICATORS of personal unease about the encounter. The explanation may be because the person you greet is someone you dislike or fear, though the shortfall signal may have as much to do with personal mood – and preoccupation – as anything else. Conversely, there is the so-called **Overkill signal**, where the greeting is too friendly, too effusive, the handshake too forcible. The overkill signal may be a simulation of sincere greeting; on the other hand, when people of different cultures or nations meet one person's shortfall may be another's overkill. See GESTURE.

Shorthand A system of rapid writing using symbols or abbreviations for letters, words and phrases; US term – *Stenography*. Among the most used shorthand systems are Pitman, Gregg and Speedwriting.

Shot In FILM making, the shot is the equivalent, in writerly terms, of a word, a phrase, a sentence or a paragraph. The director of a movie *shoots* film; each shot is the length at which a camera works continuously from a still or moving position. A 'take' may constitute a series of shots or a continuous shot. It is visually defined by the use of the *clapper board* held in front of the camera. The board has the title of the film written on it, and the number of the take; the clapper is extended and then closed at the moment of the take. Cameras roll.

There are many types of shot: low and high angle, tilted; tracking, where the camera is fixed on a *crab & track* device and follows the action into or across the picture. The zoom lens allows the CU (Close Up), MCU (Medium Close Up) and the BCU (Big Close Up). There is the wide-angle shot and the pan where the camera swings across the scene; there is the still shot and the SLOW MOTION shot. Final decisions about how long a shot will be, which shots will be used and in what order come at the *editing* stage of film-making. See MONTAGE.

Shotgun approach (to news coverage)
Term used by Terry Ann Knopf in 'Media myths on violence' in *Columbia Journalism Review*, Spring 1970, to describe the over-reporting – large headlines, large pictures and EMOTIVE LANGUAGE – by the media of certain types of events, usually crimes, political protests and racial conflict. See TABLOIDESE; SHOCK ISSUES.

Showbusiness, age of The present age of advancing communications technology has been given many titles – the Age of Information, the Telecommunications Age, the Age of the Global Village. Neil Postman in *Amusing Ourselves to Death* (UK: Methuen, 1986), calls it the Age of Showbusiness, a period in which TELEVISION dominates the lives of the community, turning people – in his view – into a population 'amusing ourselves to death'. In the Age of Showbusiness, Postman argues, all discourses are rewritten in terms of entertainment; substance is translated into IMAGE and the present is emphasized to the detriment of historical perspectives.

Postman's criticism is targeted upon the COMMERCIAL TELEVISION of his native America but his points are worth examining in a British context at a time when PUBLIC SERVICE BROADCASTING looks nervously to its future in an Age of Privatization. According to Postman, TV 'does everything possible to encourage us to watch continuously. But what we watch is a medium which presents information in a form that renders it simplistic, non-substantive, non-

historical and non-contextual; that is to say, information packaged as entertainment'. See CONSUMER SOVEREIGNTY; EFFECTS OF THE MASS MEDIA; MAINSTREAMING; PILKINGTON COMMITTEE REPORT ON BROADCASTING, 1962; PSEUDO-CONTEXT; SUPRA-IDEOLOGY OF TELEVISION; TELEVISION.

Sign In communication studies, a little word which triggers complex explanations. Father of SEMIOLOGY/SEMIOTICS, Swiss linguist Ferdinand de Saussure (1857–1913) regarded LANGUAGE as a 'deposit of signs'; he viewed the sign as a phenomenon comprising an 'acoustic image' and a concept (the thing signified). A word or combination of words in a language refers to, is an indicator of, some externally existing object or idea. Charles Peirce (1834–1914), the American philosopher and logician, posed a triangular relationship involving the activation of the sign:

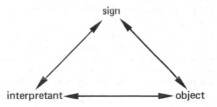

The object is that which is described by the sign, but the sign only signifies – has MEANING – in the process of it becoming a mental concept (INTERPRETANT), or what de Saussure named the *signified*. The point to emphasize here is that the sign depends for its meaning on the context in which it is communicated.

Edmund Leach in *Culture and Communication* (UK: Cambridge University Press, 1976) says signs do not occur in isolation; 'a sign is always a member of a set of contrasting signs which function within a specific cultural context.' Also, a sign only conveys information when it is combined with other signs and symbols from the same context. 'Signs signal', writes Donis A. Dondis in R. Williams, ed., *Contact: Human Communication and its History* (UK: Thames & Hudson, 1981), 'they are specific to a task or circumstance.'

Of course there are not only different kinds or levels of meaning (or SIGNIFICATION), there are many different kinds of sign. Peirce divided signs into three categories: the *icon*, *index* and *symbol*. These, like the triangular sign-object-interpretant are interactive, and they are overlapping. The icon is a resemblance or a representation of the object – a photograph or a map would constitute an ICONIC sign. An index is a sign connected or associated with its object – an indicator: smoke is an index of fire, for example. The SYMBOL may have no resemblance whatever to the object or idea. It is arbitrary. It comes about by choice, it exists by convention, rule or assent. It means something beyond itself. As Dondis neatly points out, 'Signs can be understood by animals as well as humans; symbols cannot.' They 'are broader in meaning, less concrete'.

Raymond Firth, in *Symbols, Public and Private* (UK: Allen & Unwin, 1973), adds a fourth sign type to Peirce's three – *signal*, a sign with an emphasis on 'consequential action', a stimulus requiring some response.

Signs combine to form systems, or CODES, from the basic MORSE CODE or Highway Code to, for example, the complex codes of musical notation. See ASSIGN; LANGUE AND PAROLE; JAKOBSON'S MODEL OF COMMUNICATION; TRIGGERS.

Signal The physical manifestation of a MESSAGE which allows it to be conveyed. See SHANNON AND WEAVER MODEL OF COMMUNICATION, 1949.

Significant others The analysis of the effects of a media MESSAGE, of its impact, relies on the response not only of the direct respondent, but of those persons close to, influential upon the respondent – relatives, friends, work colleagues. These are 'significant others'. In the case of a child watching TV commercials, his/her response may be conditioned and modified by parents, brothers and sisters, friends. See INTERVENING VARIABLES.

Significant symbolizers G.H. Mead in *Mind, Self and Society* (US: University of Chicago Press, 1934), uses this term to indicate how the social organization of a society, human or animal, needs the support of reliable, regular and predictable patterns or signs if it is not to be destroyed by accumulating discrepancy and misinformation. The SYMBOL or symbolizer, whether vocal sound, GESTURE or SIGN, achieves meaningful definition only when it has the 'same effect on the individual making it as on the individual to whom it is addressed'. Thus, according to Mead, a person defines him/herself by 'talking to himself in terms of the community to which he belongs'. Through contact with 'significant' (meaningful) objects of the social world a person develops a coherent view of him/herself and of his/her relations with others. See INTERPERSONAL COMMUNICATION; INTRAPERSONAL COMMUNICATION.

Signification One of the most valuable contributions made by Swiss linguist Ferdinand de Saussure (1857–1913) to the study of LANGUAGE was his idea of differentiating between the name, the naming and the MEANING of what has been named. This process enabled the linguist more effectively to examine the structural elements of communication. Saussure contrasted the *signifiant* (or **signifier**) with *signifié* (or that which is **signified**). The relationship between these, the physical existence of the SIGN, and the mental concept it repre-

sents, becomes *signification* which, for Saussure, is the manifestation of external reality or meaning. Signification, it is important to realize, is culture-specific as is the linguistic form of the signifier in each language. Saussure terms the relationship of signs to others in the sign system, *valeur*, and it is valeur which primarily determines meaning. Thus meaning is an active force, subject to constant change, the result of dynamic interaction. See SEMIOLOGY/SEMIOTICS.

Signification spiral Stuart Hall *et al.* in *Policing the Crisis: Mugging, The State and Law & Order* (UK: Macmillan, 1978) use this term for the process by which discrete, local problems and occurrences are pulled together by the media into a framework of news coverage which links these together in such a way as to suggest the existence of a more widespread and serious social problem. They argue that, for example, during the 1970s there emerged a signification spiral in which problems previously presented as atypical or parochial – such as student protest, industrial unrest, and mugging – were presented by the media as part of a wider concern – the breakdown in law and order. See SENSITIZATION.

Significs Enquiry into questions of MEANING, expression and interpretation, and the influence of LANGUAGE upon thought.

Silence, Spiral of See NOELLE-NEUMANN'S SPIRAL OF SILENCE MODEL OF PUBLIC OPINION, 1974.

Silent majority In the briefcase of every OPINION LEADER – be he/she politician, editor or TV guru – lies a hidden weapon, the 'Silent Majority'. The opinion leader claims access to the thoughts, attitudes and beliefs of those who, having no voice of their own – so the story goes – are grateful to the politicians or the PRESS for putting words and opinions into their silent mouths. They are invariably moderates; they have bags of commonsense; and what is more, they are impossible to identify. If it were possible to locate them in persons (no research has yet elicited the degree to which the silent are a majority or the majority silent) they might be perceived as, above all things, upholders of the STATUS QUO, inalienably opposed to activists, do-gooders and change agents of every type and hue.

Sincerity test (by the media) Some commentators claim that a by-product of political BROADCASTING is the way TV appearances by influential public figures are assessed by audiences for honesty and sincerity. Equally, the skilled public figure can use TV to project the desired image of honesty and sincerity in order to gain public support. See PRESIDENTIALISM.

Sins of omission In discussing the effects of TV on audiences, the PILKINGTON REPORT uses this phrase to balance the major criticism which was of 'sins of commission' – the capacity of TV to misuse its power to influence people. The sins of omission arise from the fact that many of the best potentialities of TV 'were simply not being realized', that is, programmes were relentlessly going for the largest possible audience and thus 'nearly always' appealing to 'a low level of public taste'. See BALANCED PROGRAMMING.

Sit-com Situation comedy on TV: *Steptoe and Son, Dad's Army, The Likely Lads, Rising Damp, The Good Life, Rhoda, Taxi, Porridge,* etc. – the comedy growing out of context and character, and recurringly generated or fuelled by amiable antagonism of one kind or another.

Situational proprieties Erving Goffman in *Behaviour in Public Places* (US: Free Press, 1963) employed this phrase to describe rules of behaviour common to interpersonal and GROUP situations which oblige participants to 'fit in'; to accept the particular normative behaviour suitable for a successful, DISSONANCE-free interaction. Such proprieties might be to avoid making a scene or causing a disturbance; refrain from talking too loudly or too assertively; held back from attempting to dominate proceedings or, in contrast, to check oneself from withdrawing from what is going on.

S-IV-R model of communication Derives from general theories of learning/communication, where the relationship between stimulus (S) and response (R) is regarded as providing the key to both learning and communication. Actually it is a *teaching*-orientated model rather than learner-centred, and implies a predominantly one-way traffic of information from teacher to pupil. The IV stands for INTERVENING VARIABLES, those factors in the communication situation which help, hinder or modify the response to the intended MESSAGE. These variables are innumerable: NOISE (technical or semantic), lack of motivation or concentration, personal problems and, very importantly, the influence of other people – peer GROUPS, friends, parents, etc. See COMMUNICATION MODELS; MEDIATION; SIGNIFICANT OTHERS.

16 mm FILM width generally used for sponsored and educational films and universally used by film societies. In recent years 16 mm has often replaced standard 35 mm film in cinemas which have been converted from large into small auditoriums.

Slander A false or malicious report by the spoken word or by SIGN or GESTURE. In law, slander may constitute DEFAMATION – of character or reputation – and may be subject to heavy fines. However, no legal aid is granted in the UK for defamation cases. LIBEL is the written or printed equivalent of slander.

Slang Colloquial LANGUAGE, whose words and usages are not generally acceptable within formal modes of expression. The word was not used till about 1756. Prior to that it was called *cant,* and referred to the secret language of the underworld, of thieves and rogues; also termed *argot.* Slang usually begins as in-group language, then moves into popular use. For example, the criminal world's slang nouns for policeman (*coppers, rozzers, bluebottles,* the *fuzz*), for magistrates (*beaks*), for prison (*stir, time, bird* and *porridge*) have achieved broad currency.

Rhyming slang, associated with London cockneys and subsequently Australians, uses slang words that rhyme with the intended word. Thus *apples and pears* means stairs, *trouble and strife* means wife. The point of rhyming slang is to conceal the MEANING of the language used from unwanted listeners. See COLLOQUIALISM; DIALECT; JARGON.

Sleeper effect Researchers into the responses of audiences to messages have noted how these responses can be *delayed* and only become manifest some time after exposure. This is the 'sleeper' effect. See EFFECTS OF THE MASS MEDIA.

Slider Many experiments have been conducted to investigate the effect of group pressure upon the individual and the manner in which such pressure manifests itself in the INTERPERSONAL COMMUNICATION of the group. In a typical experiment one member of the group may take on the role of slider, that is he/she will initially disagree with the majority of the group on a matter but is persuaded to agree with them. The member of the group who takes on the role of DEVIANT, however, consistently disagrees with the majority. Of those in the experimental situation some may be *naive,* that is, unaware of what is to take place in the experiment and some members may be *confederates,* that is, in league with the experimenters.

Slow-drip Term sometimes used to describe the regular, long-term coverage of certain ISSUES by the media with a view to influencing the formation of opinion; a softening-up process that builds evidence and feelings in preferred directions. The policy of appeasement towards Germany prior to the 2nd World War (1939–45) has been cited as an example. See EFFECTS OF THE MASS MEDIA.

Slow motion Has been used varyingly in the cinema to convey dream-like or fantasy situations, to emphasize reactions such as grief, bewilderment or to concentrate attention upon happenings which in real life would be here and gone before the full visual impact has been made. In contrast, **accelerated motion** has been generally used for comic effects, especially by the early silent movie comedians whose own actors' timing was rendered even more remarkable by the speeded-up action.

Reverse motion is another technique by which the cinema defies time: that which can happen can unhappen. In *October* (1927), for instance, Sergei Eisenstein (1898–1948) uses the magic of reverse motion to show a statue of the Tzar, previously smashed to pieces, miraculously restored, thus showing with impressive symbolism the restoration of the *ancien régime*, the old order.

Lastly, there is **stopped motion**, using either still photographs or stopping the action of an otherwise moving sequence by repeating the same frame when editing the FILM. The freezing of action may signal transition from one time zone to another, or may be used for special emphasis – like a fixed stare – or sometimes to underscore comic effects or impressions. See SHOT.

SMCR model of communication See BERLO'S SMCR MODEL OF COMMUNICATION, 1960.

Snap-shot Term invented by astronomer Sir John Herschel (1792–1871), writing in 1860 of 'the possibility of taking a photograph as it were a snap shot'. He may well have been referring to Thomas Skaife's *Pistolgraph* of 1858. See CAMERA; PHOTOGRAPHY, ORIGINS.

Soap opera Radio or TV domestic drama series; the term emanates from the US where such programmes have often been sponsored by big soap companies who had the housewife viewer in mind. Of the long-running soap opera in the UK, *Coronation Street*, poet laureate John Betjeman once announced, 'At half-past seven tonight I shall be in paradise'. TV's appetite for soap opera is insatiable. The TV audience for the shooting of JR in the American series *Dallas* exceeded that for the FA Cup Final in the UK. Traditionally soaps have been characterized by an immediately identifiable set-up, a stereotypical cast of characters and a distancing from contemporary reality and anxieties. However, the end of the 1980s saw the arrival of soaps exploiting social problems for all they were worth. From the BBC, *Eastenders*, featuring abortion, rape, illegitimacy, murder, robbery, incest and unemployment; from Channel 4, *Brookside*, demonstrating that Merseyside can answer problem for problem with London's East End, featuring rape, stabbings, euthanasia, homosexuality and, of course, unemployment. The BBC's import from Australia, *Neighbours*, proved it could do more than hold its own – with beatings-up, meningitis, divorce *et al*. See PARA-SOCIAL INTERACTION; PLAY THEORY OF MASS COMMUNICATION; SYNTHETIC CULTURE.

* 1. Ang, *Watching Dallas: Soap Operas and the Melodramatic Imagination* (UK: Methuen, 1985).

D. Bukingham *Public Secrets: Eastenders and its Audience* (UK: BFI, 1987).

Social action (mode of media analysis) Stresses the role of the individual as a potent force within a dynamic social system. It sees *conflict* as central to the process of change, in particular conflict between GROUPS seeking influence, power and status. Social action analysis concentrates on the media as a special group both reflecting and involved in the conflicts which concern social change, or resistance to it. A *pluralist* society, of competing ideologies and varying, changing definitions of truth and MEANING, is acknowledged by social action analysis as are the complex influences at work upon media and media audiences and the interaction between them. See FUNCTIONALIST/MARXIST (MODES OF MEDIA ANALYSIS); PLURALISM.

Social action broadcasting A broad term describing RADIO and TELEVISION programming which sets out not only to analyse current social problems and ISSUES and bring them to public attention, but to encourage people to take action in response to what they have heard or seen. Programmes range from the BBC's adult literacy series *On the Move* or *Crimewatch UK* to Capital Radio's *Helpline*. Information on social action BROADCASTING is disseminated by the National Volunteer Centre in its publication *Media Project News* which produces a twice-yearly Directory of Social Action Programmes.

Social class See CLASS.

Social influence theory See IDENTIFICATION.

Socialization The shaping of human behaviour through experience in and knowledge of certain social situations: the process by which individuals are made aware of the EXPECTATIONS others have of their behaviour; by which they acquire the NORMS, MORES, VALUES and beliefs of a social group or society; and by which the CULTURE of a social group or society is transmitted. Socialization continues throughout life as individuals change their ROLES and membership of social GROUPS.

There exist what are commonly known as *agents* of socialization. In modern industrial societies, the family, school and friendship groups are thought to be the most significant agents in shaping the behaviour of the individual. The mass media are also agents of socialization and are considered to be particularly influential in transmitting awareness and expectations concerning a wide range of societal behaviour.

Individuals and societies may undergo radical change, if so *re-socialization* may occur – the peeling away of learned patterns of behaviour and their replacement with quite different ones. There is interest as to the media's potential role in this process – its potential as a disseminator of PROPAGANDA, for example, could be of significance. Additionally, media organizations are themselves social INSTITUTIONS and as such have their own patterns of behaviour, attitudes and beliefs into which their members are socialized. The degree to which the culture of media organizations affects their output is a considerable source of interest.

Social lubricators Richard Hoggart in *Speaking to Each Other* (UK: Chatto & Windus, 1970), uses this term to describe those people involved in the research, design and presentation of material aimed at aiding the smooth running of a technologically advanced society: communications experts, public relations officers and ADVERTISING executives, for example. See PR: PUBLIC RELATIONS.

Socially unattached intelligentsia in See IMPARTIALITY.

Social system Consists of a collective of people who undertake different types of tasks in order to achieve common goals and solve common problems. The term can be applied to a group of two or more individuals, complex organizations or whole societies. For the members of a social system to cooperate, there must be a shared LANGUAGE and some cultural similarities between them, although within the overall system there may be a variety of subcultures and language CODES, as well as other individual differences.

All social systems are liable to undergo social change: a process by which the structures and functions are altered. One focus for research has been the role of the communication of INNOVATION in the process of social change. See SOCIALIZATION.

Societally conscious achievers See VALSOCIETY.

Sociodrama A structured extension of dramatic play. It differs from play only in that it involves a group situation in which a problem in the area of interpersonal relations is enacted and the observers evaluate the factors involved as well as the solution. In educational terms, it is another way of describing role play or simulation. It aids children or young adults in understanding their own behaviour and feelings as well as the behaviour and feelings of others.

Sociology French philosopher Auguste Comte (1798–1857) was the first to use the word 'sociology'. The discipline attempts a scientific and systematic study of society, employing precise and controlled methods of enquiry. It is concerned with social structure; social systems; social action; the various GROUPS, INSTITUTIONS, categories and classes which go to make up a society or SOCIAL SYSTEM; the CULTURE and lifestyle of a society and the groups of which it

is composed; the processes of SOCIALIZATION by which such cultures are communicated and maintained; and the types and allocation of social ROLES.

Social groups, their inter-relationships and INTERACTION, and their conditioning of individual behaviour could be seen as the building-blocks of the discipline.

Sociometrics (and media analysis) Sociometrics is the analysis of small GROUPS, their coherence and the interpersonal relationships and communication within them. This mode of analysis has been extended and applied within media studies to ascertain the nature of the relationships between owners of media organizations and owners of other industrial or commercial concerns and the degree to which they are interlocking. The purpose of such a sociometric *map of capitalism* is to discover whether or not shared positions in and patterns of social and economic life produce recognized shared interests and a common cluster of beliefs, VALUES and perspectives which feed back into and influence media organizations and their products.

Recent evidence suggests some overlapping points of contact. Increasingly, owners of communications concerns are also owners of other businesses, and these contacts are reinforced by overlapping directorships. Board members of top media corporations have been found to hold membership of ELITE London clubs also favoured by directors of leading financial institutions and some business corporations. Of course evidence of points of contact does not necessarily constitute evidence of shared values, beliefs and perspectives, or deliberate influence of media products.

Software See COMPUTER LANGUAGE.

Sound broadcasting See RADIO BROADCASTING.

Sound Broadcasting Act, 1972 Gave the go-ahead to COMMERCIAL RADIO in the UK. The name Independent Television Authority (ITA) was changed to Independent Broadcasting Authority (IBA), and the IBA was empowered to create a new group of contractors in up to 50 British cities to run local commercial RADIO stations and collect ADVERTISING revenue in a manner similar to that of the TV programme companies. The first commercial radio stations went on the air in October 1973. See TELEVISION ACT, 1954.

Sound, synchronous See SYNCHRONOUS SOUND.

Source An individual, GROUP or INSTITUTION that originates a MESSAGE.

Soviet Manifesto, 1928 Probably written by Sergei Eisenstein (1898–1948), and signed by him, Vsevolod Pudovkin and Grigori Alexandrov, the Manifesto was a declaration of faith in the artistic importance of cinema. It detailed the attitudes of the named directors to the processes of cinema, chiefly the commitment to MONTAGE in the light of the development of SYNCHRONOUS SOUND: 'The first experimental work with sound must be directed along the line of its distinct non-synchronization with the visual images'. See FILM.

Sovkino Organization formed after the Russian Revolution (1917) to control the new cinema of art and PROPAGANDA. In 1925, one of Sovkino's administrators tried to ban the foreign distribution of Sergei Eisenstein's *The Battleship Potemkin* completed that year, though the poet Vladimir Mayakovsky (1893–1930) had influence enough to get the decision reversed. In 1927 Mayakovsky publicly berated Sovkino for its conservatism. The battle against the Soviet bureaucrats was to be lost. Mayakovsky committed suicide in 1930, perhaps in presentiment of the Stalinist purges to come, and the end of all aesthetic freedom.

Spaghetti westerns Made in Europe, usually Spain, by Italian directors such as Serge Leone (b. 1921) whose *A Fistful of Dollars* (1967) starring Clint Eastwood was the first to be imported into the US. All spaghetti westerns contain large amounts of explicit violence. See GENRE; WESTERN.

Spatial zones Those areas and distances which individuals maintain between each other, depending on the nature of the relationship between them. Edward T. Hall, 'inventor' of PROXEMICS (See *The Silent Language*, US: Anchor Books, 1973), has specified four of these spatial zones: *intimate*, *personal*, *social* and *public* (each with a near and far phase). See DEFENSIBLE SPACE; INTERPERSONAL COMMUNICATION.

Special effects The 'real' gorilla in *King Kong* (1933) was just 18 inches high – that is special effects. Simulations of earthquakes, explosions, floods, fires, storms, of the interior of Hell, of war in space or 40 fathoms deep is the job of the special effects wizards who today command fees as great as FILM stars. Special effects can, by dazzling defiance of the possible, make the success of a film. *Star Wars* (1977), directed by George Lucas, was raised from the humdrum and the banal to the spectacular by special effects; and COMPUTER GRAPHICS have provided an exciting new dimension to the art, with, first in the field, Walt Disney's $18 million *Tron* (1982).

Speed photography See HIGH-SPEED PHOTOGRAPHY.

Speedwriting See SHORTHAND.

Spike Journalists' in-word for copy that is to be rejected. It is literally thrust on to a metal spike set in a wooden base. Once a piece of copy is 'spiked' it is 'dead'. See PRESS.

Spinning top In Russian, 'Dziga Vertov', the nickname taken by one of the most influential directors and theorists in cinema history, Denis Kaufman (1896–1954), in order to proclaim his allegiance to the idea of movement. More than anyone else, Vertov challenged the studio-bound theatrical conception of FILM-making. He plunged into the Russian Civil War (1917–21) with both camera and rifle. The camera he saw as an eye, but more wonderful, more all-seeing: 'We cannot make our eyes better than they are', he wrote, 'but the movie camera we can perfect for ever.' See DOCUMENTARY.

Spiral of silence See NOELLE-NEUMANN'S SPIRAL OF SILENCE MODEL OF PUBLIC OPINION, 1974.

Spiral model of communication See DANCE'S HELICAL MODEL OF COMMUNICATION.

Splurchase In ADVERTISING, a word invented to describe the consumer, through the prompting of psychologically orientated marketing methods, buying more than he/she expects or needs, and thus a purchase becomes a splurchase. Vance Packard gave the word currency in his seminal book on the US advertising world, *The Hidden Persuaders* (UK: Penguin, new edition, 1981). See HIDDEN NEEDS; MOTIVATION RESEARCH.

Spoiler FLEET STREET parlance for a tactic used to detract from a rival newspaper's scoop story, usually by running a different version of the story as told by lesser characters.

Spontaneous activity Alfred Schutz promoted the concept of the communicative act as being one of spontaneity. 'Every action', writes Schutz in *Phenomenology of the Social World* (UK: Heinemann, 1972) 'is a spontaneous activity orientated towards the future.' We communicate to achieve future ends, Schutz argues, and to participate in social life; to handle the world of experience. See INTERPERSONAL COMMUNICATIONS.

Spot news Term used to describe unexpected or unplanned news events, such as natural disasters, aircrashes, murders or assassinations. These are distinguished from *diary stories* which are known well in advance and can be planned for by the newspaper, RADIO or TELEVISION news team – such as news conferences, state visits, elections or budgets. The *running story* is that which is on-going and may stretch over several days or weeks, such as strikes, wars and famines; all stories that transcend the newsday cycle.

Sputnik First artificial satellite launched into space, by the Russians in 1957. See SATELLITE TRANSMISSION.

Spycatcher case A book by former British secret service employee Peter Wright, first published in the US in 1987, and banned from publication in the UK, became the centre of the most celebrated case of attempted government CENSORSHIP in the 1980s. *Spycatcher: The Candid Autobiography of a Senior Intelligence Officer* (US: Viking-Penguin, 1987) was not dissimilar in its revelations about the activities of MI5 to other books which had been permitted to appear, but Wright, having signed the OFFICIAL SECRETS ACT was deemed to have breached confidence and arguably set a precedent for other secret agents to 'spill the beans' on security. The government was determined not only to prevent publication of *Spycatcher* in the UK but to block the intentions of newspapers such as the *Guardian*, the *Observer*, the *Independent* and the *Sunday Times* to publish extracts from Wright's book. At the same time, government law officers pursued the book across the world to the courts in Australia and Hong Kong. The publicity given to the pursuit of *Spycatcher* made it a world best-seller; extracts from the book were published in the world's PRESS. Only the British people were to remain in the dark about Wright's revelations.

The government did not prosecute under the Official Secrets Act but pushed their case on the grounds of *confidentiality*, that members of the secret service, having sworn never to divulge information about their work, must – in law – be held for ever to that allegiance. The counter-arguments employed by Wright's defence, and that of the newspapers in their cases against the imposition of injunctions on publication were (1) that Peter Wright revealed activities on the part of MI5 which were in themselves illegal and (2) that the information contained in *Spycatcher* was so widely known, so widely publicized, that the British press should have the right to print it and the British public the right to read it.

In seemingly innumerable court hearings, the case for the publication of *Spycatcher* made some advances and suffered rebuffs. In December 1987, High Court judge, Mr Justice Scott lifted the injunction on the *Guardian* and the *Observer* preventing them publishing extracts from the book, with the declaration that 'The ability of the press freely to report allegations of scandals in government is one of the bulwarks of our democratic society'. Bulwark or no, the government appealed against Justice Scott's ruling, ignoring his comment that 'I found myself unable to escape the reflection that the absolute protection of the security service that Sir Robert [Armstrong, Secretary to the Cabinet] was contending for could not be achieved this side of the Iron Curtain'. The Law Lords deliberated on the saga of *Spycatcher* and in October 1988 rejected government demands for a blanket injunction against the publishing in the UK of extracts from Wright's book. 'In a free society,' said Lord Goff, one of the five Law Lords, 'there is a continuing public interest that the workings of government should be open to scrutiny and criticism.' The Law Lords attacked the Government's conduct of the litigation and its claims that it is for Government alone to judge what information must remain confidential. An estimated £3m was spent by the Government on court proceedings. This triumph for free speech was followed by government measures to revise the OFFICIAL SECRETS ACT to achieve the kind of censorship which had been so conspicuously rejected in the Lords' judgment.

Squanderbug Bites the great FILM corporations from time to time, inducing them to produce pictures at horrendous expense which are very often box-office disasters.

Stamp Duty A government tax in late 18th and 19th c. Britain on newspapers, with the express intention of controlling the numbers of papers and access to them by the general public. With news of the French Revolution (1789) across the water, Stamp Duty was raised to two pence per newspaper copy, with an additional Advertising Tax at three shillings per advertisement. In 1797 Stamp Duty was raised to three and half pence, and the hiring out of papers was forbidden. In the year of the Battle of Waterloo, 1815, the duty went up to four pence and the Advertising Tax was also raised.

The attitude of the ESTABLISHMENT to the rapid growth of newspapers had been summarized in the Tory *Anti-Jacobin Review* in 1801: 'We have always considered the establishment of newspapers in this country as a misfortune to be regretted; but, since their influence has become predominant by the universality of their circulation, we regard it as a calamity most deeply to be deplored.' Not only were heavy TAXES ON KNOWLEDGE imposed throughout the period, but subsidies or bribes became commonplace, including direct payments to journalists – to those, of course, amenable to government policies.

These measures eventually provoked what has been described as the 'War of the Unstamped', the struggle of papers unable or unwilling to pay the duties. William Cobbett (1763–1835) in his *Political Register* dropped news so as to evade tax and concentrated on *opinion*. Unstamped, and costing two pence, Cobbett's periodical achieved a sale of 44,000. 'Here, in these critical years', writes Raymond Williams in *The Long Revolution* (UK: Penguin, 1965) 'a popular press of a new kind was emerging, wholly independent in spirit, and reaching new classes of readers.'

Two of the six Acts of 1819 were directed against the PRESS and the 1820s and early 1830s featured clashes, fines, imprisonments and heroic defiance. In 1836 Stamp Duty was reduced from four pence to one penny, three years after the Advertisment Tax had been reduced from three shillings and sixpence to one shilling and sixpence per insertion. In 1853 the Advertising Tax was finally abolished; in 1855 the last penny of the Stamp Duty was removed and in 1860 the duty imposed on paper was abandoned. 'The era of democratic journalism had formally arrived', writes Joel H. Wiener in *The War of the Unstamped* (US: Cornell, 1969) 'and the daily newspaper became the cultural staple of the social classes.' See NEWSPAPERS, ORIGINS; PRESS BARONS; UNDERGROUND PRESS.

Status The concept of status derives from the work of the sociologist Max Weber, who argued that status, though linked to CLASS, is a distinct dimension of social stratification. Status is the social evaluation of an individual or group, the degree of prestige or honour that society accords him, her or it. Wealth and high income may confer status but do not necessarily do so. The reasons why individuals or GROUPS may enjoy considerable status within a community or society are complex, subject to change and derive from many sources: such as the degree of POWER or authority a person or group may have, the perceived social usefulness of the abilities of an individual or group or the level of education an individual has.

Occupation or the ownership of property may bestow status or require attributes, such as a high level of education, which themselves confer status. Hence the link between status and class.

Status may be *ascribed*, that is, based on fixed criteria over which a person may have no control – such as ancestry, ethnic affiliation, sex – or *achieved*, that is gained by endeavour or luck. Status given may not coincide with an individual's PERCEPTION of his or her status.

Status must normally be endorsed by behaviour: such as the possession of objects – status symbols, accent, manners, and social skills consistent with the status position. Much communicative behaviour is involved in the display of status, the use of accent and dress for example. The mass media carry many images of status. Advertisers in particular appeal to status-consciousness as a way of selling a wide range of products from soap to newspapers.

Status quo As things are: the way in which things are done or were done in a period of time under discussion. Within the social science disciplines the term is often used to mean the prevailing or recent social, economic or political system and its attributes. There is some controversy within media studies as to whether or not the mass media generally play an important role in reinforcing the status quo by presenting it as the 'natural' or 'real' state of things, and by rarely, in their presentation of aspects of human life, calling it into question.

Richard Hoggart in *Speaking to Each Other* (UK: Chatto & Windus, 1970) argues that the tendency to accept the status quo results in the mass media concentrating on entertaining people at the expense of exploring the nature of human existence – an exploration which might disturb the status quo. See CONSENSUS; ESTABLISHMENT.

Stenography See SHORTHAND.

Stereolithography In computer-aided design (CAD), a technique used to translate the three-dimensional IMAGE that appears on a computer screen into a scale model. This is built up of very thin layers of ultra-violet-sensitive polymers – plastic material which is changed by ultra-violet light to a solid. The light source draws a cross-section of the model on to the liquid. When this slice has hardened, another layer is added and the layers bond to create a solid form – maximum size, between 12 and 18 cubic inches.

Stereophonic sound See GRAMOPHONE.

Stereoscopy The creation of the visual illusion of relief or three-dimensions. The stereoscope was invented by Sir Charles Wheatstone (1802–75) in 1838. The process has had many applications. In photography, two separate photographs, taken from minimally different angles corresponding to the position of two human eyes are mounted side by side on a card. Viewed through the angled prisms of the stereoscope, they interact to give the appearance of depth or solidity.

In the cinema experimental processes of stereoscopy were demonstrated as early as the 1930s. It was developed as Natural Vision, or 3-D, in the early 1950s but never caught on, mainly perhaps because members of the audience had to wear special glasses. Only in Russia has a stereoscopic process which does not require the wearing of glasses been developed, yet even there it does not appear to have been widely adopted. However, 3-D (with glasses) was brought experimentally to UK TV screens by ITV in 1982–83. See HOLOGRAPHY.

Stereotype Oversimplified definition of a person or type of person, INSTITUTION, STYLE or event; to stereotype is to pigeon-hole, to thrust into tight slots of definition which allow of little adjustment or change. Stereotyping is widespread because it is convenient – unions are like this, blacks are like this, Jews are like this, teenagers, women, Scots, foreigners are like this. Stereotyping is often – though not always – the result of or accompaniment to prejudice. It serves the media well because they are in the business of instant recognition and ready cues. It is very rare that we actually *know* any stereotype: we only read of them, hear of them or have them 'framed' for us on TV. See HALO EFFECT; LABELLING PROCESS.

Stopwatch culture See IMMEDIACT.

Story appeal In ADVERTISING the hook which catches the viewer's, listener's or reader's attention; the angle or theme, which basically comes down to the posing of Who, What, Why, Where and How questions and answering them imaginatively.

Storyboard Sequence of sketches or photographs used by the director or the producer of a FILM commercial to sketch out, scene by scene, and sometimes frame by frame, the film's progression, its sight and sound.

Strategy A term sometimes used to describe a communicative act which has been planned to some extent beforehand, which is deliberate and which has a clear purpose. Strategies can become a matter of habit. An example here might be the strategy used by a door-to-door salesperson.

There are many different kind of strategies used in INTERPERSONAL COMMUNICATION and we learn to use them through experience. Some, like the greetings strategy, are commonly used by many people, some we invent for ourselves to deal with particular situations and some may be specific to certain GROUPS or circumstances.

Stream of consciousness William James (1842–1910) is thought to have been the originator of this phrase in *Principles of Psychology* (1890) to describe the flow of inner thoughts, endless, interweaving, sometimes in orderly connection, sometimes a whirlpool of confusion, working simultaneously at several levels: 'let us call it the stream of thought, of consciousness or of subjective life.' Four forms of stream of consciousness writing have been defined by critics: soliloquy; omniscient or god-like narration of the mental processes of more than one character; and both direct and indirect interior monologue.

While examples of stream of consciousness can be traced as far back as *Tristram Shandy* (1767) by Laurence Sterne (1716–68), the most famous exponent has been James Joyce (1882–1941). The interior monologue of Molly Bloom in *Ulysses* (1922) illustrates that thought, among many other important things, does not care much for punctuation. In the Penguin Modern Classics Edition, 1969, the monologue continues, unbroken, from page 659 to 704, and represents one of the great *tours de force* in literature. Virginia Woolf (1882–1941), also turned to stream of consciousness to considerable effect. Perhaps her most notable achievement in this GENRE was *The Waves* (1931), though at no time does Miss Woolf abandon all respect for punctuation.

Street culture One of a number of teenage sub-cultures whose members are mainly working-CLASS males. Activities are centred around football matches, cafes, public houses and discotheques. Films, COMICS and music associated with aggression and delinquency tend to be favoured by young people oriented to street CULTURE. This culture is thought to be strongest amongst adolescents whose limited opportunities force them to live in static, low-status social circumstances, and it contrasts markedly with the achievement orientation and behaviour of those youngsters whose opportunities are more promising. The socially static youngsters develop alternative means of achieving esteem within the sub-culture; many of these are centred upon the mostly aggressive VALUES and pursuits of street culture. See SUB-CULTURE; YOUTH CULTURE.

Stretching Or stretch-printing. Technique of adding extra frames to silent FILM footage, thus slowing down the tempo of movement on the screen. The silent movies were shot at 16 frames a second; the modern film projector operates at 24 frames a second, making everything move half as fast again as normal. Printing every second frame twice substantially removes the jerkiness of movement and the unintended comic element.

Stringer Name given in the news reporting business for a non-staff reporter.

Striped print Film to which a thin stripe of magnetic oxide has been added in the usual sound-track position alongside the picture. The sound is later recorded on to this stripe. Magnetic sound achieves a better quality than optical sound but is more expensive: unlike the optical track, it requires two further operations in addition to printing. Stereophonic sound, for example, is reproduced from 70 mm prints with four stripes, two on each side of the picture. See SYNCHRONOUS SOUND.

Structuralism A 20th c. term of wide definition to describe certain traditions of analysing a range of studies – LINGUISTICS, literary criticism, psychoanalysis, social anthropology, Marxist theory and social history. Swiss scholar Ferdinand de Saussure's *Cours de Linguistique Générale* (1916), translated *Course in General Linguistics* (1954), is probably the initial key work in this movement, later developed and diversified by Claude Lévi-Strauss and Roland Barthes. Structuralism is something of an umbrella term linked with the study of SIGN systems or SEMIOLOGY/SEMIOTICS.

Structuralists would argue that LANGUAGE has both a natural and a cultural SOURCE. The natural source refers to language as a genetic endowment of the human race, and this is framed within a NETWORK of meanings derived from the CULTURE of society. Structuralism explores the deep and often unconscious assumptions about social reality which underlie language and its use. In particular, it examines the way language is employed to construct MEANING from social events. However, assumptions about social reality are themselves also a product of social conditioning. Thus different cultures and sub-cultures – and indeed individuals – may generate different patterns of meaning from the same objective event or situation. Structuralist analysis is equally applicable to other modes of communication, such as FILM.

Student radio York University was the first in the UK to make legal broadcasts to students in higher education, in 1969, though there had been pirate broadcasters before that. The National Association of Student Broadcasting was formed in 1972; it has over 20 station members. See COMMUNITY RADIO; HOSPITAL RADIO.

Style A means by which the individual or GROUP expresses identity, attitudes and VALUES, about self, about others and about society. Style takes many forms – hair style, dress style, aesthetic style, or a complete pattern of living – life style. A teenager may adopt the style of a teenage SUB-CULTURE, in dress, LANGUAGE, behaviour for several linked reasons: to secure a sense of personal identity, to acquire a sense of belonging, of being 'in' with a favoured group, as a GESTURE of rebellion (against the *conventional* style of parents, for example, or the older generation in all shapes and forms) and to achieve *status* – that is, a status awarded him/her by others in the favoured group, and peers generally.

Defiance of society at large is often cited as a reason why certain styles are adopted; this may or may not be true in all cases, but what is certain is that society often *interprets* such styles as acts of defiance or rejection, and the arbiters in this process of interpretation (or MEDIATION) are the mass media. Coverage by the media, researchers have found, tends to overdramatize the significance of style, to create stereotypes and summon up exaggerated fears in the community (See FOLK DEVILS; LABEL LIBEL; LABELLING PROCESS; STEREOTYPE).

In the world of the arts style is that particular set of characteristics – of approach and treatment – which gives a work its identity. As with styles in hair or dress, styles are first created, then imitated. In painting, the style of Paul Cézanne (1839–1906) is highly distinctive and instantly recognizable by anyone with a particular interest in art. However, it took Cézanne many years to develop that style which was a visible manifestation of everything he believed about visual art; thus style represents the outer part of a whole structure which is made up of personality, experience, learning, theory, belief – and fused, if the style is successful.

Those coming after may slavishly imitate the style of the master or, like the cubists in the case of Cézanne, assimilate the style and then recreate it, thrusting it in new and exciting directions. See CULTURE; PUNK; YOUTH CULTURE.

* J. Clarke, 'Style', in S. Hall and T. Jefferson, eds., *Resistance through Rituals* (UK: Hutchinson, 1977).

Sub-culture Alternatives to the dominant CULTURE in society, sub-cultures have their own systems of VALUES, NORMS and beliefs and in some cases their own language CODES. Such systems often contain expressions of rejection of or resistance to the dominant culture. Members of sub-cultures are often those to whom the dominant culture awards low, subordinate and/or dependent status: youth, for example. Each sub-culture represents the reactions of a particular social group to its experience of society. Some sub-cultures and their members may be labelled DEVIANT by others in society.

It has been argued that because of the fragmented social nature of modern society, the mass media play an increasingly important role in relaying images of such sub-cultures both to their own members and to members of the dominant culture. Dick Hebdige in *Subculture: The Meaning of Style* (UK: Methuen, 1979), states that in doing so the media tend to accommodate the sub-cultures within the framework of the dominant culture, thus preserving the CONSENSUS – a procedure which he calls the 'process of recuperation'. See COUNTER-CULTURE; YOUTH CULTURE.

Subliminal Signals which act below the threshold of conscious reception. Most familiarly we use the word in reference to *subliminal advertising*, the trick of flashing up on the screen, or recording on tape, messages so rapid that they are not consciously recorded but which may subsequently affect future attitudes or behaviour.

In the UK subliminal ADVERTISING is illegal and its use in other media is banned by the Institute of Practitioners in Advertising. In the US there is no such control. Many department stores use subliminal seduction to counteract shop-lifting. Messages such as 'I am honest, I will not steal' are mixed with background music and continually repeated. One retail chain reported a drop of a third in thefts in nine months as a result of its subliminal conscience coaxing. See SLEEPER EFFECT.

Subtitle Or striptitle, a text near the bottom of the projected image, usually providing a translation of foreign LANGUAGE dialogue. These days it is possible with foreign language films screened on TV to generate subtitles electronically so that the words are not actually on the FILM itself. In some multilingual areas, such as Cairo, where three or more titles in different languages and scripts are required, subtitles are projected on to separate screens at the sides and bottom of the main screen.

Succeeders See ADVERTISING: MAINSTREAMERS, ASPIRERS, SUCCEEDERS & REFORMERS.

Sudsology Fun word to describe the 'study' of TV SOAP OPERA.

Summitese That kind of LANGUAGE – bland, elusive, vague and non-committal – which emerges from summit conferences between national leaders; usually full of high-sounding aspiration, but empty of any promise of action. The language of the STATUS QUO.

Surveillance Keeping watch; used in a media sense, the word indicates the way that listeners, viewers or readers employ the media with the aim of gleaning information from them: 'TV news provides food for thought' or 'I like to see how big issues are sorted out.' See USES AND GRATIFICATIONS THEORY.

Sykes Committee Report on Broadcasting, 1923 See BBC, ORIGINS.

Symbol Any object, person, or event to which a generally agreed, shared MEANING has been given and which individuals have learned to accept as representing something other than itself: a national flag represents feelings of patriotism and national unity, for example. Symbols are almost always CULTURE-bound. See ICONIC; METAPHOR; MYTH; SEMIOLOGY/SEMIOTICS; SIGN; SIGNIFICATION.

Symbolic convergence theory Professor Ernest G. Bormann in his article 'Symbolic convergence theory: a communication formulation' in the *Journal of Communication* (Autumn 1985), writes of 'shared fantasies' which 'provide group members with comprehensible forms for explaining the past and thinking about the future – a basis for communal and group consciousness' (See NARRATIVE PARADIGM).

Bormann, professor in the Department of Speech-Communication at the University of Minnesota–Twin Cities, posits a three-part structure to the theory: (1) the part which deals with the discovery and arrangement of recurring communicative forms and patterns that indicate the evolution and presence of a shared group consciousness; (2) the part which consists of a description of the dynamic tendencies within communication systems 'that explain why group consensuses arise, continue decline, and disappear' and the effects such group consensus has in terms of MEANINGS, motives and communication within the group: the basic communication process is the dynamic of people sharing group fantasies; (3) that part of the theory which consists of the factors which explain why people share the fantasies they do and when they do.

By 'fantasy' Borman means the creative and imaginative shared interpretation of events 'that fulfil a group psychological or rhetorical need'. What the author terms 'rhetorical fantasies' are the result of '*homo narrans* in collectives sharing narratives that account for their experiences and their hopes and fears'. Such rhetorical fantasies may include 'fanciful and fictitious scripts of imaginary characters, but they often deal with things that have actually happened to members of the group or that are reported in authenticated works of history, in the news media, or in the oral history and folklore of other groups and communities.' The sharing of fantasies brings a 'convergence of appropriate feelings among participants . . . when members of a mass audience share a fantasy they jointly experience the same emotions, develop common heroes and villains, celebrate certain actions as laudable, and interpret some aspect of their common experience in the same way.' This Bormann names *symbolic convergence*.

While the 'rational world paradigm' claims that there *is* an objective truth that speakers can mirror in their communication and against which its logic and argument can be tested and evaluated (and therefore regards MYTH and fantasy as untrue, as the recounting of falsehoods), for those giving credence to shared fantasies, 'the stories of myths or fantasy themes are central'. An underlying assumption of the theory seems to be that fantasies are not only creative but benign. It would be interesting to apply symbolic convergence theory, the notion of HOMO NARRANS, to fantasies entertained about racial superiority, where fantasy becomes a nightmare.

* E.G. Boormann, *Communicative Theory* (US: Holt, Rinchart & Winston, 1980); *The Force of Fantasy: Restoring the American Dream* (US: S. Illinois University Press, 1985).

'Symbolic annihilation of women' (by the media) See NORMS.

Symmetry, strain towards Concept posed by Theodore Newcomb in 'An approach to the study of communicative acts', *Pyschological Review*, 63 (1953). The act of communication is characterized, believes Newcomb, by a 'strain towards symmetry', that is towards balance and CONSISTENCY. See CONGRUENCE THEORY; INTERPERSONAL COMMUNICATION; NEWCOMB'S ABX MODEL OF COMMUNICATION, 1953.

Symptomatic technology See TECHNOLOGICAL DETERMINISM.

Synchronic linguistics See LINGUISTICS.

Synchronous sound In FILM, sound effects synchronized with the visual image were first used commercially in 1926, in *Don Juan*, but it was *The Jazz Singer* in November 1927 which caused the sensation among audiences and marks the birth of the Talkies. Warner Brothers had been heading for oblivion in the cutthroat world of the HOLLYWOOD studios when the company adopted a system developed by the Bell Telephones Laboratories which reproduced sound from large discs, matching sound and picture by mechanical linkage. Nothing in the cinema was ever the same again. The Talkies marked the end of many careers made in the silent era but created new opportunities for actors from the theatre, writers, musicians, vaudeville and RADIO stars.

As a technical possibility, synchronous sound had been inviting interest from movie makers from as early as 1902. In that year

Monsieur Gaumont gave an address to the Société Français de la Photographie, on film and employing synchronous sound. Indeed two years earlier Herr Ruhmer demonstrated what he called 'light telephony' to record sound directly on to the film itself – the first *sound-track*. Following the inventions of the thermionic valve by John Fleming in 1904 and the audion vacuum tube by Lee De Forest in 1907, amplification of sound by comparatively simple electric methods was feasible: the studios were simply not interested, fearing, perhaps, the impact language differences might have on the universal appeal of film as *mime*, whose only verbal language was easily translatable titling.

Though Lee De Forest's *Phonofilm* of 1923 demonstrated how light waves could synchronize sound and image, and though the Germans had developed the finest early sound system of all, *Tri-Ergon*, the continuing profitability of the silent movie blinded the studios to two significant facts: the potential of silent film had practically been exhausted; and audiences were becoming bored. *Lights of New York* (1928) was the first all-talking picture and within a year thousands of cinemas had been equipped for sound.

Warner's VITAPHONE disc was soon replaced by optical sound systems where images and sound were put together on the same film, to make the *married print* where sound synchronization with the picture could not be lost. As sound recording techniques developed, dialogue, sound effects and music were recorded separately, using a magnetic sound process, and then mixed at a later stage, thus allowing latitude for changes and creative editing.

The introduction of sound did not rescue the cinema from the general economic slump that followed the Wall Street Crash of 1929. During 1931, cinema attendances in the US dropped by 40% and in 1932 the movie business lost between $4 and 5m. However, it was probably the new dimension of sound in the cinema that enabled the industry to rally so quickly.

The Talkies interacted substantially with radio, the one drawing technical and creative ideas as well as talented personnel from the other. By 1937, 90% of US sponsored national radio programmes in the US were transmitted from Hollywood. See STRIPED PRINT.

Syntactics A branch of SEMIOLOGY/SEMIOTICS; the study of the SIGNS and rules relating to signs, without reference to MEANING.

Syntagm See PARADIGM.

Syntax The combination of words into significant patterns; the grammatical structure in sentences.

Synthetic culture The highly processed, artificial media products designed to appeal to audience stereotypes rather than individuals. Thus

greater consideration is given to the supposed desires of the target consumer GROUPS than to the material and subject matter of the product. The result, according to the critics, is that ART forms are robbed of integrity and variety and are served up as glossy, uniform packages which Richard Hoggart in *Speaking to Each Other* (UK: Chatto & Windus, 1970) describes as '. . . well-packaged emptiness', designed to catch the assumed fleeting attention and needs of a mass audience. The TV SOAP OPERA might be considered one such product.

System X A computerized TELEPHONE exchange system developed by the UK Post Office in 1971. By 1982 over £150m had been invested in the system, a sum estimated to reach £500m by 1990. Involved in the marketing of System X are major companies in the private sector. According to Patrick Fitzgerald and Mark Leopold (a former British Telecom employee) in their book *Stranger on the Line: The Secret History of Phone Tapping* (UK: Bodley Head, 1987) System X will permit the government and its agencies to monitor individual calls secretly and more easily. The INTERCEPTION OF COMMUNICATIONS ACT, 1985 does not cover the 'automatic call tracing' provided by the system: 'the [digital] tap leaves no physical presence anywhere', state the authors. If BT refused this service to government it could be caught by the safety net the 'national security' clause in the Telecommunications Act of 1984. See PABX.

Taboo In all societies or social GROUPS there is some behaviour which is considered prohibited – taboo. Often this behaviour is seen as a threat to the established order. Individuals accept observance of the taboo as a SIGN of their acceptance of group NORMS. Behaviour defined as taboo will vary from society to society and from group to group.

In modern society taboos merely restrict certain behaviour, certain LANGUAGE usage and the content of public discussions. Taboos tend to govern what is not communicated, verbally or non-verbally, in any given social situation. The word *taboo* or tabu is of Polynesian origin, thought to have been brought back to Europe by Captain James Cook (1728–79). See CENSORSHIP.

Tabloid Anything in very concentrated form; hence a *tabloid* newspaper, such as the *Daily Mirror* or the *Sun*. The word generally seems to have come to refer to the *format* of such newspapers – compressed in size. Thus the traditional broadsheet format (like that of *The Times*) was abandoned in the 1970s by the *Daily Mail* and *Daily Express*, who 'went tabloid' on 3 May 1971 and 24 January 1977 respectively.

Tabloidese Another word for JOURNALESE; in headlines and text, LANGUAGE as used by the tabloid PRESS, aiming for maximum eye-catching impact in the fewest possible words. It ranges from the witty and often poetic to the crass and the ludicrous. See UNIT HEADLINE LANGUAGE.

Tachistoscope Instrument which flashes up on a screen photographs, printed letters and words, diagrams, etc. for very short, precisely controllable intervals; used to test perceptual responses.

Tactile communication Communicating by TOUCH.

Take See SHOT.

Talloires Declaration, 1981 Concerned at the attempts by Unesco seemingly to impose upon world information systems a 'New Order' which would be characterized by far-reaching controls, representatives from news organizations of 20 countries met in the French village of Talloires in May 1981. They issued a declaration which insisted that journalists sought no special protected status – as it was planning to create – and that they were united in a 'joint declaration to the freest, most accurate and impartial information that is within our professional capacity to produce'. The declaration asserted that there could be no double standards of freedom for rich and poor countries. See MACBRIDE COMMISSION; MEDIA IMPERIALISM; NEW WORLD INFORMATION ORDER.

Talkies See SYNCHRONOUS SOUND.

Tamizdat See SAMIZDAT.

Taste In a media sense, the notion of good or bad taste relates less to aesthetic judgement than to decisions about how *much* and how *far*; the answers to these questions depend upon audience EXPECTATIONS and readiness, and the degree of access and immediacy. A photograph of an execution, reproduced in a newspaper or magazine, is sufficiently controlled by the frame of print and the fact that the event took place in the past, to escape the accusation of bad taste. However, vigorous protests went up when, on TV news, a Vietnamese prisoner had a pistol put to his head, and the trigger pulled. This was bringing, as it were, too much reality into the sitting room. It may have been the truth, ran the argument, but somehow the reproduction and presentation turned reality into theatre, indeed into macabre entertainment. As such it appeared an insult to human dignity – to that of the victim and to that of the audience cast in the role of voyeurs. See CENSORSHIP.

'Taste and Standards in BBC Programmes' A report by the BBC in 1972 for its General Advisory Council. The document emphasized the need for constant internal review and 'referral upwards' by producers of any issue which might affect the BBC's policy on matters of TASTE. See BROADCASTING STANDARDS COUNCIL.

Taxes on knowledge Government-imposed taxes and duties on the PRESS in the late 18th and 19th centuries. STAMP DUTY was levied on every copy of a newspaper printed; the Advertising Tax upon every advertisement used. The intention of the taxes was made plain at the time by Lord Ellenborough: 'It was not against the respectable Press that the Bill (Newspaper Stamp Duties Act, 1819) was directed, but against a pauper press.' That is, the radical press as represented by such editors as William Cobbett (1763–1835), Richard Carlile and Thomas Hetherington, in an age of turbulent unrest. See UNDERGROUND PRESS.

Technological determinism The view that if something is technically feasible then it is both desirable and bound to be realized in practice. In many quarters in the so-called WIRED SOCIETY of CABLE TELEVISION, SATELLITE TRANSMISSION and VIDEO there is a degree of fatalism that these things must come to pass (even if we don't want them, even if they are likely to be socially and culturally harmful). Evidence points to the fact that such determinism is only partly convincing. Much technology usage is a by-product of technology devised for other purposes. RADIO became an 'inevitability', for example, largely because its determinant was RADAR, required to fulfil military needs, while satellites had a long record of military/political functions before they began to beam sporting events to the peoples of the world.

Set counter to notions of technological determinism is a second theory, *Symptomatic technology*, which argues that technology is a by-product of a social process which itself has been otherwise determined. In *Television: Technology and Cutural Form* (UK: Fontana, 1974), Raymond Williams says that basically both theories are in error because in different ways they have 'abstracted technology from society' instead of examining the crucial interaction between them. Of course part of that interaction is the *belief* in technological determinism, and the risk of it becoming a self-fulfilling prophecy.

Technology of the media See AMSATS; BLEND; BRAILLE; CABLE TELEVISION; CAMERA; CEEFAX; CELLULAR RADIO; CD – COMPACT DISC; CELLULOID; CINEMASCOPE; CINEMATOGRAPHY, ORIGINS; COLD-TYPE TECHNOLOGY; COMPUTER GRAPHICS; CYLINDER OR ROTARY PRESS; DAISY WHEEL; DIGITAL RETOUCHING; DUAL-AUDIO TV; EARLY-BIRD SATELLITE; FACSIMILE; FIBRE-OPTIC TECHNOLOGY; FILMLESS CAMERA. GRAMOPHONE; HIGH-DEFINITION TV; HIGH-SPEED PHOTOGRAPHY; HOLOGRAPHY; INFORMATION TECHNOLOGY; INFRA-RED PHOTOGRAPHY; INTELSAT; INTERACTIVE VIDEO; IRAS; LAN; LASERVISION; LINOTYPE PRINTING; MONOTYPE PRINTING; OMNI-

MAX; PHONO-DISC; PHOTONICS; PHOTORESIST; PHOTOTYPESETTING; PRINTING; PROJECTION OF PICTURES; RADIO DATA SYSTEM; SATELLITE BUSINESS SYSTEMS (SBS); SATELLITE TRANSMISSION; SCHÜFFTEN PROCESS; STEREO-LITHOGRAPHY; STEREOSCOPY; STRIPED PRINT; TACHITOSCOPE; TECHNOLOGICAL DETERMINISM; TELAUTOGRAPH; TELEARCHICS; TELEGRAPHY; TELEPHONE; TELESOFTWARE; TELETEXT; TELEX; TELEVISION BROADCASTING; TELSTAR; TYPEWRITER; ULTRA-VIOLET/FLORESCENT PHOTOGRAPHY; VIDEO; VIDEOGRAPHY; WIRELESS TELEGRAPHY; WORD PROCESSING; WORLD REPORTER; XEROGRAPHY; ZOETROPE; ZOOM LENS; ZOÖPRAXOGRAPHY.

* No dictionary can keep up to date with the speed at which new technology is developed. The editors therefore recommend a regular scrutiny of the *New Scientist*, published weekly. Its information is reliable, its treatment lively and perceptive and clear to the non-scientific reader.

Telautograph Device for transmitting pictures electrically over distance.

Telearchics Wireless control of aircraft from a distance.

Telecommunication *Tele* means far off, at a distance; telecommunication is communication by TELEGRAPH or TELEPHONE, with or without wires or cables. In telephony and telegraphy signals are transmitted as electric impulses along wires. In RADIO and TV the signals are transmitted through space as modulations of carrier waves of electromagnetic radiation. See TECHNOLOGY OF THE MEDIA; TELEPRINTER; TELETEXT; WIRELESS TELEGRAPHY.

Telegenic Looking good on TV – a factor that has had particular significance in the domain of politics. There is no proof that it does not help to be handsome, well-groomed and appropriately clad.

Telegram A communication by TELEGRAPH; now only available for international purposes. The old inland telegram was superseded in 1982 by the **telemessage**, which is delivered with the post but transmitted to the local post office by TELEX.

Telegraphy Only after the discovery of the magnetic effect of electric current was telegraphy possible. The first **telegraph** consisted of a compass needle which was deflected by the magnetic field produced by electric currents which flowed through the circuit whenever the transmitting key was depressed and contact established. The first patent for an electric telegraph was taken out by William Fothergill Cooke and Charles Wheatstone in June 1837 and later in the same year they demonstrated a five-needle telegraph to the directors of the London and Birmingham railway. A year later the Great Western Railway connected Paddington and West Drayton by telegraph line which soon gave a considerable boost of publicity for telegraphy: in 1845 a suspected murderer was spotted boarding a London-bound train at Slough. The news was telegraphed to Paddington and the man was arrested on arrival and later found guilty and hanged.

In the US, Samuel Morse's (1791–1872) first working telegraph of 1837 depended on the making and breaking of an electric current: an electromagnetically operated stylus recorded the long and short dashes of MORSE CODE on a moving strip of paper. After much persuasion, the US Congress, in 1843, voted to pay Morse to build the first telegraph line in America, from Baltimore to Washington. It was in the following year, using the Morse Code, that Morse transmitted his famous message – 'What hath God wrought!' – on this line.

Development of telegraphy was swift. By 1862 the world's telegraph system covered some 150,000 miles, including 15,000 in the UK. A method of printing the coded telegraph messages had been invented in 1845 and was developed in the US as 'House's Printing Telegraph'. In 1850 a telegraph cable had been laid across the English Channel. In 1858 the Atlantic was spanned by telegraph cable. The **duplex telegraphy** of Thomas Alva Edison (1847–1931) made it possible to transmit two messages simultaneously over the same line. Soon, four and five-message systems followed, and ultimately the TELEPRINTER. Picture transmission by telegraphy resulted from the development work of English physicist Shelford Bidwell, the first such transmissions taking place in 1881.

Telegraphy continues to be widely used – by news services, the Stock Exchange TELEX service, public message services, certain police and fire alarm systems and private-line companies for data transmission. See MORSE CODE; TECHNOLOGY OF THE MEDIA; TELEPHONE; WIRELESS TELEGRAPHY.

Telemessage See TELEGRAM.

Telephone In his early years, a Scotsman Alexander Graham Bell (1857–1922) knew Charles Wheatstone (1802–75), co-inventor of TELEGRAPHY, and also Alexander John Ellis, an expert in sound. Ellis showed Bell that the vibration of a tuning fork could be influenced by an electric current. He was able to produce sounds very like those of a human voice. Bell, teaching deaf-mutes in Boston, Massachusetts, experimented on a musical telegraph (1872). He produced artificial 'ear-drums' from sheets of metal and linked these with electric wire. In 1876 Bell succeeded in passing a vocal MESSAGE along a wire to an assistant in another room. The first telephone switching system was installed in New Haven, Connecticut, in 1878. 100 years later, the US telephone system, largely the monopoly of the company Bell founded, was handling an average of over 240m phone conversations a day and, as Maurice Rickards points out in *The World Communicates* (UK: Longman, 1972), the telephone system had 'developed into a communications network infinitely more versatile than could have been envisaged by the pioneers'. Now telephone lines serve complex computer data systems; documents are transmitted via telephone – a scanning head records the light and shade of the document as it turns on a rotating drum, translating intensity of tone into electrical impulses for transmission over the wire to be re-translated at the receiving end. Telephone lines also carry TELEX services.

Microwave transmission techniques now allow telephone calls through air, free of wires, poles or underground conduits. Transmitting from point to point, tall towers now beam as many as 1500 calls on a single carrier wave. The London Post Office Tower has a potential load capacity of 150,000 telephone calls and capacity to transmit 100 TV channels. As Rickards says, 'the world's microwave towers, linked with each other and with communication satellites, complete a circuit almost too comprehensive to grasp.' See NETWORK; VIEWDATA.

Telephone conferencing A facility available both on many private TELEPHONE exchanges and, via the operator, on the public NETWORK; it enables the interlinking of more than two parties in a single call, each person being able to hear and address the others. A single telephone may be used at any site, or a group of people can use a loud-speaking phone. Pushbutton-activated light signals can be used to indicate to the chairperson of the conference or meeting a request to speak. It is also possible to combine telephone conferencing with a VIDEO link so that participants can see one another.

Telephone tapping See PHONE-TAPPING.

Telephone Preference Scheme (TPS) According to official instructions produced by British Telecom, TPS is 'a means of withdrawing outgoing service for most subscribers on an exchange so that service to preference subscribers may be safeguarded during civil or military emergencies, from the effects of congestion (that is, all lines engaged) or loss of public power supplies'. Every TELEPHONE subscriber is allocated a secret 'preference category'. Most people fall into Category 3, 'not entitled to preference in any emergency, civil or military'. Category 2 subscribers include 'Employers Associations' such as the Confederation of British Industries (CBI) – but not the Trades Union Congress – the homes of magistrates, sheriffs, lords lieutenant and judges (though not justices of the peace, law centres or solicitors) and the homes of mem-

bers of Parliament as well as key council officials.

Category 1 lines consist of 'only those lines required by local authorities responsible for the Fighting Services and essential public services to retain control of their organizations'.

Telephoto lens Long focal length camera lens used in photographing distant objects and scenes by enlarging the image on the film. Telephoto is a loosely applied term for all long lenses.

Telerecording Introduced in 1947, the first telerecording equipment consisted of a special 35mm FILM camera pointed at the screen. Picture quality was poor as a result of incompatibility between the camera shutter and TV's scanning process. The Ampex Corporation of American produced a definitive answer using a 'quadruplex' technique: a two-inch wide tape travelled at normal speed while a rapidly spinning drum carrying four heads recorded tracks across the tape rather than along it, thus achieving the high and constant speed required.

The Ampex machine was in service in the US in 1956 and in May of the following year Associated Rediffusion in the UK installed the first pair of recording machines in Europe. The BBC followed suit shortly afterwards.

Helical scan recorders were an advance upon the quadruplex machines. Instead of recording across the tapes, the spinning head-drum laid down tracks almost parallel to its length. Gradually, in the late 1970s, these machines took over from quadruplex though there were problems over product compatibility. Ampex and Sony agreed a common standard, known as C-format, and helical scan became the norm.

Teleprinter Telegraphically operated form of TYPEWRITER linked to national and international networks. See TELEX.

Telesoftware Some computer programs – called telesoftware – are fed directly to home computers via the TELEPHONE line or over the air. In March 1983 the BBC began the broadcast version of Telesoftware on its TELETEXT service, CEEFAX, commencing with 500 programs. Customers require a TV set adaptor which links to the BBC Acorn computer. Phone-line Telesoftware was offered by British Telecom's *Prestel* service in February 1983, with an initial library of 1000 programs.

Teletext Data in textual or graphic form transmitted via the TV screen; the BROADCASTING version of VIEWDATA which is TELEPHONE-linked. In the UK, the BBC provides its CEEFAX teletext service of information, the IBA, its ORACLE service. So far the viewer cannot 'talk back' to Teletext as he/she can with Viewdata, and information is limited to a few hundred pages. However, the service is free to those with

TV sets adapted for or produced for Teletext reception.

Telethon A live TV discussion or entertainment programme, often lasting for several hours, during which the public may ring in with questions and comments, and guest stars appear – all in aid of charity.

Television See BBC, ORIGINS; BREAKFAST-TIME TELEVISION; BROADCASTING ACT, 1980; 'BROADCASTING IN THE '90s': GOVERNMENT WHITE PAPER, 1988; CABLE TELEVISION; CHANNEL FOUR; COMMERCIAL TELEVISION; PUBLIC SERVICE BROADCASTING; SATELLITE TRANSMISSION; TELETEXT; TELEVISION BROADCASTING; TELEVISION DRAMA; VIDEO.

See also: ACCELERATION FACTOR; ADVERTISING; AGENDA SETTING; ANNAN COMMISSION REPORT ON BROADCASTING, 1977; AUDIENCE DIFFERENTIATION; AUTOCUE; BALANCED PROGRAMMING; BARDIC TELEVISION; BARB; BEVERIDGE COMMITTEE REPORT ON BROADCASTING, 1950.

BROADCASTING COMPLAINTS COMMISSION; BROADCASTING LEGISLATION; BROADCASTING RESEARCH; BUTTON APATHY; CODES; CAMERA CUE; CAMERA, TELEVISION; CAMPAIGN FOR PRESS AND BROADCASTING FREEDOM; CANDID CAMERA; CATHARSIS HYPOTHESIS; CEEFAX; 'CLEAN-UP TV' MOVEMENT; COLOUR TV; CONSENSUS; CONSPIRACY OF SILENCE; CULTIVATION; CULTIVATION DIFFERENTIAL; COMMERCIAL TELEVISION; DEVOLUTION; DIRTY MEDIUM; DRY-RUN; DUAL-AUDIO TV; DUOPOLY; FLY ON THE WALL; FORMULA BROADCASTING.

GENERAL ADVISORY COUNCILS; GLASGOW UNIVERSITY MEDIA GROUP; HANKEY COMMITTEE REPORT ON TELEVISION, 1943; HIGH-DEFINITION TV; HUNT COMMITTEE REPORT ON CABLE EXPANSION AND BROADCASTING POLICY, 1982; HYDE PARK OF THE AIR; INFORMATION TECHNOLOGY ADVISORY PANEL; INHERITANCE FACTOR; INTERACTIVE TELEVISION; INTER-CULTURAL INVASION (AND THE MASS MEDIA); INTERNATIONAL BROADCASTING TRUST; KINESCOPE RECORDING; LASERVISION; LITTLE MASTERPIECES LASTING ONE MINUTE; MAINSTREAMING; MCLUHANISM; MEAN WORLD SYNDROME; MINORITY REPORT OF MR SELWYN LLOYD; MONOPOLY, FOUR SCANDALS OF; NATURALISTIC ILLUSION (OF TELEVISION); NEWS VALUES; OPTIMUM INOFFENSIVENESS (LAW OF); ORACLE; PACKAGING; PARAPROXEMICS; PILKINGTON COMMITTEE REPORT ON BROADCASTING, 1962; POWER VALUE; PRESIDENTIALISM; PROGRAMME FLOW; QUOTAS; RATINGS, SCHEDULING; SECONDARY VIEWING; SELSDON COMMITTEE REPORT ON TELEVISION, 1935; S4C; SHOWBUSINESS, AGE OF; SINCERITY TEST (BY THE MEDIA); SINS OF OMISSION; SIT-COM; SOAP OPERA; SOCIAL ACTION BROADCASTING; SYKES COMMITTEE REPORT ON BROADCASTING, 1923; TELAUTOGRAPH; TELEGENIC; TELERECORDING; TELESOFTWARE. TELEVISION ACT, 1954; 'TELEVISION CODE OF ADVERTISING (ITCA); TELEVISION CONSUMER AUDIT; TERRORISM AS COMMUNICATION; THESIS JOURNALISM; 'THIRD AGE OF BROADCASTING'; TIE-SIGNS; TIME-SHIFT VIEWING; TRIVIALITY; ULLSWATER COMMITTEE REPORT ON BROADCASTING, 1936; VIEWDATA; VISUAL DISPLAY UNIT (VDU); 'VIOLENCE ON TV: CODES OF PRACTICE', WESTMINSTER VIEW.

Television broadcasting Technical developments in the UK, the Soviet Union and the US combined to make TV a feasibility by 1931 when a research group was set up in Britain under Isaac Shoenberg, who had had considerable experience in RADIO transmission technology in the Soviet Union. He furthered the evolution of a practical system of TV broadcasting based on a camera tube known as the *Emitrion* and an improved cathode-ray tube for the receiver. Shoenberg elected to develop a system of electronic scanning which proved far superior to the mechanical scanning method pioneered by Scotsman John Logie Baird (1889–1946) who had first demonstrated his system publicly in 1926.

The BBC was authorized by government to adopt Shoenberg's standards (405 lines) for the world's first high-definition service which was launched in 1936 – a system that proved sufficiently successful to continue in the UK until 1962, when the European continental 625 line system was introduced. In the US, TV was slower to develop. It was not until 30 April 1939, at the opening of the New York World's Fair, that a public demonstration was made by the National Broadcasting Company (NBC).

The BBC's nascent TV service closed down during the 2nd World War (1939–45) which also hampered TV development in America, though by 1949, there were a million receivers in the US and by 1951, ten million. In the UK TV, transmission resumed in June 1946.

Television Act, 1954 Gave birth to COMMERCIAL TELEVISION in the UK; the Act set up the Independent Television Authority (later to be named the Independent Broadcasting Authority with the coming of COMMERCIAL RADIO). A rigorous set of controlling rules was imposed on the Authority which required 'that nothing is included in the programmes which offends against good taste or decency or is likely to encourage or incite to crime or to lead to disorder or to be offensive to public feelings or which contains any offensive representation of or reference to a living person.'

A proper *balance* was required in subject matter and a high general standard of *quality*. Due 'accuracy and impartiality' were required for the presentation of any news given in programmes, in whatever form. There were also to be 'proper proportions' in terms of British productions and performance in order to safeguard against the dumping of American material.

Of vital significance in the Act were the elaborate precautions which were made to prevent advertisers gaining control of programme content. The governing body of ITV set up by the Act was similar in size and function to that of the BBC, with seven to ten governors each serving for five years and dismissable at the behest of the Postmaster General. Like the BBC, the ITA was to have a limited period of existence, followed by parliamentary review and renewal. See SOUND BROADCASTING ACT, 1972.

Television drama In an interview printed in *The New Priesthood: British Television Today* (UK: Allen Lane, 1970) by J. Bakewell and N. Garnham, TV playwright Dennis Potter (b. 1935) said of TV, 'It's the biggest platform in the world's history and writers who don't want to kick and elbow their way on to it must be disowning something in themselves.' While the PILKINGTON COMMITTEE REPORT ON BROADCASTING, 1962, found that the chief 'crime' of TV was *triviality*, much of TV drama (from the very first drama production on experimental TV, the BBC's *The Man with a Flower in his Mouth* by Luigi Pirandello on 14 July 1930) has been a striking exception to that judgement. In fact few might argue with the claim that TV's most substantial achievement has been to encourage a generation of quality dramatists working specially for the MEDIUM, and a canon of plays, from both the BBC and IBA companies, to rival anything produced in the live theatre during the same post-2nd World War period.

In the early days of TV drama, plays were stage-bound, or more accurately, studio-bound, both in concept and execution, taking for their model the theatre rather than the cinema, but the ideas of young directors making their mark during the 1960s, excited by the possibility of FILM drama, prevailed. Nell Dunn's *Up the Junction* (BBC, 1965) marked the first occasion when virtually the whole story was done on film. The camera was seen as as important as the pen; indeed the camera in many ways *became* the pen (See CAMÉRA STYLO). The social – and sometimes political – themes favoured by many writers and directors took the cameras more and more out of the studio and into 'real life', and many plays looked like, and had the impact of, DOCUMENTARY.

Produced by Tony Garnett, written by Jeremy Sandford and directed by Ken Loach, *Cathy Come Home* (BBC, 1966) detailed the decline into tragedy of a homeless family in affluent Britain. The sense of reality was almost unbearable: the camera was often hand-held, the scenes staged so realistically that the audience was tempted to forget it was watching something *constructed*, not something happening before their very eyes.

The intimacy, the close-scrutiny of humans under stress at which film and TV can excel, has rarely been used to more disturbing effect than with John Hopkins's quartet of plays *Talking to a Stranger* (BBC, 1966), described as the first authentic masterpiece of television. The *immediacy* of the medium was stunningly demonstrated in Colin Welland's epic *Leeds United!* (BBC, 1974) about Leeds clothing workers who struck spontaneously in 1970 for an extra 10 pence an hour: the camera became part of the ongoing action to such an extent that it was impossible to detect what had been *scripted* and what was happening for real.

Much of this kind of drama obviously grew from the opportunities of the moment, and from improvisation – a method used most notably by Mike Leigh, who works with actors for long periods before filming, encouraging them to *become* the characters and eventually invent or improvise their speech and actions. Examples of Leigh's improvised drama are *Abigail's Party* (BBC, 1976) and *Home Sweet Home* (BBC, 1982).

It is a hard task to select the outstanding TV dramas of recent years, but any comprehensive list would very probably contain David Mercer's *A Suitable Case for Treatment* (BBC, 1962), Potter's *Stand Up, Nigel Barton* (BBC, 1965), his six-part musical play *Pennies from Heaven* (BBC, 1978) and *Cream in My Coffee* (London Weekend TV, 1980), Tom Clarke's *Stopper's Copper* (BBC, 1972), Garnett and Loach's four-film drama of events in Britain seen through the lives of poor people, *Days of Hope* (BBC, 1976), written by Jim Allen, and Brian Clark's *Whose Life Is It Anyway?* (BBC, 1972) about a paralysed hospital patient demanding the right to die – not a theme, or treatment, that could in any way be accused of trivialization. The single play remains a major platform for gifted writers to display their best and most individual work, though two things ought to be pointed out: more and more TV drama is the product of a *team* of creative people, from producer to director, editor to designer, actor to composer; and TV drama has become more and more *expensive* to produce.

In *Television and Radio, 1982* (IBA), David Cunliffe, Head of Drama at Yorkshire TV, writes 'The inescapable fact is that over the last few years the television single play has spiralled in production costs and plummeted in popularity.' Having moved from the studio to location, plays have become 'nearly Hollywood-size movies'. He cites plays such as Potter's

LWT series, *Rain on the Roof, Blade on the Feather* and *Cream in My Coffee* as works which though expensive and polished appeal to 'relatively small sections of viewers'. One such play costs as much as half-a-dozen produced, years ago, in the studio – even allowing for inflation. Increasingly in the 1980s, dramatists turned to writing TV serials, which have more over-time impact and are more saleable commodities on the international programme market. Distinguished examples of serial writing are Alan Bleasdale's *Boys from the Blackstuff (1982),* Troy Kennedy Martin's *Edge of Darkness* (1985) and Potter's *The Singing Detective* (1987), all from the BBC and Alan Plater's *A Very British Coup* (1988), from Channel 4. See RADIO DRAMA.

'Television Programme Guidelines' Published in 1978 by the IBA and revised in June 1979; a codification of the principles concerning programme content on COMMERCIAL TELEVISION. While not designed 'to fetter normal editorial discretion', the Guidelines nevertheless describe 'requirements that need to be met' and 'areas where careful judgement is required on each occasion'. Among other matters, the Guidelines deal with: offence to good taste and decency; portrayal of violence; fairness and impartiality; privacy and information gathering; party politics, politicians and programmes; crime and anti-social behaviour. They have something to say about sex and nudity, bad taste in humour and the portrayal of violence (See VIOLENCE ON TV: CODES OF PRACTICE).

Telex World-wide link-up system providing a rapid means of communicating written messages via TELEPRINTER among subscribers, combining the speed of the TELEPHONE with the accuracy and authority of the printed word. A printed copy of the MESSAGE is available at both the sending and receiving teleprinters. Calls can be made to any telex subscriber in the UK and overseas 24 hours a day and messages may be transmitted to a subscriber even though his/her machine is unattended, provided it remains switched on. A TELEMESSAGE (inland) and a telegram (overseas) can also be sent from a telex teleprinter to a Post Office telegraph office or to Cable & Wireless Telegraph offices for onward transmission at normal telephone rates, and incoming telemessages can be accepted directly on the teleprinter.

Telstar Communications satellite launched on 10 July 1962; transmitted the first live TV pictures between the US and Europe. See SATELLITE TRANSMISSION.

10-codes Numerical abbreviations for messages conveyed between users of CB – CITIZENS' BAND RADIO. Developed by the US police and other RADIO mobile services, the 10-codes have been widely adapted by CBers everywhere.

Thus: 10–1 (Receiving poorly); 10–2 (Receiving well); 10–4 (OK, MESSAGE received); 10–9 (Repeat message); 10–23 (Stand by) and 10–73 (Special trap at . . .). Running parallel with this 'official' mode of exchange is a system far more colourful and very much a secret ritual of the initiated. Expressions to be found in this LANGUAGE, emanating in large part from the private world of the US truckers, are: *cooking* (driving); *flipper* (return trip); *hump* (mountain); *local bears* (local police); *negatory* (no) and *scratchin'* (vehicle moving at its best pace).

Territoriality The need in humans and animals to establish and maintain private territory. See PROXEMICS.

Terrorism as communication The main aim of terrorist activity in liberal democracies is publicity. The existence of a free PRESS, and TV and RADIO companies independent of government authority within societies which subscribe to the sanctity of the individual's right to life, provides fertile ground for headline seeking by acts of terror such as hi-jacks and abductions. 'The modern terrorist makes maximum use of mass media,' writes Dan van der Vat in *Index on Censorship*, 2 (1982). 'Little more than a century ago, before the invention of the rotary press, he would have been inconceivable; he came into his own only in the last 15 years or even less, when television became an instantaneous medium, capable of sending live pictures round the globe by satellite.' The terrorist exploits the media to further his cause: thus the question is posed, when lives are at risk, to what extent should the media withhold publicity about terrorist acts? A supplementary question relates to the perceived danger or media coverage 'setting a vogue' for such activities. See CONTAGION EFFECT.

* R.E. Dowling. 'Terrorism and the media: A rhetorical genre' in *Journal of Communication*. Winter 1986.

Text According to Tim O'Sullivan, John Hartley, Danny Saunders, and John Fiske in *Key Concepts in Communication* (UK: Methuen, 1983) text refers to '. . . a signifying structure composed of signs and codes which is essential to communication'. This structure can take a variety of forms: FILM, speech, writing, painting, records, for example. O'Sullivan *et al*. argue that the word text usually '. . . refers to a message that has a physical existence of its own, independent of its sender and receiver and thus composed of representational codes.'

Text is the focal point of study in SEMIOLOGY/SEMIOTICS. Texts are not normally seen as being unproblematic but as capable of being interpreted in a variety of ways, depending on the socio-cultural background and experience of the reader. The central concern of semiology is to discover the ways in which given texts can generate a range of meanings. See CODES; DECODER; ENCODER; MESSAGE; SENDER/RECEIVER.

Texts See OPEN, CLOSED TEXTS.

Thalidomide Case The drug Thalidomide was a tranquillizer taken by women in pregnancy. It was discovered to cause acute malformation in many new-born children. The *Sunday Times* intended to publish a series of articles based upon investigations into the Thalidomide issue, but the Distillers' Company, manufacturers of the drug in the UK, sought a court injunction preventing the newspaper making its disclosures.

It was not until 1976 that the High Court agreed to the Attorney General's submission that the *Sunday Times* now be free to publish its investigation into the Thalidomide tragedy, and the amount of compensation being considered. Thus the injunction, first granted in November 1972, waived on Appeal in February 1973, and restored by the House of Lords in July 1973, demonstrated the degree to which the courts – in this case contempt of court laws were operated – could obstruct the PRESS in matters of grave public interest and concern.

The *Sunday Times* took the case to the European Court of Human Rights which found the British government in breach of Article 10 of the European Convention on Human Rights, which guarantees freedom of the press and the right of the public to be properly informed.

Thaumatrope Or 'wonder-turner'; a small cardboard disc, having different images on each surface, threaded on two pieces of silk or string which, when twisted, creates a joining of images, thus illustrating the phenomenon of PERSISTENCE OF VISION. The device was first produced by English doctor J.A. Paris in 1826. See ZOETROPE.

Theatre censorship See LORD CHAMBERLAIN.

Theatres Act, 1968 See LORD CHAMBERLAIN.

Theories and concepts of communication See ATTRIBUTION THEORY: CENTRALITY; CONGRUENCE THEORY; CONSPIRACY THEORY; CULTIVATION; DEPENDENCY THEORY; DESENSITIZATION; DETERMINISM; DEVIANCE AMPLIFICATION; DISPLACEMENT EFFECT; DOMINANT, SUBORDINATE, RADICAL; HYPHENIZED ABRIDGEMENT; IDENTIFICATION; IDEOLOGICAL STATE APPARATUS; INOCULATION EFFECT; J CURVE; JOHARI WINDOW; MAINSTREAMING; MASLOW'S HIERARCHY OF NEEDS; MEDIATION; NARCOTICIZING DYSFUNCTION; NARRATIVE PARADIGM; NEWS VALUES; NORMATIVE THEORIES OF MASS MEDIA; PARASOCIAL INTERACTION; PLAY THEORY OF MASS COMMUNICATION; POSTULATES OF COMMUNICATION; POWER VALUE; PREFERRED READING; PRESIDENTIALISM; REFLECTIVE-PROJECTIVE THEORY OF BROADCASTING AND MASS COMMUNICATION; REINFORCEMENT; SALIENCE; SAPIR-WHORF HYPOTHESIS; SEMANTIC DIFFERENTIAL; SEMIOLOGY/SEMIOTICS; SENSITIZATION; SIGNIFICATION; SIGNIFICATION SPIRAL; SOCIALIZATION; SPONTANEOUS ACTIVITY; SYMBOLIC CONVERGENCE THEORY; SYMMETRY, STRAIN TOWARDS; TECHNOLOGICAL DETERMINISM; TERRORISM AS COMMUNICATION; TRANSACTIONAL ANALYSIS; USES AND GRATIFICATIONS THEORY; VALUES.

* D. McQuail, *Mass Communication Theory: An Introduction* (UK: Sage, 2nd edition, 1987).

Thesis journalism Term most often used critically for TV programme making as well as newspaper work which sets out with a thesis or theory to prove and then shapes the material to support the theory. See PRESS.

'Third age of broadcasting' Title and theme of a book edited by Brian Wenham, former Controller, BBC-2 (UK: Faber, 1982). RADIO, the first age; TV, the second – and now the age of CABLE TELEVISION and SATELLITE TRANSMISSION poised to break up the long DUOPOLY of the BBC and IBA.

Third Programme Now BBC Radio 3, born of the government White Paper of 1946. It was intended as a response to the change in the cultural climate considered to have been brought about in part by the war-time Education Corps and the popularization of music, ART and letters, to which the BBC itself had contributed substantially. The Third Programme was devoted entirely to high CULTURE. Radio 3 continues that ambitious tradition, though in summer it lapses (on Medium Wave) into Test Cricket commentary. The name-change took place in 1967.

* A. Briggs, *Sound and Vision: The History of Broadcasting in the United Kingdom*, vol. IV (UK: Oxford University Press, 1979).

Thought reform A EUPHEMISM for BRAINWASHING.

3-D The technique of filming and projecting movie pictures that give the illusion of being three-dimensional. See STEREOSCOPY.

Tie-signs Any action – GESTURE or posture – which indicates the existence of a personal relationship is termed a tie-sign: linked arms, held hands, body closeness (or proximity), comfortable silence between two people, instinctive reciprocal movements. *Symbolic* tie-signs are wedding rings, lovers' tree engravings, etc. See COMMUNICATION, NON-VERBAL; PROXEMICS.

Time-lapse photography See HIGH-SPEED PHOTOGRAPHY.

Time-shift viewing Made possible by the introduction of the VIDEO recorder. By recording TV programmes, the viewer is released from the schedules of the BROADCASTING companies to watch his/her programmes whenever and as often as desired.

Tokenism Support without true conviction; making a GESTURE towards a principle – of free speech and debate, equality of the sexes or the races (e.g. 'token woman' or 'token black' where males and whites dominate). The term is used by.commentators to describe semi-commitment to radical standpoints in the PRESS. The *Daily Mirror*, for instance, claims to be a paper of the Left, but its attitude is often ambivalent when faced with many of the consequences of socialist IDEOLOGY. It continues to support the routine power of capital, property and profit while deploring – in a Tokenist manner – examples of the 'unacceptable face of capitalism'.

Total communication Relates to the instruction of the deaf; specifically a manual, auditory, oral system of communication recognizing the legitimacy of the LANGUAGE of signs as an essential visual reinforcement to oral and auditory aspects of communication. Total communication takes into account the fact that language development proceeds sequentially, beginning with the more primitive or simple and then progressing to more complex and sophisticated uses of SYMBOL systems, involving all sensory modes.

Total situation See LAW OF THE TOTAL SITUATION.

Touch Not the least important of the five senses, though often the most neglected. H.F. Harlow in *Learning to Love* (US: Albion, 1971) writes of his now famous experiments with baby monkeys. He had found that the deprivation of phsycial contact resulted in a failure to learn necessary responses to their own species. They became non-sociable, were unable to mate successfully or to rear their young.

Touch is an important ingredient in the transmitting of information, especially in the young when other channels of communication such as speech are undeveloped. In western society the incidence of touching between people begins to diminish when a child reaches the age of five or six, with males being touched less than females; it increases again in the teenage period, where touching and sex become equated to such an extent that touch becomes a sexual indicator unless applied by validated 'touchers' such as doctors, tailors or hairdressers.

CLASS, status and ROLES are inextricably involved in touch-permission or touch-prohibition: a nurse may touch a patient, but it is not usual for a patient to touch the nurse, where it constitutes a trespass. Self-touching is acceptable, unless it becomes socially offensive (like nose-picking), as a form of substitution for the touch of others – face and head touching, hair stroking or hand wringing, for example.

Where we cannot touch other humans we substitute pets, stroking them and cuddling them, receiving (and perhaps giving) sensations of comfort. In illness and stress, in times of grief or great happiness, touching becomes more necessary and more acceptable. Touching communicates reassurance, affection, friendship, courage-giving, support, sharing, understanding, invitation, desire, etc. The practice varies considerably from class to class, CULTURE to culture and country to country and from hemisphere to hemisphere. See COMMUNICATION, NON-VERBAL; EYE CONTACT; GESTURE; INTERPERSONAL COMMUNICATION; NON-VERBAL BEHAVIOUR: REPERTOIRE; PROXEMICS.

Tracks In FILM making, tracks are the portable 'railway lines' along which the camera, mounted on a DOLLY, moves. The term is also used to identify separate sound reels accompanying a film. These are harmonized into one at the *dubbing* stage of film production.

Traditional transmission US linguist Charles Hockett defined 16 DESIGN FEATURES characteristic of human LANGUAGE, of which *Traditional transmission* is one, described in Hockett's 'The origin of speech', *Scientific American*, 203 (1960). This design feature refers to the passing on of language from one generation to the next. 'Human genes', Hockett writes, 'carry the capacity to acquire a language, and probably also a strong drive towards its acquisition, the detailed conventions of any one language are transmitted extra-genetically by learning and teaching.'

Transactional analysis Originally an approach to psychotherapy introduced by Eric Berne, transactional analysis is now more widely used as a technique for improving INTERPERSONAL COMMUNICATION and social skills. In essence it aims to increase the individual's awareness of the intent behind both his or her own and others' communication, and to expose and eliminate, or deal with, subterfuge and dishonesty.

The details of the framework are fairly complex and readers are referred to the works recommended below for an introduction to this area. Basically, however, transactional analysis investigates any act of interpersonal communication by considering what are called the 'ego states' of the communicators.

The hypothesis is that we are all able to function out of three 'ego states' which Berne identified as the Parent, the Adult and the Child. The states are produced by a playback of recorded data of events in the past involving real people; real times, places and decisions; and real feelings. Everyone is seen as carrying these voices inside them. We interact out of these 'ego states'.

The Parent is much influenced by the pronouncements of and examples set by our own parents and other authority figures, early in our life. It is concerned with our responsibility towards ourselves and others. It can be critical and set standards but it can also be protective and caring. The Adult within us is the part of us which rationally analyses reality. It collects information and thinks it through in order to solve problems, reach conclusions and judgements, and make decisions. The Adult develops throughout life and can arbitrate between the Parent and the Child. The Child is one of our most powerful states; it contains our feelings and carries our ability to play and act creatively. It can be spontaneous and risk-taking. It can also be rebellious or alternatively compliant or servile.

A transaction is a two-person INTERACTION in which an ego state of one person stimulates an ego state of another. Transactions are analysed by assessing out of which 'ego state' people are speaking. We can distinguish these states in ourselves and others by such non-verbal cues as tone of voice or facial expression, as well as by the verbal content of the transactions. One of the chief values of Trans-actional Analysis is that it has the capacity to help clarify communication problems.
* E. Berne, *Games People Play*, (US: Grove Press, 1964); T.A. Harris, *I'm O.K. You're O.K.* (US: Harper & Row, 1969).

Transceiver Term borrowed from technology and sometimes used in discussing general communication in order to summarize the way ENCODING and DECODING functions can be accommodated within a single organism, where sender and receiver are one and the same.

Transferability of cues See BARNLUND'S TRANSACTIONAL MODEL OF COMMUNICATION.

Triad A sub-group of three people.

Triggers Words or pictures used by the media to evoke desired responses without lengthy explanation; signs in the vocabulary of those Vance Packard has described as 'symbol mani-pulators'. Packard was, of course, referring to product marketing but in the age of TV – of trials by TV, of elections by TV – politicians and ideologies lend themselves to product marketing and presentational packaging as much as soft drinks, motor cars or soap pow-ders. See PREFERRED READING; SEMIOLOGY/ SEMIOTICS.

Two-reeler A FILM lasting about 20 minutes; usually refers to comedies of the silent era.

Two-step flow model of communication See ONE-STEP, TWO-STEP, MULTI-STEP FLOW MODEL OF COMMUNICATION.

Typage In the casting of FILM or theatre parts, shunning the use of professional actors in favour of 'types' or representative characters. The term is originally ascribed to Russian film director Sergei Eisenstein (1894-1948).

Typewriter A patent for an 'Artificial Machine or Method for Impressing or Transcribing of Letters Singly or Progressively one after another, as in Writing, whereby all Writing Whatever may be Engrossed in Paper or Parch-ment so Neat and Exact as not to be distin-guished from Print' was taken out in the UK as early as 1714, but the first practical typewriter working faster than handwriting was probably that of American Christopher Latham Sholes (1868) who, after several improvements to his machine, signed up with E. Remington & Sons, gunsmiths of New York. The first Remington machines were marketed in 1874.

1878 saw the introduction of the shift-key typewriter, followed by machines which for the first time allowed the typist to actually *see* what he/she was typing (1883). That jack-of-all-trades among inventors, Thomas Alva Edison (1847-1931) produced an electrically operated machine containing a printing wheel, in 1872, though it was many years before a commer-cially viable electric machine was produced (by James Smathes in 1920).

IBM introduced the famous 'golf-ball' elec-tric typewriter in 1961, allowing for different type faces and type sizes to be used with the same machine. Today electronic typewriters possess the mind and memory of the computer; they self-correct, they work silently, they can bank text which is recalled at the press of a button and they can print out at considerable speed. They have graduated into the *word pro-cessor*, the miracle worker every author dreams of finding one day in his/her Christmas stock-ing. See TECHNOLOGY OF THE MEDIA; WORD PROCESSING.

Typewriter culture Another term for SAMIZDAT, or unofficial publication, circulated in small numbers, often by hand, in countries that censor free speech. Where PRINTING presses are strictly licensed, the only means of reproducing works of literature and comment is by typewriter and carbon copies, though obviously much Samizdat literature is printed on unlicensed presses, illegally, and at risk of imprisonment for those involved.

Typographical culture That which was cen-trally based upon the printed word; dislodged from dominance if not superseded, by the graphic revolution caused by PHOTOGRAPHY, moving FILM and BROADCASTING.

U-certificate See CERTIFICATION OF FILMS.

Ullswater Committee Report on Broad-casting, 1936 This government-appointed committee under the chairmanship of Vis-count Ullswater was given the task of making recommendations on the future of the BBC once its first charter expired on 31 December 1936. The report praised the BBC for its impartiality and catholicity but chided it for the heaviness of its Sunday entertainment. The Charter of the BBC was renewed following the report for another 10 years; the number of governors was increased from five to seven and the ban on advertisements was to continue – though sponsorship was to be permitted in the case of TV (a right the BBC only seldom exploited).

Like reports before and after it, Ullswater made clear the very serious public responsibility of BROADCASTING: 'The influence of broadcasting upon the mind and speech of the nation' made it an 'urgent necessity in the national interest that the broadcasting service should at all times be conducted in the best possible manner and to the best possible advantage of the people'. Two other matters elicited concern. The first related to criticisms of the monolithic nature of the BBC (under the rigorous direction of Lord Reith) and the Committee recommended more internal decentralization of control, especially towards the national regions. The second concern, published in a Reservation written by Clement Attlee (1883–1967), future Labour Prime Minister, called into question the BBC's 'impartiality' at the time of the General Strike (1926): 'I think,' wrote Attlee, 'that even in war-time the BBC must be allowed to broadcast opinions other than those of the Government.' See COMMISSIONS/COMMITTEES ON THE MEDIA; PUBLIC SERVICE BROADCASTING.

Ultra-violet/fluorescent photography Used in the examination of forged or altered documents, identifying certain chemical compounds, and in the examination of bacterial colonies. See HOLOGRAPHY; INFRA-RED PHOTOGRAPHY.

Underground press Or radical, alternative or SAMIZDAT; those newspapers which are committedly anti-ESTABLISHMENT, opposing in part or entirely the political and cultural conventions of the time; often publishing information or views seen as threatening by those in authority, and likely to incur CENSORSHIP.

In the UK the so-called 'pauper press' of the 19th c., finding its readership in the increasingly literate working CLASS, was subject to harshly repressive measures by government. Editors such as William Cobbett, Henry Hetherington, William Sherwin and Richard Carlile courted arrest and imprisonment and the shutting down of their presses as a routine professional hazard. Wooler's *Black Dwarf* stirred the government to wrath with its criticism of the authorities in their handling of the Peterloo Massacre (1819). Wooler escaped LIBEL action on the plea that he could not be said to have written articles which he set up in type without the intervention of a *pen*.

Cobbett's *Weekly Political Register* had a substantial circulation despite the crippling STAMP DUTY which forced him to charge one shilling and a halfpenny per copy. Carlile's *Republican* was both republican and atheist;

the Chartist *Oracle of Reason* incurred blasphemy prosecutions while Bradlaugh's *National Reformer* declared itself 'Published in Defiance of Her Majesty's Government'. So long as radical newspapers could fight off the need to win ADVERTISING, they could prosper, despite prosecutions. They were edited by people close to the working class and they reflected the chief perspectives of the vanguard of the working class movement and directed themselves to its increased politicization.

Survival, however, depended on the ability of the radical PRESS to pay its way through circulation.

The costs of publishing and the reliance upon advertising have proved formidable barriers to underground, radical or alternative newspapers and periodicals in the post-2nd World War period (from 1945). In the 1960s they abounded – *Oz, IT, Frendz* and *Ink* – all in one way or another getting up the nose of Authority, the *Oz Schoolkids Issue* earning for itself the longest-ever obscenity trial (See OZ TRIAL).

Distribution has proved yet another hazard for the small radical press. In the UK this is practically a DUOPOLY of W.H. Smith and Menzies whose hesitancy over providing the radical press with distribution outlets has been rather more to do with a view that radicals are just not good business rather than for ideological reasons.

It would seem that the best future for alternative publications is for them to be regional or local, and several notable journals, committed to community politics, have been produced (off and on) during the 1970s and 1980s. Among these are the Welsh paper *Rebecca* ('the champion of ordinary people'), *Rochdale's Alternative Press*, Bury's *Metro News* and the *East End News*.

* S. Harrison, *Poor Men's Guardians: A Survey of the Struggles for a Democratic Newspaper Press, 1763–1973*. (UK: Lawrence & Wishart, 1974); P. Hollis, *The Pauper Press* (UK: Oxford University Press, 1970).

Uses and gratifications theory View that mass media audiences make active use of what the media have to offer arising from a complex set of *needs* which the media in one form or another gratify. Broadly similar uses have been categorized by researchers based on questionnaires or interviews. An example is the *compensatory* use of the media – to make up for lack of education, perhaps, lack of status or social success. Where the media have a *supplementing* use, the audience may be applying what they see, hear and read in social situations – as subject-matter for conversation, for example.

In 'The television audience: a revised perspective' in D. McQuail, ed., *Sociology of* the Mass Media (UK: Penguin, 1972) Denis McQuail, Jay G. Blumler and J.R. Brown define four major categories of need which the media serve to gratify: (1) *Diversion* (escape from constraints of routine; escape from the burdens of problems; emotional release). (2) *Personal relationships* (companionship; social utility). (3) *Personal identity* (personal reference; reality exploration; value reinforcement). (4) *Surveillance* (need for information in our complex world – 'Television news helps me to make up my mind about things').

Blumler and E. Katz in the book of which they are editors, *The Uses of Mass Communication* (US: Sage, 1974) emphasize the social origin of the needs which the media purport to gratify. Thus where a social situation causes tension and conflict, the media may provide easement, or where the social situation gives rise to questions about VALUES, the media provide affirmation and REINFORCEMENT.

Uses and gratifications theory is in alliance with the grand process of analysing human *motivation* contributed to by organizational theorists, psychologists and educationalists, and concerning lower and higher orders; cognitive (intellectual) and affective (emotional) dimensions; activity and passivity and external and internal responses. See COGNITIVE (AND AFFECTIVE); COMMUNICATION MODELS; EFFECTS OF THE MASS MEDIA; IDENTIFICATION; MASLOW'S HIERARCHY OF NEEDS; SURVEILLANCE.

Values Each society, social group or individual has certain ideas, beliefs, ways of behaving, upon which is placed a *value*. A collection of these values, the criteria for judgement of one often acting as REINFORCEMENT for others, may amount to a *system* of values. Such a system, if it is not to cause DISSONANCE in a person, has either to be generally consistent, or be perceived as generally consistent.

Values are not merely systems of personal belief: they represent shared attitudes within social GROUPS and society at large, of approval and disapproval, of judgements favourable and unfavourable, towards other individuals, ideas, objects (such as the value placed on *property*), social action and events. Like NORMS, values vary from one social group or society to another; and they change over time and in different circumstances.

An individual's perception and interpretation of reality will be influenced by the values of the social groups or society to which he/she belongs. The pervasiveness of such values ensures that they are enmeshed in all aspects of communication processes. The images and CODES which are the stock-in-trade of the mass media are *shaped* by value systems;

and their intention is to support and reinforce the value systems that shape them.

In his Introduction to J. Tunstall ed., *Mass Sociology* (UK: Constable, 1970), Jeremy Tunstall remarks that 'The media are saturated with social values of every kind.' These values come to the fore, achieve clearest definition, at times of crisis and conflict. An industrial strike which 'holds the country to ransom' usually brings out a bristling array of values and value judgements in the media, especially the PRESS. Obviously, two value systems are in collision. Assuming that the striker is not merely a 'subversive trouble-maker', he/she is acting from *injured* values; that is, perhaps, the feeling that his/her work is under*valued* and that this undervaluing is symbolized by underpay. Equally, the striker may *value* consultation – about new workshop arrangements, perhaps, or redundancy plans. If he/she has not been consulted, or his/her union not consulted, then something must be done about it; a protest made – a principle (or a value) fought for.

The media largely see this situation from the other end of the telescope. They see order disrupted; that is, the orderly flow of production – which is *valued* because the orderly flow of production means the orderly flow of profits. Disrupted profit is bad. It harms *monetary* value. We do not hear of this clash of values very often in the nation's press because the press is rarely in the business of putting its opponents' points of view, expressing its opponents' values. Theirs is the voice we hear; theirs the *dominant* voice.

Of course, in times of even greater crisis than a disruptive strike, such as in a war between nation and nation, the values of combat combine in a single media voice. Those expressing other values are shouted down, ignored or vilified as traitors. In such times, even the value placed upon the need for 'looking before you leap', which would in normal times be a matter for CONSENSUS, of wide agreement, may be deemed suddenly value*less*. At this point, all communication becomes PROPAGANDA. See CULTURE; IDEOLOGY; MALE-AS-NORM; MYTH; NEWS VALUES; SEMIOLOGY/SEMIOTICS; STRUCTURALISM.

Vamp Early word for sex-star in the movies. In 1914 producer William Fox (1879–1952) created a star by going to the farthest extreme away from screen-idol Mary Pickford, SYMBOL of purity and innocence, by imposing a parody of sensuality and eroticism on Theda Bara in the FILM adaptation of the Kipling poem *A Fool There Was*. The word 'vamp' was used in the publicity for the film whose financial success helped Fox set up his own studio, among the most important of the 1920s.

V-discs In 1943, during the 2nd World War (1939–45), record companies and musicians agreed to waive fees and contractual rights to a series of very high-quality musical offerings to the US forces. Such recordings, many of them by giants of the jazz world – Benny Goodman, Louis Armstrong, Duke Ellington – are now prized by collectors.

Verbal devices in speech-making Max Atkinson in his illuminating study of the speech-making techniques of politicians and other well-known contemporary orators, *Our Masters' Voices: The Language and Body Language of Politics* (UK: Methuen, 1984), analyses various forms of what the Shorter Oxford English Dictionary terms *claptraps* – linguistic or non-verbal devices to catch applause. Particularly successful, says the author, is the *list of three*, which stimulates audience response, reinforces that stimulus and then pushes it to the climax. *Antithesis* is also an effective claptrap ('I come to bury Caesar, not to praise him'). Atkinson cautions the would-be orator that these devices require skill, timing and judgement to be effective and claptrap 'always involves the use of more than one technique at a time'.

Victim funds These were organized by the UNDERGROUND PRESS in the 19th c. to help out fellow papers subjected to heavy government fines for evading the TAXES ON KNOWLEDGE – STAMP DUTY, Advertising Tax, Paper Duty and State Security System Tax. Between 1830 and 1836 at least 1130 cases of selling 'un-stamped' papers were prosecuted in London alone. See NEWSPAPERS, ORIGINS.

Video The process whereby TV programmes can be recorded on a cassette tape proved to be one of the most popular technical developments in the late 1970s and the 1980s.

Video permits TIME-SHIFT VIEWING, that is, recording TV programmes off air for later viewing. Also, it can be completely independent of the TV channels, being able to play mass-produced cassette programmes of all kinds, especially feature films. The implications for television BROADCASTING, and for the FILM industry, indeed for the survival of cinema, are considerable. Where, in the past, for example, it would have been difficult for a TV viewer to avoid at some time seeing the BBC or Independent Television News, the occasional DOCUMENTARY programme such as *Panorama* or *TV Eye*, a play by Dennis Potter, a programme on ethnic minorities on CHANNEL FOUR or an in-depth science programme such as BBC2's *Horizon*, video enables him or her to by-pass even the most casual or accidental TV encounter with communal, national or international ISSUES dealt with on PUBLIC SERVICE BROADCASTING channels. On the other hand, video enables the viewer to unburden his or her viewing life entirely from the risks of *Dallas*, quiz shows, party political broadcasts and adverts for dog and cat food.

The video CAMERA has given film makers as much freedom as the video recorder has given the TV viewer. It is lighter than traditional film cameras, cheaper both to buy and to operate and allows immediate playback. Film-making need no longer be the preserve of those with multi-million pound backing. The field is wide open to individuals, cooperatives, pressure GROUPS, clubs, schools – anyone with a case to urge, beliefs or feelings to express – to counter, at least at the level of a local community, the dominant voices of the national broadcasters or mass media communicators generally. See CAMCORDER; INTERACTIVE VIDEO; LASERVISION.

Video Box CHANNEL FOUR offers members of the public the opportunity to make their own personal comments on TELEVISION programmes, using the Video Box. One venue is the National Museum of Photography, Film and Television in Bradford (See IMEX). You step inside the box which, resembles a public phone-booth, and have 60 precious seconds to state your case. Channel 4 then makes its selection from the clamouring competition and broadcasts the results on its programme, *Video Box*.

Video-disc See LASERVISION.

Videogram Machine which translates pictures from TELEVISION into newspaper colour pictures, first used in the UK by Eddie Shah whose all-colour electronically produced *Today* newspaper was first published on 4 March 1986. The paper passed into the ownership of Australian PRESS BARON Rupert Murdoch a year later.

Video-nasties A market that developed in the 1980s of specially-made-for-video films of a singularly nasty, brutal and sexist nature. Among the most notorious nasties is *SS Extermination Camp* about atrocities performed by Nazis in an all-woman concentration camp. *I Spit on Your Grave* is about a young girl who has been gang-raped, while *Nightmares In A Damaged Brain* shows a ten-year-old boy hacking off a woman's head with an axe while she is being raped by his father. Others of equally sublime dreadfulness have been *Driller Killer* and *Snuff*. Court action in the UK in 1982 against several of these films led to their enforced withdrawal from circulation but, to the considerable disgust of Mary Whitehouse and the National Viewers' and Listeners Association – among many others – there was no order made for their destruction. However, the Conservative government brought in rigorous controls of video nasties with the VIDEO RECORDING ACT, 1984.

Video Recording Act, 1984 Passed through Parliament in the UK with all-Party support, MP Graham Bright's measure was designed to restrict the access of young persons to VIDEO

NASTIES, many of which by-passed the usual vetting process of the BRITISH BOARD OF FILM CENSORS.

The Act established by Statute an Authority (initially the BBFC) whose purpose is to classify VIDEO cassettes as suitable for home viewing and to censor those deemed unsuitable. Fines of up to £20,000 are liable for dealers and distributors breaking the law. All video works must be submitted for scrutiny, classification and certification unless they are educational or concerned with sport, religion or music.

However, if such videos 'to any extent' portray 'Human sexual activity' or 'Mutilation, torture or other acts of gross violence' or show 'human genital organs' they also have to be submitted to the censors.

See CENSORSHIP; MORAL PANIC.

* M. Barker, ed. *The Video Nasties: Freedom and Censorship in the Media* (UK: Pluto, 1984).

Viewdata Invented by British Telecom, using a TELEPHONE link to marry the home or office TV set to huge computer databanks of constantly updated information. The trade name of the service is *Prestel*, started up in 1979. Because it is possible to cross-question the computers down the telephone line, the way is open for armchair shopping. Many middle-man services can be by-passed as a result of Viewdata. You can book a holiday, check houses for sale, even summon up legal advice.

Viewers: light, medium and heavy Research into the amount and nature of TELEVISION viewing discriminates between the light viewer, generally classified as watching TV for two hours or less a day; the medium viewer, watching for between two and three hours a day and the heavy viewer watching for four hours or more a day. In the analysis of viewer response, special attention has been paid to the differences of attitude to ISSUES and controversies which can be detected between light and heavy viewers, and thus the influence TV programmes may have on attitude formation and attitude change. See MAINSTREAMING; MEAN WORLD SYNDROME; RESONANCE.

Violence and the media See BROADCASTING STANDARDS COUNCIL; CENSORSHIP; 'CLEAN-UP TV' MOVEMENT; DESENSITIZATION; EFFECTS OF THE MASS MEDIA; LONGFORD COMMITTEE REPORT ON PORNOGRAPHY, 1972; PORNOGRAPHY; REINFORCEMENT; SENSITIZATION; SHOTGUN APPROACH (TO NEWS COVERAGE); SIGNIFICATION SPIRAL; SLEEPER EFFECT; TERRORISM AS COMMUNICATION; VALUES; VIOLENCE ON TV: CODES OF PRACTICE; WILLIAMS COMMITTEE REPORT ON OBSCENITY AND FILM CENSORSHIP, 1979.

Violence on TV: codes of practice Both the BBC and the IBA have CODES of practice relating to the portrayal of violence in their programmes; each code has undergone up-datings since being drawn up in the 1960s. The publication *The Portrayal of Violence on Television: BBC and IBA Guidelines* (1980) put together the two authorities' recommendations. The BBC's 'A Revised Note of Guidance, March 1979' was based upon recommendations made by a committee chaired by Monica Sims which in turn derived criteria from earlier (1972) guidenotes. The IBA reprint 'Violence in Television Programmes', the ITV Code, was revised in 1971 and confirmed by the IBA's Working Party on the subject which reported in 1973, 1975 and 1978.

In the section 'BBC: The Portrayal of Violence in Television Programmes', the possible impact of violence on the screen especially upon 'disadvantaged minorities within the audience, including the young, the immature, the emotionally disturbed and those with aggressive tendencies' is acknowledged. There must be protection but not over-protectiveness: 'It is necessary to remove from programmes elements which might stimulate . . . dangerous or irresponsible behaviour, but at the same time, this protectiveness should be balanced by the need to portray courage, defence of the innocent, maintenance of law and order and rejection of tyranny.'

The guidelines offer the following four criteria to programme-makers: he or she must ask him/herself (1) is violent action essential to the story? (2) If essential, how much detail is necessary for the sake of clarity? (3) Am I allowing a violent act to be shown in a way that may encourage dangerous imitation by the young and immature? (4) Am I including violent action to create excitement and to hold attention?

Part two of *The Portrayal of Violence on Television* includes the ITV Code which declares 'Violence is not only physical: it can be verbal, psychological and even metaphysical or supernatural. Whatever form the violence in a programme may take its inclusion can only be justified by the dramatic or informational context in which it is seen, and the skill, insight and sensitivity of the portrayal.' The Code states that programme-makers must keep several considerations in mind: people seldom view just one programme and 'An acceptable minimum of violence in each individual programme may add to an intolerable level over a period'.

Also, 'There is no evidence that the portrayal of violence for good or "legitimate" ends is likely to be less harmful to the individual, or to society, than the portrayal of violence for evil ends.' Equally 'It may be just as dangerous for society to conceal the results of violence or to minimize them as to let people see clearly the full consequences of violent behaviour, however gruesome: what may be better for society may be emotionally upsetting or more offensive for the individual viewer.'

The authorities looked again at their codes of practice in 1983 and both concluded that they were working satisfactorily. See BROADCASTING STANDARDS COUNCIL.

Vistavision Paramount's response to 20th Century Fox's CINEMASCOPE in the 1950s. The negative was made on 70 mm stock and reduced to 35 mm during printing, to reduce graininess.

Visual display unit (VDU) The cathode ray tube or TV screen on which the data of a computer are displayed. Information can be summoned through a keyboard or worked on directly with a light pen.

Vitaphone Trade name of the first successful synchronous movie sound, introduced in 1926 by Warner Brothers. On 6 August at the Warner Theatre in New York, John Barrymore starred in *Don Juan*, to the accompaniment of a Vitaphone 16-inch 33 r.p.m. disc recording of voice and music. Curiously *Don Juan* caused less audience excitement than the Vitaphone shorts that accompanied it, such as the New York Philharmonic playing Wagner's Tannhäuser Overture. The real sensation of the Talkies was Warners' next picture, *The Jazz Singer* (1927) starring Al Jolson. There were, in fact, only 281 words spoken in the FILM, all of them ad-libbed by Jolson. See SYNCHRONOUS SOUND.

Vocal cues All the oral aspects of speech except the words themselves; *pitch* – the highness or lowness of voice; *rate* – rapidity of expression; *volume*; *quality* – the pleasantness or unpleasantness of voice tone or delivery, and *enunciation* – pronunciation and articulation. See PARALANGUAGE.

Voiceover In FILM and TELEVISION film production, voiceover accompanies what the audience is seeing with comment – explanation and analysis – without the commentator being on view. In feature films voiceover is often that of the chief character in a story though the DOCUMENTARY approach of an unidentified narrator is also common. Voiceover plays a significant role in shaping the MEANING of a film TEXT. It signals the way that audience is expected to read what is seen and heard in a programme. In this sense, voiceover closes down a text to a prescribed meaning, allowing the viewer little room for interpretation. See NARRATIVE; OPEN, CLOSED TEXTS.

Volapük Or 'World's speech'; artificial LANGUAGE invented by Bavarian pastor Johan Martin Schleyer in 1879, when it was acclaimed as mankind's universal speech of the future. See ESPERANTO; IDO.

Vox popping Collecting the opinions of large numbers of the general public (*vox populi* is Latin for 'voice of the people') in order to broadcast public reaction to a current ISSUE or topic.

'War of the Worlds' Title of the American CBS network RADIO adaptation by Howard Koch, produced and narrated by Orson Welles (1938), of H.G. Wells's famous story. Conveying the immediacy of a combat report from a war correspondent, the production actually convinced many listeners that an interplanetary war had broken out. However, reports to the effect that Orson Welles's radio 'hype' had caused panic in the streets have taken on the magic of legend, and become somewhat exaggerated in the telling. See IDENTIFICATION; PARASOCIAL INTERACTION; RADIO DRAMA.

War of the Unstamped See STAMP DUTY; TAXES ON KNOWLEDGE; VICTIM FUNDS.

Washoe See COMMUNICATION, ANIMAL.

Watchdogs Newspapers pride themselves on their role as watchdogs of injustice, abuse and corruption. Research tends to point to the media being rather less than wholly effective in this capacity; generally to follow rather than lead in the investigation of abuse and to be guilty of omission as much as commission. Robert Cirino in 'Bias through selection and omission: automobile safety, smoking' in S. Cohen and J. Young, eds., *The Manufacture of News* (UK: Constable, 1973) writes of investigations into the ways ISSUES such as inadequate car safety and smoking/lung cancer have been systematically ignored by the US mass media. Cirino reinforces the case presented by Ralph Nader in *Unsafe at Any Speed* (US: Grossman Publications, 1965), that 'by dominating the channels of communications through which the customer receives his information about automobiles, [the auto industry] has obscured the relation of vehicle design to life and limb and has kept quiet its technical capability of building crash-worthy vehicles.'

The response of the PRESS in the US to the horrors of the Vietnam War eventually became overwhelming, but not by newspapers being at the forefront of the pack of watchdogs, rather in their reaction to the growing number of wounded American soldiers returning to the States and criticizing the conduct of the war.

True 'watchdoggery' can only come about through genuine media independence – from ADVERTISING and sales revenue, from the influence of capital or institutional control. And yet, subject to all the usual constraints, the *Sunday Times* pressed on with its revelation of the THALIDOMIDE CASE and the *Washington*

Post, by uncovering WATERGATE, contributed towards the toppling of a president. See NEWS VALUES.

* J. Curran, A. Smith and P. Wingale, eds., *Impacts and Influences: Essays on Media Power in the 20th Century* (UK: Methuen, 1987).

Watergate Scene of one of history's most famous break-ins, and source of one of modern history's most dramatic scandals which eventually led to the resignation of the US president. The apartment block called Watergate in Washington DC was the 1972 election campaign headquarters of the National Committee of the Democratic Party. It was broken into in June by agents of the rival Republican Party's Committee to Re-elect President Richard Nixon. They were caught in the act as they were removing electronic bugging devices.

The ensuing cover-up was penetrated and revealed by two reporters on the *Washington Post*, Bob Woodward and Carl Bernstein, fed with significant information by a mysterious DEEP THROAT within government, possibly close to the president. A Senate investigation committee pushed fearlessly against presidential closed doors. Eventually the Supreme Court forced the White House to give access to tape recordings made, at Nixon's command, over a long period in the president's office. The tapes proved Nixon's complicity in the Watergate Affair.

He was the first president of the US to resign; if he had not resigned, he would have been impeached by Congress. His successor, President Ford, extended a blanket pardon to Nixon, but not to his associates, several of whom ended up in jail (and most of whom wrote successful books on their experiences). Watergate is varyingly cited as a supreme example of investigative journalism; a classic case study of official corruption and an alarming illustration of the paranoia that sometimes comes with power and authority. However, it is perhaps most importantly a breathtaking glimpse of the nature of open government and the potential of the democratic process. No Watergate revelations could possibly take place in the UK: the OFFICIAL SECRETS ACT would have brought down the steel curtain of CENSORSHIP long before the tide of proof of corruption swirled around the feet of a British prime minister. See SPYCATCHER CASE.

Wesley and MacLean's model of communication, 1957 In their article 'A conceptual model for communications research' in *Journalism Quarterly*, 34, B.H. Wesley and M.S. MacLean develop NEWCOMB'S ABX MODEL OF COMMUNICATION, 1953 with the aim of encapsulating the overall mass communication process. To Newcomb's A (communicator) B (communicator) X (any event or object in the environment of A, B which is the subject of communication), Wesley and MacLean add a fourth element, C. This represents the editorial-communicating function – the process of deciding what and how to communicate.

Newcomb's model represented chiefly interpersonal communication; it was a triangular formation, with A, B and X interacting equilaterally. Wesley and MacLean indicate that the mass media process crucially shifts the balance, bringing A (in this case the would-be communicator) and C (the mass communication organization and its agents who control the CHANNEL) closer together. C is both channel and mediator of A's transmission of X to B (now classifiable as audience), and B's contact with X is more remote than in the Newcomb model, if it exists at all save through the combined 'processing' of AC. FEEDBACK is represented by f.

It can be seen from the model that X need not

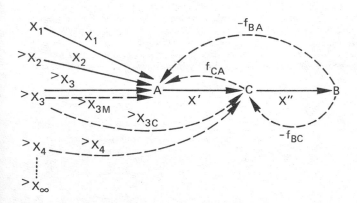

Wesley and MacLean's model of communication, 1957

go through to B via A and C but via C alone. The role of C as intermediary has a dual character, *purposive* when the process involves conveying a MESSAGE through C from an 'advocate' – a politician, for example, and *non-purposive* when it is a matter of conveying the unplanned events of the world to an audience.

The main thrust of the model appears to be emphasizing the *dependency* of B upon A and C. What is missing from the model, and what later thinking about mass media processes insists upon, are the numerous message *sources* and *influences* which work upon B other than AC, and counter-balance the influence of AC – such as the family, friends, members of peer GROUPS, workmates, colleagues, or wider influences such as school, church, trade unions, etc. See COMMUNICATION MODELS; SIGNIFICANT OTHERS.

Western Hollywood's most popularly successful transformation of the past into MYTH, with the enshrining of heroic VALUES – self-help, individualism, the legitimization of violence in the name of timeless (though rarely analysed) notions of Law and Order, and of human rights equated with access to and possession of the earth. The Western has held a firm grip on the imagination of every generation of FILM-goer since 1903 when Edwin S. Porter's *The Great Train Robbery* set the GENRE off to a brisk and colourful gallop. Like the best myths and legends, the Western told a good story and upheld (generally) the principle that Good must triumph over Evil. It has also been sustained, in a world of increasing urbanization, by open spaces and magnificent landscapes.

Some of the cinema's best directors found the Western to their liking. The greatest of these, John Ford (1895–1973), guilty more than once of if not racial prejudice, racial insensitivity, nevertheless managed to disarm doubters by the sweep of his narratives, his acute eye for detail, his humour and his search for three dimensions in his characters. His *Stagecoach* (1939) and *The Searchers* (1956) are considered to be among the finest Westerns, along with Fred Zinnemann's *High Noon*

(1952), George Stevens's *Shane* (1953) and Howard Hawks's *Rio Bravo* (1958).

As well as fine directors, the Western has commanded the talents of practically every star in the Hollywood firmament: Alan Ladd, Gary Cooper, John Wayne, Henry Fonda, James Stewart, Paul Newman, Marlene Dietrich, etc. So attractive was the form that it tempted the Italians into emulation, with their so-called SPAGHETTI WESTERNS, which drained the myth of all meaning and pumped it up with cine-blood and senseless carnage (but which just occasionally redeemed themselves with timely humour).

Westminster view Opinion that the media in the UK take their cue from and align their perspectives to the standpoint of the activities of Parliament. This produces the simplistic equation – politics equals parliament, and can result in a less than adequate coverage of political events which take place away from Westminster. See POLITICS OF ACCOMMODATION.

Whistle blowing A whistle blower is usually an individual within an organization – industrial, commercial, governmental, etc. – who can no longer keep silent about practices in that organization; perhaps because he/she perceives them as unsafe, corrupt, dishonest or misleading. Almost invariably whistle blowers act out of conscience. Their need for security is outweighed by a higher-order need, to square behaviour with a sense of VALUES (See MASLOW'S HIERARCHY OF NEEDS): they must speak out against the perceived abuse, even though their 'going public', by leaking information to the media, may result in dismissal. Almost invariably whistle blowers, however much their revelations are in the public interest, suffer for their determination to speak out. Where government practices are concerned, the would-be whistle blower faces the full battery of the law; in particular, the OFFICIAL SECRETS ACT represents a catch-all form of CENSORSHIP.

White's gatekeeper model, 1950 The existence of 'gate areas' along channels of communication was identified by Kurt Lewin in 'Channels of group life' in *Human Relations*, 1 (1947). At such points, decisions are made to

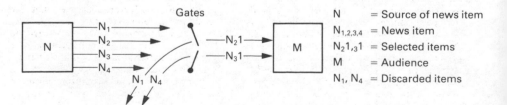

White's gatekeeper model, 1950

select out information passing through the gate (See GATEKEEPING). Lewin's particular study was concerned with decisions about household food purchases, but he drew a comparison with the flow of news in MASS COMMUNICATION. D.M. White in an article entitled 'The "Gatekeepers": a case study in the selection of news', in *Journalism Quarterly*, 27 (1950), applied Lewin's idea in a study of the telegraph wire editor of an American non-metropolitan newspaper:

Today the model is only acceptable as a starting point for analysis of the gatekeeping process; indeed it is a useful exercise for the student to build on the model by adding important factors which White does not include – such as the organizational elements of the mass communication process which constrain and direct it. The model also indicates only a single gate and a single gatekeeper, where in practice news passes through any gatekeepers, official and unofficial, direct and indirect. White's model should be studied in relation to MCNELLY's MODEL OF NEWS FLOW 1959 and GALTUNG and RUGE'S MODEL OF SELECTIVE GATEKEEPING, 1965.

Williams Committee Report on Obscenity and Film Censorship, 1979 Under the chairmanship of Bernard Williams, philosopher and then Provost of King's College, Cambridge, the Committee was set up in July 1977 by the Labour Home Secretary Merlyn Rees and reported in October 1979. The task of the Committee was 'to review the laws concerning obscenity, indecency and violence in publications, displays and entertainments in England and Wales, except in the field of broadcasting, and to review the arrangements for film censorship in England and Wales; and to make recommendations'.

Concern throughout the investigation and Report was for proposals that 'should be capable of being translated into legislation which will be rational and workable'. Among the Report's many recommendations were (1) that the existing variety of laws in the field of PORNOGRAPHY etc. 'should be scrapped and a comprehensive new statute should start afresh'. (2) Terms such as 'obscene', 'indecent' and 'deprave and corrupt' should be 'abandoned as having outlived their usefulness'. (3) The law should 'rest partly on the basis of harms caused by or involved in the existence of the material: these alone can justify prohibitions; and partly on the basis of the public's legitimate interest in not being offended by the display and availability of the material: this can justify no more than the imposition of restrictions designed to protect the ordinary citizen from unreasonable offence'. (4) The principal object of the law should be to prevent

certain kinds of material causing offence to reasonable people or being made available to young people.

The Report differentiated between the process of *restriction* and *prohibition*: 'Only a small class of material should be forbidden to those who want it, because an objective assessment of likely harm does not support a wider prohibition.' In line with this liberal stance, the Committee believed that the printed word 'should be neither restricted nor prohibited since its nature makes it neither immediately offensive nor capable of involving the harms we identify, and because of its importance in conveying ideas'. A difference is clearly recognized between the likely impact – through easy access – of pictorial material and that of reading matter which requires the extra effort on the part of the recipient of the MESSAGE to incur what the Report called the 'harm condition' – where 'members of the public are upset, distressed, disgusted, outraged or put out'.

Prohibited material 'should consist of photographs and films whose production appears to the court to have involved the exploitation for sexual purposes' of those under 16, or which 'gives reason to believe that actual physical harm was inflicted on that person'. Mindful of the readiness in some quarters to take practically anything and anybody to court for alleged purveying of harmful pornography or violent material, the Report advised that no proceedings should be instituted in respect of a prohibition offence 'other than by and with the consent of the Director of Public Prosecutions'.

On film CENSORSHIP the Report recommended that the power of local authorities to vet films 'on the basis of their powers to licence cinemas should be ended', and a statutory board be created to take up these powers and the functions of the BRITISH BOARD OF FILM CENSORS. The Film Examining Board, as the Report would have it named, would 'establish the policy and principles of film censorship within the criteria laid down by statute'.

After exhaustive analysis of often conflicting data, evidence and opinion on the effects of pornography, the Report concluded that 'the role of pornography in influencing the state of society is a minor one. To think anything else, and in particular to regard pornography as having a crucial or even a significant effect on essential social values, is to get the problem of pornography out of proportion with the many other problems that face our society today.'

The publication of the Williams Committee recommendations coincided with a change of government in the UK. No direct or immediate legislation resulted from the Report. See LONGFORD COMMITTEE REPORT ON PORNOGRAPHY, 1972.

* B. Williams, ed., *Obscenity and Film Censorship: An Abridgement of the Williams Report* (UK: Cambridge University Press, 1981).

Wipe An optical effect in cinema and TV in which an image appears to wipe off the previous image. Very widely used in films in the 1930s.

Wired world Or wired society; term used to describe the new, post-industrial economy – a telecommunications NETWORK bringing to the home multi-CHANNEL cable and satellite TV, electronic mail, push-button business transactions, all, theoretically, on a universal scale. See INFORMATION TECHNOLOGY.

Wireless telegraphy In the 1870s, James Clark Maxwell (1831–79), first professor of experimental physics at the University of Cambridge, argued that wireless TELEGRAPHY would be possible by employing electro-magnetic waves. In 1885, Welsh electrical engineer Sir William Preece (1834–1913) sent currents between two insulated squares of wire a quarter of a mile apart. Two years later Heinrich Rudolf Hertz (1857–94), German physicist, proved the existence of radio waves and in 1894 English physicist Sir Oliver Lodge demonstrated how messages could be transmitted and received without wires.

Similar pioneer work had been conducted by Italian Guglielmo Marconi (1874–1937) who arrived in England to further his ideas. Supported by the then engineer-in-chief of the Post Office telegraphs, Preece, Marconi filed an application for a wireless patent (1896) and he was soon sending long-distance messages by MORSE CODE, first across the Bristol and then the English Channel. His telegraph was used to save a ship in distress in the North Sea and it was rapidly accepted that RADIO equipment was essential on board all ships. The British Admiralty paid Marconi £20,000 a year for the use of his system in the Royal Navy.

By 1901, wireless messages were being transmitted from Cornwall to Newfoundland, tapped out in morse. A year later R.A. Fissenden of the University of Pittsburg transmitted the sound of a human voice over a distance of a mile. Further progress was made possible by the invention of the thermionic valve or electron tube, by English electrical engineer John Ambrose Fleming (1904). This device served to change the minute alternating current of a radio signal into a direct current, capable of actuating a TELEPHONE receiver or the needle of a meter. American physicist Lee De Forest improved the valve by making amplification possible. In 1910 De Forest fitted what he named a 'radio-phone' on the roof of the Metropolitan Opera House in New York,

enabling listeners to hear the voices of the singers 100 miles away.

The 1st World War (1914–18) accelerated developments in radio, where it received baptism as a weapon of PROPAGANDA – by the Germans. The future possibilities for radio were encapsulated by American engineer David Sarnoff when in 1916, he declared, 'I have in mind a plan of development which would make radio a "household utility" like the piano or electricity. The idea is to bring music into the house by wireless.'

Wireless Telegraphy Act, 1904 The result of a meeting of the major international powers held in Berlin in 1903 to prepare an international plan for the regulation of WIRELESS TELEGRAPHY at sea. The UK government required legislation in order to sign the ensuing agreements which enforced uniform rules of working. The Act established universal wireless licensing in Britain, shore and sea, granted by the Post Master General with the consent of the Admiralty and Army Council and the Board of Trade.

Word processing A method of manipulating text to produce perfect 'top' copies at extremely high reproduction speeds by means of electronic typing. The word processor is a TYPEWRITER which can display text on a TV screen, correct and alter copy electronically, store text and display text instantly and print out, in single copies or multiples. The WP system takes electronic typewriting a stage further by adding telecommunications facilities which enable the system to be hooked up to computers, dictating machines, electronic files, printers, etc. in close or distant locations. See COMPUTERS AND COMMUNICATION.

World Press Freedom Committee Formed in May 1976 to 'unify the free world media for major threats that develop'; consists of 32 journalistic organizations ranging from the American Newspaper Publishers Association (ANPA), and international PRESS agencies to the INTERNATIONAL FEDERATION OF JOURNALISTS. See MACBRIDE COMMISSION; MEDIA IMPERIALISM.

World Reporter Title of electronic publishing service begun in 1983 by the BBC in partnership with Datasolve, a computer bureau subsidiary of Thorn-EMI, offering instant access on computer terminals to world news digests. Claimed to be the first service of its kind in Europe (there are a number of such electronic news services in the US), World Reporter's initial service covered only the news summaries of the BBC's RADIO monitoring service. Even so, over 40 million words were soon data-banked, with between 10 and 20 thousand words added every day.

Writtle Britain's first BROADCASTING station was located at Writtle, Chelmsford in Essex. It was designed and run by Captain H.J. Round and built by the Marconi Company in 1920. Programmes from Writtle were lively and inventive until a monopoly of broadcasting was given to the British Broadcasting Company, later the BBC, in 1922. See RADIO BROAD-CASTING.

X-certificate See CERTIFICATION OF FILMS.

Xerography Reprographic process using a photoelectric surface which converts light into an electronic charge. Documents can be reproduced in black and white and in colour to a very high standard, reduced in size or enlarged. The electrostatic image of a document attracts charged ink powder which in turn is attracted to charged paper. A visible image is formed and fixed permanently by heating.

Yellow journalism Phrase used in the US to describe newspapers involved in the internecine (dog-eat-dog) warfare of the popular metropolitan PRESS empires of the late 19th c.; a battle which has continued to the present day with mass-circulation tabloids competing for readership with all sorts of exploitative offers, lurid revelations and blockbuster bingo.

Youth Culture Since the 2nd World War (1939–45) considerable attention has been paid to the cultures and sub-cultures of young people – to their symbols, signs, philosophies, MORES, NORMS, LANGUAGE, and music. Music is an essential part of all youth cultures and sub-cultures although the different GROUPS tend to favour different musical styles and use music in different ways.

Youth cultures and sub-cultures differ not only over time but can also differ between CLASS, sex and racial groups. Whilst they manifest significant differences there are some links between them and individuals may move from one to another. They adopt and adapt aspects of each other's cultural STYLE and those of past youth cultures and sub-cultures. The more dramatic sub-cultures have attracted attention from the media and academics. Their often spectacular modes of expression offer contrast and challenge to society, usually communicated by style – the hairstyle of the PUNKS for example. The media have been a notable *mediator* of society's reaction to such challenges, and this role has been a focus of media research. See COUNTER-CULTURE; FOLK DEVILS; MORAL PANIC; SENSITIZATION.

Zapping The practice of TELEVISION channel-switching, especially when the commercials come on; made worryingly easy – as far as the advertisers are concerned – with the arrival of remote control. In France, an anti-zapping strategy designed to keep viewers glued to the commercials was introduced in the late 1980s: individual numbers placed in the corner of the screen offer viewers bingo-style competition. A full line of numbers wins a cash prize.

Zinoviev letter, 1924 Probably forged by Russian émigrés and used as a 'Red scare' tactic by the *Daily Mail* to put the frights on the electorate immediately before the 1924 election. Labour lost the election and the Zinoviev letter probably made some difference if not a substantial one. It was a 1200 word document marked Very Secret, bearing the address of the 3rd Communist International, the organization in Moscow responsible for international communist tactics. The letter was addressed to the Central Committee of the British Communist Party and its tenor was the need to stir the British proletariat to revolutionary action against their capitalist masters. Among other recommendations, the *letter* urged the formation of cells in the armed forces – the 'future directors of the British Red Army'.

The impact of the forged letter was due to its *timing*. It was 'intercepted' by the Conservative *Daily Mail* just a few days before the election of October 1924 and published four days before Polling Day. The *Mail* used a seven-deck (or lines) headline, topping the deck with 'Civil War Plot By Socialists' Masters'. With the exception of the *Daily Herald*, the entire British PRESS swallowed and regurgitated the story. *The Times* discovered 'Another Red Plot in Germany' and on voting day the *Daily Express* warned, in red ink, 'Do Not Vote Red Today'. Labour lost 50 seats – but gained more than a million votes. See DISINFORMATION.

* C. Seymour-Ure, *The Political Impact of Mass Media* (UK: Constable, 1974).

Zircon affair *New Statesman* journalist Duncan Campbell in 1986, made a series of six TELEVISION programmes for the BBC entitled *Secret Society*. The first of these was about a Ministry of Defence project – Zircon – to put a spy satellite into space, at an estimated cost of £5m. On 15 January 1987, Alisdair Milne, the BBC's soon-to-be-dismissed Director General banned the Zircon programme on grounds of national security, a decision the *Observer* made public on 18 January.

The most notorious aspect of the Zircon affair was the police raids. Special Branch descended upon the New Statesman offices; upon Campbell's home as well as the homes of two *Statesman* journalists and finally there was a raid on the Glasgow offices of BBC Scotland, where all six of the *Secret Society* films were seized. Two days before, Milne had been sacked as the BBC's Director General.

The irony of the case is that Zircon (the project was later cancelled) was not really a closely guarded state secret; indeed the position of the proposed satellite was filed by the Ministry of Defence at the International Communications Union, an institution of which the USSR is a member. Eventually the Zircon programme was transmitted by the BBC in September 1988.

Zoetrope Or 'wheel of life'. Early 19th c. 'toy' in which pictures inside a spinning drum, viewed from the outside through slits, appear to be in motion. Invented in 1834 by Englishman W.G. Horner, the zoetrope simply but effectively demonstrated the phenomenon of PERSISTENCE OF VISION, the realization of which opened the way for the birth of cinema.

Zones In *The Hidden Dimension: Man's Use of Space in Public and Private* (UK: Bodley Head, 1966) Edward T. Hall identifies four distinct zones, or territorial spaces, in which most men and women operate. These are intimate distance; personal distance; social distance and public distance, each with its *close* and *far* phases. See PROXEMICS.

Zoom lens On a movie camera, a lens which can be adjusted automatically to give the effect of movement away from or towards the stationary camera; on a still camera, the zoom simply brings an object much closer.

Zoöpraxography Pioneer photographer Eadward Muybridge (1830–1904) was not the inventor of cine-FILM but he made the first photographic moving pictures – a process he called Zoöpraxography – 15 years before Lumière's first films. Muybridge described his Zoöpraxiscope as being 'the first apparatus ever used, or constructed, for synthetically demonstrating movements analytically photographed from life'. In 1878 he set up an experiment at Palo Alto, California, to ascertain by photography, whether all four hooves of a galloping horse were ever simultaneously clear of the ground. 24 cameras were aligned along the running track, each triggered off by the horse as it galloped past.

The Zoöpraxiscope consisted basically of a spinning glass disc bearing the photographs in sequence of movement. The disc, when attached to a central shaft, revolved in front of the condensing lens of a projecting lantern parallel to and close to another disc fixed to a tubular shaft which encircled the other, and round which it rotated in the opposite direction.

By 1885 Muybridge had produced an encyclopaedia of motion: men and women, clothed and unclothed, performed simple actions such as running, drinking cups of tea or shoeing horses; and a massive and varied study of animals and birds in movement. His carefully catalogued work was published in 1887.